THE OBAMA YOU DIDN'T KNOW:

PRESIDENT OBAMA AND OTHERS IN THEIR OWN WORDS

BY AVINOAM SAPIR

The Obama You Didn't Know:
President Obama and Others in Their Own Words
by Avinoam Sapir

Published by the Laboratory For Scientific Interrogation
P.O.Box 17286
Phoenix, Arizona, USA
Email: info@LSISCAN.com
www.LSISCAN.com

Printed in Israel

ISBN 978-965-572-785-2

Acknowledgement

I would like to thank my wife Leah Sapir who not only did fact checking, correcting errors and omissions, but also contributed her own insights into the text. Her diligent work on the manuscript helped the final product to be clearer to the reader, and also to be more accurate in both content and language.

About the author – Avinoam Sapir

Avinoam Sapir served in the Israeli Military Intelligence Unit 8200 (SIGINT).   He holds a B.A. in both Psychology and Criminology, and an M.A. in Criminology. His M.A. thesis was on "Interrogation in Jewish Law".

Mr Sapir worked as a polygraph examiner in the Israeli Police Department, and as a polygraph examiner in the private sector.

During the past few decades, Mr Sapir has conducted training in interviewing for various government agencies in Israel, the US, Canada, and several other countries around the world.

He developed the SCAN technique by conducting extensive research into verbal communication, looking into the linguistic behavior used by people in communication. SCAN (Scientific Content Analysis) analyzes a text or statement strictly according to the words used. The SCAN technique is currently being used in many police departments and other government agencies in many countries.

Mr Sapir's first book, "Linguistic Archeology", analyzes the text of the book of Genesis, as a demonstration of the use of SCAN in analyzing an ancient text. The book was published in Hebrew in Israel with the title "What Does the Bible Conceal?"

Mr Sapir's second book, "'Intelligence' vs Common Sense", compares the successes, weaknesses, and failures of the Intelligence organizations in the US and Israel. It is based on an analysis of memoirs written by the former directors of various intelligence organizations in both countries. It also discusses the question of Russian interference in the 2016 elections and possible "collusion".

Mr Sapir and his wife have 3 children and several grandchildren. They divide their time between the US and Israel.

Table of Contents

Introduction

When writing about a political figure, the messenger is as important as the message. After all, nobody is objective, and each writer brings into the writing not only his own knowledge, but his past, his set of values, and his way of perceiving reality. Therefore, I need to outline for the reader who I am.

I was born and raised in Israel, and became a naturalized US citizen in 1988. When voting in the US, I do not support a specific party, but I have always voted according to the person running for office. For example, I voted for Bill Clinton, and then I voted for Bush.

In 2008, I wanted to know who Candidate Obama is, so I set myself to reading the two books he had published: "Dreams from My Father" and "The Audacity of Hope". I was impressed by his analysis of the situation, as he was very accurate in reporting the situation as it is. However, the remedies he offered were not the right ones for the country. At the same time, I didn't vote for Senator McCain either, as I didn't think that he had the right temperament to be president. The same happened in 2012. I didn't vote for President Obama, and I didn't vote for his Republican opponent Mitt Romney. I didn't think that Romney was the right person.

My view of the US

I came to the US in 1981 to teach my course on interviewing and interrogation. Since then, I have studied the US laws regarding interrogation, as well as the history and the culture of the US. I have read many books, and I have listened to many audio classes.

I was very impressed by the Founding Fathers of the US. They "came alive" for me in my studies, and I equated them to the Biblical prophets Isaiah and others. Their wisdom reached the level of prophecy.

Since I come from Israel, I also studied how US presidents and political dignitaries have related to the Holy Land, from the time of US independence till the present time. I was impressed by one important point. It didn't really matter whether or not the current president was "good for Israel". What mattered was whether the president was good for the US. This is important not only for the US. One can say that the rest of the world needs a strong US economy, as the US is the engine of most of the global economic activity.

There is a saying in economics that when the US sneezes, the rest of the world gets pneumonia. It is all about the economy.

President Truman recognized Israel when it became independent. He had presided over ending the Second World War, bringing the soldiers back home, and entering the Korean War. I once went to visit his presidential library in Independence, Missouri.

President Eisenhower was not that friendly to Israel, but he was a great US president. I went to visit his presidential library in Abilene, Texas. President Eisenhower saw himself as the president of peace, and he rejected the temptation to enter the war in Vietnam. Great president.

Then President Kennedy came and brought the country into Vietnam. He was photogenic, young, and promising, but he was not good for the country. Three years of his presidency left a legacy of war, internal strife, and trouble.

The next two presidents – Johnson and Nixon – had to deal with the Vietnam War and the super inflation that was caused by the Arabs quadrupling the price of oil. The economy at the time suffered. The same happened with President Carter.

President Reagan was very friendly to Israel, and he also won the Cold War, but at the same time he put the US into very serious debt. He almost took the country into bankruptcy.

His successor, President Bush 41, was very much against Israel, but he was a good president for the US. Although he went to war (Desert Storm), he got the funding from other countries, so there was no debt.

President Clinton was great for the US economy, and he actually reached a surplus in the budget.

President Bush 43 was a major disaster. He entered two wars while reducing taxes, and buried the country in so much debt, that it is doubtful if the country would ever come out of it.

But if President Bush doubled the national debt from 4 trillion to 8 trillion in eight years, President Obama surpassed him by increasing the national debt to around 20 trillion. It is a point to note that President Obama inherited the financial collapse occurring under President Bush. In essence, both presidents – Bush and Obama – were equally bad for the economy.

When I became a US citizen in 1988, the US was one of the strongest countries economically. The dollar was very strong, and American tourists spent US dollars overseas. The impact of this strength was evident in the stores. It took only thirty years, and the US dollar lost all of its strength, to the point today that today the US dollar and the Euro have almost the same value.

How could a country lose its strength in just thirty years? There is a reason for it.

During the last thirty years, US companies started to outsource their manufacturing to overseas. Factories closed, and employees were sent to unemployment. I couldn't figure out – how could the leadership of the country allow something like this to happen?

In comparison, Israel asked Intel to build a huge plant in Israel, and the country gave the company exemption for ten years from local taxes. The government only wanted Intel to provide 1,500 good paying jobs for employees in Israel. The Israeli government encourages companies to come in, offering the companies exemption from taxes, as long as jobs move in; and then the employees with these good jobs will pay taxes. But in the US, the system was reversed. The companies shipped the jobs out. It came to a point that there was almost no manufacturing done in the US, unless it was somehow connected to the defense industry. That's why refrigerators are still being produced in the US, as there is a component in the refrigerator that is important in the defense industry. But otherwise, everything went away.

This process went on regardless of whether the president was a Democrat or Republican. President Clinton was the first to sign the NAFTA agreement that shipped many jobs to Canada and Mexico. It came to a point that new cars have no sign indicating what is the percentage of US production that was involved in producing the car; the sign only says the percentage of "North American" components involved, as "North American" includes Canada and Mexico. The car industry is around 15% of the US economy, so it creates a significant loss if these jobs move to Canada or Mexico.

The research behind the book

It is said in intelligence that 85% of all information comes from "open sources". This means newspapers, magazines, and books. In my research to find out more about President Obama, I set myself to reading books written by President Obama, by his wife, and by people who worked with him on his campaign and at the White House. I also read books by other people who interacted with him, whether they were Americans, or leaders of other countries, such as Canada, the UK, Germany, and Israel. There is so much information that it is very easy to drown in all the information available.

It was a very long process. First, I needed to read the book, to highlight the quotes I found to be important (a very subjective process), and then to sort the quotes of each book by topics. Once all the books were done this way, I had to merge corresponding descriptions from all the books together, to get the picture.

It was a very tedious job, but as Mark Twain once said that a successful job is more "perspiration" than "inspiration". You have here the product of this long research.

What Do We Know About President Obama?

Background

David Plouffe, Obama's campaign manager before the elections of 2008, stated that people's knowledge of Obama is very limited. People only know what the news media writes about him (DavPl 82). If so, relying upon the news media is not the best way to know a person. The most one can know is only what the person wants others to know about him.

The former French president, François Hollande, found that the real Barack Obama is very different from the public persona Obama projects (Hollande 83-84). In many words, Hollande said that while the "public" Obama is very outgoing and charming, the "personal" Obama is very reserved and actually the exact opposite from what the public sees. David Litt, Obama's speechwriter, explained this point by the fact that Obama derived his energy from the enthusiasm of the audience, that he "thrived" on it (DavidL 98).

Taking into account what both Plouffe and Hollande are saying - two people who met Obama in person, and the first even worked with him extensively - we can ask, do we really know who is President Obama?

There is a lot of information available about Obama. It is in the two books that he published before he was elected president, in his wife's book, and in several books published by people who worked with him during his campaign, and during his presidency. There are numerous speeches that he gave before and after he was elected. We can also obtain information by using the SCAN technique to derive information from the language Obama uses, and from the way he chooses what to include in the text ("The Editing Process").

Physical description

Michael Oren, Israel's ambassador to the US, who met President Obama numerous times, described Obama as being a man who moves around with ease, and is ok with his own body (MicOr 62).

It is the same description given by Ben Rhodes, longtime aide to President Obama (BenR xviii). Rhodes even equated Obama to a basketball player who plans how to spend his energy according to the time of the game (BenR xviii). We will see later on, that Obama does extensively use basketball language. Valerie Jarrett, who was a close friend of the Obama couple, beginning even before the Obamas got married, said that one can easily judge Obama's confidence just by watching the way he walks (ValJ 196).

Obama's smile

Obama's smile is a main feature in most of the descriptions people give.

Obama's wife Michelle commented on how wide Barack's smile is (MichO 103). Jarrett went further to describe his smile as a "thousand-megawatt smile" (ValJ 125). Plouffe described it as "a cat-that-ate-the-canary smile" (DavPl 89).

Jarrett described her first meeting with Obama. At the time, he was Michelle's fiancé, and Jarrett was offering Michelle a job. Michelle told Jarrett that her fiancé (Barack) wanted to talk with her to make sure that Michelle will be ok. Jarrett said that Obama's smile contradicted her expectations of him (ValJ 108). Jarrett also observed once seeing Obama's eyes smiling (ValJ 121).

David Axelrod, Obama's strategist, mentioned that there were times when Obama was smiling before answering. (Axe 202). Was it a reflex to give him time to phrase his answer?

Plouffe reported the same - Obama laughed before answering (DavPl 280).

In fact, we find Obama smiling at times when he is under pressure. Axelrod described a stressful situation in which Obama talked with a "thin smile" (Axe 334). Plouffe described a situation in which Obama's body language showed the stress Obama was having. Obama leaned back, exhaled, and smiled, before answering (DavPl 150). Plouffe produced another occurrence in which Obama smiled, while Plouffe knew that Obama was stressed (DavPl 197).

Robert Gates, Obama's first Defense Secretary, a leftover from the Bush administration, described a gift he brought President Obama from China.

It was a small backpack with Obama's picture on it, dressed in a Mao jacket and wearing a PLA hat. Gates presented it to Obama, saying that the souvenir would confirm what the Republicans were thinking of him. Obama just laughed (RobG 528)

In his book "Dreams from My Father" Obama described an event in which his mother demanded answers to a situation in which one of Obama's friends had been arrested on a drug charge.

Obama gave his mother his "reassuring smile". Obama went on to explain his smile to the reader, admitting that his smile was a "tactic", a "trick" he had learned for calming people around him. He had found that they would not be afraid of "a well-mannered young black man who didn't seem angry all the time" (BO DFMF 94-95). Obama said that his mother, knowing her son well, was not fooled by his smile.

There are different views of Obama's smile. John Kerry attributed warmth to the smile (JohnK 343). On the other hand, James Clapper, Director of National Intelligence, labeled Obama's smile as being a "patented" one. Clapper went on to say that he had no doubt that Obama "choreographed" his smile to put Clapper "at ease" (JC 129).

David Litt, who was one of Obama's speechwriters, with a great deal of access to Obama's time, described Obama's ordinary laugh as being "an act of judgment as much as reflex" (DavidL 185).

Litt described one time in which Obama laughed freely. It was at a time in which the team discussed a slide they had prepared showing both Obama and Netanyahu, the Israeli prime minister. The team saw that in the angle Obama's picture was taken, Obama resembled Hitler. When Obama was told about it, he laughed.

At this point, Litt went on to give the reader a "verbal video": Obama clasped his hands together. He raised his feet, and rocked back into the couch cushions (DavidL 185). Litt said that this was the only time that he ever saw Obama laughing so freely (DavidL 185).

Ben Rhodes describes almost the same situation. Before Obama was to give a speech in Berlin, Rhodes went to inform Obama that one of the quotes in the speech resembled something that Hitler had said.

When Obama was informed of it, he reacted with what looked like a "cathartic full-body laugh". Rhodes concludes it by saying that "the absurdity of the situation", instead of making Obama angry, relaxed him (BenR 27)

These two last examples might be a reflection of what Litt described as Obama's "sense of gallows humor" (DavidL 236). Valerie Jarrett described Obama's idea of a good movie as one that depicted a lot of suffering and "ends with everybody dying" (ValJ 287).

Confidence and Modesty

There are several reports of how Obama's body language reflected self-confidence.

Hillary Clinton remarked on Obama's confidence (HRC 15). David Axelrod gave his first impression of Obama as a young man who has the confidence of a much older one (Axe 119). James Clapper related to the way Obama decorated the Oval office. He said that it projected Obama's confidence although with the sense of being more "relaxed" (JC 130).

While he was described as being confident, there are also reports that Obama was not "overdoing" his confidence, or displaying "arrogance" (Axe 119). Clapper observed the same - confidence with "humility" (JC 130). Clapper also quoted Obama telling the intelligence community: "I don't know how astute a consumer of information I am, but I can tell you I sure do rely on it." (JC 147)

Obama described himself to Samantha Power as being more of a "vehicle", than focusing on himself (SamP 147-148). He also told her that he is not "some big original thinker". At the same time, he described himself as one who can "listen well" and "synthesize ideas", and that he knows "how to communicate" (SamP 148).

Being relaxed

"Relaxed" is an adjective attributed to Obama by several people around him. Hillary Clinton described Obama as "relaxed and rested" (HRC 15). John Kerry described him as "…loose and relaxed…" (JohnK 348).

We see the same with David Plouffe (DavPl 62), Axelrod (Axe 438), and Samantha Power (SamP 145, 318). Axelrod even described Obama as being relaxed at the time he had problems with Congress (Axe 438).

William Burns from the State Department, who held the talks with Iran, described his conversation with Obama at the White House: "Over a relaxed conversation, we covered everything from our daughters and the current NBA season…" (WillB 381).

Temperament

In his book "The Audacity Of Hope" Obama brings his wife as one who can give "testimony" that he is not one who gets emotional over things (BO AOH 21).   Obama once told Axelrod that he can "chill" about things (Axe 261).   Axelrod even coined the label – "the famously chill Obama" (Axe 358).

Axelrod described Obama as "reserved" (Axe 177) just as the French President did. It impressed Axelrod that Obama didn't give in to provocations (Axe 264); he described Obama's "steady temperament" as one of the best assets of the campaign (Axe 264).

David Plouffe talked of Obama's mood as "not too high and not too low" (DavPl 136). In other words, "calm demeanor" (DavPl 215). Plouffe gave the same description two months before the Democratic convention (DavPl 285).   Valerie Jarrett, Obama's close aide, gave the same description as the others, even when Obama was late to show up for a primary debate (ValJ 124-125). John Kerry concurred with Plouffe and Jarrett (JohnK 343, 348).

William Burns, State Department employee, described Obama as one who was not into "melodrama" (WillB 250-251). No wonder William Burns describes Obama's "effective relationship" with German chancellor Angela Merkel, who was like Obama in that sense (WillB 273).

Jarrett also said that Obama "never once yelled at us, and he rarely complained" (ValJ 183). Alyssa Mastromonaco, who worked with Obama as a scheduler, agreed with the same description as Jarrett (AlyM

32). Plouffe also said that the campaign employees didn't have to worry about Obama's reactions (DavPl 59).

Dealing with Success

Plouffe even coined the phrase "No Drama Obama culture" (DavPl 269). He gave his readers examples of how it manifested itself. He quoted Obama, who said "Just don't gloat..." (DavPl 187). Obama also told him that he is not into "daydreaming" over future success (DavPl 252).

Axelrod reported how Obama was cool when he reported to him success in the primary (Axe 146). Axelrod explained that Obama was not into "giddiness or elation" (Axe 146).

Dealing with failure

In his book "The Audacity of Hope", Obama talked about his fear of losing an election (BO AOH 105). He went on to describe the problem that loss of an election poses for a politician, since it is "on public display" (BO AOH 107).

And in fact, Obama did lose an election early in his political life – to Bobby Rush in Illinois. Valerie Jarrett described Obama's reaction to this failure. Although Jarrett expected Obama to be feeling down about it, he was not. She assessed his lack of emotion to it by saying that he had already moved on (ValJ 114).

Plouffe also commented on Obama's "terrific speech" after the loss in the New Hampshire primary, saying that anyone who had listened to Obama that evening wouldn't have known that it is a concession speech (DavPl 151). It seems that the speech was more of a cry for future battles. Obama told Plouffe after that loss: "I actually think this is for the best." (DavPl 153) It was similar to what Axelrod said, that not only did Obama not dwell on failure, but he actually "lifted everyone around him" (Axe 255).

When contemplating his run for presidency, Obama told Jarrett, "I'm OK with knowing that if I lose this race, I'll have to find a new career..." (ValJ 120). She attributed his attitude to possible failure partially to "temperament", but also to his upbringing, where his mother and grandparents sent him the message that he could do whatever he was aiming for (ValJ 121).

Susan Rice said that Obama dealt with bad news with "equanimity" and not emotionally (SusanR 355). Like Jarrett, she attributed this ability of his to "his cool temperament and rationality" (SusanR 355).

Obama on emotions

In his book "Dreams from My Father" Obama mentioned Lolo, his Indonesian stepfather, and his grandfather in Hawaii as his role models, although he describes them as men that he "…might love but never emulate…" (BO DFMF 220).

Saying that, Obama brings his stepfather's message to him about women. When his stepfather talked about Obama's mother, he labeled her as having a "a soft heart", and that his stepfather saw this as a "good thing" in a woman, but not in a man, who should have "more sense" (BO DFMF 39). In fact, Obama commented that he did not find even once that his stepfather talked about his own feelings. Moreover, his stepfather didn't show any sign that emotions ruled him (BO DFMF 40). Obama also mentioned that his stepfather instructed him on how to manage his own emotions (BO DFMF 38).

His stepfather gave the young Barack a lesson about life: "Men take advantage of weakness in other men. They're just like countries in that way… Better to be strong… If you can't be strong, be clever and make peace with someone who's strong. But always better to be strong yourself. Always." (BO DFMF 41).

His stepfather's message remained for life, personal and political. Years later, David Cameron, prime minister of the UK, said that Obama gave him the same message: "You'll find that people will use your strengths as your weaknesses and vice versa." (DavCam 248)

His stepfather was not the only one who "instructed" him about emotions. When Obama visited Kenya, his grandmother gave him some information about his own father. She told him that his father did not want people around him to know him. It came to a point that he even looked away when people talked to him so they wouldn't know what he thought of what they said (BO DFMF 406).

Years later, in Hawaii with his grandparents, Obama learned to hide his own "feverish mood" (BO DFMF 87).   In his last two years in high school, after he stopped communicating with his father in Kenya, Obama learned "not to care" (BO DFMF 93).

Poker face

Axelrod describes his inability to detect whether Obama "was panicking or even taken aback" when facing bad news (Axe 334, 437).   Valerie Jarrett, his close aide, said the same.   She labeled her efforts to read Obama's face as "fruitless" (ValJ 213).

Jarrett described a time in which she sat close to Obama at the Oval Office, trying to figure out if he is really as calm as he appears.   Obama interrupted her and asked her what she was doing.   She answered that she wants to make sure that he is indeed fine.   He answered in the affirmative, telling her to stop staring at him (ValJ 214).

Jarrett gave an example of Obama's ability to maintain his composure.   The night of the raid in Pakistan to capture Osama Bin Laden, Obama spoke at the White House Correspondents' Dinner and made a very "witty speech".   Jarrett said that nobody in the audience could have known from Obama's behavior that anything important was happening elsewhere (ValJ 213).

The report of David Litt, Obama's speechwriter, resembles those of Axelrod and Jarrett in saying that there was a time that both he and Obama entered into "a staring contest".   Obama asked Litt what he was doing, and Litt responded by saying, "I'm just watching."   Obama later said that Litt makes him nervous (DavidL 4).

Susan Rice said that Obama's "complaint" against her was she cannot maintain a poker face.   He criticized her constantly for letting her emotions come through her facial expressions (SusanR 388).

There is only one time in which Susan Rice gave a sign she could detect Obama's emotions on his face, describing his "stiff upper lip" – right after the victory of Donald Trump in the 2016 elections (SusanR 456).

David Litt, who was in close proximity to Obama for two years, professed to read Obama's body language well - unlike Axelrod, Jarrett, and Susan Rice. When Obama finished a successful speech, his right hand would tap on the podium (DavidL 98). Litt also reported a time in which Obama's face talked volumes of the fact that he didn't want to be where he had to be (DavidL 102). And Litt said that he could tell when Obama was "phoning it in" – Obama's half smile. Litt even read Obama's language to know when Obama was on edge: the words "Now look" at the beginning of every sentence, and the "uh" sound (DavidL 150).

Obama the Spockian?

Litt described Obama as "a Spock-like president" (DavidL 209). Jeffrey Goldberg, who wrote an article about "The Obama Doctrine" in "The Atlantic" in April 2016, also described Obama as "Spockian".

Both Litt and Goldberg gave the image of Obama as the Star Trek character Spock, who is strictly ruled by logic and reason. And in fact, Goldberg quoted Obama admitting to him that there are times in which Obama was not sufficiently tuned to other people's feelings.

Robert Gates, Secretary of Defense, phrased it differently when he complained of lack of "passion" in Obama (RobG 298).

Samantha Power said that when she asked Obama how a certain thing felt to him, Obama didn't know what she was asking. When she repeated her question, he still couldn't answer. Instead, he asked what does she mean. She again had to clarify that she is inquiring about his emotions.   The most Obama could come up with was "I don't know" (SamP 166-167)

Is Obama really Spockian? Is he detached from emotions? Other reports about him do not support this conclusion.

Before Obama's acceptance speech at the Democratic convention in Denver in 2008, he showed signs of emotions. Axelrod said that while rehearsing the speech, Obama asked for a few minutes to be by himself with no people around him (Axe 302).

Hillary Clinton reported a time in which it was clear to her that Obama was struggling to control his emotions – when he pledged help to Haiti after the earthquake (HRC 530-531).

Crying

In his book, "Dreams from My Father" Obama mentioned two times that he cried: once at a church (BO DFMF 295), and the other at a cemetery (BO DFMF 429). Hillary Clinton listed Obama among several presidents who showed emotions in public (HRC WH 123).

Plouffe described Obama crying when he talked of his grandmother's passing away (DavPl 367). Obama told Axelrod that he had to struggle to keep from crying when he visited a wounded soldier in Afghanistan (Axe 452). After winning the Iowa primary Obama was "red-eyed" (DavPl 137).   During the drive "tears were streaming down his face" (ValJ 140). Jarrett also talked of Obama's crying after his reelection in 2012 (ValJ 258).

During the campaign for the US Senate, Valerie Jarrett confronted Obama at one point, telling him that he seemed to be indifferent. Obama sat silently for a moment and then tears came into his eyes (ValJ 126).

Anger

Crying is not the only emotion that Obama expressed. Anger was another. And it is interesting to witness **how** he expressed his anger.

Robert Gates, Obama's first Secretary of Defense, said that Obama expressed anger, although he rarely heard him swearing (RobG 298).

Edward Snowden revealed that the US was tapping the phones of leaders of other countries, among them Brazil. Obama met the Brazilian president, who complained very angrily of this invasion of privacy. Susan Rice said that the more the Brazilian president complained, the "cooler" Obama became. Obama even responded "antiseptically", with "a calm, low voice". However, Rice could tell that Obama was "royally pissed…" by these complaints of the Brazilian president and other leaders (SusanR 358). Elsewhere, Rice also mentioned that Obama's usual verbal response when he was upset was: "I'm aggravated" (SusanR 418).

UK Prime Minister David Cameron gave the same description as Rice. Talking on the phone with Obama about Libya, Cameron quoted a piece from the BBC, where a US official had contradicted what Obama said. At this point, Obama became quiet and spoke slower than normal, and it was clear to Cameron that he "was clearly fuming" (DavCam 270).

Both Samantha Power and David Axelrod described Obama demonstrating a flash of anger. (SamP 242, Axe 180). Axelrod reported being in shock when Obama responded in anger, not only nonverbally, but also verbally by using foul language (Axe 465-466).

Axelrod said that Maureen Dowd, the reporter who wrote of how Michelle was talking negatively about Obama, "got under Barack's skin" (Axe 294). And Obama reacted to her in a way that was "rarely seen" (Axe 294).

David Plouffe described a situation in which, although Obama was laughing, Plouffe knew that Obama was "rattled" (DavPl 197). He also reported a time in which Obama was annoyed and "increasingly on edge" (DavPl 219).

All of the above refer to situations in professional life. We have one description by Obama himself in his book of an emotional reaction within his own family, at his wedding. Some of the guests were flirting with his sister Maya, at which time Obama "started to grumble" (BO DFMF 440).

Shifts in Moods

Robert Gates mentions something less known about Obama's smile – the high speed at which the smile can vanish, leaving behind "a glacial look". Gates compared this phenomenon of Obama to Margaret Thatcher, the "Iron Lady" of Great Britain. Gates said that it was "no fun" to witness such a swift change of mood (RobG 300).

Axelrod produced a contrast in Obama's emotions between public and private life. While in public Obama was interacting "warmly", and was "moving and evocative" with others, in private he was "reserved" and "restrained" (Axe 264, 317-318). Axelrod's description is almost identical to the description of the French president Hollande after meeting Obama: "He does not like to confide in people, let alone show his feelings. He is a friendly but reserved guest." (Hollande 83-84)

David Plouffe, Obama's campaign manager, gave a description of a swift mood shift from one day to another. One day, Obama was a "tired, uninterested speaker", and the next day, he was the exact opposite (DavPl 42). Plouffe said that it was a pattern for Obama to change once the "red light went on" indicating that taping is taking place. Obama confirmed it (DavPl 114).

David Litt gave other examples of "rapid" changes in mood. Litt said that Obama could come from "a deadly serious meeting on Afghanistan" to record a happy birthday greeting to Michael Jordan, and go back to "a solemn tribute to our troops" (DavidL 216).

People person

Axelrod said that Obama was "comfortable" with people. Axelrod attributed it to the fact that Obama's background took him into different continents, and he was okay in all of them. (Axe 137).

Axelrod talked of Obama's empathy, and quoted Obama telling him that his (Obama's) mother emphasized to him to always put himself "in the other person's shoes" (Axe 139).

Aloofness

Ben Rhodes talked of Obama maintaining "a sense of privacy" along with having a large group of friends, bringing Obama to see himself as an "outsider", and other people to see Obama as "aloof" (BenR 47). Samantha Power labeled Obama as "a recluse" (SamP 153).

Obama saw other people as "unnecessary distractions" (BO DFMF 3). He enjoyed talking with people, but only briefly. If the conversation moved to anything dealing with "familiarity", he would move "to excuse [him]self". His solitude was "the safest place [he] knew" (BO DFMF 4).

In his second book, which he wrote a few years after getting married, he talked about himself in politics, saying that he answers only to his "own conscience" (BO AOH 134). Axelrod described this trait by saying that although Obama enjoyed people, he didn't have the "grab-your-elbow, stare-into-your eyes shtick of a Bill Clinton" (Axe 459).

Arm on the shoulder

Axelrod described Obama putting his hand on Axelrod's shoulder (Axe 147). Obama did the same on another occasion when he told Axelrod not to worry (Axe 159). Plouffe says that Obama "grabbed [his] shoulder and looked into [his] eyes" (DavPl 386). Valerie Jarrett says that while the two sat together on the couch, Obama had "one arm draped over [her] shoulder" (ValJ 291-292). Samantha Power reported the same (SamP 263).

When Obama and Hillary Clinton were arguing on the tarmac, Obama put his hand on her shoulder, which Axelrod explained as Obama's attempt "to calm things down" (Axe 242). Plouffe described it a bit differently after seeing a re-enactment of the event by Obama and Axelrod: that Obama's hand was not on Hillary's shoulder, but on Hillary's arm (DavPl 120). This was not the only physical contact between Obama and Clinton. In her book she reported a time when the two of them were on a trip overseas, and Obama put his arm around her (HRC 233)

Michael Oren reported that in his meeting with Israeli prime minister Benjamin Netanyahu, Obama put his arm around Netanyahu's shoulder (MicOr 222).

Obama describes this as an "unconscious habit", realizing that it could make people around him feel "more than a little uneasy" (BO AOH 47).

Other physical contacts

Axelrod reported that in a meeting between Obama and his opponent during the campaign for the US Senate, Obama "jabbed" Keyes "in the chest with his finger". While Axelrod used the word "jabbing", Obama used the word "poked", describing it as "…a bit of alpha-male behavior …" (BO AOH 211). Axelrod said that one time Obama grabbed his shirt "for emphasis" (Axe 383).

Valerie Jarrett said that when Obama encountered her assistant Kathy, he would always give her a "fatherly kiss on the forehead" (ValJ 174). Michael Oren said upon Obama being introduced to Oren's sister, he kissed her on the cheek and hugged her (MicOr 310). Samantha Power said that when Obama met her while she was pregnant, Obama embraced her warmly and "sized up" her tummy (SamP 242).

David Cameron, prime minister of the UK, took a flight with Obama on Air Force One. When he suffered from jetlag, Obama offered Cameron his bed. When Cameron leaned back on the bed, Obama tucked him in with a blanket (DAVCAM 341).

In summary, we find contradictory reports. On one hand, we see a person who is "aloof" and "reserved" in private. On the other hand, we see a person who invades the personal space of people around him.

Skipping small talk?

Hillary Clinton described Obama as one who was used to skipping small talk (HRC 15). In John Kerry's words, Obama "doesn't beat around the bush" (JohnK 406-407), and quickly gets to the point. Susan Rice and Samantha Power confirmed this trait (SusanR 343, SamP 323).

As we have reports that he skipped small talk, we also have the opposite reports.

Clinton described a meeting between Obama and the Burmese leader saying that the two leaders talked about their dogs (HRC 114). William Burns reported that in his meeting with Obama at the White House, the two of them talked about family and the NBA, along with the reason for the meeting – the Iran negotiations (WillB 381).

Two sides of Barack Obama

Till this point we have seen Obama exhibiting a duality in each trait attributed to him. Obama is confident and modest, or confident and shy. Obama is a recluse and private, but invades other people's private space. Other observers close to him nailed it right.

Ben Rhodes, Obama's long time aide, talked of Obama being "reticent" at times and "bold" at other times (BenR xix).   John Kerry called Obama "a profile in contrasts" (JohnK 343).

Obama told Axelrod: "There was an old critic who said, 'Everything is either a comedy or a tragedy, and the difference is whether you are on the inside, or on the outside, looking in'. I try to remember that, and step outside on those tough days and see the absurdity of some of these scenes." (Axe 458)

Obama talked of this trait of his in his book "Dreams from My Father". Others noticed that part of him "remained removed, detached, an observer among them" (BO AOH 206). Axelrod described Obama as being both a "participant and an observer" (Axe 184).

After he was elected president, Obama said, "Each day, it sinks in a little bit more. But there are still moments when it seems like an out-of-body experience." (DavPl 386)

Talking about Himself in the Third Person

There are several instances reported of Obama talking about himself in the third person, avoiding use of the pronoun "I".

Axelrod quoted Obama saying, "It turns out that being Barack Obama is a pretty good gig in and of itself." (Axe 202) Obama did the same when quoting people who talked about him: "…Here's this young, untested guy who was a state legislator just a few years ago. We're not ready to say, after two contests, that he's ready. We want to see more." (Axe 255) Obama also told Axelrod to send Axelrod's wife a message: "Tell her the commander in chief probably hates it as much as she does." (Axe 397)

Valerie Jarrett quoted Obama saying, "Had there not been a Mayor Washington, there might not have been a President Obama." (ValJ 65) Samantha Power said that she got an email from Obama saying, "**Your candidate** needs to do better in the polls so you don't have to be so defensive." (SamP 175)

Jeffrey Goldberg, in his article in "The Atlantic" (April 2016) quoted Obama: "I want a president who has the sense that you can't fix everything."

Being controlled

Hillary Clinton in her book "What Happened?" talked of Obama being as "controlled" as she is . She went on to describe in detail what she meant by being "controlled": "He speaks with a great deal of care; takes his time, weighs his words." (HRC WH 122) Axelrod said that Obama's complaint against him was that Axelrod "was instinctive and undisciplined" (Axe 278).

Just as with self-control, so was Obama in controlling others. Obama told Plouffe that it was not easy to "give up control" (DavPl 6). Clinton said that when Obama offered her to be his Secretary of State, he "literally wouldn't take no for an answer" (HRC WH 53).

Valerie Jarrett said that when her daughter was planning her wedding, her daughter decided **not** to have a wedding cake. Obama insisted and argued with her that there should be a wedding cake. Jarrett's daughter didn't give in. (ValJ 255)

Samantha Power was on the phone with her stepfather, who was babysitting for her baby while she was at the White House. Power was trying to explain something to him, but he didn't understand her. At this point Obama intervened. He took the phone, introduced himself as the president, and went on for three minutes to instruct the babysitting stepfather on how to do things (SamP 322).

Axelrod was friendly with the reporter Maureen Dowd, who wrote a non-flattering article on Obama. It bothered Obama to the point that it was "a minor source of tension" between Obama and Axelrod (Axe 294).

The trait of control was not only in private life. It extended also to the way Obama ran his presidency. Robert Gates quoted John Podesta, in charge of the transition team, telling him that "the Obama team tend to be control freaks" (RobG 275). According to Gates, Obama's White House was "centralized and controlling in national security" (RobG 585).

Sense of Humor

David Cameron, prime minister of the UK, related to Obama's great sense of humor (DavCam 154). Michael Oren, Israeli ambassador to the US, talked of Obama's "impeccable comic timing" and joking even when the joke targeted himself (MicOr 62).

What about laughing at others' expense?

Obama was "equal opportunity" in joking at the expense of others - Democrats and Republicans, and even people who worked inside the White House.

Axelrod said that Obama once joked about Axelrod's hair by comparing him to the North Korean leader Kim Jong-Il (Axe 412). When Jarrett's dress flew up due to the helicopter blades, and Rahm Emanuel saved her from embarrassment by pulling her dress down, Obama "laughed" at her catastrophe (ValJ 196). Ben Rhodes commented how Obama called Susan Rice's attention to Rhodes's socks (BenR xi).

Samantha Power said that when her husband Cass broke a glass at the White House, Obama said, "Leave it to Cass to break the White House.'" (SamP 322) Power also said that Obama would "joke" when she didn't say anything in a meeting: "Are you sick, Power?" (SamP 509).

William Burns, who had to deal with the authorities in Russia to release the plane Senator Obama was flying in, commented that thereafter Obama reminded him of the problem they had in Russia, calling it, "You're not going to pull another Perm on me, are you?" (WillB 245).

Obama also "joked" about the Republican Speaker of the House of Representatives John Boehner, who was very tanned, by saying, "That's not a tan, it's rust." (MicOr 206)

Susan Rice was also the target of Obama's laughing at her own expense. Obama commented numerous times on how short she was (SusanR 2). She called it "a recurrent annoyance" in their relationship. Obama also laughed at her shoes, and at holes in her jacket (SusanR 353).

Obama even "joked" about Rahm Emanuel's losing his right middle finger in an accident, by saying that the accident also impacted "half of [Rahm's] vocabulary" (MicOr 103).

Beck Dorey-Stein, a stenographer at the White House, brings an event in which she was running on a treadmill, and Obama came to run on the adjacent treadmill. He commented on her running by saying, "I thought you'd be faster than that." If this was not enough, Obama called the attention of the agents in the room to it, saying, "Hey, guys, don't you think she could have run a little faster?" Everyone laughed, except the target of the joke. She was in shock. She went on to say that Obama addressed her again, saying, "You could have gone a little faster." She described herself as being "speechless and starstruck and want to pass out" (FCO 40). Later on, in her book, she labeled Obama's behavior as "trash-talk" (FCO 318).

David Litt, Obama's speechwriter, brought his family to the White House to meet Obama. During the photo shoot Obama criticized Litt about his appearance in front of his family. And if that was not enough, Obama told Litt's parents that their son is a good writer but "he's a little absentminded" (DavidL 232).

Litt commented on Obama's extraordinary ability to pick up in every human being their "most cringeworthy trait". Litt said that although Obama was not "mean", even so, "behind his **trash talk** inevitably lay a kernel of deeply personal truth" (DavidL 232).

One might wonder if all this "joking" at the expense of others, was the reason that brought Susan Rice to describe Obama as "**wicked** smart" (SusanR 19).

Honesty

Axelrod quoted Obama as saying on the campaign trail that American lives were "wasted" in Iraq. Axelrod labeled it as "a small yet significant gaffe" (Axe 218).

Was it really a "gaffe"? When Obama gave his speech in Chicago against the Iraq war in October 2002, he related to his grandfather, who fought in the Second World War in Patton's army. He said that his grandfather "did not fight in vain."

It was clear that Obama was comparing soldiers who "did not fight in vain" during the Second World War, to the soldiers who were about to embark on a war in Iraq that **would be** "in vain". That was his opinion, and he was honest about it. It was only because his speech in 2002 used high language and long sentences, that he could say this without anyone picking it up. But in Ames, Iowa, he used "wasted" – language that everyone could understand, and as such easily picked up.

Axelrod said that the campaign didn't want to restrict Obama's "candor or spontaneity", but the "slip" in Iowa was a "wake-up call" that Obama needed "discretion and discipline" (Axe 219).

At one point, Obama said of people in small towns in the Midwest that they "…get bitter, they cling to guns or religion…" (DavPl 216). When confronted with what he said, Obama at first tried to explain it, but very quickly he moved on to admit that he did "mangle the words". He said he "had misspoken" (DavPl 216), but in actuality, he said what he actually believed, as we will see later on.

After several times in which he said that he would not run for president, and then he decided to run anyway, Obama expected he would have to deal with the question of why he changed his mind. Plouffe reported that in their internal discussions, Obama suggested "a novel approach" – to tell the truth. Plouffe concluded by saying that for the average person such an approach would not be that unique, but that politicians tend to deny "the obvious" (DavPl 6).

Obama was also honest on the campaign trail when he acknowledged that his campaign didn't have a plan for healthcare (Axe 222). After debates,

Obama rated his performance accurately, even when he didn't perform well (Axe 222, 468, 470, 471; DavPl 47). In summary, Obama was not shy in taking responsibility for lukewarm performance (DavPl 58, 216, 217).

Obama expected honesty from others as well. Jeffrey Goldberg in his article "The Obama Doctrine" in "The Atlantic" (April 2016), said that Obama told King Abdullah II of Jordan that he had heard that Abdullah had complained to friends in the US Congress about his leadership. He told the king that if he had complaints, he should raise them directly.

Being honest is commendable, but we have two reports in which Obama's honesty was out of place.

David Cameron, prime minister of the UK, said that Obama told him in front of the others present: "David, I think you're wrong and naïve…" Cameron was upset that Obama was criticizing his country in front of the other European leaders, which was "deeply embarrassing" (DavCam 587).

William Burns described Putin as being a "kid in the back of the classroom with an attitude problem". Obama mentioned this image later on in public (WillB 281).

Burns labeled this behavior by Obama as "undiplomatic". But is it only "undiplomatic"?

Background information

The legal definition of "truth" is to tell the truth, the whole truth, and nothing but the truth. This is what any witness in the courtroom is asked to do. However, the social definition of truth is different. One should tell the truth, but not necessarily all of it.

The message parents give their children is: "I want you to tell me that you did it, and if you tell me I will not punish you this time. It is more important for me that you will be truthful, than to punish you."

In fact, the value of being truthful is value number one in society. People can understand almost any misdeed, but they cannot tolerate lying.

When a person is caught lying, there is no way to recuperate from this situation.

However, parents later balance this with another message to their children. There would be a time in which a parent would tell the child: "You shouldn't have said that. When you said that, you embarrassed yourself, and you embarrassed me. You should have remained silent." And the child defends himself, "But you always told me to be truthful," to which the parent responds, "Yes, but not about everything. There are some things that you should keep to yourself. Don't tell everyone everything you know." And in fact, there are situations in life in which one can defend himself by saying, "I didn't lie to you. If you were to ask me I would have told you, but you didn't ask me." In other words, we defend ourselves in lying by omission and not be commission.

We might wonder why Obama is sometimes "undiplomatic", instead of incorporating this "balancing message" ("Be truthful but don't say everything") in his behavior.

Daylight

David Plouffe, when bringing in another person to help him manage the campaign, said that "…we made sure there was no daylight between us…" (DavPl 269)

The concept of "daylight" means that if there are disagreements between the two people, or two parties, the two of them should not air disagreements to the outside world. Their disagreements should stay only between the two of them. As Michael Oren, Israeli ambassador to the US, explained it, "daylight was bad and darkness – that is, the absence of open disagreements on policy – optimal." (MicOr 88) In simple language, "daylight" means: "Don't wash your dirty laundry in public."

In a meeting between Obama and the leaders of American Jewish Organizations, Obama said, "When there is no daylight, Israel just sits on the sidelines and that erodes our credibility with the Arabs." (MicOr 87)

Oren, who is a historian, explains the impact that "daylight" in the US-Israel relationship regarding peace issues (unlike defense issues) would have on the Arab Middle East.

According to Oren, "daylight" in the Middle East simply does not work. In his words: "A friend who stands by his friends on some issues but not on others is, in Middle Eastern eyes, not really a friend. In a region infamous for its unforgiving sun, any daylight is searing." (MicOr 88)

Obama on Reason and Common Sense

In his book Obama says that humans have "only our own reason and our judgment to rely on" (BO AOH 89). He champions the cause of liberalism, since liberalism is "grounded in reason and fact" (BO AOH 24). He also binds "reason" and "science" together (BO AOH 219).

It is important for him that his position would "make sense" (BO AOH 119). The phrase "It makes sense" is frequently used by Obama (Axe 255). He also quotes himself as saying, "It made no sense to me. No sense." (BO DFMF 265)

David Cameron, prime minister of the UK, commended Obama for having "buckets of common sense" (DavCam 154). Alyssa Mastromonaco, who worked with Obama for many years, named her book, "Who Thought This Was a Good Idea?"

Wisdom

Obama said of himself: "I think I'm reasonably smart" (Axe 304). His game of choice for leisure time was Scrabble (BenR xii).

Several people concurred with Obama's self-evaluation. David Cameron, prime minister of the UK, commended Obama's ability to provide "brilliant analysis of the most complex situations" (DavCam 154). James Clapper, who was Director of National Intelligence (DNI), described Obama as being "cerebral" and not making decisions on "a gut call" (JC 326-327). Axelrod also labeled Obama as being "brainy" (Axe 120), and a "rationalist" (Axe 373).

Steve Harper, prime minister of Canada, said on one occasion that Obama was the "most articulate individual in the room" (StephenH 125).

David Plouffe also talked of Obama's "sound analysis and research" (DavPl 381). Valerie Jarrett labeled Obama as being "a devout believer in reason" (ValJ 235). Susan Rice talked about Obama's "rationality" and his "formidable intellect" (SusanR 355).

Hillary Clinton, who served as Secretary of State in Obama's first term, said that she had learned how to appeal to Obama's "highly analytical mind" (HRC 193).

Axelrod's first impression of Obama was of the wisdom of a much older person (Axe 119). Leon Panetta, who was CIA Chief during Obama's first term, and Defense Secretary during the second term, said that he was impressed by Obama's "quick grasp of the budget" (LeonP 191).

Other adjectives used for describing Obama were "shrewd" (Axe 120, HRC 17), and "wicked smart" (SusanR 19).

Decision Making

Robert Gates, Defense Secretary, described Obama as the most "deliberative president" (RobG 299).   William Burns, who served under both Secretary Clinton and Secretary Kerry, and was instrumental in reaching the agreement with Iran, commented on Obama's decision-making process. Burns listed several stages in the decision-making: "rigorous review of the facts and problem", "patient examination of the various options", "careful attention to second- and third-order consequences", and "'buttoned down' execution of decisions" (WillB 251). Burns also added that Obama's advisors were "…avoiding analytical or procedural shortcuts." (WillB 250-251). Burns connected the "disciplined decision-making" to "disciplined implementation" (WillB 251).

David Plouffe, Obama's campaign manager, said that Obama was not into "rash decisions" (DavPl 286). Plouffe rated this slow process as being "taxing in terms of time" (DavPl 337). William Burns wrote that while this slow-motion decision-making process was "usually one of the strengths" of Obama, it could also be a "weakness" as it could be "a substitute for action, or a dodge" (WillB 252-253)

Plouffe and Burns were not the only ones who were frustrated by this slow motion. James Clapper said that Obama did not reach any decision during a meeting – that Obama preferred to think of it after the meeting was concluded (JC 152). Samantha Power quoted Obama saying at the beginning of a meeting that he didn't expect a solution at that meeting (SamP 507). Michael Hayden, who was NSA and then CIA Chief at the G.W. Bush administration, said that people in the intelligence community complained of the endless meetings (MH2 37).

Michael Oren, Israel's ambassador to the US, labeled Obama as one who "prefer[s] contemplation to leadership", and quoted critics who called Obama "The Analyst in Chief" (MicOr 236).

Obama himself was sometimes frustrated by the long deliberation process. Obama told Samantha Power: "I rack my brain and my conscience constantly. But I can't answer in practical terms what we can do." (SamP 508)

Gates, on the other hand, didn't see anything wrong in deliberating for a long time. He was against those who criticized this slow motion process (RobG 299). Gates also commended Obama for it, and he said that when it was time, Obama made a decision, even "a life-and-death decision" (RobG 299). Once Obama had reached a decision, according to Gates, he didn't "have a second thought or look back" (RobG 300).

Hillary Clinton said that Obama wanted to make sure that every option was discussed before reaching a decision (HRC 133), and that Obama listened to all arguments during the decision-making process (HRC 147).

Obama expressed in his book the idea that being smart is not a prescription for success. In his words: "How can someone so smart fall so badly? It made no sense to me. No sense." (BO DFMF 265)

Axelrod concurred with this point, evaluating Obama's decisions: "Few of the decisions he had made would satisfy the politics of the moment. But at home and abroad, Obama was playing a longer game." (Axe 402)

What exactly is Axelrod saying in this evaluation? That Obama's decisions might not be good for the present time, but they would be relevant for the "longer game". And if so, how would we know if his decisions were the right ones? When will the "longer game" be over? In one year? 10 years? In our life time?

Summary

The highlights of Obama's personality are:

1. He does his best to hide his emotions. He does his best to maintain a "poker face".
2. He describes himself as being "removed, detached, an observer". He acts as a "participant-observer". Obama has said that he "steps outside" on tough days.
3. He is controlled in the way he talks.
4. Although he has a steady temperament, he also has flashes of anger.
5. He has quick shifts in moods.
6. He invades other people's personal space.
7. He ridicules other people's physical appearance.

One should wonder if there is any common denominator that can stand behind these "symptoms".

Child Abuse

In fact, there are several signals in Obama's two books, published before he was elected, that indicate that Obama might have been a victim of sexual abuse.

Signal No. 1

There are numerous points in which Obama related to himself by using the word "child". One should note that the word "child" (instead of the word "son" or other synonyms appropriate to the context) indicates grave danger to the person. In many cases, the word "child", which negates the gender, reflects past sexual abuse. [See more about the word "child" in the LSI Newsletter Anthology, and in the book "Linguistic Archeology".]

The following are the places where Obama uses the word "child":

1. "I remembered the stories that my mother and her parents told me as a **child**…"
   (BO DFMF xiv)
2. "A separation occurred, and he returned to Africa to fulfill his promise to the continent. The mother and **child** stayed behind…"
   (BO DFMF 10)
3. "… I can retrace the first steps I took as a **child**…" (BO DFMF 23)
4. "…looking after the knowing, dark-eyed **child** that my sister had become" (BO DFMF 75)
5. "…but I knew with the unerring instincts of a **child**…" (BO DFMF 78)
6. "…the same images that my mother had offered me as a **child**" (BO DFMF 134)
7. "What is a family? Is it just a genetic chain, parents and offspring, people like me? Or is it a social construct, an economic unit, optimal for **child** rearing and divisions of labor?" (BO DFMF 327)
8. "At first I reacted to all this attention like a **child** to its mother's bosom…" (BO DFMF 328)
9. "I saw that my life in America—the black life, the white life, the sense of abandonment I'd felt as a **boy**, the frustration and hope I'd witnessed in Chicago…" (BO DFMF 430)
10. "It was the same appeal that the military bases back in Hawaii had always held for me as a young **boy…**" (BO AOH 31)
11. "…got passed on to my mother. Her own experiences as a bookish, sensitive **child** growing up…" (BO AOH 203)
12. "As the **child** of a black man and a white woman…" (BO AOH 231)
13. "…and perhaps because I had lived much of my life as an only **child**…" (BO AOH 338)
14. "I felt as well the mark that a father's absence can leave on a **child**" (BO AOH 346)

Please note the following:

1. Points 7 and 8 talk about "child" in general, and not relating necessarily to Obama himself.

2. There is only one place in which Obama used the word "boy" instead of the word "child". It is in the context of him combining "the black life, the white life, the sense of abandonment I'd felt as a **boy…**" – quite likely he is referring to the time he was with his white grandparents, without his mother being present (**"sense of abandonment"**).

Signal No. 2

One should note that an "open statement" is not a list of activities that are an answer to the question of "what happened?" An "open statement" is a "list of summaries". For example, when a person says "I returned home," this is not one activity. "Returning home" includes the activities of parking the car, getting out of the car, locking the car, and going inside the house. When a person says "I went to sleep" this is not one activity. Some people take a shower. Others prepare themselves for sleep during a length of time. Some read in bed, and then they fall asleep.

It is important to know that when a person mentions in an "open statement" the activity of "opening/closing doors," which can be expressed simply by "I went into the room," for example, it should serve as a signal that the person might have been sexually abused in childhood. Victims of sexual abuse remember one point all their life. When the door opened the crime started, and when the door closed the crime ended.

In his book "Dreams from My Father" there are several places where Obama mentions the activity of opening/closing doors.

1. "I went into my room and **closed the door**." (BO DFMF 60)
2. "When I entered the elevator, I stood without pressing the button. **The door closed, then reopened**, and an older Filipino man who lived on the fourth floor got on." (BO DFMF 64)
3. "At night I would **close the door** to my room…" (BO DFMF 85)
4. "I **opened my door** to see Toot entering their bedroom to get dressed for work." (BO DFMF 87)
5. "**He opened the door** for me, then paused. 'By the way, what church do you belong to?'" (BO DFMF 274)
6. "Rinsing my face in the sink, I put water on for tea, then **opened the door** that led into the yard." (BO DFMF 308)

7. "As we got up to leave, the old man said something else, and Roy nodded his head before **closing the door** behind us." (BO DFMF 388)

Signal No. 3

Obama said that he has "…little sympathy for those who would enlist the government in the task of enforcing sexual morality" (BO AOH 335).

He listed the "personal decisions" that "society has a right and duty to step in". These include: "child abuse, incest, bigamy, domestic violence, or failure to pay child support" (BO AOH 335).

Generally speaking, the order of listing might reflect the set of priorities for the person. Usually, what is listed first is more important than what is listed second, and so on.

See for example, a list given by Valerie Jarrett: "Law school, work, marriage, baby, bliss. I'd pursued my plan…" (ValJ x). In this list, it is clear that she is listing them chronologically.

In comparison, let's see another list, given by Alyssa Mastromonaco, an assistant to the president for scheduling: "I like my house and my husband and my cats and my job" (AlyM 135). Here, we can see that her house is listed first while her husband is listed only second.

Returning to the list provided by Obama, it is clear that the list does not go from the light to the heavy, or from the heavy to the light. "failure to pay child support" (listed last) is less serious than "incest" (listed second, and not first). One should note that for Obama "child abuse" is listed first – most important.

Summary

In analyzing statements we should never go by one signal. One signal might not mean much. However, when we have an accumulation of signals, then we can say that we are reaching the level of the information being definite.

These three signals together are a very strong indication of past sexual abuse. With that in mind, one can look upon the several symptoms in Obama's behavior, and understand that quite likely Obama had a need to hide his emotions. But like many other victims of sexual abuse, Obama lost the awareness of boundaries in society. He lost the ability to respect other people's personal space. He needed to control his anger, but his anger shows up verbally by ridiculing other people's appearance.

As we continue into the material, we will see additional signals in behavior that will support this understanding.

More About President Obama

President Obama the Orator

"Words alone cannot meet the needs of our people. These needs will be met only if we act boldly in the years ahead…" (President Obama in his speech to the Moslem world in Cairo, Egypt, June 4, 2009).

Valerie Jarrett, the Obamas' close friend, titled her book – "Finding My Voice". Jarrett considers three speeches Obama gave to be milestones in Obama's development: the keynote speech at the Democratic National Convention (Kerry's campaign) in Boston in 2004, the "Yes, We Can" speech after his loss in the New Hampshire primary, and his "Race Speech" in Philadelphia in March 2008. Jarrett saw these three speeches as a process in which Obama "had found the voice". These three speeches enabled Obama to create a coalition of people from different backgrounds, shades and colors, a coalition that carried him into his presidency (ValJ 156).

Speeches for Obama are "storytelling" for him, the reason for existence. Obama expressed this idea in a conversation he had with Ben Rhodes, his speechwriter. According to Obama, "storytelling" distinguishes between humans and animals. Without "storytelling", Obama told Rhodes, "We're just chimps." (BenR 373)

Obama's wife Michelle described Barack's fascination with the pen by saying that Barack was free with his emotions only in writing. (MichO 119).   She attributes this trait to his personal history. He corresponded with his mother in far-away Indonesia while he was in the US with his grandparents. This correspondence accustomed him to the idea that one shows emotions in writing. It was the background for Obama's having a "deft and easy way with words", as Michelle described it (MichO 215).

Michael Oren, Israeli ambassador to the US, labeled it as "Abracadabra", which he describes as an ancient Aramaic word standing for "I speak therefore I create" (MicOr 96). Obama told Axelrod that he distinguished between talking to people in person while campaigning in the US, and the speeches in which he talks "values" (Axe 470).

According to Rhodes, speeches were a main tool in Obama's presidency. The objective of a speech was to "reorient" US foreign policy and domestic policy, not only for the population at large, but also for the government bureaucracy (BenR 49).

A speech was also a way to deal with a problem or scandal. David Litt, Obama's speechwriter, talked of Obama's reaction to the brewing scandal of Reverend Jeremiah Wright with his inflaming rhetoric about the US and race. Obama's way to calm down the situation and eliminate the scandal was with a speech. This speech was, in Litt's words, "a sober, thoughtful, thirty-eight-minute address" titled "A More Perfect Union" (DavidL 99), also known as "the Race Speech".

A speech was also a way to deal with tragedy. When Congresswoman Gifford was shot in the head in Tucson, Arizona, Obama quoted from the book of Job, addressing the need to find meaning in pain. The speech was rated as equal to Dr. Martin Luther King's speeches (MicOr 206).

For another tragedy, a massacre in an African American church in Charleston, South Carolina, committed by a white man, Obama gave a eulogy at the church. Litt described Obama's performance there as being one of a "crossover artist, as much professor as pastor, as much Kennedy as King". According to Litt, Obama even borrowed the "cadence" from previous African American leaders and preachers. He ended his speech by singing "Amazing Grace" (DavidL 284).

For major speeches, such as his speech on receiving the Nobel Peace Prize, or his "Race Speech" in Philadelphia, Obama wrote his speeches by hand – not on a computer, but in handwriting. He usually did it at night, and many times he ended his speeches close to the deadline, close to the day of the speech, and he delivered the text on a yellow legal pad, "with his neat handwriting" (BenR 80).

David Plouffe, Obama's campaign manager, considered Obama to be the best speechwriter on the campaign, a point Plouffe said was unique among political campaigns. Plouffe saw it as a huge advantage, since by going over the text for major speeches, Obama actually owned the speech as if he had written it himself (DavPl 40).

Axelrod described Obama's preparation for a speech. When determining the content, Obama made the text come alive by including the lives of people encountered on the campaign trail (Axe 172). It was not only "content". In a way, it was a verbal TV show.

But Obama was not satisfied with only the content. Obama cared a lot about words (BenR 49). He had a strong belief in the power of words (MicOr 96). Obama in his book labeled his communication style as "overly verbose" (BO AOH 120). Jeffrey Goldberg of "The Atlantic" implied in his article that John Kerry's "vaulting oratory" resembles that of Obama.

Obama also took into consideration the meaning of the words, the way they sound, and the tempo in delivering them. Axelrod said that Obama considered how each word played against another (Axe 172). In other words, Obama used all the components of language – content, sound, and pace.

David Litt, Obama's speechwriter, outlined an important point that can be easily be observed in Obama's speeches. The text includes very long sentences, to the point that one can easily say that Obama talks in paragraphs, instead of sentences. Beck Dorey-Stein, a stenographer at the White House, quoted Obama as saying that "We just try to get our paragraph right." (FCO 139)

Litt, as a speechwriter, observes that most speakers do not prefer long sentences. In fact, every teacher in school will instruct the students to break their thoughts into shorter sentences, as short sentences make the text easier for the reader to follow. It also helps the speaker to breathe naturally between sentences.

But Obama did not limit himself to short sentences. Litt compares Obama to a sports car that can take a turn in the road even at a high speed. Litt talks about Obama using pauses, and even "beats within the words", not subjected to the regular punctuation, to better deliver the words. Litt describes how Obama would raise and lower his voice, captivating the listener with the text (DavidL 98-99). Alyssa Mastromonaco describes Obama as a "brilliant orator" (AlyM 49).

Plouffe says that Obama didn't do it with "fire-and-brimstone". He would first call for quiet in the room, and when he started to speak, the audience was totally attentive (DavidPl 57).

Plouffe also described a meeting where the campaign team and Obama went over the text of an important speech Obama was due to deliver in Iowa before the first primary contest.
They went over the text of the speech "line by line". Obama also practiced reading it.   After all, if sound and pace are as important as content, practicing the sound of the speech is critical (DavPl 110-111).

People paid attention to other sounds as well in Obama's speeches. Laura, Valerie Jarrett's daughter, had watched Obama on TV a few days before his "keynote" speech in 2004, and she noticed that he said "um" frequently. She mentioned this to her mother Valerie, who relayed the comment to Obama (ValJ 129).

Litt observed Obama's body language, and could determine from his behavior at the end of each speech if it was successful, not only by the audience's judgment, but by Obama's own judgment. If it was a successful speech, Obama would "…give the podium a satisfied little thump with his right hand". Litt interpreted it as a sign that Obama was satisfied with his own performance. If, on the other hand, Obama knew it was not a good speech, there would be no "little thump" (DavidL 98).

A Speech and its Impact

When reading the two books that Obama wrote and published before his election as president, I found it necessary to break up each paragraph into sentences, in order to enable myself to get the full meaning of what Obama had said. And if it is difficult to understand him in reading, one can only imagine the difficulty his audience will have while listening to a speech in real time. In other words, the way Obama wrote his "paragraphs" would sometimes prevent people from understanding him in full. When he named his Philadelphia speech "A More Perfect Union" – the speech that later became known as the "Race Speech" – it was not easy to grasp the full meaning of the anger within the African American community that Obama was talking about. But the speech served its purpose. The speech stopped in its tracks the brewing scandal about Reverend Jeremiah Wright.

Litt talks about the impact of Obama's speeches on the audience. In spite of the audience being "captivated" – and in this case, this included Litt himself – Litt testified that he later couldn't remember a word (DavidL 21).

Litt went on to say that even the most "well-crafted presidential address" could not bring any change in the course of events (DavidL 99). He also commented that the most Obama's speeches could do was to remind the converts why they believed in Obama, but there was no speech that could convince the "unpersuadable" (DavidL 102).

Litt summed up Obama's presidency as follows:

"Barack Obama's election was a triumph of hope. But his presidency was a triumph of persistence" (DavidL 303).

So we see that even for David Litt, Obama's presidency was not a "triumph of hope". And in fact, Litt expressed openly his disappointment with Obama's presidency. In his words, he started as an "Obamabot" but he didn't end as such.

Obama himself said in his speech in Cairo, Egypt: "Words alone cannot meet the needs of our people. These needs will be met only if we act boldly in the years ahead…"

President Obama and Basketball

The only picture Obama has together with his father is where the two of them are standing by the Christmas tree, and 10-year-old Barack holds an orange basketball, his father's gift for him for Christmas (BO DFMF 70). Basketball is strongly connected to his missing father.

The basketball court is also the place where Obama could have "a community of sorts" (BO DFMF 80). The young boy, with his father gone, his mother far away, living with his grandparents, needed a community to belong to. It was where a black boy, raised by his white grandparents, found a place where "blackness couldn't be a disadvantage" (BO DFMF 80).

Basketball was also a game where Obama, the logic and reason person, the one labeled as "Spockian" could play "with a consuming passion" (BO DFMF 78). In summary, basketball and passion are one and the same. In high school Obama played with his high school basketball team in a state championship in Hawaii (Axe 235).

Obama's wife Michelle grew up with her brother Craig, described by Barack as "a basketball star" (BO DFMF 79). Basketball was what Michelle used as a litmus test to find out if Obama is the right guy for her. Michelle asked her brother Craig to play basketball with Barack, and to see Barack's personality as it is expressed on the court (MichO 131).

We know that Barack passed the test, as the two of them did marry each other. We should note Craig's comments after the game/test. Craig concluded that Barack has "guts", although Barack was no "ball hog" (MichO 131). Barack talked in his book of his "limited talent" (BO DFMF 78).

Another basketball player close to Obama, Susan Rice, mentioned in her book the use of sports to assess a person. The professional tennis coach Nick Bollettieri watched her play and assessed her very quickly, saying that she is "fiercely competitive and a sore loser". Rice concurred with this assessment wholeheartedly (SusanR 12).

Obama commended Rice on her tennis game, and on being a good basketball player. He attributed to her the adjectives "fearless" and "tough". Rice concurred with Obama, saying that the basketball game taught her to be "fearless". But the game taught her a lot more. Playing as a point guard taught her to play with a team, lead a team, and to "lose with grace". She considered the basketball court as important as her academic studies in teaching her "leadership" (SusanR 86-87).

As Obama played basketball with Michelle's brother, so he did with Susan Rice's brother (SusanR 344).

When Obama came to Washington DC as a new senator from Illinois, he used a basketball metaphor to describe his view of his coming to the Senate as a "rookie":

"…the rookie who shows up after the game, his uniform spotless, eager to play, even as his mud-splattered teammates tend to their wounds" (BO AOH 19).

We find that many of Barack's friends were actually his teammates on the basketball court. For example, Marty Nesbitt, who attended the first meeting in Chicago to discuss the potential run for president, was Barack's neighbor and "basketball-playing buddy" (Axe 190).

Before his keynote speech at the Democratic National Convention in 2004, Obama likened himself to Lebron James, the basketball player. Reporters asked Nesbitt what he thinks of Obama comparing himself to Lebron. Nesbitt answered that Obama can carry a game, and "he always gets the shot" (OA 151).

David Axelrod, Obama's top strategist, likened Obama to Michael Jordan, who once said, "When the game gets close and something big is on the line, it all slows down, and I see things better." (SamP 176)

Axelrod said that in order to calm Obama down before any debate, the team played basketball with him (Axe 242). Obama also had his "traditional primary day basketball game" (DavPl 199).

Obama played basketball with the soldiers in Afghanistan and Iraq during his visits there. He was proud to mention that he managed there to score "the first three-pointer" he tried (DavPl 276).

Not only did playing the game relax him, but even talking about it was a relaxing activity. Valerie Jarrett said that before his well-known "race speech" in Philadelphia, Obama had a small talk with Eric Holder about basketball (ValJ 147). After the speech, Holder said that they couldn't understand how he was talking basketball before such an important speech (ValJ 148).

William Burns, from the State Department, the point man for the negotiations with Iran, said that he and Obama had a very relaxed conversation covering everything "from our daughters and the current NBA season to the Iran negotiations" (WillB 381).

David Plouffe said that once the New Hampshire primaries were over, the heavy traffic prevented them from going on their way. The team stayed at a gym and played basketball. Plouffe said that Gibbs used the opportunity to teach Obama how to throw a football in a spiral, an activity that Obama was eager to learn (DavPl 144).

Even when Obama was not playing basketball, he moved like a basketball player (BenR xviii).   Rhodes also described Obama as "an athlete who'd just finished a game." (BenR 388)

As President

David Litt, Obama's speechwriter, divided the White House personnel into those who liked basketball, and those who only pretended to do so. He added that in "Obamaworld" there was no third option (DavidL 248).

Samantha Power said that Obama arranged a basketball court near the White House lawn. It was a place to play with other administration people. Playing there gave her relationships she couldn't have achieved in any other way (SamP 254).

Power said that basketball was the game for Obama throughout his life. However, once he became president he preferred golf, and the reason he gave Power was that when playing golf he was outside and not in a golden cage (SamP 230).

Obama took David Cameron, UK prime minister, to a basketball game in Dayton, Ohio. Throughout the game Obama explained the rules of the game while Cameron only pretended to understand (DAVCAM 341). The basketball game was one of the activities that the two leaders shared (DAVCAM 343).

Cameron also mentioned that Obama invited him to talk while the two of them were exercising on a treadmill – "treadmill bilateral" as Cameron called it. Cameron commented that this exercise produced a major benefit for him. While normally Obama talked "at great length" (as we established earlier, in "paragraphs" and not sentences), the exercise on the treadmill forced Obama to be more "concise" (DAVCAM 343).

Excelling at basketball, according to Obama, deserved the Presidential Medal of Freedom. Obama gave that honor to Michael Jordan (ValJ 200).

Barack and ESPN

Obama in his book talked about the pleasure he gets from watching "a well-played baseball game" on TV (BO AOH 31).

Axelrod told Obama that since he, Obama, likes "to play hoops and watch ESPN", a normal activity for a regular guy, he might be "too normal to run for president." (Axe 202)

David Plouffe said that the TV on the campaign bus was tuned to ESPN throughout the entire campaign (DavPl 188).   According to Plouffe, a night of ESPN is the best reward for Obama on winning a debate (DavPl 346).

Plouffe also brings an example that after a debate, Obama was more interested in talking about baseball than about the debate. Obama even asked Plouffe if he, Plouffe, would prefer "winning the election or the World Series?" (DavPl 361)

John Kerry met Obama during the transition period after Obama won the 2008 elections. On the wall there was a television set tuned to a football game (JohnK 348).

Obama also talked of working on the draft for a speech while he was watching a basketball game (BO AOH 356). He turned off the TV only when he actually began to write the speech.

Obama talked of watching a football game while his daughters were in the room (BO AOH 61). When he visited Iraq, he had difficulty in sleeping at night (jetlag?) so he watched the Redskins game (BO AOH 300).

Politics and Diplomacy as Sports

For Obama, politics were "a full-contact sport". He compared politics to basketball in the sense that both have "the sharp elbows" and "the occasional blind-side hit" (BO AOH 17).   He saw the elections as winning the "semifinals" while healthcare legislation (Obamacare) was the "finals" (Axe 485).   When commending his team he said that "Everybody really lifted their game." (DavPl 279)

Obama decorated his Oval Office with "a pair of Muhammad Ali's red boxing gloves" (SamP 284).   He labeled the last two years of his presidency as "the fourth quarter" (SamP 528).   Susan Rice described Obama as "the classic closer - a fourth quarter player" (SusanR 427).

Basketball Language

Throughout his campaign and his presidency, Obama used basketball language, and at times he borrowed metaphors from other sports, such as football and baseball.

Michael Oren, Israeli ambassador to the US, quoted Obama telling the Israeli Prime Minister, "The United States intends to pursue a full-court press in offering assistance to Israel." (MicOr 194) Oren said that he was not sure that Netanyahu would understand the metaphor, but it seemed to Oren that Netanyahu (who spent many years in the US and graduated MIT) seemed to understand.

Not only Obama used basketball language. People around him did so as well. Samantha Power used the same metaphor when talking of the US push to reach an agreement with Iran. She said that they were "in a relentless, full-court press" to achieve that agreement before Obama would leave office (SamP 530).

Oren quoted McDonough, Obama's Chief of Staff, as telling him, "America wants to move the ball steadily up the field, run down the clock, and make a touchdown." (MicOr 284)

A foreign leader who knew this about Obama's language could use it to his advantage. David Cameron, UK Prime Minister, was not known to be heavily into sports, but he said that when he talked to Obama he used "sports language": "I used a baseball analogy to convey the merits of staying: we just needed one more home run." (DavCam 281)

ISIS

Obama equated ISIS to a "jayvee team" (quoted by Jeffrey Goldberg in "The Atlantic"). Rice said that in December 2015, Obama instructed his administration to "put ISIS in a box" by the end of his term (SusanR 422). In fact, Rice talked about the US success in doing so (SusanR 423). Samantha Power also used the "penalty box" metaphor, when for a time she was suspended from the campaign (SamP 199).

Obama also used another metaphor for ISIS, not from sports, but from movies – a Batman movie, "The Dark Knight". Obama equated ISIS to "the Joker" in the movie: the one who "comes in and lights the whole city on fire". (quoted by Jeffrey Goldberg in "The Atlantic")

Basketball language

The ball was a frequent metaphor in the language of Obama and his people.

The ball

Before going on a stage to deliver a speech to millions of Americans, Obama told Axelrod, "Just give me the ball," while he illustrated with his body "taking an imaginary shot at a basket" (Axe 312).

David Plouffe, when talking to Obama, used the same language. He told Obama that when the red light is on (in a debate or a speech), "you're alone with the ball. You either make the shot or miss it…" (DavPl 362). In discussing policy with Plouffe, Obama said that he could make a specific argument, but that "it puts too much spin on the ball" (DavPl 324).

Susan Rice uses a very rich sports language. When talking of presenting the president with the results of discussions, she describes doing it "without any 'spin on the ball'" (SusanR 390).

Rice compared her position as National Security Advisor to performing as a "'point guard' who calls the plays, runs the offense, and passes the ball." At times she also played a "'shooting guard' – the player on the team most expected to drive to the basket and score" (SusanR 427).

Rice talked of "driving down the court to the bucket" (SusanR 14). She talked of the "ball" being in her "court" (SusanR 264). She also used sports metaphor in talking to Obama during his run for presidency. She equated the idea of a trip overseas too early in the campaign to be equivalent to "running the 1982 Berkeley lateral play through the Stanford Band at halftime rather than in the last seconds of the game" (SusanR 94). When describing this afterwards, she commented that the group's familiarity with college football enabled her point "to land its punch" (SusanR 95).

Samantha Power, describing the lingo used at the NSC, said that when they got what they wanted at the UN, they didn't want to "spike the ball", and if they needed to get instructions from the State Department or from the White House, they needed to "'tee up' the issue" (SamP 218).

It seems that the "ball" is a fixture in US politics, regardless of the party. Nikki Haley, who was US ambassador to the UN during the first two years of the Trump administration, talked in her book about running for governor of South Carolina. She talked about being able to "move the ball" (NikkiH 246).

Taking a shot

When talking with Axelrod of his plan to run against an incumbent in the elections for US Congress, Obama told Axelrod, "I'm going to take a shot." (Axe 122) Obama also equated his run for US Senate as taking "one last shot" (Axe 123).

Michelle in her book said that when Barack was considering running for president, her brother Craig told her: "…if Barack's got a shot, he's got to take it…" (MichO 224)

When Obama gave Samantha Power instructions on how to negotiate with the Russians at the UN, he instructed her, "don't overshoot the runway" (SamP x), but at the same time he also said, "don't undershoot the runway either" (SamP x).

Play point

Before meeting with President Bush, McCain and other leaders, to discuss the financial crisis, Obama told Plouffe that he would "play point at the meeting" (DavPl 342).

In describing the election campaign, Plouffe wrote about "the home stretch", and said that the campaign "had only to block and tackle well" in order to win the presidency (DavPl 363). In describing their strategy in the campaign, Plouffe said that they "threw long" (DavPl 368). And when referring to Rahm Emanuel, a candidate for Chief of Staff, Plouffe said that "In baseball, a five-tool player refers to someone who excels at just about everything." According to Plouffe, Rahm was such a player. (DavPl 372).

President Obama and Movies

Movies served Obama throughout his life as metaphors. Obama's wife Michelle said in her book that Barack would sometimes jokingly compare her family to the Cleaver family of Mayfield USA, in the TV series "Leave It to Beaver" (MichO 172).

Obama's wife said that Barack liked "dark, dramatic movies" (MichO 113). For example, he liked watching the Sopranos (MichO 211). Valerie Jarrett said that Obama liked movies "with a complicated plot that involves a great deal of suffering and that ends with everybody dying" (ValJ 287)

Obama used movies as metaphors in politics. For example, he describes President Reagan as having a "John Wayne, 'Father Knows Best' pose" (BO AOH 31).

Jeffrey Goldberg, who interviewed Obama extensively, describes an episode in which he told Obama that the Middle East for Obama is what the Mob was for Corleone in the movie "The Godfather, Part III". Goldberg started to quote Corleone saying in the movie, "Just when I thought I was out…" and Obama finished the quote by saying, "It pulls you back in". (Goldberg, "The Obama Doctrine" in the magazine "The Atlantic")

Jeffrey Goldberg also quoted Obama talking about ISIS, and quoting from the Batman movie "The Dark Knight", equating ISIS to "the Joker" in the movie, in the sense that ISIS had the potential to set the whole area on fire. (Goldberg, "The Obama Doctrine" in the magazine "The Atlantic")

Obama mentioned the importance of movies when he talked at the "Shoah (Holocaust) Foundation dinner. He described how, due to the movie "Schindler's List", the "world eventually came to see and understand the Holocaust like never before..."

Samantha Power mentioned that Obama liked to quote a scene from the movie "The Departed". When an officer messed up during a stakeout, his fellow officer was shouting at him. When the officer asks him, "Well, who the f*** are you?", the fellow officer answers with, "I'm the guy who does his job. You must be the other guy." (SamP 267)

Axelrod quotes Obama paraphrasing a quote from the movie "Risky Business": "I mean, sometimes you just have to say, 'What the f***.'" (Axe 206).

When he was talking of his weak performance at a debate, Obama brought a scene from the movie "Tin Cup", in which the character in the movie just changed the way he wore his cap on his head, to be able to succeed. Obama concluded by saying, "He didn't change anything, really, but his head" (Axe 470).

Ben Rhodes says that after the 2016 election victory of Donald Trump, the one "...who represented every political, economic, and social force that his own identity opposed", Obama jokingly quoted Corleone, saying "I feel like Michael Corleone, I almost got out" (BenR xix).

Who is Michelle?

In his book "Dreams From My Father" Obama described his wife as having "wit, grace, candor". Axelrod said that Michelle was "…a warm, whip-smart, and often hilarious person…". According to Susan Rice, Michelle was the funniest person she knows (BO DFMF xvii, Axe 277, SusanR 378).

Susan Sher, a top lawyer in the city of Chicago, sent a note to Valerie Jarrett in 1991 recommending Michelle for a job, saying, "Very impressive! Bright, mature…". Jarrett herself gave her own first impression of Michelle's personality: "…composed demeanor… a firm handshake, made direct eye contact, and exuded a confidence…". After meeting with Michelle, Jarrett remarked on Michelle's maturity, unexpected at such a young age (ValJ 105, 106, 107).

Michelle's background

In an appearance as First Lady at a conference for "Working Together to Address Youth Violence in Chicago" on April 10, 2013, Michelle declared that Chicago is her hometown. She was born and raised in Chicago, and built her career there. She married and raised her children there. She also said that her children still refer to Chicago as "home".

Obama in his book "The Audacity of Hope" mentioned that Chicago of today has a very strong upper middle class of African American professionals, including doctors, lawyers, and others. He also mentioned that these successful people didn't use race or discrimination as "an excuse for failure" (BO AOH 240, 241).

But Chicago is a very big city. Michelle came from the "South Side of Chicago". She twice mentioned it in her speech at the Democratic National Convention in 2008, and several more times later on as First Lady, when she spoke at two schools in African American neighborhoods in the Washington DC area (Anacostia High School on June 11, 2010, and Ballou High School on March 30, 2011). In Michelle's words, "Chicago is truly a city of neighborhoods… where walking just a few blocks can put you into an entirely different world of experiences." (Speech in Chicago, April 10, 2013) The South Side of Chicago was a badge of honor for her.

What do we know of the South Side of Chicago, or any other inner city in the US?

South Side of Chicago

Obama said in his book that there has been a deterioration in the condition of the inner city poor. There is also a recognition within the African American community that the conditions are "spinning out of control". He said that many African Americans criticize, although only in private, the "work ethic, inadequate parenting, and declining sexual mores" in their own community (BO AOH 249, 251, 254).

Obama even gave specific details to explain this deterioration. At the time Obama wrote his book, 54 percent of all African American children lived in single-parent households, compared to about 23 percent of all white children. Obama attributed it to the "casualness toward sex and child rearing among black men", a fact that makes African American children more vulnerable (BO AOH 333, 245).

Children living with single mothers are five times more likely to be poor than children in two-parent households. Children in single-parent homes are also more likely to drop out of school and become teen parents, even when income is factored out. And the evidence suggests that on average, children who live with their two biological parents do better than those who live in stepfamilies or with cohabiting partners. (BO AOH 333-334)

Obama pointed out that one out of three black men will go through the criminal justice system during their life time. More than a third of black males are unemployed in some Chicago neighborhoods. The infant mortality rate among poor black Americans is equal to the mortality rate in Malaysia, a third-world country (BO AOH 251-252).

Education on the South Side of Chicago

The "inadequate parenting" that Obama mentioned includes parents being unable to help their children financially, and "lack of emphasis on educational achievement". In the neighborhood where Michelle grew up, the average African American family watches television more than eleven hours per day (BO AOH 243, 245, 244).

It is a neighborhood where the schools do not prepare students for college; and where Michelle's classmates teased her for studying hard. Teachers told Michelle that she could not aim high as her grades were not good enough.   It is a neighborhood where kids don't speak proper English. When Michelle's parents required her to speak English correctly, the other kids criticized her for talking "like a white girl" (Michelle, 3/30/2011, Michelle 6/11/2010, MichO 40).

What brought Michelle to achieve so much?

The answer is: her parents, who had big dreams for Michelle and her brother Craig. They wanted her to graduate high school and go to college. Her mother taught her to read before she entered kindergarten, took her to the public library and sat with her while she sounded the words on the paper. They had a dictionary and the entire "Encyclopedia Britannica" at home. In short, her parents "invested" in her (Michelle, 6/27/2013, MichO 4, 40).

A Case Study – Ben Carson

Ben Carson grew up in the inner city of Detroit. He was raised by a single mother after his father left them to live with another family he already had elsewhere. His mother worked two jobs to support Ben and his brother. The only government help they received was food stamps.

In his book "Gifted Hands", Ben Carson says that when he was at the bottom of his class, he accepted that it was the place that he deserved to be. He accepted that he was "dumb". His lack of performance reinforced his own understanding that white kids were smarter than black kids (BenC 27).

But Ben Carson's mother cared about the success of Ben and his brother, even though she herself had only a third grade education.

When she came home in the evening from her two jobs, she was very tired, but the first question she asked him was: "What did you learn in school today?". When he didn't do well in school, she insisted that he should learn the multiplication table. When he complained that this was too hard, she told him: "You can't go outside and play until you learn your times tables." (BenC 22, 31)

She insisted that Ben and his brother should not watch more than three TV programs a week. Instead, she demanded that they should read two books a week and produce a book report for her on these books (BenC 32, 33).

She often quoted to him the poem "You Have Yourself to Blame". And when he told his mother that he wants to be a doctor, and asked her if that was possible, she answered: "Bennie, listen to me. If you ask the Lord for something and believe He will do it, then it'll happen." In reply to these words, he said: "I believe I can be a doctor," and she concluded by saying, "Then, Bennie, you will be a doctor." (BenC 60, 25)

Ben Carson went on to graduate Yale, to complete medical school, and to become a prominent neurosurgeon.

The Talmud says: "Do not neglect the children of the poor, for from them will go forth the Law." (Babylonian Talmud, Nedarim, 81a:2.) i.e. Jewish tradition teaches that even a poor child can grow up to be an illustrious scholar.

Another Case Study – Deval Patrick

Deval Patrick, in his book "A Reason to Believe",[1] describes his journey from the South Side of Chicago to become the first African-American governor of Massachusetts.

Deval's parents separated after his musician father went away to pursue his career in music, and left Deval's mother with her two children to live on their own.   The single mother, living on welfare, had to return to live with her parents.

Deval described his family as having one vision: "to no longer be broke". Deval explained his grandmother's terminology: "broke" was not the same as "poor" – a term that his grandmother refused to use. While "broke" was temporary, "poor" meant permanent (DPatrick 6).

---

[1] Deval Patrick, "A Reason to Believe: Lessons from an Improbable Life", Broadway Books, New York, 2011

Deval's mother worked as a clerk, and at the same time she took night classes to achieve her GED. She later got a job at the post office with better conditions (DPatrick 19).   When he was a very young kid, six or seven, his mother took him to listen to Dr. Martin Luther King Jr. He didn't remember the words, but he remembered the "sense of optimism" (DPatrick 195).

His mother wanted to take her children out of the neighborhood, at least for the summer, so one summer she sent them to a Bible camp in Michigan for two weeks (DPatrick 22).

While his mother was trying to elevate them, his father saw any attempt to get better schooling as a "final surrender to capitalism… to the white power structure, to the institutions that had oppressed blacks forever" (DPatrick 128).

Values at home were important, and Deval said that "table manners, respectfulness, and homework" were a priority, and not "poverty, deprivation, or social justice". He said that he was lucky that nobody at home discouraged his wish to go to college. Although he was surrounded by people "who had every reason to curb my dreams" they did not. All of them drilled into him "to reject the cycle of despair" and the gift that they gave him in his childhood was that he "could shape [his] own destiny" (DPatrick 22, 31, 32, 33).

His teachers in school saw his potential and recommended that he would go to a boarding school in Massachusetts. When he came back home, his sister said that he talked like a white boy. His grandmother responded with, "He speaks like an educated boy." (DPatrick 40)

The subtitle of his book is "Lessons from an Improbable Life". He came from "a broken home and in poverty", but still he graduated Harvard College and Harvard Law School, and moved on professionally.

Besides commending his family for the values and "gift" they gave him, he commended his teachers both in his Chicago schools and in the boarding school at Milton, for the foundation and love they gave him. He mentioned his sixth-grade teacher, for whom teaching was not only facts and figures, but also "imagination". He had other teachers who became his surrogate parents (DPatrick 27, 45, 46).

Although people think that being sent to the boarding school at Milton was the factor that catapulted him in life, he rejected this assumption, as back home he had people who had "high expectations" for him. His school was "a launching pad", but he had "some spring in my legs" (DPatrick 57).

After graduation he volunteered in Egypt. His time there, and the poverty he saw there, brought him to conclude that it made his "own experience growing up in Chicago seem small and insignificant" (DPatrick 84).

Deval was in the audience when Obama gave his keynote speech at the Democratic National Convention in Boston in 2004. He was impressed that Obama "invoked the language of idealism", and Deval felt that it was time that there should be "a voice that blended optimism with pragmatism" (DPatrick 204, 207).

He met Obama and gave him his points on how to run: "run like you're willing to lose", "run the grassroots", "keep [your] rhetoric positive and high-minded" (DPatrick 212-213).   Obama might have done it anyway, but one might still wonder if Deval gave Obama the winning formula.

Michelle – Ben – Deval – Summary

These are only three examples, and could be considered "anecdotal evidence", but one striking conclusion comes out of these three successful life stories: reading books and stimulating the brain with information is essential to developing the brain at a critical time – young adulthood.

We find it with Michelle, whose parents made sure that the entire Encyclopedia Britannica would be available at home for the children to use. We find it with Ben Carson's mother, who insisted that they would read books each week, and provide book reports to her. We find it with Deval, whose teachers stimulated his "imagination".

Even Michelle, in her college thesis, included the number of books at home as a factor to check in the questionnaires she conducted.

The neuroscientist Daniel Levitin said in his book[2]:

> "…we now know that students who do well in school often have advantages that other students lack, such as parents or older siblings who value education, who help them with their homework and teach them ahead of time what they'll encounter in class." (Levitin 121)

Michelle Obama - Educational History

Michelle Robinson grew up in "a too-small house with not much money in a starting-to-fail neighborhood". In Barack Obama's words, she was raised in a "bungalow-style house". She was "a daughter of the South Side" of Chicago (MichO 416, BO DFMF 439).

Michelle's father, a city employee, struggled with multiple sclerosis throughout his life. The Robinsons couldn't afford to buy a house on a mortgage, as they couldn't rely upon the father's salary to be stable. There was always the fear that a sudden deterioration in his debilitating disease would prevent them from making the monthly payments.

But the guidance of Michelle's parents, and Michelle's own efforts, brought Michelle to be in the top ten percent of her class, and to make the National Honor Society (MichO 65).

Michelle enrolled in Princeton, following the footsteps of her brother Craig. Realizing that she came from an inner-city high school, she got ahead by "putting in extra time, asking for help when I needed it, and learning to pace myself and not procrastinate" (MichO 78).

While she extensively covers in her book her time at Princeton, her study at Harvard Law School is described by merely one paragraph. Moreover, while her account of her life at Princeton consistently uses the first person pronoun "I", the paragraph about Harvard Law School uses only the second person "you".

---

[2]Daniel J. Levitin, "Successful Aging: A Neuroscientist Explores the Power and Potential of Our Lives", Dutton, 2020

After she graduated Harvard Law School, she got a job at a prestigious law firm. She labeled her progress from college to law school to the law firm in Chicago as a "direct arrow shot of my trajectory from Princeton to Harvard to my desk on the forty-seventh floor…" (MichO 97).

At the law firm she was appointed to mentor a summer intern who was between his first and second year at Harvard Law School - Barack Obama.

Michelle's Personality

Michelle describes herself in her book as one who is "fanatically devoted" to neatness and who craves "routine and order". She is "a detail-oriented person" who needs to have a file for everything, and each file must be "labeled and alphabetized". She also has a "to-do list" in her head (MichO 200, 191, 89, 80).

She labels herself as a "planner" who feels that everything must be planned. Chaos agitates her, and this is the reason she gives for why she hates politics – because life in politics is not "neat", as schedules and plans in politics change all the time. Valerie Jarrett said that Michelle had no patience for the "underbelly of politics" (MichO 190, 64, 170, 64, 63, ValJ 154).

She learned this very early with her childhood friend Santita, Jesse Jackson's daughter, who introduced her to political life.

She writes that "tardiness drove me nuts", and she considered it "hubris". She describes at length the fact that Barack was late for their first meeting at work. But as the years went by, this "disregard for punctuality" became "a straight-up aggravation" (MichO 96, 202).

Michelle sees herself as smart and analytical, although she admits that logic is not the only engine for her. She is also motivated by her wish to get other people's approval (MichO 91).

She is "hard-driving", and has a "power walk", even during her leisure time (MichO 199, 105).

Even as an adult, she continued to hold worries from her childhood, and because of tragedies that brought death to people around her, she learned that the "world could be brutal and random", and that a person's hard work does not guarantee success in life (MichO 230, 225).

Michelle Obama – Racial history

Background

During the 2008 presidential campaign, Obama needed to respond to inflammatory remarks by Reverend Jeremiah Wright. In his speech at the National Constitution Center in Philadelphia on March 18, 2008 (the "race speech") he said:

"I am married to a black American who carries within her the blood of slaves and slave owners, an inheritance we pass on to our two precious daughters."

He went on to say that race and racism in the black community, even among those "who did make it", still continues to dominate their life, and to "define their world view".

He added that the anger in the black community might not surface in public, but is present "in the barbershop or the beauty shop or around the kitchen table."

While these are certainly general examples of places where people tend to chat and discuss the things that bother them, there is also a personal aspect. Michelle mentions in her book that Barack "spent time in the barbershops", so it is quite likely that when he mentioned "barbershops" he was thinking of a place that he himself frequented. And by extension - the beauty shop is quite likely where Michelle went, and the kitchen is quite likely where the two of them got together (MichO 98).

Michelle

Michelle connects her own educational history to race and racism throughout elementary school, high school, and even at Princeton University.

Elementary school was in her neighborhood, and she lived through the time of a major migration in the city of Chicago. Many white families migrated to the suburbs, followed by black families with means. From 1950, from the time before her parents moved to the neighborhood, till she graduated high school, 30 years later, the neighborhood changed from 96% white to 96% black. Still, during these years, Michelle felt that "Everyone seemed to fit in, except for me." (MichO 19, 41)

Her high school years were at Whitney Young, a school located right between the North (rich) and South (poor) sides of Chicago. There she was introduced to the fact that the city had what she called "black elite" – children of doctors, lawyers, and other professionals, all of them African Americans. Although at first she doubted her ability to compete with the others, she tried hard, and her grades, if not the very best in class, were very close to the top.

Michelle said that with her high school being located at the line of separation between the North and South sides, it should have been 40% white, 40% black, and 20% others, but in fact it was 80% black.

Princeton was the first educational institution where Michelle was in a dominantly white school. Only nine percent of her first year class were black. At Princeton Michelle felt that she is not only representing the South Side of Chicago, but representing her race as well. Being at the dorms, far away from home, there was no excuse of distance to prevent her from establishing friendships with others, black and white alike. But in fact, Michelle didn't have many white friends, adding that it was not because the others boycotted her. It was her own fault as she was "cautious" (MichO 72, 80, 75).

Michelle mentions a thesis she wrote in her senior year at Princeton. She describes it as a "survey" of African American alumni's attitudes towards racial identity. The exact title of the thesis was: "Princeton-Educated Blacks and the Black Community"[3] (MichO 263).

---

[3]

https://www.politico.com/story/2008/02/michelle-obama-thesis-was-on-racial-divide-008642

Michelle said that she couldn't understand why the conservative media portrayed her paper as "some secret black-power manifesto". In her defense, she said that she was twenty-one years old, and it was only "college-age me" (MichO 263).

What exactly did Michelle write? She wrote of her feelings of alienation at the bastion of whites. She felt more of a "visitor" than one who belonged there. She was surprised how people who were supposed to have an open mind, related to her first as black, and only second as a student (MO thesis 2).

Michelle mentioned the writings of Stokely Carmichael, who defined "separationism" as "a necessary stage for the development of the Black community before this group integrates into the 'open society'." (MO thesis 7-8).

Carmichael started his political journey as a member of Martin Luther King's civil rights movement, advocating the integration of blacks and whites in the US. However, he later joined Louis Farrakhan, the leader of the extremist "Nation of Islam", and advocated establishment of a "black entity" within the US. The majority of whites perceived Carmichael as a symbol of black extremism.

In her thesis, Michelle mentioned that Carmichael had emphasized "the need for Blacks to separate themselves from White society in order to strengthen the Black community." (MO thesis 26-27)

Michelle conducted a questionnaire survey among Black Princeton alumni, and concluded that those who spent more time with Blacks and/or had a more separationist ideology were more motivated to benefit the Black community than those who spent more time with Whites and/or were more integrationist (MO thesis 38-39).

Many years later, in writing her book "Becoming" (published after eight years of White House life) Michelle related to her graduation from Harvard Law School and joining the law firm Sidley & Austin in Chicago: "Now you're one of them… You've joined the tribe." (MichO 92)

But the fact that she graduated Princeton and Harvard, did not make Michelle an "elitist". In a campaign appearance she rejected this title attributed to Barack, and said that even though she graduated from these prestigious colleges, she saw the world via the "lens" she grew up with. She didn't forget her upbringing on the South Side of Chicago. She still saw herself as part of that community (Axe 276-277).

Michelle, who "joined the tribe", and became "one of them", summarized it by saying: "I had everything I was told I should want – a fancy job at a prestigious law firm, a big office, a nice paycheck." But something was still missing: "passion". Michelle decided to reject that "tribe", and to stop being "one of them". She quit her job at the law firm, and accepted a lower-paying job at the city administration, run by Harold Washington, the first black mayor of Chicago. She wanted to give to others (Michelle, 5/18/2013).

Angry Michelle?

Michelle started her book by bringing what her "detractors" were saying – that she is an "angry black woman". She responded in a lawyer-like way: "I've wanted to ask my detractors which part of that phrase matters to them the most – is it 'angry' or 'black' or 'woman'?" (MichO x)

Axelrod related in his book to a video that was circulating on the internet. In the video, Michelle denied the claim that Barack was an "elitist" (as mentioned earlier). But what bothered people was not the words she used, but the way she said them. According to Axelrod, people thought that Michelle was "angry". David Plouffe and Valerie Jarrett also mentioned the same video in their books. Plouffe wrote that there was a campaign against Michelle, claiming that "she was too angry". Jarrett wrote, "The words in her speech weren't angry, but her demeanor made them seem as if she was." (Axe 277, (DavidPl 301, ValJ 155).

Michelle was called to the campaign headquarters, to what she labeled as an "intervention", at which time the video was played for her without the sound. She was asked to watch her own body language, to see the impression that the audience was getting from her. She saw herself talking (no sound) "with intensity and conviction and never letting up" (MichO 267).

It was not "anger" for Michelle, but "intensity". And she might be right.
Body language is not so easy to determine. What seems "angry" to one
person, might appear as "intensity" to another. Axelrod saw Michelle as
"warm, whip-smart, and often hilarious", but he also added that when she
is angry, she goes all the way (Axe 277).

Michelle, when comparing herself to the "cool" Barack, said that when
something gets her angry, she feels a "fireball…exploding" to the point
that she might not even remember later what she said in the heat of the
argument (MichO 160).

Michelle and campaigning

Obama's first political campaign was for the Illinois senate. Michelle
said that she helped him with his campaign – she collected signatures,
she knocked on doors, and listened to people. She even enjoyed the
campaign (MichO 184).

Once Obama was elected and started to commute between Chicago and
Springfield, he was absent from home most of the week, from Monday
afternoon till Thursday night. At this point, she said that she felt "a first
flicker of resentment" about Barack being so involved in his job, and
being away from home.

Three years into Obama's service, he decided to run for US Congress
from a district represented by the incumbent Bobby Rush. For this race,
which was the only one Obama lost, Michelle does not say anything
about whether she helped the campaign. However, she did write
extensively about how she was hurt by the attacks against her husband –
especially since these attacks came from other African American leaders
(MichO 198).

Michelle said that she "doesn't recall" the first time Barack raised the
possibility that he wants to run for the US Senate. Her response to this
was very negative. They were already busy enough (MichO 203).

At this point of time, she started complaining a lot more about him being
so busy and away from home. She devotes several pages in the book to
outlining all the hardships she faced from his political life (MichO
203-211).

In 2002 they convened a meeting of close friends to discuss the possibility of this new campaign. At the meeting she agreed to let him have his wish with one important condition: if he loses, he would leave politics altogether, and get another job. In her description of the meeting, she repeats this condition twice more to emphasize its importance to her (MichO 213).

Moreover, in this campaign, Michelle was passive. Axelrod described her as "one notable absentee" in the campaign (Axe 136).

This was the campaign that brought Obama to be elected as US Senator in November 2004.

Summary

Till this point, there had been three political campaigns. One was for the Illinois Senate, a campaign in which she was very active. This campaign involved a local district in the Chicago area, quite likely representing a mostly African American population. Once he was elected, she complained of his absence with "a first flicker of resentment".

The second campaign was for the US House of Representatives. She doesn't mention that she was active in this campaign, but she was emotionally involved. A district for the US House of Representatives is also largely local, and although it is larger than a district for the Illinois Senate, it is still from the Chicago area.

The third campaign was for the US Senate, a campaign in which she was a "notable absentee". She devotes several pages to complain about Barack's absence from home. This campaign openly branches out to the entire state of Illinois, including the central and southern areas of the state, that are predominantly populated by whites.

Is it possible that Obama's wish to branch out and represent not only areas with a large African American population, but to represent whites as well, brought Michelle to be a "notable absentee"? She justifies her lack of participation in the campaign by complaining extensively of his absence from home, although she didn't do so for five years while he was serving in Springfield.

Running for President

While Michelle participated in Obama's campaign for the Illinois Senate, and she didn't take part in his campaign for the US Senate, she did participate very actively in the presidential campaign. Axelrod commented on it, saying that Michelle changed from being a "reluctant conscript" in 2007, to become a very active campaigner in the 2008 campaign (Axe 4).

But it didn't start this way. He wanted to run, but she didn't want him to. Moreover, she realized that in this upcoming campaign, not only would she be required to support him from behind the scenes, but she would need to be very active and to be right front and center on the stage (MichO 223, 224).

In fact, she said that she supported his decision to run because she "loved him and had faith in what he could do", but also because she didn't expect him to win. She even said that she would have been "content to lose the election". In many words, she said she wanted him to lose! (MichO 226, 275)

Still, she was campaigning. During the campaign, Maureen Dowd of the New York Times published an article (April 25, 2007), with the headline: "She's Not Buttering Him Up". In the article Dowd quoted some things that Michelle had said about her husband the candidate.

"I have some difficulty reconciling the two images I have of Barack Obama. There's Barack Obama the phenomenon. He's an amazing orator, Harvard Law Review, or whatever it was, law professor, best-selling author, Grammy winner. Pretty amazing, right?

"And then there's the Barack Obama that lives with me in my house, and that guy's a little less impressive. For some reason this guy still can't manage to put the butter up when he makes toast, secure the bread so that it doesn't get stale, and his 5-year-old is still better at making the bed than he is."

In her book, Michelle defended herself by saying that she wanted other people to see her husband as human. Assuming the quotes are accurate, there is no other way to understand them than to say that they show negativity and bitterness towards her husband (MichO 241).

The article by Maureen Dowd angered Obama a lot, and he even expressed his anger openly when she came to interview him. Moreover, later on, Obama criticized Axelrod for being friendly with Dowd. (Axe 294)

But in fact, Michelle was consistent in making jokes about her husband, even after he became president and she became First Lady.

In an appearance in front of students at the Martin Luther King Jr. Magnet High School, in Nashville, Tennessee, on May 18, 2013, she wanted to reinforce the point that failure does not mean that one should give up. She listed several famous people who failed before they became successful – such as Steve Jobs and Oprah Winfrey. Then she moved on to add one more name: "…this guy, Barack Obama…", and she added, "I could take up a whole afternoon talking about his failures… and now he gets to call himself my husband."

She continued by saying, "All jokes aside…" but the question is: was she really "joking"?

Although Michelle campaigned throughout the country in 2008, her behavior exposed the fact that she didn't want him to win. It is no wonder that she found it necessary to say in her book that she voted for him in November 2008 (MichO 273).

She says that she wanted to "reclaim" the life they had, before her husband became "a man with two families" – one of which was Michelle and the girls, and the other was the voters. But the fact is that in her book, her complaints about political life are minimal, and during the first five years of Barack serving in the Illinois Senate, she put her complaint in one sentence. However, once he went on to the national arena, running for US Senator, and later for President, the volume of her complaints became deafening (MichO 275, 213).

Is it possible that there was another reason for Michelle's wish for her husband to not win?   Is it possible that she wanted him to devote his political life to focusing on the Chicago area, where the African

American community was quite large, and not to spend his energy nationally, at the expense of the African American community? This is very similar to the theme of the thesis she wrote as a student at Princeton.

US Holidays in the Memoirs of Barack, Susan Rice, and Michelle

Background

Christmas is a US federal holiday, and can easily be considered as the most important US holiday. However, since its origin is in the Christian religion, we should consider in this very short check only two holidays that are specifically American in nature – Independence Day (the Fourth of July), and Thanksgiving.

Personally, I don't celebrate Christmas, and I don't compare Christmas to Chanukah. Although the two holidays have a tradition of lights in the winter, their origins are very different.

On the other hand, I do celebrate both the Fourth of July and Thanksgiving. In our family we celebrate each of these holidays with a festive dinner including the "traditional" foods for each, and we also greet each other with the Hebrew greeting "Chag sameach" (Happy Holiday). And if my teaching schedule will take me on the road on Thanksgiving, I will make sure to have turkey even while I am on the road; and my wife and I will have a "delayed Thanksgiving dinner" of roast turkey with all the side dishes when I am home.

I see the Fourth of July as an opportunity to show my appreciation for the existence of the United States; and I see Thanksgiving as a beautiful tradition to thank the Almighty for all the good He has given us in our lives – something that we should actually do every day. In fact, in the Jewish tradition, we begin the morning with "Modeh Ani" – giving thanks to the Almighty every single morning upon waking up.

Fourth of July

Although Obama did not mention his own celebration of the Fourth of July in his two pre-presidency books, he did mention in his first book that his grandparents had told him about their childhood memories of living in a small town at the time of the Great Depression. Their memories included Fourth of July parades (BO DFMF 13).

In his second book, "The Audacity of Hope", Obama included Fourth of July parades as one of the activities that a politician would include in maintaining his name recognition. He also mentioned the Fourth of July as the day that his daughter Malia was born (BO AOH 103, 339).

Susan Rice served as US ambassador to the UN in the first Obama administration, and as National Security Advisor during Obama's second administration, beginning this job on July 1, 2013. She mentions that on July 4 (interestingly, using this term instead of the more usual "Fourth of July") Obama "was due to host" a family celebration for his daughter Malia's birthday, and in the evening, thousands of military families for the fireworks display at the White House (SusanR 349).

Question: why to "host" a family birthday celebration? Why not say to "celebrate"? And since the verb "host" is extended to the second part of the sentence, Rice avoided attributing the verb "to celebrate" the Fourth of July in regard to Obama.

For comparison, earlier on the same page, Rice mentions her family tradition of marching with neighbors in the local Fourth of July parade. In fact, she describes it as the "Independence Day parade".

Susan Rice also talked of "Thanksgiving dinner" in which she and her mother were able to cooperate, and she mentioned her father and mother joining their family for Thanksgiving (SusanR 228, 250).

Michelle Obama

Unlike Susan Rice, Michelle does not mention any Thanksgiving dinner at all. She only mentions Thanksgiving at the time she was First Lady, talking of "the most ridiculous ritual of the office", which was pardoning a turkey from being served for Thanksgiving dinner (MichO 392).

As for July 4, for Michelle it is the day that her oldest daughter was born. In a caption to a family picture in the center of the book she wrote: "The Fourth of July always gives us a lot to celebrate, since it's also Malia's birthday." (MichO 190)

She mentions attending a Fourth of July celebration in Butte, Montana while on the campaign trail in 2008. She writes: "For me, the Fourth of July 2008 was the most significant threshold we'd crossed" – and then she immediately explains that this is because it was the tenth anniversary of them becoming a family (MichO 251, 254).

Michelle writes that because Barack was campaigning, he couldn't take time off to celebrate Malia's tenth birthday at home; talking like an outsider or even a foreigner, she adds that he couldn't walk away from "what was the country's most symbolic holiday" (MichO 253).

She talked about the line separating individual and public celebrations. Indeed, there were signs of "Happy Birthday Malia" in Butte, but it was in the context of a public celebration; while she wanted to have it as a family celebration – just a birthday party for Malia (MichO 253)

This is the only time in her book in which Michelle mentions being present at a Fourth of July celebration before becoming First Lady. Realizing that the book is an "open statement", and "edited" by the subject – meaning, nobody says everything, but we should still ask the question: is it possible that it was the first time in her life that a Fourth of July celebration was significant for her?

Michelle and massacres in the US

Michelle talks in her book of three major violent events (2 massacres and one individual murder) – Newtown Connecticut; Charleston, South Carolina; and one murder in Chicago.

Newtown, Connecticut – December 2012

This massacre is registered in her book as the only time in which the president sent for her to come to the Oval Office during the daytime. When Obama gave his remarks, she commented on the fact that she was "not ready". And when the president went to Newtown to attend a prayer vigil, Michelle didn't join. She was so shaken by the event that she had no strength to be there (MichO 376, 378).

Charleston, South Carolina – June 2015

This massacre at an African Methodist Episcopal church was committed by "an unemployed twenty-one-year-old white man" who came into the church during their Bible study group, sat with the group for a while, and then got up and killed nine of them.

For this massacre, Michelle said, "Late in June 2015, Barack and I flew to Charleston, South Carolina, to sit with another grieving community…" (MichO 396)

Hadiya Pendleton in Chicago – January 2013

Hadiya Pendleton, a fifteen-year-old girl, was murdered in a public park in Chicago.
She was with a group of friends who were mistaken for being gang members, and she was shot in the back by a gang member while she was running away (MichO 380). She was one of three people who were killed in Chicago that day (MichO 381).

Michelle said that she went to Hadiya's funeral "…because it felt like the right thing to do". Moreover, she invited Hadiya's parents to attend the President's State of the Union Address, and also hosted the family at the White House for Easter (MichO 381, 382).

Hadiya's murder registered strongly in Michelle. A few pages after the above description, and after describing a meeting with high school students on a visit to London, she writes:

"Two months after Hadiya Pendleton's funeral, I returned to Chicago," "In the wake of Hadiya's death…" (MichO 384)

In a speech Michelle gave to "Working Together to Address Youth Violence in Chicago" on April 10, 2013, she said:

"…Hadiya's family was just like my family. Hadiya Pendleton was me, and I was her."

Michelle wanted to give meaning to Hadiya's life by encouraging others "to dream as big as she did, and work as hard as she did, and live a life that honors every last bit of her God-given promise."

Later the same day, she also went to address the students at the William R Harper Senior High School in Englewood, a neighborhood on the South Side of Chicago (MichO 385).

In her address, she realized that for the students in the school she represented not only the South Side of Chicago, but also the establishment in Washington DC. Her speech reflected this dual representation.

She emphasized to them that their school afforded them everything needed to succeed, and that there were many among the school's teachers who cared for them and wanted them to succeed (MichO 387). She also went against the idea that an African American kid in the US was destined to fail, since this idea in itself is the prescription for failure (MichO 388).

But when a kid in the audience asked her whether anything would be done about the problems they faced, such as gang violence in their neighborhood, she answered:

"Honestly, I know you're dealing with a lot here, but no one's going to save you anytime soon. Most people in Washington aren't even trying. A lot of them don't even know you exist." (MichO 387).

We should note that this is in answer to a question, so at this point Michelle was not talking from prepared notes written by a speechwriter. She answered with what came into her mind at that moment.

But a more basic question is whether it is true that "most people in Washington aren't even trying. A lot of them don't even know you exist."

Michelle herself had organized and spoken to a group of prominent Chicago organizations and citizens earlier the same day, with the goal of raising money to reduce gun violence. President Obama also spoke frequently about initiatives to reduce gun violence – for example, in a speech at the White House on January 16, 2013; in a speech in Minneapolis on February 4, 2013; in a speech in Denver on April 3, 2013; and on many other occasions. Certainly Michelle had to be aware of this.

In other matters, Michelle herself, in a speech she gave on September 15, 2010 to the Congressional Black Caucus Foundation Legislative Conference, mentioned that the federal government funds school lunches for 31 million kids.

So when Michelle talked to the high school students in 2013, she had to be aware that even though the federal government does not focus on individual kids, the administration – regardless of whether it is Democrat or Republican – devotes a large amount of the federal budget to support low income families, and this includes the African American communities. School lunches are only one example of how the administration in Washington cares about low-income families, many of whom are African American.

Summary

Michelle mentioned two massacres and one individual murder.

Newtown, Connecticut – she was so shaken by the event that she had no strength to be there (MichO 376).
Charleston, South Carolina – "Barack and I flew to Charleston, South Carolina, to sit with another grieving community…" (MichO 396).
Hadiya Pendleton in Chicago – she went to the funeral "…because it felt like the right thing to do" (MichO 381).

There were two massacres and one murder. The first (Newtown) was a white killing whites. The second (Charleston) was a white killing African Americans. The third (Chicago) was an African American killing an African American.

Michelle and the US

Michelle was quoted as saying on the campaign trail in Madison Wisconsin in February 2008: "For the first time in my adult lifetime I'm proud of my country." (Axe 277, DavidPl 301, ValJ 152-153)

In her book, Michelle brought the full quote of what she said:

"What we've learned over this year is that hope is making a comeback! And let me tell you something, for the first time in my adult lifetime, I'm really proud of my country. Not just because Barack has done well, but because I think people are hungry for change. I have been desperate to see our country moving in that direction, and just not feeling so alone in my frustration and disappointment. I've seen people who are hungry to be unified around some basic common issues, and it's made me proud. I feel privileged to be a part of even witnessing this." (MichO 259-290)

Question: why did she restrict the sentence to "my **adult** life"? Why not to say "my life"?

Michelle and language

Michelle used the words "country" and "nation" numerous times [See Appendix].

Discussion

We should disregard the first two quotes as they are in the introduction to the book. The rest of the book goes chronologically, according to the time in her life.

Michelle used the word "country" once when talking about the riots "across the country" (3) after the murder of Martin Luther King. She next used the word "country" when talking about programs for gifted students "around the country" (4), and later (5) when she talked about Jesse Jackson (father of her friend Santita) running for president. We should note that in #3 and #5 the word "country" is used in conjunction with two African American leaders – Martin Luther King and Jesse Jackson.

The next time she used the word "country" is when she decided to take the LSAT test so she call enroll in "the best law schools in the country".

She used the word "nation" for the first time when her husband was running for president, just before the first primary test in Iowa.

She used the phrase "**our** country" seventeen times.

She used the phrase "**my** country" three times.   The first is in the well-known quote when she said, "For the first time in my adult lifetime, I'm really proud of **my** country" (MichO 260).

The other two places are:

1. "I loved **my country** for all the ways its story could be told" (MichO 416)
2. "The responsibilities I've felt – to Sasha and Malia, to Barack, to my career and **my country**…" (MichO 418-419)

Please note the following:

1. Both places are towards the end of the book, representing the time that was towards the end of her husband's presidency.
2. In the first quote the term "my country" is used in the past tense – "I **loved** my country".
3. We should note the order of listing in the second quote where "my country" appears last. It is quite understood and even expected that her daughters and her husband will be listed first. After all, family comes first. But we should note that "career" is listed before "country".

   This is similar to her saying about her childhood: "As we grew, we spoke more about drugs and sex and life choices, about race and inequality and politics." (MichO 25) Note that "politics" is listed last.

Michelle and "country" - more

In her speech to the Democratic National Convention in 2008, the convention in which her husband Barack Obama was nominated by the Democratic party to be the candidate in the upcoming elections, Michelle several times referred to the US with the words "country" and "nation".

1. "That is why I love **this country**."

2. "And in my own life, in my own small way, I've tried to give back to **this country**…"
3. "…each of us has something to contribute to the life of **this nation**."
4. "It's what he's done in the United States Senate, fighting to ensure the men and women who serve **this country**…"
5. "to make health care available for every American, and to make sure every child in **this nation**…"
6. "…to hold us together as **one nation** even when we disagree."
7. "…and became the first voices in this chorus for change that's been echoed by millions of Americans from every corner of **this nation**."
8. "How this time, in **this great country**…"

We should note that she did not use the possessive pronoun "my" (singular) or "our" (plural) in any of these places.

Michelle as First Lady

There are several speeches Michelle gave as First Lady.

Even as a First Lady we can still see several occasions in which she used the phrase "**the** country". However, there are also several places in which "**our** country" entered her language.

The first one was at the Bust Unveiling of Sojourner Truth on April 28, 2009. In these brief remarks, she said, "Forever more, in the halls of one of **our country's** greatest monuments of liberty and equality…", and she did use the possessive pronoun "our".

She did the same on another occasion, when she spoke to the Congressional Black Caucus Gala, Washington Convention Center, Washington, DC, on September 23, 2012.

In this event she said several times:

1. "They came because they believe that there is no higher calling than serving **our country**, no more noble a cause than that of our fellow citizens."

2. "Whether our sons and daughters who wear **our country**'s uniform…"

One can say in these two events she talked to an African American audience, and hence "our country". But the fact is that in this last event she also said,

1. "It's about who we are as Americans."
2. "It's about doing everything we can to carry on the legacy that is our inheritance not just as African Americans, but as Americans – as citizens of the greatest country on Earth."

It is clear from her language that she **can** identify as an American. We should note that in the second quote she not only expressed both the African American and American identity, but she acknowledged being a citizen "of the greatest country on Earth."

She also used "our country" on two more occasions.

The first was at the Democratic National Convention in Charlotte, North Carolina, on September 4, 2012, when she said:

"I love that for Barack, there is no such thing as "us" and "them" – he doesn't care whether you're a Democrat, a Republican, or none of the above; he knows that we all love **our country**."

In this speech she also expressed again her identity as an "American" – "It is who we are as Americans."

Now we can return to the sentence she said during the campaign: "For the first time in my adult lifetime I'm proud of my country." (Axe 277, DavidPl 301)

In the campaign, and later on in her position as First Lady, the process reinforced her identity as an "American". The campaign, indeed, was the "first time" she felt she could be proud.

Summary - Michelle and the US

When she describes the campaign before Obama's second term as president (2012), Michelle begins by talking about history. Although she is familiar with US history, still, she felt closer to her own history, and as she said, "it wasn't that of presidents or First Ladies" (MichO 365).

She went on to say that she could relate to the story of Sojourner Truth better than to the story of John Quincy Adams; and to Harriet Tubman more than to Woodrow Wilson. She was more familiar with the struggles of Rosa Parks and Coretta Scott King than those of Eleanor Roosevelt or Mamie Eisenhower. (MichO 365-366)

In other words, her own history was the history of African Americans. But if she would stop here, the story would not be as complicated.

After Barack and Michelle took a trip to Kenya in August 1991 to visit his family there, Michelle described her feelings about that trip. Before the trip she assumed that she would feel some connection to the continent from which her ancestors came.   But the visit gave her a feeling of sadness, as she got the sense of being "unrooted in both lands" (MichO 160).

When Michelle said during the campaign, "For the first time in my adult lifetime I'm proud of my country", she expressed her true feelings and attitude towards the US.   She did relate a lot more to her own heritage. She was the product of the African American community of the South Side of Chicago. She never forgot where she came from. And during the campaign, seeing people of all colors and races joining her husband with his message of hope and change, she could relate to the US as her own country ("my country") (Axe 277, DavidPl 301).

As First Lady, talking to an African American audience, she was finally able to feel that she and the audience are not only African Americans. They do not have only one identity. They are also the "citizens of the greatest country on Earth."

The Marriage of Barack and Michelle Obama

Introduction

Michelle dedicated her book, "Becoming", to "the folks who raised me…"
To "my circle of strong women…"
To "my loyal and dedicated staff…"

Then she moves on:

"To the loves of my life: Malia and Sasha, my two most precious peas…"
"…and finally, Barack, who always promised me an interesting journey."

He did promise, but did he deliver on his promise?

Michelle and Barack

Michelle met Barack when she was asked to be his mentor at her workplace, the "high-end law firm called Sidley & Austin" (MichO 92). Barack at the time had completed his first year at Harvard Law School. He was to be at the law firm for the duration of the summer, and then to return to continue his studies at Harvard for two more years.

Michelle starts the chapter on her meeting with Barack by writing in capital letters: "BARACK OBAMA WAS LATE ON DAY ONE" (MichO 94). If one doubts the significance of this fact, Michelle says that her secretary knew that being on time was very important to her, and being late "drove her nuts". Moreover, she saw his being late as "hubris" (MichO 96).

Since she writes the book after their long journey that brought them to the highest level of politics – the office of the president of the US – did she capitalize this sentence about his "tardiness" as an omen for the future? As if she tells herself: I should have known even then!

It didn't take long before the two started dating.   When he returned to Harvard they were "**a** long-distance couple" (MichO 151-152). Once he graduated, he came back to her (MichO 151).

And she continues: "I **loved** him. I felt **loved** by him." (MichO 151)

In fact, again, she is writing her book after 26 years of marriage and 8 years of being First Lady, looking back to the time before they got married. But why does she use past tense? Why can't she say, "I loved him then as I love him today"? Why is "love" in the past tense?

Moreover, why can't she say, "We loved each other"? And if she didn't want to use the pronoun "we", why couldn't she say, "I loved him and he loved me"? She only talked of love from her point of view.

She continues by saying that once he was back from college, they could be "a short-distance couple" (MichO 152).

Why not to say, "we could be a real couple," or even, "we could be together"?
Why doesn't the word "distance" vanish once he returned to Chicago?

Would a couple living in the same city, and even living together (as she says that he moved into her place) describe their relationship as a "short-distance couple"?

Getting Engaged

After a few months of a "short-distance" relationship, while they were at a restaurant celebrating Barack's completing the bar exam, Barack brought up the topic of marriage by saying that he "didn't really see the point."

Michelle responded by asking, "If we're committed… why wouldn't we formalize that commitment?" Although they had discussed this in the past, they continued into "the old argument" regarding the significance of marriage, and whether it is even necessary. Michelle describes their conversation as "not fighting" but "quarreling… attorney-style".
Knowing Obama to be the "chill" and "not too high and not too low" guy, as described by Axelrod and Plouffe, it is no wonder that Michelle says that she was the one who was more emotional, and who did most of the talking. This continued until the waiter brought a dessert tray with a silver lid. When he lifted the lid, she saw a small box with a diamond ring (MichO 156).

Was it funny? Did he need to "torture" her before giving her the ring? Knowing that there is an aggressive streak in his personality (as seen in his ridiculing people to their face, and shaming them) we should not be surprised.

Interestingly, Barack was not the one who lifted the lid to offer her the ring. The waiter lifted the lid. Only afterward, Barack "dropped to one knee" and asked her to marry him.

The Wedding

Although Obama initially said that he is not interested in the details of the wedding, still, knowing his controlling personality (remember the cake at the wedding of Valerie Jarrett's daughter), we shouldn't be surprised that Michelle says he gave his opinion about every single detail, even the most minute one (MichO 164).

She ended this description by saying, "I had faith in **this** union, faith in **this** man." (MichO 165)

One should note the use of "this" for the "union" and the "man" indicating a missing possessive "my"/"our" in both cases.

The wedding was performed at the sanctuary of the Trinity Church and conducted by Reverend Jeremiah A. Wright, Jr. (BO DFMF 440)

At the party, Obama's half-brother raised a toast "To those who are not here with us", (quite likely referring to the deceased father and the large family in Kenya) to which Obama responded with, "And to a happy ending" (BO DFMF 442).

Knowing Obama's fascination with movies, and using scenes from movies as a point in conversations, one can understand why he would look upon his own wedding as "a happy ending". Still, the question can be asked, why would a wedding be called an "ending". When a couple builds their future together, it is more likely to be considered the "beginning" of a mutual life, and not an "ending".

Life After the Honeymoon

Background

Before they got married, Obama committed himself to writing a book about race relations. However, he didn't deliver. The publisher cancelled the contract and asked for the advance payment to be refunded. Obama had no choice, but to find another publisher that would agree to take the project. Still, he needed to write the book (which later became "Dreams from My Father").

"Dreams from My Father"

Six weeks after the wedding, Obama had an idea for how he would be able to finish the book, an idea that Michelle said "seemed to suit him perfectly". He would do it "in isolation" so he could concentrate on the project. Obama's mother rented him a cabin on the beach, far away from "everyday distractions" but also far away from Michelle. (MichO 170).

The bride of six weeks defended her husband by saying that he was not the one who had rented the cabin – it was his mother. But there is one major point missing from this description. Michelle does not mention any prior conversations between them on how to deal with the unfinished book. Obama did not ask his wife for any input on what, where, and when to do the project. He came to her one day with this idea, with a ready-to-execute plan, as his mother had already rented the cabin.

And where did this "little cabin" happen to be?

Would "his mother" choose a place somewhere in the US? Would it be in his home state of Hawaii? And if not Hawaii, maybe somewhere in the sunbelt, in the south of the US?

No. The place that his mother chose was on the island of Bali, Indonesia (170-171).

Bali has a reputation for being the capital of an easy life for tourists, and the capital of drugs and sex.

Six weeks after the wedding Obama vanished for five weeks.

Michelle equated these five weeks to being like an "all-nighter" in college to prepare for a test, or to finish a paper before a deadline. She defended him. She even suggested that he did it "out of kindness" – to spare her the "chaos" of writing the book (MichO 171). Still, she called this Bali book project a "honeymoon with himself" (MichO 171).

Obama returned from Bali "looking tanned" (MichO 171), but the book was not really finished. It was "**basically** finished" (MichO 173)

Going away to Bali was not the only time Obama was away from his wife. Michelle said that he liked to play basketball with his friends in "what little leisure time he had" (MichO 212). Obama also liked to work out at the gym on Thursday before coming home. When he would arrive, he often found her already asleep (MichO 204)

Obama did the same while being president. He would find time during the day to play golf to be able to relax (MichO 363). As we saw earlier, sports were a big part of Obama's life.

Obama in the Illinois Senate

During the time Obama served in the Illinois Senate, he was in Springfield, the capital of Illinois, from Monday to Thursday night, the time when the Senate was in session. In addition, he increased his activity at the University of Chicago, where he was teaching. Michelle and Barack had "a standing date night" on Friday (MichO 184-185). In Michelle's words, her husband was "oversubscribed and away a lot" (MichO 201).

And as time went on she became more and more upset. From only teasing him about being late, it became an "aggravation" (MichO 203). This brought her to give us Obama's dictionary - "On my way" was an expression of optimism. "Almost home" was only a "state of mind" (MichO 204). In other words, she stopped believing him.
She summed it up by saying that her husband was "a man with two families". He needed to split his time between her and the girls, and his constituents from the South Side of Chicago (MichO 213).

Question: Would the spouse of a politician label his/her spouse as having "two families"?

Life inside the White House

Life inside the White House presented a challenge for Michelle. She wanted to feel like her own self, to remain "Michelle Robinson from the South Side" (MichO 361). Although they had been married for many years by that time, she still didn't forget her origin as "Robinson".

She outlines for us the daily schedule inside the White House. Obama was working many hours, "until 1:00 or 2:00 in the morning" (MichO 349). There were two exceptions: the family dinner, to which – despite his general tendency to be late – he now came on time (MichO 307). The second exception was that he always took a break in the evening to give Michelle and the girls a good night kiss (MichO 349).

One major point bothered Michelle. During their eight years at the White House she felt that she and her daughters were only "supporting players", a position she didn't want her daughter to accept as normal. She felt that a family should not necessarily "revolve around the man's needs" (MichO 306).

Being together

Four months after the elections, Obama took Michelle on a date, to have dinner and see a show in New York City (MichO 323). It was not that simple to arrange. A trip for the president requires meticulous planning, and arranging the Secret Service detail (MichO 324).

Michelle gave a very detailed description of the conversation during dinner. She started by saying that the conversation was "light". She then described how, four months into the presidency, the two of them were going through a period of transition, "retrofitting" in her language; and that they needed to "…figur[e] out how one identity worked with the other and what this meant inside our marriage." (MichO 324)

In this description she talks of two identities, and the need of each one to deal with the other. But at this point it is not clear if the two identities are hers and Barack's, or, maybe she means two identities of Barack? i.e., one is Barack, the person, and the other is Barack the president. We should remember that during the campaign she also talked of the two Baracks she knew. One was her husband, and the other was the politician that the masses knew,

The ending of the sentence – "and what this meant inside our marriage" – tends to support the second interpretation, that these were the two identities of Barack, as their marriage was listed separately from the two identities.

She goes on to say that "…there was almost no part of Barack's complicated life that didn't in some way impact mine" (MichO 324).

We should note the following:

1. She refers to several parts of Barack's life. This again supports the possibility that the two identities mentioned earlier are of Barack.
2. This is the first time during Barack's journey into politics, first as a state senator, and then as a US senator, and now as president, that she labeled his life as "complicated".

    She didn't do so when he was a state senator, or when he became a US senator. She only described his life as "complicated" fourth months into his presidency.

    It is a point to explore what might have changed once they moved into the White House.

Communication between the two

When she describes their date at the New York restaurant, she mentions all the "shared business" they could have talked about, but she intentionally did her best not to bring it up during their time at the restaurant. After all, she wanted the conversation to be "light" (MichO 324).

She added that this was her strategy, not only for that evening. In general, during their time at the White House, she did not want to talk "business" during their personal time together, as she wanted total separation between the White House business and their own personal life.

This means that their dinner was like an island, separate from the events going on in the outside world, or in the White House, the "West Wing", or the Oval Office. She wanted "fences" and "boundaries" between their personal life (mainly dinner) and Obama's professional life (MichO 346). At their family dinners, they would listen to their daughters talking of their time in school (MichO 347).

As for White House business, if she had anything to discuss with the "West Wing", she left it to her "staff" to discuss it with Barack (MichO 325).

Not only did she not talk with him directly, but it comes across that he didn't consult her, or ask her for her opinion, before making major decisions. For example, she was "surprised" when he chose Hillary Clinton as Secretary of State (MichO 335).

There are two times she mentions that Barack shared information with her. The first was about the raid on Osama Bin Laden. One evening after dinner was over, and their daughters went on their way, Obama told her that they might go to capture Bin Laden, although she immediately tells the reader that "he needed no input from me." (MichO 346) After the raid, Barack told her: "We got him, and no one got hurt." (MichO 363)

The second time was after the Newtown massacre. She said that her assistant came to tell her that "Barack was in the Oval Office by himself", and he wanted her to come "right away" (MichO 376).

Question: Why did she have the need to insert the phrase "by himself"? To the reader it sounds as if it is "unnecessary".

Note: what seems to the reader as "unnecessary" is only "unnecessary" for the reader, but it is "necessary" for the writer. We should consider this sentence as a very important sentence. Later on, we will address this issue separately.

Once Barack called her, she talked of her feelings: "My husband needed me." (MichO 376) Earlier, she had related to her position in her husband's life as being a "supporting player", but now she was "needed".

She added one more point: "This would be the only time in eight years that he'd request my presence in the middle of a workday." (376-377)

This does not mean that she wasn't in the Oval Office at all. But this was the only time that he requested her presence there.

The Newtown massacre was an event that "shattered" the separation she established between their personal and professional life. "Windows" and "fences" were down (MichO 377).

Earlier, she talked of the need to establish "fences" and "boundaries", and now she added that "windows" existed. Barack's life at the Oval Office was not opaque to her. She had "windows" to look into.

Back to Osama Bin Laden

Michelle said that when Barack told her about the capture of Bin Laden, he "was coming out of **our bedroom**" (MichO 363).

There are several other places in her book where Michelle refers to the bedroom / bed:

1. "I walked down the stairs from **our bedroom** with the dogs following on my heels." (MichO xii)
2. "I found him sitting at his desk, looking over the text of his victory speech in the little book-strewn office adjacent to **our bedroom** – his Hole." (MichO 276)
3. "…just down the hall from **the master bedroom**." (MichO 290)
4. "…and into **our** strange new bed." (MichO 303)
5. "**Our bedroom** had not just a king-sized bed…" (MichO 304)
6. "**The master suite** in the residence…" (MichO 305)

Please note the following:

1. There are two places where she uses "the" and not "our" – when she talks about "the master bedroom" (3) and "The master suite"

(6) inside the White House, describing the outline of the place. In the other four places, besides the text in the present location, we find the use of "our".

2. Generally speaking, there is a difference between couples' language and the language of singles. A single person would say "**my** bed", "**my** bedroom", while couples would say "**the** bed", "**the** bedroom". It is rare, if ever, to find "**our** bedroom" inside an "open statement" (when talking to strangers).

    Whenever "our" appears in an "open statement" it would raise the suspicion of possible divorce or adoption present in the background.

3. She does talk of "my bedroom" for the time before the presidency, the time she said that most of the week she was alone.

In 2010, Barack signed "a new child nutrition bill", that was important to Michelle. She reports that Barack "joked to reporters", saying, "Had I not been able to get this bill passed, I would be sleeping on the couch." (MichO 348)

Was it only a joke? Or, was it a reflection of "our bedroom"?

Michelle's Marriage to the President

In general, she described her marriage to Barack as "coexistence" (MichO 81; 131; 214) which sometimes interfered with their "shared life" (MichO 214).

When talking about being married to the president, she said:

"When **you**'re married to the president, **you** come to understand quickly that the world brims with chaos, that disasters unfurl without notice. Forces seen and unseen stand ready to tear into whatever calm **you** might feel." (MichO 342)

Note that she used the pronoun "you" instead of the pronoun "I", contradicting the linguistic formula of commitment – "First Person Singular ("I") past tense". This makes this text "unreliable".

In summarizing her life as "First Lady", Michelle said that she was "something of a curiosity", as she was "a black First **Lady**, a professional **woman**, a **mother** of young kids" (MichO 372).

She used the words "lady", "woman", and "mother", but the word "wife" is missing!

She also avoided using the word "wife" when talking about her life after the White House years, when she doesn't need to be a "political **spouse**" anymore (MichO 418).

Bringing the dogs into the White House brought "lightness", and they served as proof that the White House was a "home" (MichO 392). Without the dogs, would it not have been a "home"?

Life After the White House Years

In the "Acknowledgements" at the end of the book she writes: "My husband, Barack, my love, my partner of twenty-five years and the most lovingly committed father to our daughters, has been a life partner I could only have imagined." (MichO 423)

Question: Why is "lovingly committed" only reserved for "our daughters", and not to her?

Other People Around President Obama

Susan Rice

Susan Rice came from an African American family. Both of her parents were highly educated. Her father, a descendant of slaves, got his Ph.D. in economics, and served in high positions in the government. Her mother, also highly educated, was on several corporate boards, promoting education for African American students. The family was upper middle-class, and employed a housekeeper to take care of all household chores (SusanR 26, 38-39, 57).

When Susan was 10 years old, her parents separated due to her mother's "illicit affair" with a white man, labeled by Rice as a "WASP", whom the mother married after the divorce was finalized (SusanR 70).

Years later, after a long relationship with her white boyfriend from college, Susan and her boyfriend married and had two children; in her words – "white-looking black kids". Since they were "mixed-race children" (remember Obama?) it was difficult for her to impart to them the African American experience, a sense of their history and responsibilities (SusanR 218-219).

The main message that Rice's parents gave her and her brother was education and service. Education was the most important as it was the key to success in life.

Rice attended prestigious private schools from pre-school till high school. She then went to Stanford University in California, but after her high school, the National Cathedral School (NCS) "Nothing in life has seemed hard." She continued her graduate studies at Oxford University in the UK, where she received her Ph.D. in 1990 (SusanR 99, 119).

Rice's first job in government, when she was twenty-eight years old, was at the National Security Council during the Clinton administration. She went on to become a regional Assistant Secretary of State, and during the Obama administration she served as US ambassador to the UN during Obama's first term, and National Security Advisor during his second term.

Who is Susan Rice?

There are several traits that Rice attributes to herself that mirror those of Obama.

The first one is that she is a fact-based person. Afraid of failing due to her parents' divorce, she wants to make sure that her decision is the right one, and to do so, she needs to be fully informed (SusanR 100).

This reminds us of the long discussions in the White House before President Obama would make a decision, a process that at times was long and draining.

As a derivative of the first trait (fact-based), comes the second one – the meaning of leadership. It is not the great performance of one player of one instrument, but it is a "symphony" playing in harmony. Again, she mirrors the evaluation of the long process Obama instituted in the White House on the way to reach a decision. Not only to make sure that the decision is the right one, but to ensure that the bureaucrats involved in the process will accept and implement the decision. In summary, "the most enduring outcomes are not always the swiftest ones." (SusanR 203)

Another trait she shared with Obama is control. She was a control freak on grammar and punctuation, especially the use of commas. She wanted to ensure that any paper coming out of her office would be perfectly written (SusanR 356).

Self-declared as a "tomboy" and not "acting like a girl", it bothered her that her brother criticized her for "acting like a girl" during the time she was attacked after Benghazi. Her brother saw her treating the mission as more important than her self- preservation, an attitude that her brother told her that a man wouldn't have (SusanR 56, 304, 335).

Even so, she experienced the difficulty of being a woman working in a male-dominated environment. However, she didn't encounter any sexual harassment, except for "crude jokes, loose hands, and obnoxious comments" which she managed to deal with (SusanR 85).

It is interesting to note that she mentions that at the White House Correspondents' Dinner in 2015, Trump approached her, gave her an "unsolicited hug" and told her that she was "doing a great job for the country." She writes that she felt as if she had been "molested" (SusanR 382).

She was stressed when she was scheduled to throw the ceremonial opening pitch for a baseball game at Nationals Park, but she "didn't let womankind down". She could "report to the president that [she] hadn't humiliated him or [her]self" (SusanR 341-342).

Rice is not only a woman. She is also African American. She labels herself as "a confident black woman", who judges herself according to her own inner scale, and not by what others think. (In the words of Warren Buffett – according to an inner scorecard.) The fact that she kept going in spite of hardships gave her the sense of "personal triumph". Others did not make her a victim (SusanR 38, 75).

At Stanford she told her classmates that although she accepted her being black to include history, burden, and responsibility, still the fact that she went through her life in a majority-white environment made her feel "uncertain and uneasy" (SusanR 103).

This does not mean she was hesitant to use her "blackness" as a weapon. There were times that she used colorful language to tell people, "Kiss my black ass." It was a sort of mantra for her. It came to a point in which one of her deputies gave her an ink stamp with the letters "KMBA". She also used Obama's language – "getting shit done" – when the Supreme Court upheld the Affordable Care Act (Obamacare). In her farewell party at the UN, the Russian ambassador said that he could not find some of her language in the Oxford dictionary (SusanR 353, 427, 299).

She commented that people who do not know her misread the fact that she is not smiling, interpreting it as anger (SusanR 224)

The fact is that people in the government criticized Rice for being confrontational. She found out that people saw her as "brash, demanding, impatient, hardheaded, and unafraid of confrontation". Her superior at the State Department during the Clinton administration told her that she alienated most of her team; that she is "hard-charging and hardheaded" and intimidating. There was a time in which she showed her middle finger to a superior while he was talking. She had to learn how, within the government, to choose her enemies wisely. (SusanR 170, 191, 198, 203)

Susan Rice and Basketball

On the back cover of her book "Tough Love" the insert gives some information about the author, saying that she is "…a long-retired basketball player."

Rice describes herself as an "inveterate tomboy" who avoided "prissy, girly" activities.
Very early in age she liked throwing a football, which was her favorite activity. She was proud that she was not throwing "like a girl" (SusanR 56, 304).

Sports in general, and basketball in particular, are a theme mentioned throughout her book. Her nickname was "Spo", short for "Sportin" (SusanR 80).

Her father would sometimes take her and other children to the Washington Bullets basketball games (SusanR 68).

Basketball was a school of life for her, showing her how to play with a team, how to win, and even how to lose – with grace. Playing point guard at the basketball court taught Rice more about leadership than she attributed to her academic studies (SusanR 86-87).

Her high school basketball coach had a major influence on her, and kept in touch with her for years beyond high school. She even mentioned "love" when talking about her.

There was one time when her coach called her by a racist label, and she responded with an expletive. Interesting to note that Rice didn't blame her coach for it, nor was she hurt.
She understood that quite likely it was her coach's upbringing that caused it. She was even sorry when her coach moved away from the school to another position. Still, her coach kept in touch with her by letters, telling her the same message her parents gave her: "be Susan Rice always".
Many years later, during the Benghazi incident after which Rice was attacked, her coach sent her a letter expressing regret for hurting her

years earlier in high school. Rice mentioned that she still keeps the letter close to her (SusanR 86-87).

Basketball is one of the ways Rice related to people. In describing her brother, she mentions that he played basketball and other sports. Although her brother didn't want to go to the same university she attended (Stanford), and instead chose Yale, he became the starting point guard on the varsity basketball team. When talking of her friend Andrea, she commended her for being a better player than herself (SusanR 102, 87-88).

When Rice studied at Oxford University in England, she also played on the Oxford women's varsity basketball team. She played as a point guard with a team of mostly American players (SusanR 113). In describing her other activities, she mentions, "off the basketball court and outside the library…" – giving primary importance to the basketball court by listing it first (SusanR 115).

One summer during her studies at Oxford, Rice and her boyfriend went on a trip together to China, where they shot hoops with the Beijing Work Unit women's basketball team. She also played basketball with her friend's students (SusanR 116-117).

There is no mention of any basketball activity between her description of the above-mentioned trip to China, and the time she became US ambassador to the UN during the first term of the Obama administration. She does mention that she was at the State Department during the Clinton administration, and Secretary of State Madeleine Albright was a family friend and a mentor to Rice, but still no basketball activity is mentioned.

One should note that an "open statement" is not reality. It is only "subjective reality". It means that what we encounter in an "open statement" is only what the person has decided is important to be mentioned. And we see that Rice mentioned basketball quite a bit during her life until getting her Ph.D. degree, and she returns to mention basketball once she is at the UN during the Obama administration. During the eight years of the Clinton administration, and her work as Assistant Secretary of State for African Affairs – no basketball is mentioned. During the eight years of the Bush administration – no basketball is mentioned. Once Obama entered the picture, basketball returns to the center of attention.

During her time at the UN there were annual basketball games where the US Mission staff played against the UN security guards (SusanR 304).

When she "came back" (name of chapter) from New York to Washington DC to serve as
National Security Advisor, and she received Secret Service protection, she asked that her code name would be "Point Guard" (SusanR 384).

In choosing this name, she compares her position as National Security Advisor (NSA) to her position as "point guard" on the basketball court. The point guard, like the NSA, is not a "glory position". He/she is not the one who scores nor the one who receives attention. The NSA is the one who manages the players as a team, to ensure high efficiency. The same is true of the point guard who has to see the whole picture, determine the moves, organize the offense, pass the ball to the shooters, and in essence to be the team leader. She played that position in high school and at Oxford, and it prepared her for her position at the National Security Council (SusanR 384-385).

Rice's Relationship with Obama

Rice met Obama in 2004, when he was a candidate for the US Senate from Illinois. In early 2007, when Obama had already decided to run for president, he asked Rice to lead his foreign policy team, and she happily agreed (SusanR 221).

After he was elected president, Obama offered Rice the position of US ambassador to the UN. She had wanted the position of National Security Advisor, and she requested it based on her "candid relationship" with Obama. She consulted her family friend and mentor Madeleine Albright, Secretary of State during the Clinton administration, who advised her to take the UN job (SusanR 130).

Although she was the lead of the foreign policy team, still Obama consulted Rice on a domestic/foreign policy issue. He asked Rice for her opinion on the possibility of him offering Hillary Clinton the job of Secretary of State (SusanR 130).

In late 2011, while she was UN ambassador, Obama met Rice and offered her the job of World Bank president. In many words she refused. Interestingly, although elsewhere she describes his tendency to move straight to the point when talking business, in this case he first held a small-talk conversation with her before mentioning the World Bank. He opened the conversation by asking her how she was doing and how her family dealt with her being far away from them. It should be noted that he didn't ask her how she was doing being far away from her family, but only how her family is doing with her far away from them. He also asked her a "business" question – if the White House is supporting her; and then one more personal question – how she is doing after the loss of her father (SusanR 303, 343).

During the campaign of 2012, Rice "didn't see much" of Obama, as he was on the road campaigning, and she was in New York (SusanR 315).

Benghazi

Benghazi is the event that brought Susan Rice's name to the knowledge of the average American citizen.

Background

On 9/11/2012, the US consulate in Benghazi, Libya, was attacked, and four US diplomats were killed. The information that the US Intelligence Community initially put out was that the attack was quite likely a violent demonstration that was triggered by a video insulting the prophet Muhammad. Susan Rice appeared on several TV shows that weekend, and repeated this incorrect assessment. In fact, the attack was a pre-meditated attack held on the anniversary of 9/11, and with the intention of killing US personnel.

One should take into consideration that the Benghazi attack took place only a short time before the 2012 elections, and the Republicans used the Benghazi attack as a card in the campaign. They attacked Susan Rice as if she was the one who had made the mistake, although she was only the administration's public face to the media regarding this incorrect assessment.

Rice, Obama and Benghazi

During a debate with the Republican candidate Romney, Obama very strongly defended Rice. Later on, he challenged the Republicans to forget Rice and to attack him personally (SusanR 316, 319). On her part, Rice assessed that the attacks against her, mostly by Senator McCain, who had lost the elections to Obama in 2008, were due to her closeness to the president, and to the fact that she had attacked McCain in the 2008 campaign (SusanR 323).

One month after the Benghazi attack, Rice was invited to lunch with National Security Advisor Tom Donilon. President Obama "popped in" and expressed his support for her and encouraged her: "Stay strong, Susan." Obama supported Rice both privately and publicly. Obama called her and told her, again, to be "cool" and to listen to Jay-Z music to relax, which she said she did (SusanR 315-316, 330).

After the elections, Rice was called to the Oval Office to have "a rare, off-the-calendar, private meeting". Obama raised the idea of Rice replacing Donilon as the National Security Advisor (NSA) when Donilon would resign. Although a date was not set at the time for the conclusion of Donilon's term, this eventually happened the following June. It is a point to note that while Rice called this section of the book "Coming Back", she quoted Obama as telling her in May to prepare to "come **home**" (SusanR 342, 344).

The description in Rice's book of Obama's announcement of her appointment is very poetic. It was "on June 5, 2013, in the White House Rose Garden, fully in bloom on a perfect Washington summer day" that Obama announced, "I'm absolutely thrilled that she'll be back at my side." (SusanR 344)

On her entering "Obamaworld", Obama commended Rice on her tennis and basketball games, mentioned that he played with Rice's brother "occasionally", and that sports is in her family – "throwing the occasional elbow – but hitting the big shot" (SusanR 344).

Rice's Closeness to Obama

Rice said that her mind and Obama's "worked in similar ways". She could predict with accuracy what Obama was thinking, and even how he would phrase it, even "verbatim". Although she wondered about this ability of hers, she didn't tell others about it. She attributed it to the fact that they thought alike (SusanR 221).

This ability of hers helped her to serve as "surrogate" to Obama. On the website of the Obama White House, there are many speeches that she gave to different groups, even to groups that did not deal with national security. By comparison, while her predecessor is listed with one speech, Rice is listed with a double-digit number of speeches.

As National Security Advisor, she sat in the meetings in the Oval Office very close to the president, a location where the two of them could "exchange notes" and which enabled her to gauge his approach to the issues at hand. The two of them were even able to communicate "without reliance on words" (SusanR 349).

Rice also talked of the fact that neither of them was a "morning person". She describes Obama's schedule in the morning: getting up at 7, working out, breakfast, reading material, and showing up at the office at 10. His schedule "suited [her] just fine" (SusanR 352).

A senior person from the National Security Council usually accompanies the president when he travels. However, during August, when the president went on vacation in Martha's Vineyard, Rice herself joined him. She gave the reason as "bad things often happen in August", and listed the 1998 embassy bombings that had occurred over 20 years earlier (SusanR 350).

We saw earlier that she complained of Obama's talking about her short height. At the morning daily briefing he would frequently comment on her height and her clothes, and the clothes of the other participants in the meeting. In return, she would comment on his appearance as well, although she admits approving of his tan suit, while not liking the usual navy or gray ones. Once on St Patrick's Day, she pointed out that his tie was actually "teal bluish", when he was expected to wear green. When he objected that the tie was green, she held it close to his face to prove the point, even asking other people nearby for their opinion. Obama went to change his tie. The event repeated itself with the same tie a year later (SusanR 353-354).

Closeness vs. Proximity to Obama

There are several places where Rice talks about her closeness to Obama. There are four places in which she used the words "close" and "closeness" in reference to him:

1. "Throughout my time in New York, I benefited from being perceived as **close** to President Obama..." (SusanR 246)

2. "I also recognized that I was irresistible to Fox News, given my relatively high profile as Obama's U.N. ambassador and my perceived **closeness** to the president going back to his 2008 campaign." (SusanR 317)

3. "Perhaps he [=McCain] also sought retribution for my **closeness** to the man who defeated him..." (SusanR 323)

4. "...though I find it somewhat hard to believe that neither my race, my gender, nor my perceived **closeness** to the president..." (SusanR 334)

However, towards the end of the book, in the chapter called "The Fourth Quarter", dealing with the last two years of the Obama administration, Rice changed her language. In talking of the US-China relations, she said:

"...were meant to underscore the importance the Chinese assigned to the U.S.-China bilateral relationship and their understanding of my **proximity** to the president of the U.S." (SusanR 435).

She changed her language from "closeness" to "proximity". There is one more place in the book in which she used the word "proximity" in reference to a person, when she talked of her conversations with the Iranian ambassador at the UN:

"Early in my tenure, due to my trusted role in the administration and my **proximity** to the Iranian ambassador in the relative discretion New York afforded…" (SusanR 263).

It is quite evident that the word "proximity" is less than "closeness". The question is: does the change of language indicate that while she was in China she talked with them about Iran, or would it indicate that there was a decrease in the closeness of the relationship between Obama and Rice?

In fact, she mentioned that a week before the 2016 elections there was a French delegation in Washington checking on the mood before the elections. While everyone else in the administration estimated that Hillary Clinton would win, Rice said that she is not so sure of Clinton's win. She had the same conversation in Abu Dhabi with the local ruler. She said that Trump had "a decent chance" to win. (SusanR 454).

Does it mean that the "closeness" between Rice and Obama had changed? This could explain the change of language from "closeness" to "proximity".

Summary

There are several personality traits that both Obama and Rice share. The most apparent one is their love of basketball – a major point in "Obamaworld". They also shared several personality traits – fact-based, same approach to leadership, and emphasis on control.

In Obama's books there are also signals that Obama quite likely was a victim of sexual abuse, a point that might have contributed to him losing boundaries. It is expressed either verbally (ridiculing people) or even physically, by invading their personal space (=touching them).

Are there signals in Rice's language of the same?

Two points come to mind right away:

The first, she didn't encounter any "sexual harassment" except for "loose hands" (SusanR 85). In other words, "loose hands" (=touching her) is not considered in her point of view as "sexual harassment". The second, when she reported that Donald Trump had hugged her at the White House

Correspondents' Dinner, she felt she was "molested" (SusanR 382). "Molestation" is a very strong word to define a hug in public, when she even admits that "the hug was not too close". On the other hand, she does not define "loose hands" as either "sexual harassment" or "molestation".

(Interestingly, the word "molest" appears only one other time in the book: there is a place where she describes the family dinners at her grandparents' home in the summer. Guests included her father and uncles, and even neighbors, such as a Jamaican lady and a gay couple. Rice describes how she and her brother "learned the rich family lore and how to consume the entire contents of a lobster, leaving no portion unmolested." It is strange why she would use this term for the lobster instead of "untouched" or "uneaten".)

Rice and the word "child"

There is another signal indicating that quite likely Rice was a victim of sexual abuse.

1. "Still a young **child**, Maris had internalized the distress that had infused our household." (SusanR 11).

2. "As a child, I didn't fully appreciate the extraordinary lengths to which my grandparents went to ensure that their children went to top colleges…" (SusanR 27)

3. "Nothing was more arresting for me as a **child** than the first images of man walking on the moon." (SusanR 53)

4. "As a **child**, I witnessed film of napalm attacks, air raids, close combat, Cronkite's nightly body count, the full brutality of war." (SusanR 53)

5. "All the violence, the fractious debates, and the Washington political dramas gripped me as a **child.**" (SusanR 54)

6. "Even as a young **child**…" (SusanR 57).

7. "Looking back, I do not recall a time, even as a **child**..." (SusanR 61).

8. "...and the whacky marching band whose albums I was given as a **child**..." (SusanR 91).

9. "It was a fascinating look at activism during a period I'd witnessed through a **child**'s eyes..." (SusanR 101)

10. "...Stanford gave me the opportunity to catch up to Johnny, who, as a **child**, had developed greater comfort and clarity about race." (SusanR 102)

11. "Born jaundiced and skinny with gorilla-length arms, Jake developed unevenly as a **child.**" (SusanR 213)

Two people with the same background (African American community), both highly educated, both of them into basketball, sharing important personality traits, and both having signals of sexual abuse in their past. And the two of them could communicate "without reliance on words" (SusanR 349).

Samantha Power

Samantha Power was born in London and spent her first years in Ireland. Both of her parents were studying medicine at the time, and later became doctors. But her father was an alcoholic, who did not actually practice medicine after receiving his degree. Her parents separated when she was nine years old, and her mother took Samantha and her brother and immigrated to the US. Both of her parents loved sports, and her mother religiously ran six miles each day, early in the morning – quite likely a point that impacted Power's focus on sports for life (SamP 3, 8, 11, 14, 16).

Once in the US they settled in Pittsburgh. Her eighth grade was in Atlanta where her mother had accepted a job at the faculty of Emory University School of Medicine. She attended Lakeside High School, a school that had a reputation for both academics and athletics. She mentions that three of her closest friends in high school were gay (SamP 37).

Upon graduation she attended Yale University, where she participated in writing at the Yale Daily News, and during summers she interned at radio stations. Her years in college were the period of international events such as the Tiananmen Square in China, and the fall of the Berlin Wall. On graduation she was admitted to the Carnegie Institute in Washington DC.

She moved on to be a journalist during the conflict in the Balkans, and mainly in Bosnia. This brought her later to research and publish her book "A Problem from Hell" about genocide in Bosnia and Rwanda. Her book was her key to meet Senator Obama.

Sports

In Pittsburgh, she integrated herself into the American culture, playing baseball and basketball. In high school she was the starting shooting guard on the basketball team, and she spent hours and hours practicing. Sports was also her main activity in college, from basketball to many other sports. But sports was not enough for her. She asked herself what is out there for her beyond sports. (SamP 21, 27, 37, 43).

Sports and relationships

Sharing the focus on sports brought her to date her first boyfriend in college. They were together for three years and then separated. She met a former high school basketball player, but they decided to be just friends. She fell in love with an actor. Their first date was at a Mets game in New York City. When the actor left her, she felt crushed. Her basketball friend helped by taking her to shoot baskets (SamP 44, 48, 136-137, 158, 159).

She met her future husband, a fellow campaign advisor to Obama, who was a squash player like herself; and like her, he was a "compulsive Red Sox fan". They started texting as the Red Sox began their triumphant 2007 playoff run. Later on, she described a romantic evening as playing squash (SamP 169-170, 171, 196).

She bonded with Obama over basketball (SamP 194).

Meeting Obama

The first time Samantha Power heard the name Obama was at the July 2004 Democratic National Convention where Obama gave the keynote speech. Power was captivated by his oration and message. But in November 2004 President Bush was reelected, a point that she describes, in many words, as depressing. A colleague suggested that she should contact the newly-elected Senator Obama. In March 2005 she received an email from his office requesting a dinner meeting (SamP 143).

In spring 2005 they met. It is interesting that till this point her account mentions the month of each time-milepost, while here she only mentions the season – the spring.

She brought a long list of questions to ask him, but she found instead that he had plenty of questions about her own history – if she was good at basketball (she was about to enter "Obamaworld" and this was the key), her experience at Harvard Law School (mirroring his experience), about story telling (she had published a book, as he did). She notes, though, that although she was curious about his father and the parallels to her own father, they did not talk about that. (SamP 145).

She commented instead about her impression of Obama's mother as a brave woman, and Obama responded that his book "Dreams from My Father" was primarily about his mother (SamP 146).

Several points in this conversation open windows that demonstrate Obama's inner process.

Concerning his personality – she asked how he avoided having "too big a head", in view of the attention he received from the media. He shared with her his assessment that his election as a Senator was mainly a result of other events at the same time. He saw himself as a "vehicle" to address people's "hunger" for authenticity, only "filling some kind of void". He evaluated himself as able to listen and communicate, while minimizing his thought process. They discussed the possibility of him running for President in 2008, which had already been suggested by others, but he said he did not plan to run. (SamP 146-148, BO AOH 18).

Concerning a lack of emotions on his part, at least as seen on the surface – he asked "a bit coolly" why she cried when she heard that the US was intervening in Bosnia. When she said it was out of relief, he only responded with "Hmm" (SamP 146).

He analyzed Kerry's loss in the 2004 elections, concluding that Kerry hadn't clarified what he was standing for. He felt that once a person finds his truth, people will follow, even if they don't agree with it (SamP 148).

Concerning his long and thorough decision-making process – Obama criticized the US war policy in Iraq for not anticipating correctly all future consequences. The two shared their frustration in dealing with symptoms rather than the cause of a problem. She related to Bosnia while he related to his work as a community organizer in Chicago.

Concerning his need for power and control – although he had entered politics to pursue real change, he still had frustrations as a US Senator, although different ones from before. A major source of frustration for him was that as a new senator he had no power at all, since the Senate as an institution relies mainly on seniority (SamP 148).

Obama didn't shy away from sharing with her his own personal life. He talked of missing his two daughters, who had stayed behind in Chicago.

His routine enabled him to spend time with them on Monday night and return from Washington on Thursday night, and he concluded that his wife "is carrying us" (SamP 147).

Power ended her description of the conversation by saying that she was inspired both by Obama's leadership style and his personality. She felt that she would not only be able to learn from working with him, but she would also participate in whatever he did; and so she offered to work with him (SamP 149). Outside the restaurant, he gave her his email address and cell phone number. He would talk to his chief of staff about bringing her "on board" (SamP 150).

Senate Years

Since she had published a book on genocide, and had sent him the book as a "resume", Obama asked her to help him with his book "The Audacity of Hope" by going over the content. As for her, since she wanted to be part of whatever he did, they found that the book project was serving both of them.

He sent her drafts, and she sent him back edits and suggestions. Since Obama used to write his book during nights and weekends, these were the times they communicated about his book. Usually, he sent her the material very late after watching ESPN, the sports channel, which she watched as well. She realized that this collaboration on the book was more important than anything else she did in the Senate office. Working with Obama gave her the feeling that she was getting to know him, not only as a politician or leader, but also as a person. For example, she noted his personality trait of delaying the completion of his obligations till close to the deadline (SamP 149, 165-166, 176).

They had many talks in his Senate office, and their conversations were both political and personal in nature. Her book about genocide gave people the impression that she is "hawkish". Obama told her that in talking with her he found that she is not as "hawkish" as people think. She agreed with him, saying that she didn't think that the US should use military force (SamP 227, 306).

He talked with her privately of his feelings towards the debates in the primaries, and she shared with him her evaluation of his performance in the debates. She felt she could read him a lot better than before. She could feel the gradual process of him changing from being a professor to becoming a candidate who connected with people (SamP 176).

Obama gave a speech at the Save Darfur Coalition rally at the National Mall in Washington, DC, in April 2006. In his speech he recognized Power as "a wonderful friend" and recommended that people should read her book (SamP 162).

Phone calls

Obama phoned Power quite a bit. When he landed back in Chicago after the above-mentioned rally, he called her to say, "That was quite something. You should feel really good about what happened out there."

It should be noted that he talked about what she should feel, and not what he felt. When she hesitated, he acknowledged that just giving a speech "doesn't necessarily bring you exactly what you want", but it gives "fuel" to keep moving. She thanked him for his "involvement" in the cause, and "after hanging up" ("unnecessary connection" indicating sensitivity) she slept for a long time (SamP 165).

She called him to let him know that she is returning to teach at Harvard. Obama, in his "complete honesty" approach told her that he hadn't expected her to be useful to him in Washington. He moved to lessen the impact of his harsh words by saying that he didn't mean to hurt her (which he did), but he didn't have the power as a senator to use her properly. Afterwards he called her in Massachusetts, asking her about the new book she was working on. When she asked him in reply how she can help him, he responded that he didn't need any help. He only wanted to know how she was doing (SamP 166).

She wanted him to run for president. When he called her in November 2006 with "great news", she was sure he was going to tell her that he had decided to run. Instead, he told her about the success of his book. She did not know whether he was really excited about the book, or if he was "messing with [her] head". But she mentioned the exact date, December 12th, 2006, when he called her with "the real call": "We're pulling the trigger on this thing". He added that this information was still confidential, and they would announce it in mid-January (SamP 168).

David Plouffe, Obama's designated campaign manager, said that the critical phone call he received from Obama saying that he had "crossed the Rubicon" was only on January 6.   Samantha Power got the news of Obama's running around three weeks before Plouffe did (DavidPl 27).

She also had a dream in which she was responsible for Obama taking the wrong train to reach a major fundraiser. She concluded it by saying that her subconscious was telling her that Obama made a mistake in trusting her (SamP 168).

During the campaign Obama called Power to share with her his feeling of how he saw the race, and the prospect of losing. In one of the phone calls he shared with her how he was "worn down" by being away from his family (SamP 174).

When Obama was declared a winner at the Iowa caucus, he went to the podium to give his victory speech. A short time beforehand, Samantha had shared with Obama the "romantic news" that Cass was now her boyfriend. While Obama was on the podium, about to give his speech, he looked back into the people behind him and spotted both Samantha and Cass. He pointed to both her and Cass, and she understood it to be a sign for her that she and Cass were the real good news of the evening. He smiled broadly at them, turned to the podium, and started his speech (SamP 180).

When Obama was declared a winner in the national elections, she waited in line to congratulate President-elect Obama. He gave her "a deep hug" across the barrier, saying, "This is something, huh?" She could feel how he was "truly alone", and that "the usual spark of mischief in his eyes" had vanished.   Obama was reserved, and it seemed to her that he was saying "goodbyes" and not "hellos" (SamP 201).

A few days before his inauguration he called again, sharing with her the pressure he was under, making sure that all his friends and family would be at the festivities. "It's like a wedding," he said (SamP 207). We should remember how he looked at his own wedding as a "happy ending" and not a "beginning" (BO DFMF 442).

Emails

After a TV interview with Power, Obama sent her an email telling her she didn't have to be so defensive of him.   Talking about himself in the third person, he called himself "your candidate". Power said that she couldn't stand the thought of Obama's losing the election (SamP 175).

After the final debate before the Iowa caucus she emailed him her positive feelings about his performance in the debate, and he emailed back "Just gimme the ball" (SamP 176).

When she met her future husband Cass, Power emailed Obama about her "romantic news". He was busy with the campaign in Iowa, but he called her as soon as she sent the email. When she told him it was Cass, his first reaction was: "Cass?! Cass Sunstein? He's a total slob", and the line went dead. A little while later called her again, apologizing for losing the connection, and said: "What I should have said is: This is wonderful news! Cass is one of the most brilliant, creative, and kind people I have ever met. Congratulations". He ended the conversation by saying, "Don't f*** this up." (SamP 178-179).

She took inventory of her life saying:

> I had worked for three years with the **person** who could well become the next leader of the free world. And I was falling in love with a remarkable **man** who appeared to love me back (SamP 180).

During the campaign there was a time in which the campaign had to freeze Power out due to her attacking Clinton, calling her a "monster". She called that time – "my exile". During that time she got an email from Obama telling her not to avoid interviews, and not to "crawl under a rock", as it would not be good for either her or him. She referred to him as "**my** Robert Horry". Horry was a professional basketball player who had the reputation of having "last-second jump shots" and who achieved seven championships. She emailed Obama saying "Every time I'm slumping toward self-immolation, you land that 22-footer from the corner as time expires." (SamP 194)

When he won the Wyoming caucus, she got an email from him saying:

> "Wanted to check in with you to make sure you're ok. I know this whole thing [=her exile from the campaign] is shitty. But I hope you know how much I love and appreciate you, that all this will blow over, and that we are going to change the world together. In the meantime, enjoy your travels, make sure Cass [=her future husband] spoils you, and let me know if you want to talk at all." (SamP 193)

She wished him luck a few hours before his well-known "race speech" dealing with Reverend Jeremiah Wright. He emailed back joking, "This whole Reverend Wright thing was an elaborate ruse to take people's attention off you!" (SamP 195).

On the night that Obama got enough delegates to be nominated by the Democratic party, he emailed her saying that the best part of being nominated is getting her back from exile into the campaign (SamP 197).

Once she was back at the campaign headquarters, she emailed him thanking him for bringing her back. He emailed in response that she had never been "off the team" and was only using the time to find "true love" – letting her future husband enter her life (SamP 198).

Their email connection ended with Obama's election, and he sent her an email saying that he was giving up his personal email account (SamP 202).

White House Years

Before the elections she had direct access to him via email. However, after the elections she didn't have his email address, as only a few people had it. Their interactions were limited in numbers (SamP 238).

When she was pregnant, and the two of them had a private moment in the Oval Office, Obama asked her when she was due, and even joked saying "I think Barack would make a great name." She had wanted to talk about politics with him, but she later told her husband that she understood that Obama needed to talk about baby names instead, to have some freedom from the constant pressure (SamP 227).

There was a time in which Obama pulled her aside and warned her that there are rumors at the White House that she might be leaking information to the media due to her previous connections with the media and other organizations. She promised him that she will never leak anything (SamP 229).

A few days before flying to Norway to receive the Nobel Peace Prize, he saw her exiting the West Wing as he was arriving. He stepped out of his car and called to her, "We need to talk." (SamP 262)

Although his regular speechwriters were working on a speech for him to give on receiving the prize, Samantha had prepared a long memo with her own suggestions. She took the opportunity of this "talk", on the day before his flight to Norway, to give him her memo. The next morning he told her that he might need to bring her on the flight as a "stowaway", and soon thereafter she got the invitation to go on Air Force One (SamP 263).

Obama invited her to lunch in May 2010. She describes the seating arrangement. It was a small room near the Oval Office, with a table that could seat 6 people. He was sitting at the head of the table, and she was at the other end. She commented that he "felt far away".

He started by saying that he doesn't talk with her much, and he wanted to know her opinion of what they were doing right or wrong, and "what ideals we have betrayed lately." It seems as if he treated her as his moral compass. Their conversation dealt with US foreign policy in the Arab Middle East (SamP 283-284).

After his reelection in 2012, Obama went on a trip to Burma, a trip that Power organized with the Burmese leader Aung San Suu Kyi, a winner of the Nobel Peace Prize. On the way home, Power perceived Obama as being "in high spirits". He invited her to his personal cabin on Air Force One and asked her what job she would like in his second term (SamP 320).

David Litt, Obama's speechwriter, gave a description of the five sections on Air Force One. In the back of the plane was the section reserved for reporters, followed by a section reserved for VIP guests. The third section was for the White House personnel, then a section that included the conference room, where Obama either worked or relaxed. At the front of the plane was the president's "fully appointed office with a small private bedroom attached" (DavidL 190).

Later on, Power and her husband were invited to dinner at the White House. This was the time that Obama ridiculed Power's husband for breaking a glass. "Leave it to Cass to break the White House." (SamP 322)

Obama invited her to have a talk with him in a separate room. She was nervous as to what he might have in mind, thinking she might have made some mistake, but it was for the purpose of offering her the position of US ambassador to the UN (SamP 323).

Her job at the UN called for a more thorough security clearance vetting than the one she had when she got her job at the National Security Council. Obama told her that they need to know everything about her including "sex, drugs, or taxes".

Note the order of listing, with sex as number one.

She said that Obama "saw [her] face fall". When he asked her why, she said that in her early years she had dated "a lot of the wrong guys". Obama responded, "Well, unless you dated Yasser Arafat, I think we'll be okay." At the end of the evening, Obama told her to think while he gave her "a parting kiss on the cheek" (SamP 323-324).

A few days later, in the Rose Garden at the White House, Obama introduced Power saying:

> "One of our foremost thinkers on foreign policy, she showed us that the international community has a moral responsibility and a profound interest in resolving conflicts and defending human dignity . . . To those who care deeply about America's engagement and indispensable leadership in the world, you will find no stronger advocate for that cause than Samantha." (SamP 326)

He confirmed that she was a moral compass not only for him, but for his administration as a whole.

When people at the White House complained about the way she was dealing with adversaries at the UN, mainly the Russians, Ben Rhodes told her that Obama defended her, saying that she was doing exactly what he expected her to do (SamP 421).

While on a visit in Cameroon, their car had an accident and hit a young boy. That night she received an email from Obama:

> "I'm so sorry about today—heartbreaking. I know you know rationally that bad stuff like this happens, and there's nothing you could have done differently to anticipate it. But given the emotions it surely evokes, it's worth hearing from your friend that I don't know anyone who cares more about people, and your work saves countless lives, and I couldn't be prouder of you. So hang in there. Much love." (SamP 485).

Childhood

Background

We already found that Obama and Susan Rice shared two major points: basketball, and possible child abuse in the past, besides other personality traits that both of them share.

Samantha Power shared with Obama the issue of basketball. The question now is: did she also share with him the issue of child abuse in the past.

Symptoms

Power in her book described two major symptoms that she experienced that eventually brought to seek help via therapy.

The first one was what her boyfriend in college called "lungers". She found it difficult to breath normally. She emphasized that it was not identical or even similar to asthma. She felt as if her lung (hence the name) shrank and she couldn't take in enough air. Her reaction to this symptom reinforced the connection between this symptom and social environment. Whenever "somebody" wanted to get close to her, and started to talk about a future together, the "lungers" returned.   Instead of seeking help, she tended to push away the person closest to her (SamP 47, 125).

It happened again when she returned to her second year in Harvard Law School. The "lungers" returned in full steam.   While at Yale this symptom was manageable, but at Harvard it immobilized her. She tried yoga, but it didn't help. She sought medical help and was prescribed anti-anxiety medicine, which helped her. But she still didn't explore the reason for the "lungers" (SamP 116-117).

When her friend suggested that she should go for therapy, she ridiculed the idea, saying that her "screwed-up dating life" is connected to her father. When she did go to therapy, the first question the therapist asked her was to talk about her father, a question which brought her to cry for quite a while (SamP 125-126).

She also reported another symptom – pain in her lower back. Her friend suggested to connect both symptoms to her father's death (SamP 158-159).   She went into intensive therapy while working with Obama. The realization of the connection between the symptoms and her father's death brought her to experience "telling dreams", one of them already described earlier, where she dreamed that her mistake caused Obama to lose the presidency (SamP 167-168).

After her son was born, she could sit still with no symptoms, not "lungers" and not back pain (SamP 247).

Power quotes two sources to show the importance of her leaving her father back in Ireland and moving to the US (SamP 192, 194). Is it her leaving him behind that created the symptoms? Or, maybe, is it something much deeper?

Her father was an alcoholic and spent a lot of time in a pub drinking. When she was very young, he even took her to the pub with him, and left her to read books in the basement of the pub while he was drinking with his friends upstairs.

She also reported another behavior of his. When he returned from the pub, even after midnight, he would come into her room and wake her up.

Sometimes he wanted to talk with her about her day, and at times even took her and her brother for a ride in his car.   She also reported an event, after her parents had separated, when she was in her pajamas next to her dad in the large bed he had shared with her mother during their marriage. (SamP 10, 24).

He died while Samantha was in high school in the US. When he was found dead, he was in the bed that had been Samantha's, and not in his own bed (SamP 30).

Before moving to the US, her parents battled over custody of the two children, a battle that went up to the Ireland Supreme Court due to her father's appeals.   The battle ended when the court gave the mother permission to remove the children from Ireland and take them far away to the US (SamP 14). There must have been something very serious to justify distancing the children from their father to another continent.

Child abuse - language

There are several places where Power labeled herself as a "child", a label usually used by victims of sexual abuse.

1. "Even as a **child**, I could tell he was the man in the room that people most wanted to please." (SamP 4)
2. "He drank too much and clearly didn't do much work, but he had infinite time for me – a **child**'s only true measure of a parent." (SamP 14)
3. "…but like a **child** who has just noticed her blinking, and suddenly begins to do it intentionally, this activity only caused me to focus more on my breathing…" (SamP 116)
4. With my heartbreak so close to the surface, the feeling of loss I had experienced as a **child** became easier to reach." (SamP 160)
5. "Because we were expecting a **child**, we had started to receive gifts…" (SamP 232)
6. "I had never not worked; from the time I was a **child**…" (SamP 247)
7. "With rare exceptions, though, I did not feel distracted at work because I now had a **child**. If anything, motherhood made me more focused and efficient, given that every extra hour at the office meant another hour away from **my son**." (SamP 251)

8. "I remembered the gratitude I felt as a **child** when Mum scored a seat in the upper decks of Pittsburgh's Three Rivers Stadium for a Pirates game." (SamP 464)
9. "During the tense drive, I began to make deals with God – as I had done as a little **girl** when I first moved to Pittsburgh." (SamP 544)

We should note that she became a "girl" (and not "child") only when she was already in the US.

Opening/closing doors

Power mentions the activity of opening/closing doors several times in her book. This activity, when it is mentioned in an "open statement" (and a book is an "open statement"), indicates that the speaker/writer quite likely experienced opening and closing doors in childhood as a meaningful activity. Opening the door started the crime, and closing the door ended it.

The following are the places where this activity is mentioned:

1. "I needed to be alone. Mum walked out, **closing the door behind her.**" (SamP 29)
2. "When she **opened his unlocked front door**…" (SamP 30)
3. "When I left the *U.S. News* office and the **doors** to the elevator **closed** behind me…" (SamP 64)
4. "After the guard **opened the door**…" (SamP 343)
5. "When I would read the details of some new massacre, I often **closed my office door**…" (SamP 504)

Samantha Power – "Man" vs. "Person"

Her father

1. "Even as a child, I could tell he was the **man** in the room that people most wanted to please." (SamP 4)
2. "My grandfather accurately saw his new son-in-law as a **man** who needed to be taken care of." (SamP 5)
3. "…I only remember my father, the first **man** I loved" (SamP 10)
4. "…that I was the daughter of a **man** he had once watched hold forth at Hartigan's." (SamP 193)

Her Stepfather

5. "…by the **man** with whom Mum had become romantically involved" (SamP 12)
6. "As we exited the baggage area, I recognized the middle-aged, medium-built **man**…" (SamP 16-17)

Boyfriends

7. "after I got back together for the third time with a **man** I knew was bad news…" (SamP 125-126)
8. "The **man** in question was a thirty-eight-year-old actor from the midlands of Ireland, whom I met while he was performing on Broadway." (SamP 158)
9. "I had been involved with a **man** who claimed he was divorced from his wife, but I later learned they were only legally separated." (SamP 324)

Her husband

10. "'This is a **man** completely in my corner,' I wrote in my journal." (SamP 178)
11. "I had worked for three years with the **person** who could well become the next leader of the free world. And I was falling in love with a remarkable **man** who appeared to love me back." (SamP 180)
12. "…I allowed a **man** I might otherwise have pushed away to take care of me." (SamP 198)

Obama

13. The **man** before me was outwardly the same **person** I had worked with …" (SamP 200)
14. "He had always been a solitary **person**…" (SamP 201)
15. "…the only **man** in the world who would be *President of the United States*" (SamP 201)
16. "The **man** who sat before me in the President's chair looked and sounded just like the **man** I had worked for in the Senate and on the campaign." (SamP 225)

17. "I pointed out that, for a **man** who prided himself on gathering his 'Team of Rivals' before making hard decisions…" (SamP 238)
18. "For a split second I thought, 'Don't ruin this nice moment with a **man** who never gets a break.'" (SamP 242)

Biden

19. "Having observed Biden in debates in the Situation Room, and from just chatting with him during chance encounters in the West Wing, I was struck by the extent to which the **man** I saw up close resembled the public Biden…" (SamP 341-342)

Trump

20. "Instead, we were about to elect to our highest office a **man** who had boasted about forcing himself on women. I was deeply shaken." (SamP 534)

Discussion

1. Her father received the title "man" and there are enough signals to indicate that something was not right between them. Her stepfather received the title "man" and he was romantically involved with her mother (SamP 12).
2. Her boyfriends and her husband are expected to receive the title "man".
3. When she talks of both her husband-to-be and Obama, her husband-to-be is a "man" while Obama is a "person" (SamP 11).
4. On the day Obama was elected president, he was both a "person" and a "man" (SamP 13,14). Thereafter, he is only labeled as a "man".

Reginald Love

Introduction

Reginald (Reggie) Love was not a household name in the US during the Obama administration. There were other people who were more well-known, and in the news media quite a bit, as the public face of the administration. Two of these were Hillary Clinton, as Secretary of State, and Susan Rice, as US ambassador to the UN during Obama's first term, and as National Security Advisor during his second term.

However, there were other people, more in the background, who were important inside the White House. For example, Valerie Jarrett was considered to be one of the most influential people in the White House (DavidL 48). Another one was Reginald (Reggie) Love, who accompanied Obama during the campaign of 2008, and later on in his presidency.

Axelrod described Reggie's relation to Obama as being "**always** alongside the candidate." Plouffe described it in different words: a "**close**, full-time personal aide" (Axe 235, DavPl 57).

Hillary Clinton said that Reggie "rarely left Barack's side" (HRC 2). During his service, Reggie visited every state in the US, visited 65 countries, and traveled 1.8 million miles. For comparison, as Secretary of State, Hillary Clinton visited 112 countries and traveled nearly one million miles, close to a million miles less than Reggie (Reggie 201, HRC xi). Clinton, as Secretary of State, used the Secretary of State plane for her overseas trips. Reggie flew on Air Force One with Obama.

Whenever Clinton came to meet with President Obama, and while she waited for her time to go in, she talked with Reggie. She was very interested in Reggie as a person. She asked him about his life, traveling, and family (Reggie 168).

Reggie was the "gatekeeper" to the Oval Office (Reggie 6, 161). His office was only five-steps away (Reggie 150). Realizing that, generally speaking, power in the White House is measured by the proximity of the person's office to the Oval, one can easily conclude that Reggie was at the center of power.

Reggie was not only five steps away from the Oval. He was inside the Oval.

At one time there was a large wildfire in Israel that destroyed a major forest area and also caused many deaths. The fire departments in Israel did not have sufficient airplanes and other equipment to fight such a large fire, and requested help from other countries, including the US. Michael Oren, the Israeli ambassador, met President Obama in the Oval Office to deliver Israel's request for such help.

Present at the meeting were the President, Reggie, and Oren. The president told Reggie to write down the items requested, and to make sure that Israel will get "whatever it needs".   Along with writing the items, Reggie was also in charge of making sure that the various US departments would deliver the equipment, and Oren commended him by saying that he "faithfully carried out his presidential instructions." (MichO 193, 194)

Hillary Clinton on Reggie

Hillary Clinton mentioned two people who, after the elections of 2008, were instrumental in setting up a meeting between President-elect Obama and herself: Huma Abedin, who had worked for her since she was First Lady in the 1990s; and Reggie Love, Obama's aide.

She described Huma Abedin as her "traveling Chief of Staff" and gave accolades saying that she is a "savvy, indefatigable, and gracious young woman". For Reggie she only mentioned that he was a "former Duke University basketball player" (HRC 2).

In view of the significance of basketball in "Obamaworld", the fact that Reggie was a former basketball star at Duke who had played big-time college basketball and football, gave him a major advantage in getting into the inner circle close to the candidate, and later president, and even inside the Oval Office (DavPl 57, Axe 235).

There are differences in the way Clinton described Huma and Reggie:

1. Huma Abedin is introduced by her full name – first name and last name; Reggie is introduced by his nickname and last name. His full first name is "Reginald".

   One can say that this is the way "Reggie" was known. However, the difference still exists.

2. Huma received a title - "traveling Chief of Staff", while Reggie did not receive a title, although David Plouffe introduced him as a "full-time personal aide" (DavPl 57).

   The lack of a title might indicate an inability to give a title, due to some information that the person does not want to, or cannot, label.

3. Huma Abedin is described as one who "worked" for her, while she didn't say that Reggie "worked" for Obama. For Reggie she only said that he "rarely left Barack's side".

4. Huma received several adjectives, while Reggie is only mentioned by his resume: a "former Duke University basketball player". For comparison, while Clinton labeled Abedin as "indefatigable", David Plouffe labeled Reggie as "renowned for working hard", and "seemed to require zero sleep" (DavPl 57).

   One can say that she knew Huma quite well as they had been working together for many years. However, if Reggie "rarely left Barack's side", and Hillary was Secretary of State for four years, and worked with Obama very closely, she met Reggie several times. And Reggie talked of her conversations with him. She must have had an impression of him. However, no such impression is mentioned in this short introduction..

5. Huma received the adjective "young", while Reggie did not, although in reality he was young.

6. Huma received the title "woman", while Reggie didn't receive the title "man".

Huma and Reggie

Reggie and Huma had frequent encounters during the 2008 campaign, in connecting the two competing candidates.

In one event that took place on the tarmac of the airport in Washington, DC, the planes of the two candidates were parked close to each other. Huma approached the Obama plane, indicating she wanted to talk. Reggie went downstairs to the tarmac to meet her and to ask her what's going on. Huma said that Clinton wanted to talk with Obama. Reggie reached for his cell-phone to contact Obama, who was still on his way; but at that moment Obama's car came along, and Obama went to talk with Clinton.

During this encounter the Obama team was observing the encounter from the plane, and although they were too far away to follow the words spoken, they still could see that the encounter was very heated. Huma and Reggie were standing on the tarmac close by, and by the accounts they were looking up while witnessing the encounter (DavPl 119, Axe 242, Reggie 166-167)

The meeting on the tarmac between the two candidates was significant to Obama. It signaled to him that he was going to win the nomination of the Democratic Party, because Clinton "had unraveled" while he "was keeping his cool" (Reggie 167).

When it later became clear that there was no way Clinton would be able to overcome the gap in delegates that Obama had accumulated in the long primaries contest, Clinton conceded and accepted that Obama was going to be nominated at the convention.

At that point Huma and Reggie went to dinner at a well-known restaurant in DC. Huma was accompanied by Anthony Weiner, while Reggie was with "a friend". This meeting drew the attention of the gossip columns in the news media (Reggie 167).

This was not the only time that Huma and Reggie were instrumental between Obama and Clinton. After the elections of 2008, they were the ones who established the phone call from Clinton to the president-elect, to congratulate him on his victory (HRC 11).

What do we know about Reggie?

Reggie Love, twenty-four years old , is described as "physically imposing" at six-foot-four, but soft-spoken (DavPl 57, Axe 235, MicOr 193).

Reggie's background was similar to that of other successful African Americans described earlier, such as Michelle Obama, Susan Rice, and Ben Carson. Reggie came from a family that promoted education. Both of his parents were college graduates, and his mother insisted that he should succeed in his studies (Reggie 175).

Reggie graduated Duke in 2005, majoring in political science. During his studies he played college basketball and football. Upon graduation, Reggie used his basketball connections to circulate his resume in the Congress corridors. It didn't take long, and Reggie got a phone call from the office of the new Senator from Illinois – Obama.

Although Reggie at the time quite likely didn't know of the "Obamaworld" fixation on sports in general, and specifically on basketball, still at the time of writing his book Reggie attributed the forwarding of his resume to Obama's office to the fact that he was a former basketball and football player; that he was African-American; and that he had graduated from Duke University with a political science degree (Reggie 2).

Meeting Obama the first time

Reggie described in detail what he wore to his first interview with the Senator. He described the suit, the tie, and the shoes. He summed it up by saying that he looked "sharp" (Reggie 1).

The interview

In Reggie's words, it was less of a job interview and more of the two of them "eyeing each other" and "sizing up" (Reggie 2).

The questions Obama asked were not about what the future employee could offer, but what mattered to Reggie, and what he wanted to do in his future.

When Reggie said that he is interested in learning about the political process, Obama replied that it is a lot easier to learn as a young man than when you are thirty-five years old . Obama concluded with, "maybe we'll work something out." (Reggie5)

Reggie started as an intern in Obama's Senate office. At first he worked with Alyssa Mastromonaco, taking calls from constituents and dealing with email addresses, and as Mastromonaco was the scheduler of Obama's trips, Reggie worked with her on managing Obama's political trips and planning his book tour to promote his book "The Audacity of Hope". In May 2006, when Mastromonaco transferred to the Hope Fund, Reggie went along with her as her deputy (AlyM 134, AlyM 151, AlyM 160, Reggie 62).

Once the campaign for president moved into high gear, and the candidate's time was the most important "asset" of the campaign, they needed someone to take care of the candidate's needs while on the road, including food, laundry, etc. This position, also called "bodyman", was offered to Reggie.

When Reggie was offered the position, he described his appearance again. He described his shirts, pants, neckties – brand and type (Reggie 83).

Being a "bodyman" meant that Reggie was at Obama's side not only during daytime, but sometimes even in the middle of the night. Being a "bodyman" also meant that what the boss says becomes the employee's "whole existence". Reggie became what Obama called "his 'iReggie'" (Reggie 6, 62).

Reggie would ride along with the campaign manager in the same car with the Obamas. Valerie Jarrett reported that on the night of the caucuses in Iowa, Barack, David Plouffe, Reggie Love and herself arrived at one of the caucus locations (DavPl 136, ValJ 139).

His constant proximity to the candidate allowed Reggie to observe the campaign from the balcony of the theater, and at times even to give his outlook on what is going on (DavPl 57, 136).

In a way, Reggie was not only a "bodyman". Just as the barber in a barbershop who stands behind the client can be a great listener for what the client has to say, so was Reggie who sat in the back and could be not just a listener, but also a cheerleader.

Reggie's close and constant presence around Obama brought Obama to share with Reggie his thoughts about the events surrounding them.

After the encounter with Hillary on the tarmac at the airport in Washington DC, Obama told Reggie that the way Hillary behaved told him that he would win the nomination, since she was "unraveled" while he remained cool (Reggie 167).

After the economic meltdown, just before the elections, Obama shared with Reggie his feelings of being upset that the ones who created the problem will be not be impacted as the rest of the population (Reggie 158).

After the victory in the elections of 2008, Obama shared with Reggie the burden that he felt in being the commander in chief, a position that brought Obama to feel that he is responsible for every soldier in the US armed forces (Reggie 162). Obama shared with Reggie another responsibility of his – solving problems. Since people under Obama solved the easy problems, any problem that came all the way up to the president was due to be "doozy" and required immediate attention (Reggie 152).

It was not a one-sided relationship. Reggie could contribute to Obama as well. When Obama in the company of Reggie met Jay Z and Beyoncé Knowles at a restaurant in New York, Obama asked Reggie to tell him what are the seven best songs of Jay Z, which Reggie provided (Reggie 188). Reggie also showed Obama how to use cloud computing, Dropbox, and his iPad. On the other hand, when Reggie thought that Paul Newman was only a manufacturer of salad dressing, Obama imparted to Reggie his knowledge of movies, listing several movies which Paul Newman had starred in (Reggie 189).

How did it start?

Being a "bodyman" meant taking care of food, carrying luggage, babysitting for children when needed, and many other tasks that fell into his lap. Reggie became an expert on luggage and packing, using different brands of luggage. It showed him that what seems insignificant can be very significant (Reggie 7, 130).

Although the relationship between Obama and Reggie had started as "chilly", a relationship of "boss and assistant", in time they grew closer to become "friends", and even "close to family" (Reggie 79-80, 6).

The gym on the road

In history there is no way to play "what if?" History takes its turns, and nobody can say what would have happened otherwise. The same is true for the question: what would have happened if Obama wouldn't have had the trait of "tardiness", which Michelle labeled as "hubris"?

Obama did tend to be late wherever he went, and since the candidate's time was the most important "asset" of the campaign, something had to be done about it. And once Obama "lost track of the time" while he was at the gym.

Marvin Nicholson, Obama's trip director, told Reggie that in the future he should go to the gym along with Obama. Obama was an early riser in the morning, as well as being late to go to sleep, and insisted on having at least one hour in the gym each morning. The visits to the gym every morning gave Obama and Reggie time to chat in a "relaxed setting" ((Reggie 64).

Although each one of them preferred different kinds of exercise, still, exercising together allowed for a break from the tense atmosphere of the campaign. They were able to talk about anything not related to the campaign, among them "exercise philosophies", sports, and "pop culture". At times Obama asked about Reggie's past experience in basketball and football (Reggie 64-65).

Being in charge of keeping time was not restricted to the gym. Reggie was also in charge of keeping time during the meetings Obama had with voters at different campaign stops. Reggie would stand to the side or to the back of the room, and maintain eye contact with the candidate. It was his responsibility to signal to the candidate when they were "out of time" (Reggie 78).

Playing basketball

On the campaign trail, they had a "tradition" to play an informal basketball game on the day of a primary. Reggie mentions that this began on January 3, 2008, the day of the caucus in Iowa. (His mentioning the date might be due to his good memory for dates, especially birthdays.) Reggie mentioned that it was Obama's idea – since they were not permitted to campaign on the day of a caucus or primary, they should play a game of basketball in the meantime (Reggie 78).

Till this point, Reggie used basketball as a metaphor for being a "bodyman". He described his position in the campaign as taking the ball from half court and bringing it into the basket. As the candidate's time-keeper, one might wonder if Reggie was comparing Obama to the ball (Reggie 6).

The Iowa caucus was a milestone in their relationship. Basketball was not a metaphor anymore. Basketball was the foundation upon which their relationship developed. And they played "a *lot* of basketball" (Reggie 7) [italics in the original].

Since, in Reggie words, "nothing connects people like athletics", basketball changed everything. Obama could see Reggie's competitiveness, his love for the game, and commitment to it. (Reggie 79-80, 81). All three of these mirrored Obama in full. Competitiveness was Obama's strong trait, and basketball was not just a "game" for Obama, but a sense of belonging.

While playing basketball together, Reggie could see in Obama what others did not. The two of them could use "expletives" freely without being concerned how others see it (Reggie 7). In this way, basketball was freedom for Obama. As we learned earlier, for Obama, basketball was "a true passion", a sense of community.

For Reggie, basketball was "meditation", and an activity that helped to "set [his] head straight". During his years in college, it was his "home away from home" (Reggie 35).
If the Iowa caucus day was a milestone, the New Hampshire primary was another one. Matt Rodriguez, state director for the Obama campaign in New Hampshire, suggested to "shoot hoops on the campaign". Rodriguez's idea was to have a way to connect with the voters. It also brought Reggie and Obama to connect (Reggie 73-74).

Reggie attributed the effect of basketball on the strength of their friendship to their mutual love of basketball. Although there was a gap in age, in culture, and life stages, basketball was the "common ground" for the two. Basketball brought Reggie to compare Obama to his legendary coach from college, the one he worshipped throughout his book, describing the life lessons he gave him, just like his parents.

Hoops and basketball games gave Obama an escape from the tense atmosphere of the campaign. Basketball became not only an "icebreaker" for the two, but also an "escape" for the candidate (Reggie 73-74).

They also shared basketball by email. Reggie mentions that Obama once emailed him statistics of a basketball player, and Reggie responded with the statistics of another player. This brief exchange of emails produced a different dimension between them, since it did not involve schedule or assignments. "Fun" entered the picture, along with some competition between the two (Reggie 74).

They played with different groups. When playing with future voters, they made sure not to play the very best, so as not to lose their vote. There was a game in which Obama was injured and required stitches, and there was another game in which Reggie was injured, requiring stitches as well. Obama, true to his nature, as described earlier, told Reggie that it was lucky that he, Obama, was not the one who got injured (Reggie 75-76).

There were occasions when basketball dominated Obama's mind. On one occasion, Obama and Marvin argued about Marvin's claim that he could beat Obama at basketball. Moments later, Obama began a speech, and he later shared with Reggie that throughout the speech he was thinking about what Marvin had said (Reggie 79).

Obama's basketball game gave Reggie a window to evaluate Obama. Reggie considered Obama to be "a very unselfish teammate", who cared more about the team winning than about his own achievement. Reggie comments that the same was true in politics as well (Reggie 143).

Being basketball buddies "upgraded" Reggie's position. When Obama saw a special new outfit that Reggie was wearing, he commented on it. Obama liked the tie, and even borrowed it later to wear it himself. Reggie's opinion on clothes became important for Obama. When Obama dressed before a major event, he would ask Reggie for his opinion on how he looked. If everything was okay they would "fist bump" before Obama went on the stage (Reggie 84-85). It was also true before the swearing in as President (Reggie 148).

On Election Day, back in Chicago, they played basketball with Obama's friends and supporters (Reggie 142-143). After the elections, Reggie flew with President-elect Obama to DC. During the flight, Obama talked about a basketball player who was a friend of Reggie's; about "predictions for the NBA season"; about Lebron; and then "out of nowhere" Obama told Reggie, "You're coming with me, right?" to which Reggie responded in the affirmative. Obama gave Reggie "a fist dap" and the deal was sealed (Reggie 145).

Obama and Reggie at the White House

The time at the White House started with a tour of the building on the first weekend, given by the White House curator to the trio of POTUS, FLOTUS, and Reggie. (Reggie 150).

Reggie was known as "the guy who plays basketball with the President", but he was not only Obama's basketball buddy. He was the president's "touchstone for normalcy". He was with Obama even during his own private time, like eating lunch alone. It came to a point that Reggie could read Obama, the one with the poker face, the "Spockian", very well. One look at Obama, and Reggie knew everything. In a way, Reggie became a sort of extension to Obama (Reggie 6-7, 71).

Obama and Reggie and Boundaries

Reggie labeled himself as one who wants to test the boundaries and limitations. When he was a kid, and he faced a certain situation in which there were no rules, Reggie would "push the boundaries" until he "found the line". He also said that at times he crossed the line (Reggie 26).

Reggie described an event where he pushed the boundaries, and crossed a line – an event that he labeled as "the most humiliating event" of his life. While at Duke, after he had gotten drunk at a party, there were pictures circulating that showed Reggie "passed out" with other "drunk dudes" who were pretending to "straddle" his face. He also called it – "my passed-out butt on that green futon" (Reggie 43-44).

Did Reggie push the boundaries with Obama?

Reggie said that the campaign rule was that nobody should enter the candidate's hotel room without the candidate's permission. Reggie even gave the reason for this rule: respect for the candidate, and a "formal boundary" that was kept religiously.

But there was a night in which the candidate was awake till 4am writing a speech. At 7am Reggie went to wake him up to get ready for the speech, since he needed to be on location at 8. Reggie knocked on the door and rang the doorbell. Since there was no answer, and it was a large suite, Reggie asked the agent guarding the room to let him inside. Previously Reggie had called it a "massive suite", but once he was in the "entryway" he changed his language and began to refer to it as a "room".

Could Reggie have used the phone to ring for a long time to wake up the candidate? He could. But he didn't. He walked into the "room"/"suite" in spite of the explicit order not to do so.

Reggie did not keep up the "formal boundary" mandated by the campaign. Yet what is missing from Reggie's account is any reprimand for his behavior, either by the candidate, by the campaign, or even by himself! Reggie afterwards writes that Obama woke up, the speech went well, and he "had a small part in making [it] happen." (Reggie 194-195)

Reggie also describes a similar event, but reversed – in which it was Obama who crossed the boundaries.

There was an event in Florida when Reggie's old friend came to visit him, and she decided to stay for the night. In the morning, Obama used the Secret Service keys to enter the room. Although Reggie heard "the most peremptory of knocks" (which according to Reggie's account was after Obama had already entered the room), the candidate charged into the room and started talking to Reggie about the schedule. Reggie's friend was in bed with the covers up to her throat. When Obama saw the woman in bed he immediately apologized and left the room.

The event didn't end there. When Obama told the team that he was exhausted from the campaign, Reggie "chimed in" and said, "You know, sir, if it's any consolation, I'm having the time of my life." Obama responded that improving Reggie's love life was not a consolation for him (Reggie 29-30).

Ben Rhodes, Obama's speechwriter, reported another event that took place before the candidate Obama was to give a speech in Berlin, Germany. Rhodes went over the speech, and its translation to German, and after googling a certain word, he found that it was a term that was used by Hitler in a speech at the German parliament, the Reichstag.

Rhodes emailed Reggie to ask if he could meet Obama to discuss the issue. Reggie told him that the two of them, Obama and Reggie, wear after a workout and that Rhodes should stop by his suite. Rhodes even emphasized: "Not Obama's – Reggie's".

Rhodes went to Reggie's suite and saw Obama sitting by a small desk reviewing the speech on the laptop, while Reggie was lying on the bed looking at his blackberry.

The next sentence in Rhodes' account is that the curtains were drawn to prevent any "external audience".

When Obama and Reggie joked about the error, Rhodes concluded his description of the conversation by telling them the word was "problematic", and in doing so he volunteered himself "as straight man" (BenR 26-27).

Question: Is this event one of the reasons that Rhodes described Obama at the beginning of his book as "A man constantly in the public eye who hid important parts of himself" (BenR xviii)?

Reggie and the word "woman"/"women"

It is clear that Reggie's book is mainly about his time with Obama the candidate, and later president. In addition, Reggie mentions his parents and his coaches as significant people who influenced him in life Reggie (8).

Reggie uses the word "woman"/"women" to describe his grandmother (89) (he also called her "superwoman") and his mother (175,177) – women in his life who gave him empathy (173).

Reggie uses the word "woman"/"women" in regard to women's rights – "women and LGBT populations" (113), and "LGBT, immigration, women's rights…" (Reggie 121)

Reggie uses the word "woman"/"women" while talking to Jay Z saying, "You never let another man massage your woman's feet" (189).

Reggie uses the word "woman"/"women" in regard to "men and women" serving in the military (42, 162, 163).

Reggie uses the word "woman"/"women" in connection to Obama – "men and women" in the corridors of Congress when he came to his first meeting with Obama (4);
Edith Childs, a woman who led the participants in a cheer of "fired up and ready to go" at an Obama campaign stop (126); women who wanted to hug the candidate (138); and when quoting Michelle Obama talking to him about finding a woman (174).

Reggie uses the word "woman" to refer to women in his social life - talking in general of "a woman I was charmed by" (Reggie 129) and "women" who expressed interest in him (Reggie 161).

There are only three women in his personal life, other than his family, who are mentioned in his book. Two of them are mentioned by name:

Erin, who influenced him to get the job with the Obama campaign, and is introduced with the description "I was dating a young woman named Erin" (15); and Lydia Guterman, who is described as his "ex-girlfriend" and "a smart and beautiful woman" (70).

The third is the one who was in his bed when Obama unexpectedly came into his room in the morning. She is referred to only as "an old friend", "my friend", and "she" (Reggie 29-30).

In the beginning of his book, Reggie says that his parents and his coaches influenced him, and later in the book he talks of his time with Obama as the period that brought him to maturity, and to become a "man".

Erin is related to his decision to join Senator Obama's office, but Lydia is not. She is also not connected to his parents, to his coaches, or to Obama the candidate and later president.   Still, Lydia is mentioned as one "who constantly pushed me to be better personally, athletically, and academically". By saying this, Reggie "elevated" Lydia to be as important as his parents, coaches, and Obama.

Lydia shared with Reggie that she had started to date women, and that she is going to attend a march in Washington, DC, to rally for LGBT rights. When Reggie asked her "why would you want to waste your time on that", she very forcefully argued with him. Moreover, other members of the campaign who had heard his side of the phone conversation, told Reggie that he should be more compassionate towards "what is important to other people", and Reggie conceded that he was wrong.

In a way, mentioning Lydia in the book does not serve the main theme of the book, but it does serve the cause of LGBT, who are mentioned twice more in the book.

Summary

One point distinguishes Obama's childhood from that of Reggie. Obama came from a broken home, being raised by his single mother and grandparents. Reggie was raised by a two-parent family. On the other hand, there was one point that the two of them shared about their childhood.

In talking about his father, Reggie said that his mother never spanked him. This was his father's job. Reggie also mentioned that when he was in grade school, his father left his belt on the doorknob when he went to work in the morning, signaling to the young Reggie what would wait for him if he would misbehave. And Reggie did misbehave (Reggie 175, 90).

Both Obama and Reggie were interested in basketball; both of them were likely to have been abused in childhood; and both of them, at times, crossed the line, crossed boundaries.

President Obama and Race

Being born to a father from Kenya and a mother from Kansas, Obama had to struggle with his mixed heritage. In his book, "Dreams From My Father" he talks about Malcolm X's autobiography.

Malcolm X wished that he could eradicate "the white blood that ran through him" which was a result of violence. Obama could identify with this wish, realizing that he would have to live with his mixed heritage throughout his journey in life (BO DFMF 86).

Obama also talked of his bloodline as coming from all over the globe (BO AOH 331), and he felt had to shift back and forth between his black and white worlds (BO DFMF 82).

In essence, both Malcom X and Obama considered their genetic heritage to be a major factor in their life.

Obama was raised by his white mother and white grandparents (with a short interval of being with a stepfather in Indonesia). Still, the adults in Obama's life talked positively of his Kenyan father. Moreover, his white mother exalted the fact that he has black heritage. She talked with him in superlative terms of his father's inheritance and destiny (BO DFMF 51).

But one fact could not be disregarded. His father was not there in his life (BO DFMF 26). When he was two years old, his parents separated and his father returned to Kenya, and "the mother and child stayed behind" (BO DFMF 10).

At the age twelve or thirteen Obama stopped talking of his mother's share in his physical constitution. He didn't want feel as if he is "ingratiating" himself to whites. At that age, Obama started to become more attached to his black world. Or, as Ben Rhodes described it:

"Obama became centered in his own identity as an African American, joining a continuum of those who had suffered oppression but managed to achieve change through nonviolent mobilization." (BenR 48)

But even feeling attached to his black identity, and able to "embrace [his] black brothers and sisters", sharing with them a "common destiny",

Obama realized that he does not really represent "the black American experience" (BO DFMF xvi).

Dealing with Discrimination and Prejudice

Obama said that since people cannot be immune to the stereotypes that culture constantly provides, prejudice does exist (BO AOH 235).

Even with this prejudice in existence, the city that Obama knows best has many African American professionals, to include doctors, lawyers, and many others (BO AOH 240), and none of these successful people used discrimination as an excuse to not do their best to be successful. He attributed to this generation the complete rejection of any limits on their way to success (BO AOH 241).

Michelle Obama, who graduated Harvard and became a lawyer, described in her book, the influence of her mother on her upward mobility: the way her mother tutored her, and insisted on her doing her best to succeed in the general American society (MichO 4).

Michelle also described the way her parents taught her to speak – "Our parents had drilled into us the importance of using proper diction, of saying 'going' instead of 'goin' ' and 'isn't' instead of 'ain't.' We were taught to finish off our words." It came to a point in which one of her cousins asked Michelle - "How come you talk like a white girl?" Michelle concluded it by saying, "We seemed to be related but of two different worlds." (MichO 40)

When talking about college, Michelle said that "whatever deficits I might have arrived with, coming from an inner-city high school, it seemed that I could make up for them by putting in extra time, asking for help when I needed it, and learning to pace myself and not procrastinate (MichO 78).

Towards the end of her book, Michelle summarized her success in life: "My early successes in life were, I knew, a product of the consistent love and high expectations with which I was surrounded as a child, both at home and at school" (MichO 383), and "Education had been the primary instrument of change in my own life, my lever upward in the world." (MichO 401)

Susan Rice, an African American who served as US ambassador to the UN in Obama's first term, and as National Security Advisor in his second term, described in her book the message about discrimination she received from her parents.

Her father's message was, "Don't take crap off of anyone" (SusanR 14), and "don't let anyone demean" or "define" her (SusanR 69).

Rice's parents insisted that she should "honor" her heritage, "value" herself, do her best, and not let anyone else tell her that she cannot achieve something (SusanR 19).   Her parents insisted that "good education, economic stability, and physical security" is all she needs to succeed in life (SusanR 22).   She internalized these values as her own, and refused to accept that her appearance (as an African American woman) would be "her" problem (SusanR 38).

Nikki Haley was born to Indian-American parents, was elected as governor of South Carolina, and later served as US ambassador to the UN in the Trump administration. Haley described in her book the discrimination that she had to deal with due to her being "brown".   The message that her parents gave her: "Your job is not to show people how you are different. Your job is to show them how you are similar." (NikkiH 23) Another message her parents gave her was: "Whatever you do, be great at it, and make sure people remember you for it." (NikkiH 247)

Valerie Jarrett describes her experience growing up as an African American girl. Her father, a doctor, found a job in Iran, as it was a place where they were willing to hire a black doctor.

Before she went to college, her mother sat with her with a spreadsheet of how much each class she is going to attend is costing them. Her mother said that she realizes that going to college can be fun, but if she plans to skip classes, her mother wanted her to know how much her absence from class costs (ValJ 33). Jarrett couldn't let her parents down. She had to succeed. Before taking the bar examination she knew that failure was not an option (ValJ 40).

In summary, although prejudice "still exists", a person's success in life is dependent mainly on the upbringing that the person's parents impart to them in childhood.

Obama also brought statistics to show that the African American middle class had grown fourfold in a generation (BO AOH 242).

Obama's election as president

Leon Panetta, CIA Director and later Defense Secretary under Obama, connected Obama's election as president to the US Supreme Court decision against school segregation fifty years earlier. Panetta saw these two points as milestones in the process of growth of the US as a society (LeonP 191).

Obama related to the significance of his being elected as president. Obama told Axelrod before the elections that the day he would take the oath of office as president of the United States would change the way millions of kids, including African American and Latino kids, would look at themselves (Axe 199). Obama recalled what an African American man had told him about the election of Harold Washington, an African American, as mayor of Chicago: "People weren't just proud of Harold. They were proud of themselves." (BO DFMF 148)

David Cameron, prime minister of the UK, met Obama at the time Obama was a senator from Illinois. He asked Obama if he (Obama) could win the 2008 presidential election. Obama responded that there were several "things" to overcome: the "inexperience thing", the "black thing", and the "Muslim thing" (DavCam 153-154).

There were many around Obama who didn't believe that the election of a African American as president is even possible.

Samantha Power said that many experts, along with millions of Americans, didn't believe it was possible for an African American to be elected as president in "a majority-white country with deep racial fault lines" (SamP 179).

Valerie Jarrett said that such an outcome didn't enter her "wildest dreams" (ValJ 112). She expressed the same doubt in regard to Obama running for the US Senate in 2006 (ValJ 119). Even after Obama was elected, Jarrett knew that race would be a feature to remain throughout Obama's presidency (ValJ 133).

Susan Rice joined Jarrett in the same doubt. And when Obama was elected she couldn't stop crying the night and the day after the election (SusanR 232-233). Samantha Power told Obama that his election was something "too big to comprehend" (SamP 200).

When John Kerry came to congratulate Obama and said the words "Mr. President", Obama "arched his eyebrows slightly, as if to say, 'What a crazy world this is.'" (JohnK 351).

David Plouffe, Obama's campaign manager, in describing Obama's decision to run, wrote: "Barack Hussein Obama… was running for president of the United States. With little more than hope in his sails." (DavPl 27).   When describing election night, Plouffe wrote that the country had just elected "an African American man, born to a Kenyan father and a Kansan mother" (DavPl 1).

Obama's primary campaign strategy

Since Obama's campaign team accepted that race played a part in American politics (Axe 170), Obama's campaign had to adjust its strategy in order to win, especially in the first state to start the long race – Iowa. Iowa is not a primary state, but a caucus state. Iowa is also a state with a "90 percent white" electorate (ValJ 134), and it is a "rural state" (ValJ 140).

David Plouffe said that the campaign team believed that their "fervent grassroots support" was an advantage in caucus states (DavPl 94). And since Obama was an African American candidate campaigning in a mostly white state, the campaign had to expand the number of people coming to the caucus, or, in Plouffe's language, to change the electorate completely. They needed to reach younger whites, independents, and African American voters.

They started with around ten thousand e-mail addresses, a list that grew by mid-2008 to over 5 million (DavPl 237). On the day of the caucus, Plouffe gave the numbers. While in 2004 the number of people who

came to the Iowa caucus was 120,000, in 2008 the number was double –
240,000.

Samantha Power quoted Obama as saying that his victory in Iowa was his
most favorite night of his entire political career, even more than the night
of November 4, 2008, when he was elected president (SamP 180).

Obama and Race

Two events during the campaign brought the issue of race to the front –
Jeremiah Wright and Obama's wife, Michelle. (The events concerning
Michelle are discussed in the chapter "Who Is Michelle".)

Jeremiah Wright

The "Jeremiah Wright Event" dominated Obama's campaign for a while.
On March 6, 2008, Rolling Stone magazine published an article by Ben
Wallace-Wells titled "Destiny's Child" – a profile of Barack (Axe 212).

Note: the article was originally published under the title "The Radical
Roots of Barack Obama", but the magazine later changed the title to
"Destiny's Child".

The article produced very inflaming quotes from a sermon Wright had
given, quotes that Axelrod labeled as "raising hell" instead of hope (Axe
212):

"Fact number one: We've got more black men in prison than there are in
college. Fact number two: Racism is how this country was founded and
how this country is still run! We are deeply involved in the importing of
drugs, the exporting of guns and the training of professional KILLERS…
We believe in white supremacy and black inferiority and believe it, more
than we believe in God… We conducted radiation experiments on our
own people… We care nothing about human life if the ends justify the
means!"
"The government gives them the drugs, builds bigger prisons, passes a
three-strike law, and then wants us to sing 'God Bless America'? No, no,
no, God *damn* America!"
"The USA of KKK."

"We have supported state terrorism against the Palestinians and black South Africans, and now we are indignant because stuff we have done overseas is now brought back into our own backyard. America's chickens are coming home to roost." (Axe 212, ValJ 148, ValJ 144-145, DavPl 206)

Plouffe noted that the very last two sentences were given right after 9/11.

If these quotes were not enough, Reverend Wright spoke later at the National Press Club in Washington, DC. Wright added to his list that the US government was the one responsible for AIDS in the African American community, and he even showed the audience what he meant by saying "America's chickens are coming home to roost" by dancing like a chicken (ValJ 148).

The Campaign's Initial Reaction

The campaign knew that these sermons by Wright were floating around (DavPl 206), but they didn't relate to them. Rolling Stone magazine brought these sermons to the "mainstream consciousness", which produced "chaos" and fear (DavPl 210).

Valerie Jarrett labeled the sermons as "an existential threat" to the campaign. She even concluded that the campaign was "toast" (ValJ 149).

Obama's Initial Reaction

Initially Obama said that he "didn't recall" these sermons.(DavPl 208).

David Plouffe quoted Obama saying:

"I don't recall any of these parts of these sermons… From time to time – and it was fairly rare – Wright would say something I thought crossed the line or was even in poor taste. I would often come up to him after and say so, and he and I would sometimes have heated disagreements. But I'm positive I never heard anything like this."

Assuming it is an accurate quote we should note three points in Obama's language:

"Wright **would** say something… I **would** often come up to him… and he and I **would** sometimes have heated disagreements."

Using "would" violates the formula of "first person singular past tense". Obama avoided using past tense ("Wright **said** something… I often **came** up to him… and he and I sometimes **had** heated disagreements"), and by doing so, Obama reduced commitment to the content of these sentences, making these sentences "unreliable".

No. 2: Obama said, "But **I'm positive** I never heard anything like this." Why to add the phrase "But I am positive"? Why not to say simply, "But I never heard anything like this." By adding "I'm positive", Obama, again, reduced commitment to the content of this sentence, making it, again, "unreliable".

No. 3: Obama said, "But I'm positive I **never** heard anything like this" – Obama couldn't say, "But I didn't hear anything like this." Note that the word "never" is not strong as "didn't".

And Obama continued telling Plouffe:

"I went much less frequently in recent years…" Obama implied here that the quotes produced from Wright's sermons might have been delivered at the time Obama was not there.

Please note that SCAN does not deal with what a person implies. SCAN only deals only with what people say. Obama couldn't say that he wasn't there at the time the sermons were delivered. He wanted the listener (Plouffe in this case) to conclude that he wasn't there, but he couldn't bring himself to actually say it.

And Obama continued telling Plouffe:

"But these excerpts simplify Wright. **Most** of his talks are about love and support and fairness. It's a wonderful church community with a pastor who is **mostly** positive but can draw outside the lines sometimes."
(DavPl 208)

And here, Obama moved to defend Wright, and he labeled the hatred expressed by Wright only as a tendency to "…draw outside the lines sometimes".

This was Obama's initial response internally, talking to Plouffe, his campaign manager.

Why Would Obama Minimize Wright's Message?

We shouldn't be surprised by Obama's reaction and response to Plouffe. In his book "Dreams from My Father", Obama extensively talked about the Trinity Church and its leader, Jeremiah Wright.

Obama described a sermon Wright gave titled "The Audacity of Hope". He later borrowed this title to be the title of his own book, his second one.

Obama quoted Wright who said:

"It is this world, a world where cruise ships throw away more food in a day than most residents of Port-au-Prince see in a year, where white folks' greed runs a world in need, apartheid in one hemisphere, apathy in another hemisphere … That's the world! On which hope sits!" (Bo DFMF 292-293)

Wright also talked of "…Sharpsville and Hiroshima, the callousness of policy makers in the White House and in the State House."

Obama ended his description by saying that "the stories of strife became more prosaic, the pain more immediate." (BO DFMF 292-293)

Obama quoted Wright talking about "Sharpsville and Hiroshima", and "callousness of policy makers in the White House". This is Wright, but what does Obama think of "policy makers in the White House"?

US Guilt According to Obama

In his book, Obama opened a window to his thinking about the US. When talking about the area of Aceh in Indonesia, Obama said that the atrocities committed by the Indonesian army (murder, rape, and others) were done with the knowledge of US administrations, "if not outright approval" (BO AOH 276).

Obama also said that past US administrations had ignored the "legitimate aspirations" of people around the globe, a behavior that made the world more dangerous (BO AOH 280).

"Manifest destiny" for Obama was "bloody and violent conquest". He compared this conquest to slavery, both of which contradicted principles upon which the US was established (BO AOH 281).

Obama's US Guilt List went on – the US tolerated and helped "thieves" and "thugs" as long as these opposed the expansion of communism. The US was involved in removing democratically elected leaders, like in Iran in 1953, causing repercussions that are still felt in the present (BO AOH 286).

Obama talked of the tools used overseas by the US government that impacted the way US governments treated the American people – the way US governments suppressed criticism, manipulated the public to support "questionable policies", or to simply cover up fiascos (BO AOH 287).

Although he referred to Nixon and Kissinger's bombing campaign in Cambodia as "morally rudderless", he labeled their foreign policy as "tactically brilliant"; but at the same time he accused them of abusing the American people (BO AOH 288).

Obama didn't spare Reagan, who according to Obama had "blindness" to misery all around the world (BO AOH 288). Reagan's list of sins included support for the apartheid regime in South Africa, funding of El Salvador's death squads, and the invasion of Grenada (BO AOH 289).

Obama attacked the American drug companies, since they prevented other countries, like Brazil, from producing generic AIDS drugs that could have saved millions of lives (BO AOH 318).

Obama also attacked the International Monetary Fund and the World Bank, two financial institutions under US leadership that that caused "enormous hardship" to "ordinary citizens" (BO AOH 318).

In summary, both Wright and Obama criticized the US. The only difference between them is their language. While Wright used "incendiary language", Obama used professorial language that reduced the impact on the listener.

As for condemning the US, Obama did a better job, language-wise. In content, it was not much different from Wright.

Many years later, when Obama was already president, he went around the globe with an "apology tour". The conservative Canadian Prime Minister Stephen Harper listed this "apology tour" by Obama as one of the reasons that brought many Americans to view their own country as one that "lacked confidence in itself" (StephenH 49).

Obama's Public Response to Wright

Obama told the campaign team not to worry. "We are taking the trash out today. It won't be fun but we'll be stronger for it." (DavPl 210)

And Obama went to use the most powerful tool in his arsenal – the power of the speech.

Obama prepared a speech which was later called "The Race Speech"

Obama's "Race Speech"

Obama's speech, which he delivered at the National Constitution Center in Philadelphia on March 18, 2008, includes three major themes:

A more perfect union
Slavery still impacts society
Anger in the black community

"A More Perfect Union"

Originally, the phrase referred to the fact that a confederation of thirteen independent states, as the American colonies were at the time of independence, was not conducive to efficient governing or the free flow of trade between the colonies and Europe. Alexander Hamilton described the confederation as "a monster with thirteen heads." There was a need to create "a more perfect union" to address the chaos that existed within the colonies, and between the colonies and the outside world. The preamble to the US constitution mentions "to form a more perfect Union" as one of the constitution's goals – i.e. to enable the thirteen colonies, now states, to go from chaos to unity.

However, the former Constitutional Law professor, Barack Obama, borrowed this phrase from the preamble to the constitution and used it to describe the situation of the African American community in the US.

Initially the African Americans were slaves, and the Civil War brought their freedom; but it was not a complete freedom, as the southern states created the Jim Crow laws to restrict their rights. For a time, "separate but equal" was considered legal; and only in the 1960s, the time of Martin Luther King, John F Kennedy, and Lyndon Johnson, the US Congress legislated the laws that granted full integration of the African American community, and forbade any discrimination due to race or other issues.

Still, Obama described a situation in which the African American community **today** is not equal to the white one. He gave statistics to support this view. "The average black wage is 75 percent of the average white wage; the average Latino wage is 71 percent of the average white wage. Black median net worth is about $6,000, and Latino median net worth is about $8,000, compared to $88,000 for whites." (BO AOH 242-243)

In a speech given on July 19, 2013, President Obama pointed out that it is only a process: "…we're becoming a more perfect union – **not a perfect union**, but a **more** perfect union."

Obama elaborated on this concept of a "more perfect union" in a speech given on February 18, 2016: "There's a gap – there always will be – between who we are and the 'perfect union,' that ideal that we see. But what makes us exceptional, what makes us Americans is that… that gap gets smaller over time. And it's that effort to form a 'more perfect union' that marks us as a people."

Returning to Obama's "Race Speech", we can see that the only fault Obama found in Jeremiah Wright's speech is that he didn't recognize this process:

"The profound mistake of Reverend Wright's sermons is **not** that he spoke about racism in our society. It's that he spoke as if our society was **static**; as if no progress had been made; as if this country – a country that has made it possible for one of his own members to run for the highest office in the land and build a coalition of white and black, Latino, Asian, rich, poor, young and old – is still irrevocably bound to a tragic past."

Slavery still impacts society

In his "Race Speech", Obama tied all the statistics about the African American disadvantage in the American society to his second main point – that slavery still impacts society:

"But we do need to remind ourselves that so many of the disparities that exist between the African American community and the larger American community today can be traced directly to inequalities passed on from an earlier generation that suffered under the brutal legacy of slavery and Jim Crow."

Obama went on in his speech to give examples:

"Segregated schools were, and are, inferior schools. We still haven't fixed them, fifty years after "Brown v. Board of Education". And the inferior education they provided, then and now, helps explain the pervasive achievement gap between today's black and white students."

Earlier in life, in his book, he gave personal examples: "…security guards tailing me as I shop in department stores, white couples who toss me their car keys as I stand outside a restaurant waiting for the valet, police cars pulling me over for no apparent reason" (BO AOH 233).

Slavery in the present time

Obama went one step further – not only talking about the impact of slavery, but also bringing the concept that the African American people identify with the slaves of the past. In other words, the African Americans feel that they are the slaves of the past.

In 2009, in talking to the NAACP Centennial Convention, Obama described his visit to the Cape Coast Castle, in Ghana, "…where captives were once imprisoned before being auctioned…"

Obama ended his description by concluding: "I was reminded that no matter how bitter the rod, how stony the road, **we** have always persevered."

By using the "we", Obama included himself in the group of the captives before being auctioned. He identified himself with the slaves.

In 2012, at the Groundbreaking Ceremony of the National Museum of African American History and Culture at the National Mall, Obama said that he wanted his daughters "…to see the shackles that bound slaves on their voyage across the ocean…" and that he wanted his daughters "…to appreciate this museum not just as a record of tragedy, but as a celebration of life." It was not just a tragedy of the past, but it is a celebration in the present.

In 2016, at a Black History Month Reception, he was clearer about this concept: "**We'**re the slaves who quarried the stone to build this White House…"

In the same speech, when he was talking about the young generation of today, he praised them by saying, "They don't see themselves as distant from that history – they are participants, making history. It's alive, something that we have the power and the responsibility to shape and to wield."

The history of slavery, and its impact on today, and even the feeling of identification with the slave of the past, brought Obama in his "Race Speech" to deal with the third issue of his speech – the anger in the African American society.

Anger in the black community

In his "Race Speech", Obama said: "For the men and women of Reverend Wright's generation, the memories of humiliation and doubt and fear have not gone away; nor has the anger and the bitterness of those years. That anger may not get expressed in public, in front of white co-workers or white friends."

The anger in the African American community is not a new theme; Obama mentioned it in the two books he published before he was elected president.

In his first book, "Dreams from My Father", Obama described an event that happened while he was in New York City, even before he went to Chicago to become a community organizer.

He took his white girlfriend to see a new play by a black playwright. It was a "very angry play", although it was "very funny", and Obama considered it as "typical black American humor".

When the play was over, his white girlfriend asked him why black people were so angry all the time, to which Obama responded: "it was a matter of remembering – nobody asks why Jews remember the Holocaust." (BO DFMF 211)

In his book he quoted people who considered the need of African American people "to let off a little steam every once in a while" (BO DFMF 203).

Obama described what Reverend Philips told him in Chicago. The Reverend equated the anger of African American Muslims to his own, an anger that he understood will stay with him for life, and the only thing he could hope for is to learn to control it by using prayer (BO DFMF 273).

Returning to Obama's "Race Speech", we can understand why Obama said:

"…the anger is real; it is powerful. And to simply wish it away, to condemn it without understanding its roots, only serves to widen the chasm of misunderstanding that exists between the races."

After recognizing the existence of the anger in the African American community, Obama talked of how this anger manifests itself in public (i.e. Jeremiah Wright):

"And occasionally it [=the anger] finds voice in the church on Sunday morning, in the pulpit and in the pews."

In his eulogy in 2015 for the people who were killed in an African American church in South Carolina, Obama talked of the Church as an institution in the African American community:

"Over the course of centuries, black churches served as 'hush harbors' where slaves could worship in safety; praise houses where their free descendants could gather and shout hallelujah, rest stops for the weary along the Underground Railroad; bunkers for the foot soldiers of the Civil Rights Movement."

According to Obama, the church in the African American community is not only an institution of religion. It is an institution of social justice.

Why was there surprise in the news media and the general US public about this anger? It was not new. It was and it is always there. It only came to the forefront of consciousness of white people during Obama's campaign.

Did Obama know of Jeremiah Wright's words at the time he attended the Trinity Church?

Although when talking to Plouffe he was evasive, in his speech Obama changed course, language-wise. When talking to Plouffe earlier about of his knowledge (or lack of it) regarding Wright's message, Obama avoided using past tense, and instead repeatedly used "would". But in his speech Obama confessed:

"For some, nagging questions remain: Did I know him to be an occasionally fierce critic of American domestic and foreign policy? **Of course**. Did I ever hear him make remarks that could be considered controversial while I sat in the church? **Yes**. Did I strongly disagree with many of his political views? **Absolutely**..."

At this point, Obama moved to use a dual approach, which he also used in many other issues. On one hand he would condemn, and on the other he would praise.

Orly Azoulay, an Israeli jounalist, in her book about Obama, quoted Obama's classmate, Kenneth Mar, who later became a professor at Harvard. "It was difficult to classify him. He always said that one can see the issue in a certain way, but there is also another side, and one needs to look upon things from different angles." (OA 132)

Professor Mar also said that Obama "...could give everyone the feeling that he agrees with him, but he was also a little bit mysterious. Even those who were close to him didn't know for sure what exactly he is thinking." (OA 132)

Back to Obama's "Race Speech"

In his speech Obama continued, "...Reverend Wright's comments were not only **wrong** but **divisive, divisive** at a time when we need unity; **racially charged** at a time when we need to come together..."

Now Obama moved on to commend the Reverend: "...a man who spoke to me about our obligations to love one another; to care for the sick and lift up the poor." A man who served the community "...by doing God's work here on Earth – by housing the homeless, ministering to the needy, providing day care services and scholarships and prison ministries, and reaching out to those suffering from HIV/AIDS."

Till this point, we can see that Obama is juggling between condemnation and praise of the same person. He then explained why, saying that Wright is not different from any other black church: "Like other predominantly black churches across the country, Trinity embodies the black community in its entirety – the doctor and the welfare mom, the model student and the former gangbanger."

This is similar to what Valerie Jarrett said in her book: "In black churches in America, there's a tradition of fiery rhetoric that serves to validate the pain of a people who have long suffered injustice in order to motivate them to rise above it." (ValJ 145)

Expanding on this theme, Obama continued: "The church contains in full the kindness and cruelty, the fierce intelligence and the shocking ignorance, the struggles and successes, the love and, yes, the **bitterness** and **biases** that make up the black experience in America."

And Obama continued: "Not once in my conversations with him have I heard him talk about any ethnic group in derogatory terms or treat whites with whom he interacted with anything but courtesy and respect."

It should be noted that Obama mentioned in his book that Wright, after his military service in the Marines, was "...dabbling with liquor, **Islam, and black nationalism** in the sixties" (BO DFMF 282).

Valerie Jarrett quoted Wright talking of his joint trip with Louis Farrakhan to Libya to meet with Mu'ammar al-Gadhafi (ValJ 144).

Wright, who was "...dabbling with... Islam and black nationalism in the sixties" and who went together with a well-known virulent anti-Semite to visit the Libyan dictator, is described by Obama as one who didn't "...talk about any ethnic group in derogatory terms..." Obama might be reporting it accurately but this is quite unlikely.

Moreover, as a community organizer in Chicago, Obama reported his conversation with another reverend, Reverend Smalls, who told him:

"...the last thing we need is to join up with a bunch of white money and Catholic churches and Jewish organizers to solve our problems." (BO DFMF 161)

Reverend Smalls is not Reverend Wright. But still Obama reported a Reverend in Chicago who talked in "derogatory terms" of "white money and Catholic churches and Jewish organizers".

In his speech, Obama continued: "I can no more disown him than I can disown the black community."

Obama had said a moment earlier that "Trinity embodies the black community in its entirety". Therefore, to disown Wright would amount to disowning the entire black community.

And as he cannot disown Wright and Trinity Church, he also:

"…can no more disown him than I can disown my white grandmother – a woman who helped raise me, a woman who sacrificed again and again for me, a woman who loves me as much as she loves anything in this world, but a woman who once confessed her fear of black men who passed her by on the street, and who on more than one occasion has uttered racial or ethnic stereotypes that made me cringe."

If in the last paragraph, Obama minimized Wright's words, by equating Wright to his own white grandmother, now he moved on to the other side – condemnation. Wright's remarks:

"…expressed a profoundly distorted view of this country, a view that sees white racism as endemic and that elevates what is wrong with America above all that we know is right with America…"

Summary

Obama, in his language, identifies with the African American community of today, and even identifies with the slaves of the past. But as he said in his book, he still cannot feel that he is able to represent the African American community, as he shares mixed "bloodlines", and he was raised by his white mother and grandparents. Therefore, he is split into two. On one hand, he can talk of the pain of the African American community, but on the other hand he can see how the American community at large offers the African American people the mobility to join the rest of the society. That it is a process. It is not static. "A **more** perfect union".

Slavery in the past of two communities

Every year, the Jewish people celebrate Passover, the holiday of freedom from slavery in Egypt. In the text that is read at the festive meal ("the seder"), it is said that each one of us should perceive himself as if he himself came out of Egypt. And in fact, there are Jewish communities where the family even "re-enacts" the exodus from Egypt. But note that the text does not say that each one should perceive himself as if he himself **was a slave** in Egypt – only that he himself **came out**.

Both communities relive an event in the past – slavery. Both communities were freed from slavery, but not on their own. The Israelites were freed by the Almighty, Who fought the Egyptian Pharaoh with the ten plagues, bringing Pharaoh to expel the Israelites. The narrative of the Biblical text says openly that the Israelites were bystanders in this struggle. They were not participants.

The same applies to the African American community. The Civil War brought their release from slavery (although they did not achieve true equality until the 1960s). The African Americans were not involved in the struggle as a group. Even though there were some African Americans who were soldiers in the Union Army, as a group they were bystanders, just like the Israelites in Egypt.

The difference between the two groups is that the Israelites identify with the freed slaves, while Obama identifies with the slaves during slavery.

It should be noted that the news media reported how each year Obama and the White House staff celebrated the holiday of Passover. Since several members of his close team were Jewish, one can easily assume that the message of freedom appealed to Obama. But we find that Obama paraphrased the message of freedom into being the message of slavery.

Passover and Jewish Slavery

Background information

Within the Haggadah (the text read at the seder) there is a song which is sung by all present: "V'Hi She'amda".

A literal translation of the first line is: "And it is this that has stood for our Forefathers and us…" What is "this"? It refers to the covenant between the Almighty and the Jewish people. In this covenant, the Almighty promised the Jewish people that in spite of all the hardships, He will not forget His people.

The full text of the song is: "And it is this [covenant] that has stood for our Forefathers and us. For not just one enemy has stood against us to wipe us out. But in every generation there have been those who have stood against us to wipe us out, and the Holy One Blessed Be He saves us from their hands." [Translation courtesy of Aish HaTorah https://www.aish.com/h/pes/f/hh/48959161.html]

President Obama and Jewish Slavery

David Litt, Obama's Jewish speechwriter, and another Jewish colleague prepared a text for the president's pre-Passover message. The speech that they presented to Obama included part of the above-mentioned song.

"In every generation, there are those who have tried to destroy the Jewish people." (DavidL 103)

Please note that the main point of the song is not the suffering of generations. The main point of the song, which actually starts the song, is the reference to the covenant that guaranteed the continued existence of the Jewish people despite all the persecutions. The two Jewish speechwriters omitted this important part of the song. In other words, the religious message was absent while the suffering and the threat of annihilation still remained.

[Note: In his book David Litt describes his relationship with his Christian girlfriend. When talking about Christmas he said, "We already have a Christmas… It's called Yom Kippur." (DavidL 207) To label Yom Kippur as the equivalent of Christmas is a fundamental misunderstanding of Yom Kippur – a day of fasting and atonement. When he visited his girlfriend's parents for Christmas, he commented, "Christmas was the most Jewish thing I'd done in months." (DavidL 224) In summary, David Litt was completely detached from his own Jewish heritage, yet he was the messenger of Jewish heritage to President Obama.]

When Obama reached this place in the prepared text and encountered this line from the song, he commented, "Isn't that line kind of a downer?… I mean, this is supposed to be a party, right? What's the deal? Like, 'Everyone's out to get us, have some matzo.'" (DavidL 103)

David Litt's response to this comment by Obama was, "In fact, that was exactly the deal. POTUS had summed up five thousand years of Jewish history in just eight words."

But the fact is that this was not "the deal" at all. And Obama, presented with a partial, misleading quote, misunderstood Jewish history in entirety. The Jews do not celebrate their suffering. They celebrate their rescue as a nation (even if sometimes not as individuals).

Litt continues his description of the event. Obama asked for a pen to change the text, and he revised it to his liking:

"In every generation, there are those who have targeted the Jewish people for harm."

And Litt comments: "In just five minutes, he rewrote it to express the same idea, but in far more measured tones." (DavidL 104)

In fact, it was not the same idea.   Obama was presented with a partial, misleading quote, and he moved to minimize the message of the text. No "destroy". No "wipe out". Only "targeted for harm".

In other words, Obama acted as he did with Jeremiah Wright's inflammatory words. Instead of using harsh words, as Wright did, he talked of "a more perfect union".

For an African American President who looked upon slavery as being in present tense, why would he move to diminish the suffering of another community?

If this was not enough, in an interview after a Jewish deli in France was attacked and several Jews were killed, Obama said:

"Look, the point is this: my first job is to protect the American people. It is entirely legitimate for the American people to be deeply concerned when you've got a bunch of violent, vicious zealots who behead people **or randomly** shoot a bunch of folks in a deli in Paris." (An interview with Vox on January 23, 2015).

Randomly? The deli (actually a kosher supermarket) was named "Hypercacher", i.e. "hyper kosher". Even its name indicated that it was a Jewish store with all-Jewish customers.

Obama omitted the fact that the deli was attacked specifically because it was a Jewish establishment. And he should have known it. After all, his Daily Briefing gave him that information.

We are only facing two incidents in which Obama minimized the idea that Jewish communities are being targeted not only for "harm", but targeted to be killed, or in the language of the Passover Haggadah – to be "wiped out" or "destroyed". While two incidents are only anecdotal evidence, it is still alarming.

President Obama and Religion

In his book "Dreams from My Father", Obama emphasizes the importance of religion in American life. He produces statistics showing that the percentage of Americans who believe in God is in the high nineties, and that more than two-thirds belong to a church. The belief in angels is far beyond the belief in evolution, and attending church regularly is the most important point that divides Americans – those who attend, and those who do not (BO AOH 201).

Obama considers the strong attachment of Americans to religion to be due to the need to reduce loneliness, and to have something beyond everyday life. Americans, according to Obama, want to know that someone cares and listens to them, and that their lives are not leading to "nothingness" (BO AOH 202). In other words, Americans want to find meaning in life.

Throughout the description by Obama of Americans' religious lives, he uses the pronoun "they", and not "we".

Obama also talks of the dangers of religion. According to him, history has shown that religion can lead to "self-righteousness, closed-mindedness, and cruelty" (BO AOH 56). Obama the historian goes on to describe the Founding Fathers of the US as people who rejected the idea of "absolute truth" or "the infallibility of any idea or ideology or theology" (BO AOH 93).

One should note the order of listing – idea first, ideology second, and theology last. Generally speaking, the order of listing in a sentence might reflect the order of importance to the writer/speaker.

Obama, quite likely with cynicism, gave an example of football players who "point to the heavens after every touchdown", thinking that the Almighty is "calling plays from the celestial sidelines" (BO AOH 198-199).

In his book "Dreams from My Father", Obama said that in Indonesia he attended both Muslim and Christian schools. In the Muslim school, the teacher complained to Obama's mother that her son is not "respectful" (BO DFMF 154).

In the Catholic school, during prayer, Obama would pretend to pray. While others closed their eyes, Obama was looking around and he didn't see any angel present in the room (BO DFMF 154).

Obama said that his grandparents were not really into religion. His grandmother was "too rational" to be religious. His grandfather was too tolerant to others to be dogmatic in religion (BO AOH 203). These traits of both of his grandparents were passed on to his mother, who looked upon religion with "respect" but was still "detached" (BO AOH 204). Still, his mother was very "spiritual" (BO AOH 205).

His absentee father was "a confirmed atheist" who looked upon religion as "superstition" (BO AOH 204).

In his childhood, religious texts of all religions were on the shelf (BO AOH 203-204). His mother "dragged" him to church on holidays, but also to the Buddhist temple, the Shinto shrine, and other religious sites. She considered it a matter of culture rather than belief (BO AOH 204).

This might be the background for Obama saying that democracy "demands" that religious people should transform their view of life into "universal" rather than "religion-specific values" (BO AOH 219).

Skepticism and Doubt

Obama says, "…based on my experience as a senator and lawyer, husband and father, Christian and skeptic…" (BO AOH 9).

Please note the following:

1. The order of listing of traits inside the sentence might reflect the priorities in Obama's life. As he did earlier, Obama listed religion at the end of the list.
2. Obama didn't label himself only as "Christian". He labeled himself as "Christian and **skeptic**".

He expands on this "skepticism" by saying that his commitment to religion did not mean that he abandoned "critical thinking" (BO AOH 208). This theme was repeated in his speech as President (Keynote

Address at the Call to Renewal Conference in Washington DC, June 28, 2006) when he said, "Faith doesn't mean that you don't have doubts."

Obama himself realized that "Christian" and "faith" do not go along with "skeptic" and doubt". In his book he brings the accusations against him by his opponent in Illinois, who accused of Obama of supporting a lifestyle that contradicts the Bible, and that Obama is against the idea that life is sacred (BO AOH 212).

When Obama describes his response, he writes, "What could I say?" Not wanting to "impose [his] religious views on another" he replied with "the usual liberal response" that "we live in a pluralistic society". But he also understood that his opponent's accusations implied that he, Obama, lives with "doubt", and that he is not really a "Christian" (BO AOH 212). Obama didn't deny these accusations, as he acknowledged throughout his book, and later in life.

Obama says that he believes in "evolution", "scientific inquiry", "global warming", and "free speech"; and he is against government imposing religious beliefs on the citizen (BO AOH 10).

Again, notice the listing: "evolution" is listed first, while "religious beliefs" are mentioned only at the end of this long sentence. Obama said that the ability to tell stories is what makes us humans. Without this ability, "We're just chimps." (BenR 372-373)

Joining the Church

While he was a community organizer in Chicago, Obama went to talk with one of the Reverends to recruit him in his project to promote social change. Towards the end of the conversation, the Reverend asked Obama which church he belongs to. When Obama said that he "attend[s] different services", the Reverend repeated his question, to which Obama responded in the negative. At this point, the Reverend told Obama that if he wanted to succeed in his job as a community organizer, he should belong to a church (BO DFMF 274). Obama concurred with this opinion when he said that he was drawn to the "African American religious tradition" due to its power in promoting social change (BO AOH 207).

An alderman on the Chicago City Council, Toni Lynn Preckwinkle, evaluated Obama as one who calculated all his steps with the view of how each step in his life journey would help him to progress to the next level. Preckwinkle felt that Obama had joined the Trinity Church for political reasons. The Trinity Church drew many important people to its activities, and his membership there would help his campaign of networking in the African American community (OA 142).

Obama and the Jews

Background information - US Jewish people

The organized Jewish population in the US is divided into three main branches –Orthodox, Conservative, and Reform. There are also many who are "unaffiliated".

The main differences between these three branches are as follows:

The Orthodox adhere to all the rules and regulations that are mandated by the Torah (the first five books of the Jewish Bible), along with all the derivatives of these rules as they were mandated by the rabbis throughout generations. Adaptations to modern times are made according to these guidelines.

The Conservative movement accepts the Torah's divinity, but are more liberal in making adjustments of the rules and regulations, according to what they consider to be required by modern times.

The Reform movement does not accept the Torah's divinity. They perceive Judaism as being a cultural and social bond between people who share the same history. They place more emphasis on the humanism in the Torah, and will call for "Tikkun Olam" (improving the world), even in objectives that contradict the Torah itself.

Jews in Obama's life

The first time Obama mentioned the Jews in his book "Dreams from My Father" was when his maternal grandfather counted as his close friends the Jews he had met in the furniture business (BO DFMF 17).

Obama's connection to Jews extends to his childhood.   When he was eleven years old, he attended a summer camp. One of the counselors in the camp, an American Jew, had visited Israel with his family quite a bit. This counselor told the young Obama of his impressions of his visits.

The counselor's impressions included the idea of returning to the Jewish historical homeland, the connection between the displaced Jewish people and their land, and how the displaced Jews had succeeded throughout history in preserving their culture and their bond to their heritage, in spite of all the difficulties and suffering they had endured (OA 218).

Philip Roth, a Jewish-American author, published numerous books that were later on made into movies. Leon Uris, another Jewish-American author, published several best-sellers. Two of these that stand out are: "Exodus", the fight to return to the Jewish homeland, which was controlled by the British before Israel's independence, in spite of the British prohibition on this return; and "Mila 18", the Jewish revolt in the Warsaw Ghetto against Nazi Germany's attempt to destroy the Ghetto and its residents.

Both of these authors shaped Obama's emotional world. Obama said that he had sympathy for Israel, sympathy for the suffering and sorrow of the Jewish people, and sympathy for the people who had returned to their homeland (OA 218).

Obama mentions in his book that one of the Reverends whom he met in his activity as a community organizer told him that he is serving a good cause, but the Reverend cannot cooperate with him, as a Jewish community organizer was the one who had recruited Obama, and the Reverend did not want "white money and Catholic churches and Jewish organizers" helping the African-American community (BO DFMF 161).

When Obama was serving as an Illinois State Senator, one of the local African American rappers criticized Obama in his songs. He accused Obama of being too friendly to Jews, and therefore the African American community cannot rely upon him (OA 228).

When campaigning in the Jewish community, Obama defended his record by saying that his Jewish friends in Chicago knew that he talked against anti-Semitism, especially in his own community, when it was not convenient to do so. Obama said that he is aware that the Jews think that he listens more to the Muslims, while the Muslims think he listens more to the Jews.

Obama's wife, Michelle, has a cousin, Rabbi Cypress Funye, who is the rabbi of the Beth Shalom Bani Zaken Ethiopian Hebrew Congregation. As Funye got older he became attached to Judaism.   When he decided to convert to Judaism, his mother and Michelle's father gave him their blessing.

In the 2008 elections, Obama received 78% of the Jewish vote. The cover of one of the 2011 editions of *"New York"* magazine described Obama as "The First Jewish President" (MicOr 268).

But Michael Oren, Israeli ambassador to the US, who described the above-mentioned magazine cover in his book, felt the need to add, "That was true if being Jewish in America meant recoiling from military power, territorialism, nationalism, and a sense of tribe." (MicOr 268)

When Obama gave a speech at the Israeli embassy in Washington DC, on the occasion of the "Righteous Among Nations Award Ceremony" (January 27, 2016), Obama mentioned an event during the Second World War when a Nazi officer demanded that US prisoners would surrender the Jewish soldiers among them, and if the American officer would not comply, the Nazi officer would shoot him. The American officer, a Christian, replied, "We are all Jews."

Obama said: "…Master Sergeant Roddie Edmonds… looked evil in the eye and dared a Nazi to shoot. His moral compass never wavered. He was true to his faith, and he saved some 200 Jewish American soldiers as a consequence… I cannot imagine a greater expression of Christianity than to say, I, too, am a Jew."

Obama also related to anti-Semitism at that time by saying, "When any Jew anywhere is targeted just for being Jewish, we all have to respond as Roddie Edmonds did – 'We are all Jews.'"

This should remind us of the European newspaper after 9/11 whose headline was: "We are all Americans."

A year later, on January 25, 2017, already out of office, Obama said at the Temple Emanuel in Manhattan, "I'm basically a Liberal Jew." (Haaretz, January 26, 2108)

In fact, from the start of his presidency, Obama surrounded himself with several liberal Jews – Rahm Immanuel, his Chief of Staff; David Axelrod, his strategist; and Ben Rhodes, his Deputy National Security Advisor and speech writer.

Obama and the Holocaust

Obama in his book "Dreams from My Father" said that when he took his white girlfriend to watch a show by an African American playwright, Obama admitted that it was an "angry" play, but "very funny". According to Obama, it was "typical black American humor" (BO DFMF 211).

After the show the girlfriend asked Obama why African Americans are "angry all the time", to which Obama responded that "nobody asks why Jews remember the Holocaust." (BO DFMF 211)

Obama mentioned the Holocaust quite a bit when he talked to Jewish audiences.

When Obama visited the Buchenwald Concentration Camp (June 5, 2009), he mentioned his great uncle, who was part of the 89th Infantry Division that liberated Ohrdruf, one of Buchenwald's sub-camps.

At the Righteous Among Nations Award Ceremony at the Israeli embassy (January 27, 2016), Obama said more about his great uncle – "…hearing the stories of my great uncle who helped liberate Ohrdruf, part of Buchenwald, and who returned home so shaken by the suffering that he had seen that my grandmother would tell me he did not speak to anyone for six months, just went up in his attic, couldn't fully absorb the horror that he had witnessed."

It is no wonder that in his speech at Buchenwald, Obama talked against Holocaust denial saying, "To this day, there are those who insist that the Holocaust never happened – a denial of fact and truth that is baseless and ignorant and hateful. This place is the ultimate rebuke to such thoughts;

a reminder of our duty to confront those who would tell lies about **our** history."

His great uncle, who saw the effect of the Holocaust on the ones who still remained alive in Buchenwald at the time of liberation, made the Holocaust for Obama an American history – "**our** history".

Obama and Islam

In an interview with George Stephanopoulos on ABC News on September 7, 2008, Obama said, "What I was suggesting – you're absolutely right that John McCain has not talked about **my Muslim faith**…"

Although Obama said "my Muslim faith", in fact he was addressing the issue of others suspecting him of being a Muslim. And although the interviewer corrected him by saying, "Christian faith", Obama went on to explain, "…what I think is fair to say is that coming out of the Republican camp, there have been efforts to suggest that perhaps I'm not who I say I am when it comes to my faith, something which I find deeply offensive…"

In his book, Obama describes his visit to a barbershop on arrival in Chicago. When the barber asked for his name, he replied with his first name: "Barack". The barber asked Obama if he is a Muslim, to which he responded, "Grandfather was." (BO DFMF 148-149)

One should note that Obama didn't say "yes", and did not say "no". Instead, he said ambiguously, "Grandfather was." Why is this "ambiguous"? In Islam, religion goes by the father. If your father is a Muslim, you are a Muslim. This fact would be well-known to any Muslim. Therefore, if the barber were Muslim, he would have concluded that Obama had just told him that he is a Muslim as well. But if the barber was not a Muslim, he would have concluded that Obama had answered in the negative.

Actually, Obama couldn't say "yes", and he couldn't say "no". His father started his life as a Muslim, but later became "a confirmed atheist" (BO AOH 204).

Between the time of this conversation at the barbershop, and the time he ran for office in Illinois, Obama joined a church, got baptized, and got married in the church.

Obama introduced himself to the Muslim world in his speech in Cairo, Egypt, in June 2009 by saying, "I am a Christian, but my father came from a Kenyan family that includes generations of Muslims. As a boy, I spent several years in Indonesia and heard the call of the *azaan* at the break of dawn and at the fall of dusk."

As a community organizer in Chicago, Obama encountered both Muslims and Christians as part of the African American community. A Muslim told Obama that he had grown up as a gang leader, and if he hadn't "found religion" by becoming a Muslim, quite likely he would have been dead (BO DFMF 196). As a president, Obama acknowledged that many in the African-American community in Chicago "found dignity and peace" in the Muslim religion (Cairo speech, June 4, 2009).

Christians and Muslims in Chicago shared something in common – anger. Obama quoted a Reverend who told him that the anger of the Muslims was "his own anger", that the Reverend could not get away from; the most he could do is to learn to control this anger by use of prayer (BO DFMF 273).

In some cases there was mobility between Christianity and Islam. In a conversation with Obama, Reverend Jeremiah Wright listed "the former Muslim" among other groups looking for their place "in a Christian church" (BO DFMF 283) .

What is Islam according to Obama?

In his remarks to the Islamic Society of Baltimore, Maryland on February 3, 2016, Obama said, "…the very word itself, Islam, comes from salam – peace."

One should note that this is a common mistake, to associate "salam" and "Islam". It sounds the same, but they are not the same.

In Arabic, several words might come from the same basic root word, but each one of them can mean something entirely different. While "salam" indeed means "peace", "Islam" means "surrender". The believer surrenders himself/herself to Allah.

One should note that the slogan that "Islam" is the "religion of peace" is only promoted in the west. It will not be heard anywhere in Arab or Muslim countries, as they know it is not true. But the Muslim communities in the west, whether in the US, Canada, UK, or other western countries, tend to promote this falsehood, because to the ears of the western person it sounds nice.

So when Obama said, "The standard greeting is as-salamu alaykum – peace be upon you," he is right. However, promoting the wrong interpretation of Arabic is misleading. In fact, in Arab and Muslim countries, another slogan is recited: "The Law of Mohammad is in the sword."

In his remarks at the 2015 Iftar (end of fast) Dinner at the White House on June 22, 2015, Obama said, based upon a quote from the Koran, that "…we affirm that, whatever our faith, we're all one family."

Again, one should realize that the Koran distinguishes sharply between the believer (i.e. the Muslim) and the non-believer, the infidel. All the instructions given in the Koran are meant for the believer, and the non-believers do not enjoy the rights given to the believer. In other words, while a western Christian, like Obama, will look upon humanity and say that, "whatever our faith, we're all one family", a Muslim will not think that and will not say so at all.

Obama felt the need to explain the contradiction between saying that Islam is the religion of peace, and the fact that a lot of violence has been generated in the Middle East, a region where Islam is supreme.

In his well-known speech in Cairo, Egypt, attempting to approach the Muslim world with a message of peace, Obama emphasized that his approach is based upon what he labeled as "what Islam is, not what it isn't."

In other words, an American Christian president is telling his audience that there are at least two versions of Islam, and he is the authority to tell them which version is the genuine one. And Obama continued in his

Cairo speech to tell the audience that he considers it to be part of his responsibility as president of the United States, to fight against negative stereotypes of Islam wherever they appear.

In another appearance by Obama, this time in Baltimore, Maryland, Obama told the Islamic Society of Baltimore (February 3, 2016) that "a small fraction" of Muslims advance a "perverted" Islam. In a later interview, Obama repeated this idea in different words – "a tiny faction", and this time he specified that it is "violent, radical, fanatical, nihilistic" (Jeffrey Goldberg, "The Obama Doctrine", "The Atlantic", April 2016).

Obama in his book "The Audacity of Hope" says that he is upset with the Muslim influence on Indonesia. In the past the Islam of Indonesia was very moderate and tolerant (the culture of the south Pacific islands). However, due to large investments of the Wahhabist clerics of Saudi Arabia to build Islamic schools that teach and educate children in the extreme interpretation of Islam centered in Saudi Arabia, Indonesia became more "militant, fundamentalist" (BO AOH 278). Interesting to note that in his book, Obama didn't attribute this fundamentalist Islam to Saudi Arabia. He preferred instead to call it "Middle East".

Obama even gives examples of how this extreme Islam has attacked anyone who was different. In other words, in his book it is clear that Indonesia became a country that negated the mantra that "whatever our faith, we're all one family."

Obama and 9/11

One should realize that when talking to an audience of Muslims, Obama wants to connect with them. And 9/11, planned and executed by Muslims (15 of the 19 terrorists were Saudis), presents a problem. Let's examine the one-sided speech Obama gave to Muslims.

In a speech at the White House for the evening dinner at the end of the Ramadan fast (Iftar), Obama talked to a Muslim audience. In his words, 9/11 was executed by Al-Qaeda, which "is not Islam". According to Obama, Al-Qaeda is "a gross distortion of Islam". If anyone had any misunderstanding of what Obama was saying, he moved on to clarify himself: that Al-Qaeda "are not religious leaders – they're terrorists".

He even found it necessary to tell his Muslim audience that among the victims of 9/11 there were Muslims as well (Speech August 13, 2010).

If this view by Obama regarding Islam is accurate, one should wonder why Muslim clerics and leaders anywhere outside the US do not share Obama's views?

One year later (Speech August 10, 2011), Obama again spoke about the Muslim component of 9/11. He didn't mention the terrorists who committed the mass massacre, but spoke only about the victims: "Muslim Americans were innocent passengers on those planes, including a young married couple looking forward to the birth of their first child. They were workers in the Twin Towers – Americans by birth and Americans by choice, immigrants who crossed the oceans to give their children a better life. They were cooks and waiters, but also analysts and executives."

Besides talking about the victims, Obama spoke about "…the heroes who rushed to help that day and all who have served to keep us safe during a difficult decade. And tonight, it's worth remembering that these Americans were of many faiths and backgrounds, including proud and patriotic Muslim Americans."

And Obama continued, "Muslim Americans were first responders – the former police cadet who raced to the scene to help and then was lost when the towers collapsed around him; the EMTs who evacuated so many to safety; the nurse who tended to so many victims; the naval officer at the Pentagon who rushed into the flames and pulled the injured to safety. On this 10th anniversary, we honor these men and women for what they are – American heroes."

True. They are heroes. But does this description give a full picture of 9/11?

And how did the Muslim world respond to this terrorism?

In his remarks to the Islamic Society of Baltimore, Maryland, on February 3, 2016, Obama said, "But across the Islamic world, influential voices **should** consistently speak out with an affirmative vision of their faith. And it's happening."

He also said, "Muslim political leaders **have to** push back on the lie that the West oppresses Muslims, and against conspiracy theories that says America is the cause of every ill in the Middle East."

And although he mentioned "…Muslim clerics who teach that Islam prohibits terrorism, for the Koran says whoever kills an innocent, it is as if he has killed all mankind," he "forgets" to tell his audience that in defining "innocents", the Koran distinguishes between the Muslim and the infidel, and that there is a dispute, even at the UN, of what is "terrorism".

Obama and Dr. King

At the same speech to the Islamic Society of Baltimore, Maryland, Obama said, "Dr. King was joined by people of many faiths, challenging us to live up to our ideals."

Really?

There is a description of Dr Martin Luther King's "March on Washington", where he made the famous "I have a dream" speech. (https://www.infoplease.com/history/us/civil-rights-march-on-washington)

"The March on Washington represented a coalition of several civil rights organizations, all of which generally had different approaches and different agendas. The "Big Six" organizers were James Farmer, of the Congress of Racial Equality (CORE); Martin Luther King, Jr., of the Southern Christian Leadership Conference (SCLC); John Lewis, of the Student Nonviolent Coordinating Committee (SNCC); A. Philip Randolph, of the Brotherhood of Sleeping Car Porters; Roy Wilkins, of the National Association for the Advancement of Colored People (NAACP); and Whitney Young, Jr., of the National Urban League."

"The speakers included all of the "Big Six" civil-rights leaders (James Farmer, who was imprisoned in Louisiana at the time, had his speech read by Floyd McKissick); Catholic, Protestant, and Jewish religious leaders; and labor leader Walter Reuther. The one female speaker was

Josephine Baker, who introduced several "Negro Women Fighters for Freedom," including Rosa Parks."

Note that in this description we have "Catholic, Protestant, and Jewish religious leaders" No Muslim leader is mentioned.

Susan Rice, President Obama's national security advisor, gave a speech to the AIPAC Annual Meeting in Washington DC on March 02, 2015, in which she gave more information on the Jewish participation in the Selma march.

> "This weekend, President Obama will travel to Selma, Alabama, to mark the 50th anniversary of the historic marches there. He'll pay tribute to those brave souls who took enormous risks for civil rights, including Jews and rabbis from across the country – from St. Louis and San Francisco; the Northeast and the Deep South. They faced tear gas and billy clubs, Torahs in hand. They were jailed. They conducted Shabbat services behind bars, and they sang "Adon Olam" to the tune of "We Shall Overcome." They broke the Fast of Esther in prison. They even started a trend. Some black marchers, moved by the solidarity of their Jewish brethren, started wearing yarmulkes – they called them "freedom caps."

> "As you recalled last night, one of those on the front lines in Selma was the great teacher, Rabbi Abraham Joshua Heschel. After marching across the Edmund Pettus Bridge with Dr. King, he reflected, 'our legs uttered songs. Even without words, our march was worship.' Our march was our worship."

But Muslims were present there.

"...the march was also condemned by some civil rights activists who felt it presented an inaccurate, sanitized pageant of racial harmony; Malcolm X called it the 'Farce on Washington,' and members of the Nation of Islam who attended the march faced a temporary suspension." (https://www.infoplease.com/history/us/civil-rights-march-on-washington)

Obama and Radical Islam

Ben Rhodes said that Obama read an article in the newspaper by Thomas Friedman, titled "Say It Like It Is," criticizing the Obama administration for avoiding use of the term "radical Islam" when fighting terrorism. In response to the article, Obama told Rhodes, "I didn't realize that we were being so politically correct in talking about Islamic extremism." (BenR 313)

Michael Hayden, who was Director of both the NSA and CIA during the Bush administration, said that clearly the Obama administration refused to say the words "radical Islam", and cynically Hayden said that Obama preferred to relate to it as "free electrons or something" (MH2 - 53).

Hayden produced several reasons why Obama didn't use the "explosive" term "radical Islam"; among them, that Obama didn't want to insult Muslims. Hayden, who wrote his book to attack Trump after the 2016 elections, felt that it was "an opportunity lost" and it actually "invited" Trump to use the language that he used. As Hayden phrased it, "in the eyes of some, gave it legitimacy" (MH2 - 54).

James Clapper, Director of National Intelligence in the Bush administration, joined Hayden's view that Obama should have used the right phrase "Islamic extremists". Clapper felt that in fighting one should know exactly who is the enemy, and even call it as such. But Clapper thought that Obama was more concerned with being nice to Muslim governments that "repudiated the terrorists". (JC 331)

Since Clapper used "governments" in the plural, I wonder if he could give the number of how many Muslim governments did in fact "repudiate" the terrorists.

One should note that Muslim countries in the UN did their best to diminish the definition of "terrorism", so it will not include, for example, any terrorist act that is being used by "oppressed people". It came to a point that the UN definition of terrorism is practically meaningless.

Michael Oren, the Israeli ambassador to the US, commented on President Obama's first trip overseas – to Turkey. Turkey is a Muslim country whose constitution mandates the separation of religion and state. Obama "expressed admiration for Turkey's democracy" and its leader Erdoğan. Oren points out that under Erdoğan, Turkey had jailed more journalists than either China or Iran. When Turkish students asked Obama to respond to an outburst by Erdoğan against Israel, Obama said only, "I wasn't there." (MicOr 51)

President Obama's Views

The Individual vs Government

Point to consider: "For the poor shall never cease out of the land…" (Deuteronomy 15:11)

Obama asserts in his book that capitalism enables "social mobility", as it is a system that enables any person to advance in society if they are willing to invest time and energy. (BO AOH 151).

He also acknowledges that the success of the US economy throughout generations, since the birth of the country, was due to individuals "pursuing their own vision of happiness" (BO AOH 150).

In addressing specifically the African American community, Obama acknowledges that "social mobility" in the US brought the African American middle class to grow fourfold in a generation, and to cut poverty within the African American community by half.   In addition, he attributed the success of African Americans who advanced in society solely due to their own individual efforts, as these successful people rejected "any limits to what they can achieve". As an example, he mentions Chicago, a city that has many African American professionals, including doctors and others (BO AOH 242, 241, 240).

One only needs to look at Barack and Michelle Obama's lives, coming from Chicago, for examples of this basic truth.

But Obama does not stop with attributing success to the individual's own efforts. He has one additional message. Obama believes that if one wants to guarantee "social mobility" in society, one cannot leave it only to the individual. For the best results, we need not only the individual's efforts but also the intervention of the government. Government cannot remain passive; it has the responsibility to intervene in the free market to prevent fraud, mishaps, and failures (BO AOH 153).

When declaring himself a Democrat, Obama asserts that values, mutual responsibility, and social solidarity are not only dependent on religion, neighborhoods, workplaces, and families. He feels that government should have a say as well. In his words: "…government can play a role in shaping that culture for the better – or for the worse." (BO AOH 63)

Obama brings examples from US history in which the government intervened and instituted mechanisms to protect the citizen. He lists President Teddy Roosevelt, who introduced limits on monopolies, and laws to protect the citizens against faulty food and merchandise, such as the establishment of the Food and Drug Administration (FDA), and others.

He also mentions FDR and the Great Depression. This brought about Social Security and others laws that "fundamentally changed the relationship between capital and labor" (BO AOH 154).

If one wants to summarize what Obama says, one only needs to go to his speechwriter David Litt, who described the role of government by saying, "The most sacred piece of Democratic orthodoxy was that government could improve people's lives. The most sacred piece of Republican orthodoxy was that it could not." (DavidL 211)

The African American Community

Obama brings statistics to show the economic gap "…between the living standards of black, Latino, and white workers". He lists several social and cultural issues that contribute to this gap. For example, watching TV for longer hours, smoking cigarettes, eating fast food, and also "lack of emphasis on educational achievement" (BO AOH 244-245).

He also mentions the collapse of two-parent households in the African American community, and other social problems that have made African American children "more vulnerable" (BO AOH 245).

Then, after stating that cultural and social issues contribute to the lack of progress among many minorities, Obama turns around to negate and reject this altogether. He asserts that these factors do not have much to do with the economic gap between minorities (African Americans and Latinos) and whites; and that this gap is not due to race, but to economic issues: "downsizing, outsourcing, automation, wage stagnation, the dismantling of employer-based health-care and pension plans, and schools that fail to teach young people the skills they need to compete in a global economy." (BO AOH 244-245)

So what is it for Obama? Is it the individual efforts that bring about success? Is it the society whose values guarantee the individual's success? Or, is it the government that should intervene to influence morals and values?

Obama on Society

In describing his study of law at Harvard, Obama outlined quite a cynical approach to the law. According to him, the law serves the ones in power, to explain to those who are not in power, why their condition is wise and just (BO DFMF 437).

He continued with this theme in his second book, talking of the ones on the top of society doing their best to maintain their wealth and status at all costs, while keeping the ones on the bottom of society in their position (BO AOH 215).

Obama attributed his concern for those who do not have, to his mother. She was the one who imprinted in him his values, and among them was to stand up for the disadvantaged. (BO AOH 29). It is no surprise that Obama, being described as the epitome of logic and reason, expressed anger at the policies that favor the rich over the average citizen (BO AOH 10).

In summary, the themes that Obama advocates in his book should remind the reader that in some quarters of academia they would be classified as "class warfare".

If one has any doubt about what Obama meant by his cynical view of the law – society divided by class – one only has to listen to Obama when he talks about people's "modest" hopes, that are the same "…across race, region, religion, and class". Race is first place in his list, but class is also listed, even though it is in the last place (BO AOH 7).

David Plouffe, Obama's campaign manager in 2008, quoted an argument Obama had on the campaign trail. Obama argued with a citizen about his tax plan, and in his argument Obama used the phrase "redistribute the wealth" – a phrase known in socialist circles (DavPl 359). Again, it is another example of "class warfare". Plouffe said that he, Plouffe, "blanched at the choice of words", but he calmed down when he realized the voters didn't care.

Obama listed "hot-button issues" that define the political divide in the US – "affirmative action, crime, welfare, abortion, and school prayer…" (BO AOH 32-33).

He considers the three issues of "class", "poverty", and "welfare" to be matters that government needs to deal with, in order "to lift large numbers of our fellow citizens out of poverty", and it can only be done with broad political support (BO AOH 41).

But the existence of a gap between the rich and the poor does not mean that there is a war between them. Obama writes: "Most rich people want the poor to succeed, and most of the poor are both more self-critical and hold higher aspirations…" (BO AOH 51).

Being in politics required Obama to approach rich donors to fund his political campaign, and this presented a problem for him. He found himself in the company of "people of means", who were the ones who could write checks to his campaign, but they also talked with him using "the perspective of their class". Being with these rich people made him feel that he was becoming more like them. In other words, he was influenced and impacted by their company. The more he was in politics, and the more he needed the help of the rich, the further away he became from his view of class gaps and class warfare, and the anger over "class", "poverty", and "welfare" (BO AOH 113, 114).

Obama acknowledges that government policies that encouraged "social mobility" did in fact succeed in pulling "the large majority of blacks and Latinos into the socioeconomic mainstream within a generation". Still, he thinks that government should do more. The government should allocate more budgets towards educating the poor, and "…to ensure that every child is loved and cherished". One should wonder if government should replace parents to give every child the feeling of being "loved and cherished" (BO AOH 248-249, 215).

Obama: "If you've got a business - you didn't build that"

Till this point, we see a duality in Obama's approach. On one hand, Obama recognizes the power of the individual in society to guarantee one's own success, and secure "social mobility". On the other hand, Obama talks of the need of the government to intervene by allocating more budgets to educate the poor.

But Obama went one step further. In a campaign stop in Roanoke, Virginia, on July 19, 2012, Obama said the following:

[Note: when Obama's opponent used the highlighted quote against him, Obama responded by saying that the quote was taken out of context. Therefore, the following is the entire quote.]

> *"There are a lot of wealthy, successful Americans who agree with me - because they want to give something back. They know they didn't - look, if you've been successful, you didn't get there on your own. You didn't get there on your own. I'm always struck by people who think, well, it must be because I was just so smart. There are a lot of smart people out there. It must be because I worked harder than everybody else. Let me tell you something - there are a whole bunch of hardworking people out there. (Applause.)*
> *"If you were successful, somebody along the line gave you some help. There was a great teacher somewhere in your life. Somebody helped to create this unbelievable American system that we have that allowed you to thrive. Somebody invested in roads and bridges. If you've got a business - you didn't build that. Somebody else made that happen. The Internet didn't get invented on its own. Government research created the Internet so that all the companies could make money off the Internet.*
> *"The point is, is that when we succeed, we succeed because of our individual initiative, but also because we do things together. There are some things, just like fighting fires, we don't do on our own. I mean, imagine if everybody had their own fire service. That would be a hard way to organize fighting fires.*
> *"So we say to ourselves, ever since the founding of this country, you know what, there are some things we do better together. That's how we funded the GI Bill. That's how we created the*

middle class. That's how we built the Golden Gate Bridge or the Hoover Dam. That's how we invented the Internet. That's how we sent a man to the moon. We rise or fall together as one nation and as one people, and that's the reason I'm running for President - because I still believe in that idea. You're not on your own, we're in this together."

Note that Obama repeated the same theme that he used in his two books: that success is not just the result of the individual who invested time and energy to succeed. It is also the result of the government who created the right environment to help people advance in society.

But in this quote he went one step further. He **negated** the efforts of the individual. It is **only** team effort.

Warren Buffett

What does Warren Buffett, the multi-billionaire from Omaha, Nebraska, have to do with President Obama? A lot!

One cannot understand the dichotomy Obama presented between the individual's effort and the government's intervention without looking into Warren Buffett's life.

Warren Buffett built a business empire from scratch. He started very young, and gradually he used his business skills and intuition to amass many large corporations that are held by his company – Berkshire Hathaway.

Buffett, now in his eighties, donated the overwhelming majority of his stocks to the Bill Gates charity fund. He is a Democrat, and contributed money to Obama's campaign. Obama and Buffett met several times during Obama's presidency.

Buffett also shared two themes with President Obama. The first is that the US tax code is against the working class. While Buffett pays less tax on his income, as it is income from stocks, his secretary – relatively speaking – pays more tax than he does. This refers to the percentages required by the tax code, as everyone understands that his tax bill is in the millions, while his secretary's tax bill might be in the hundreds. But she pays a higher percentage of her income than he does.

The second is that although the individual is responsible for his own success in life, still the businessman takes advantage of the government investment in infrastructure. Who paid for the highways that enable the shipping of the merchandise? Who built the bridges? And so on.

President Obama used these two themes in his speeches. When he started his speech in Roanoke, Virginia, by saying: "There are a lot of wealthy, successful Americans who agree with me – because they want to give something back," quite likely he was referring to Warren Buffett.

This is not a "guess". President Obama, in his State of the Union Address, invoked the "Buffet Rule".

The text in full is as follows:

"Tax reform should follow the Buffett Rule. If you make more than $1 million a year, you should not pay less than 30 percent in taxes. Now, you can call this class warfare all you want. But asking a billionaire to pay at least as much as his secretary in taxes? Most Americans would call that common sense."

But would Warren Buffett agree with Obama that he didn't build his own business empire? Very unlikely. The concept is correct. Everything is a product of the multitude. In every development in any field, whether it is in business or in science, a person is "standing on the shoulders" of the ones who came before him. But would this mean that the person "didn't do it"?

Inner and Outer Score-cards

Although Warren Buffett didn't write a book, there is a book titled "The Snowball: Warren Buffett and the Business of Life", written by Alice Schroeder (Bantam Books, 2008). The book is practically an autobiography, as Buffett sat with the author, and the book includes many quotes by him.

In the book, Buffett says that the entire human population is divided into two main groups: those with an "inner score-card", and those with an "outer score-card". Those with an inner score-card feel that whatever happens to them is based solely on their own efforts, while those with an outer score-card feel that they are subject to outside influences that determine whether or not they succeed in life. It is no surprise that Buffett lists himself in the first group.

The neuroscientist Daniel J. Levitin in his book "The Organized Mind: Thinking Straight in the Age of Information Overload" (Dutton, 2014) mentions a "critical point" that influences workers' productivity: "locus of control" (DanielL 287).

As with Buffett's score-card analogy, Levitin describes people with an "internal locus of control" as those who are responsible for their own life and success. These people will classify success as "I tried really hard", while failure will be "I didn't try hard enough."

On the other hand, people with an "external locus of control" are influenced by others.   These people will classify success as "It was pure luck", and failure as "The competition was rigged" (DanielL 288).

Levitin says that experience is not going to influence this way of looking at success or failure. This means that "internals" will not become "externals", even if experience only gives them hardships and failures. The opposite is also true. "Externals" will not change their attitude and become "internals" even when they succeed (DanielL 289).

Levitin adds that these two types of personality are the extremes, but most people are on a continuum between these two.

Is Obama "internal" or "external"?

It is quite a surprising question to be asked of someone who ran for the position of US President, a position considered to be the leader of the free world.

"You didn't build that", although it is accompanied by the opposite message, is clearly the words of an "external". But this is just anecdotal evidence, based upon only one point. One should not accept one point as meaningful. Are there are other instances in which Obama expressed himself as "external"?

In regard to his successful campaign that brought him to be elected as a US Senator from Illinois, Obama said in his book that his "campaign had gone so well that it looked like a fluke." He quoted reporters who said that he was "the luckiest politician in the entire fifty states". Quite likely this assessment was due to the fact that the campaign of his Republican opponent imploded because of a scandal. Obama added that some of his staff were angry at such an assessment, but Obama himself said that his success was "almost spooky good fortune". He summarized by saying that his victory "proved nothing" (BO AOH 18).

At the time Obama was running for the US Senate, John Kerry was running for president. In a stop in Illinois, Kerry met Obama and was impressed by him. Not long after this meeting, the Kerry campaign offered Obama the opportunity to give the keynote address at the Democratic National Convention in Boston in July 2004.

This speech, with its themes and oratorical excellence, catapulted Obama to the national stage, and immediately he became the focus of attention of the news media and national politicians as a possible candidate to run for president.

David Axelrod, Obama's strategist, said that both Harry Reid and Chuck Schumer, both of whom were leading Democratic senators, asked for a meeting with Obama, and in the meeting they told him that he should run for president (Axe 181).

This is not to say that Obama didn't think of it before these two senators showed up. There is a report by Craig Robinson, Michelle Obama's brother, who said that right in their first or second meeting Obama told him that he plans to run for politics, "…and who knows, I might be president some day." (OA 139-140)

After the keynote speech, there was a major wave of support from the news media, which joined forces with the Democratic establishment to push Obama to run for president.

Was it Obama's idea to give the keynote speech at the Democratic National Convention? No. Did the speech give him national attention? Yes. Was it "almost spooky good fortune", and did his victory "prove nothing"? Or, maybe the content and the delivery were Obama's doing, and his success was what brought him to the attention of the country?

Both Axelrod and Plouffe remarked in their books that Obama hesitated a lot before giving the green light to run.   They realized that Obama needed to get Michelle's consent for him to be absent from home for two months, and to subject their family to the hardships of a presidential campaign.

In history there is no "what would happen if…", but as it happened before Obama was elected as senator in 2004, when his Republican opponent's campaign imploded, so too happened just before the 2008 elections – the financial meltdown, presided over by a Republican president. Moreover, Obama's opponent, John McCain, who ran with the slogan "Country First", announced that, for the good of the country, he would suspend his campaign. Since Obama didn't agree to suspend his campaign as well, McCain returned to the campaign trail. Did this impulsive and erratic behavior help McCain? Quite unlikely.

Did Obama look upon the results of the 2008 elections as his own doing? Or did he feel, as he said about his election in 2004, that it was "almost spooky good fortune", and his victory "proved nothing"?

There is another instance in which President Obama negated the efforts of the individual. In a political rally in Jacksonville, Florida, for candidate Hillary Clinton, five days before the elections of 2016, Obama talked against Clinton's opponent – Donald Trump.

"He says he thinks that's a sign that he's a smart businessman. **But if you've been given so much** and you give back so little, that's not a sign of a good businessman to me."

We should note that Obama didn't say, "If you are making so much…" Obama talked as if Trump's wealth had fallen upon him from nowhere. Although it is true that Trump's father helped him start his business, nobody would dispute the fact that Trump increased his wealth due to his own efforts and skills.

As president, Obama was quoted as saying that "nothing comes to my desk that is perfectly solvable." He added that "Any given decision you make, you'll wind up with a thirty to forty percent chance that it isn't going to work." (Quoted in "the Organized Mind", page 219.)

The feeling of not being able to influence reality is definitely the feeling of an "external".

President Obama's Policies

Introduction

In this section we will examine the policies of Obama as a senator, candidate, and then president in regard to four different issues: globalization, climate change, immigration, and health care.

We will examine each one separately, and then we will see how these four issues produce one impact on the US economy and society.

We will start with globalization, and as a derivative we will discuss climate change, which is a global issue. We will continue with immigration, and we will conclude with what was labeled as President Obama's "signature" legislation – health care, also known as "Obamacare".

Globalization

In listening to voters while running for the US Senate, Obama listed "loss of manufacturing jobs" very early in his book "The Audacity of Hope". It was one of the challenges of globalization he acknowledged (BO AOH 6, 40-41).

On one hand, globalization has produced lower prices for goods, even luxurious goods, and increased the standard of living of the lower levels of society.

At the same time, globalization has brought US companies to send jobs away. Millions of people lost their jobs, while these jobs went to millions of others in faraway places like China, although at lower pay. Those in the US who didn't lose their jobs, could not compete with the lower pay elsewhere, which meant that their pay didn't increase as expenses did, especially health care. In other words, globalization suppressed the salaries of the workforce employed in the US.

As an example of this outcome, Obama mentions the closing of plants in the Chicago area, including the South Side neighborhoods, an area dear to him. Chicago was only one example. The workers at Maytag in Iowa, who found themselves irrelevant and unemployed, were another (BO

AOH 145, 146, 148, 149, 150, 156). The process spread throughout the US. It is estimated that around sixty thousand industrial plants closed down in this process.

But manufacturing jobs were not the only ones to vanish overseas. Many jobs in the service sector went to faraway countries. Anyone who needed technical support for their computer, found that the "support rep" on the phone could barely speak understandable English. It came to a point that Dell began to offer its customers a new "American Warranty" at an additional cost. This means that when calling a service center, only a customer with this additional warranty would be able to speak to a support rep whose native language is English (BO AOH 158).

Obama acknowledged that one of the core components of the Democratic Party strongly resisted this trend, as globalization mainly affected the blue-collar union workers. For them, "free trade" meant only one thing – "disaster" (BO AOH 147, 172).

Obama knew that the organized labor resisted the free trade agreements. When the free trade with Central American countries (CAFTA) was on the table being discussed, the representatives of the labor unions met Obama, trying to recruit his support for their position. The union, that represented the people who were most affected by the process of closing plants, did not want more of the same process. The representatives asked to add to the agreements clauses that would put the American workers and the foreign ones on the same footing. And Obama listed the unions' concerns:

> "…stronger labor protections in countries that trade with the United States, including rights to unionize and bans on child labor; improved environmental standards in these same countries; an end to unfair government subsidies to foreign exporters and nontariff barriers on U.S. exports; stronger protections for U.S. intellectual property; and – in the case of China in particular – an end to an artificially devalued currency that put U.S. companies at a perpetual disadvantage." (BO AOH 172)

Obama agreed with all of the labor unions' concerns. Still, he felt that even if all the measures they wanted would be added to the treaties, it would not change "the underlying realities of globalization" (BO AOH 172).

Obama listed all the components in society that supported free trade: policy makers, the press, and the business community. Only one component was missing, and the most affected ones: the blue-collar employees, who would either lose their jobs, or find that their salaries are being suppressed while their expenses go up. In other words, they would be "squeezed" very tightly (BO AOH 173).

[Note: one should consider this point in coming to decide if Obama is "internal" ("internal locus of control"), viewing himself as being able to influence reality, or if he is "external" – accepting as a fact that reality controls him.]

It is interesting to find that David Plouffe, Obama's campaign manager, described a heated debate between Obama and Clinton in Myrtle Beach, South Carolina, before the primaries in that state. Both candidates accused each other of "selling out American workers" (DavPl 158).

Obama realized the effects of unemployment and suppressed salaries that globalization produced – stress and instability for millions of Americans. Economic frustration started to boil over, and brought people to "turn on each other". In other words, angry people were all over the place (BO 149).

Till this point, Obama accurately described the situation in the US when he as a senator was considering running for president. This was 2006, a long time before the economic meltdown of 2008.

Stephen Harper on Globalization

Stephen Harper was the Prime Minister of Canada for 10 years, many of which were during Obama's term as president. In his book, he talked about globalization.

Harper's evaluation of the situation was identical to Obama's. Globalization was not working for many people in the US and Canada. While a billion people worldwide came out of poverty, the income of people in the west was suppressed, while the cost of living rose, or even declined; and this was especially true in the US, particularly for working class people, and mainly in the manufacturing sector. Globalization, Harper said, produced real "losers", not imaginary ones, mainly among the non-college-educated workers, and he brought statistics of the US labor force to support his evaluation (StephenH 2, 16, 17).

While both Obama and McCain accepted globalization as engraved on stone, as a dogma, Harper is more of a realist. First, he disputes the idea that the world is "post-national". Or, in other words, as if it is some ambiguous entity that is above the nation state. Nationalism for him is an essential part of society (StephenH 7).

As we saw how both opponents in the 2008 elections perceived globalization the same way, so Harper called a spade a spade. Both establishments of the two big parties in the US embraced the same policies, and Harper named them: trade deals, deficit financing, high levels of low-skilled immigration (legal and illegal), weak financial regulation, and corporate bailouts (StephenH 11).

In Harper's evaluation, both trade deals and unskilled immigration produced **a huge gap between the voting public and the elected representatives**. In such a situation, the political establishment wants to sweep this gap under the carpet, and is interested only in gains in the stock market, while **the working people felt rejected, neglected, and forgotten**. The public, using "populism", put this gap right in the center of attention (StephenH 13, 17).

This is the reason, according to Harper, that Trump's message of bringing jobs and manufacturing back to the US was a winning mantra (StephenH 17).

Back to Obama

Both Obama and Harper produced the same evaluation of the US economic situation. Actually, Obama was no different than Trump in correctly reading the map. It comes to a point in which any reader of Obama's book might think that Trump was talking to him. Maybe even Trump read Obama's book.

Where Obama differed from Trump or Harper was that Obama moved further to give his assessment of the future of the US in the age of globalization. Obama said: "A strategy of doing nothing and letting globalization run its course won't result in the imminent collapse of the U.S. economy." (BO AOH 148)

In the Intelligence Community, there is a difference between evaluation of data versus assessment of the future. While data-based evaluation, as Obama produced, is accurate, an assessment of the future is without any foundation. Maybe there will be no imminent collapse. But what about gradual collapse? And what about the anger building up among the unemployed, and those who are employed with decreased salaries?

Obama moved on to say that the US cannot return to protectionism or to raising the minimum wage. According to Obama, globalization is here to stay (BO AOH 158).

Accepting globalization as if it is engraved in stone is the point of view not only of Obama the Democrat. His Republican opponent in the 2008 elections said the same. For McCain, globalization is not a "policy", and one cannot withdraw from it, as one cannot withdraw from the weather. Going against globalization is "anti-historical hysteria" (McCain 302).

But reading Harper's book, one can understand why Harper says that if a policy is not working for the people, one does not move to change the people; one has to change the policy. In his book, Obama outlined a program to change the people.

In his words, Obama said that the US needed to invest in "education, science and technology, and energy independence" (BO AOH 159).

While "science and technology, and energy independence" address "infrastructure", "education" addresses people. Education is a nice mantra, but when people lose their jobs, one should not come and talk about better education of the young in elementary and high schools, or even in colleges. It sounds nice, but one does not talk about long term solutions while the people are sitting at home, unemployed and depressed.

Rahm Emanuel, the first White House Chief of Staff in Obama's first term, co-authored a book with Bruce Reed, titled "The Plan: Big Ideas for America". One of his ideas was to guarantee college education for all people in the US. After all, college education is the line between poverty and middle class, so if everyone would get a college education, there would be no poor people. Right?

It is right and wrong at the same time. It is true that a college education marks the poverty line, with people who have a college degree above the line, and people without a college degree below it. But it is wrong for the mere fact that the US economy needs millions of workers who do not have a college education, and their salaries are above what college-educated people receive. The auto industry is 15% of the US economy, and workers who manufacture cars receive great pay, unless their jobs are shipped to Canada and/or Mexico under the trade deal of NAFTA, promoted by Democratic president Bill Clinton.

The trucking industry has a shortage of drivers, estimated to be around one million. Truck drivers have great pay. One only needs to drive on the interstate and to read the signs on the back of almost every truck calling for people to work for them.

What about the call centers giving support to computer owners? Does an employee there need a college degree? And there are numerous sectors of society in which low-skilled people are needed, and some even train new people to work in the industry.

The Main Problem with Globalization – China

In the book that he published in 2006, Obama talked of the dilemma the US faces with China. On one hand, the US cannot compete with China by reducing wages in the US, and on the other hand, the US cannot move into protectionism, by returning to trade barriers. In other words, Obama accepted the situation as is, and he gave up on any possibility that the US would be able to rectify the problem (BO AOH 158).

In the same book, Obama talked of factories moving to China, an economic phenomenon that illustrates that the US cannot control its destiny (BO AOH 264).

What happens if one side to a conflict plays by the established rules while the other side does not? Even in times of war, the international community established some norms that should be adhered to when two sides want to kill each other. Are there such norms when there is a trade war?

Hillary Clinton, as Secretary of State, talked of the importance of convincing China to play by the rules. She listed several things that the Chinese are doing to harm others: discriminatory trade practices, manipulating the value of their currency, and allowing tainted food and goods to reach consumers. But the Chinese avoided entering any discussion about their behavior (HRC 43, 492).

Susan Rice, National Security Advisor during President Obama's second term, talked of other problems with the Chinese: theft of intellectual property, and the disadvantageous restrictions it places on US businesses operating in China (SusanR 433, 436-437).

While both Clinton and Rice labeled Chinese behavior as "theft", Canadian Prime Minister Stephen Harper described it in harsher language, as "industrial **espionage**, and intellectual **piracy**" (StephenH 44-45).

In other words, While the US called it "free trade", it was not "free trade" for the Chinese. For them, it was "unfair trade" – you open your markets to us, while we close our markets to you. Harper called it "economic nationalism, commercial imperialism, and domestic protection" (StephenH 44-45).

While listing this Chinese behavior, Rice said that she and President Obama believed that the US should expand cooperation with the Chinese. Harper labeled this US attitude as being "apologists" for the Chinese behavior. It bothered him that the Republican party in the US had the same attitude (SusanR 434, StephenH 45).

Harper described the economic conference in Davos in 2016 where the Chinese president gave a speech against protectionism, while the "liberal globalists" among the reporters did not bother to ask him why China does not open its own market to the outside world (StephenH 120).

In summary, the school bully (China) was hurting others, and the teachers and the principal are only talking with the bully, allowing him to continue his wrong behavior.

And when the US and China reached an agreement that both sides will not use cyber to steal intellectual property, the most that the US intelligence community could report was not elimination of the practice, but "a marked reduction" of such behavior. Rice herself emphasized that there was not "complete elimination" of such behavior (SusanR 439).

Summary

Globalization is a great example to illustrate Obama's intellectual integrity in analyzing a situation correctly with all its implications. At the same time, it is a great example of how a personality trait (being "external") would take the person away from the desired solution.

Obama at the UN

2010

President Obama entered office in January 2009, but his first appearance before the UN General Assembly was in September 2010. In his speech, Obama talked of the "age when prosperity is shared", an age that mandated global cooperation to spur growth.

He talked of resisting "protectionism", and even looking to expand more multinational trade and commerce, stating that the objective is "not only for all Americans, but for peoples around the globe".

2011

In 2011 he talked of the extraordinary achievements of "open markets" that lifted hundreds of millions of people from poverty.

Financial crisis was evidence that the fates of all nations are "interconnected". In this interconnected economy, "nations will rise, or fall, together".

He mentioned his plan to put Americans back to work, and at the same time he emphasized that the US "commitment to prosperity" requires working together with emerging economies to bring about "rising standards of living".

2012

He related briefly to the US partnership with the G20 to "keep the world on the path of recovery".

2013

He talked briefly of an "integrated global economy".

2014

Already in his second term of presidency, Obama gave accolades to the era as "the best time in human history to be born" when people are more literate, healthy, and free to pursue their dreams.

This is also the first time that Obama mentioned "pervasive unease" due to "new dangers" that made it difficult for any single nation to insulate itself from global forces. He also talked of a broader problem – the inadequacy of the present international system to keep pace with the interconnected world.

He talked of the junction the world had reached – either to move forward with the international system, affirming "collective responsibility to confront global problems" that had produced so much progress, or to move backward, to the time of instability. He declared that for the US the choice is clear – "We choose hope over fear."

Since he talked of the US as being "a Pacific power" it is clear that when he mentioned the junction the world is facing, he related to China, as he demanded "that all nations abide by the rules of the road".

2015

Obama's appearance at the UN General Assembly in September 2015 was three months after Donald Trump's announcement of his candidacy for president, and it is easy to observe the change of tone in President Obama's speech. If in 2014 he sounded the first alarm of not all countries abiding by the same rules, in 2015 Obama was actually addressing US internal opposition to globalization.

He talked of "global capital flows" weakening the bargaining power of workers, and accelerated inequality. He mentioned the "increasing skepticism" of globalization in the most advanced democracies (i.e. the US).   He talked of "polarization", "movements on the far right", "stopping the trade that binds our fates to other nations", and "building of walls to keep out immigrants". In summary, he came out at the international arena, the United Nations, to talk against candidate Trump's agenda.

He talked of the "integrated world" in which "we all have a stake in each other's success", and we cannot go back ("external", right?) on "integration". He praised "cooperation over conflict", labeling it "strength" and not weakness.

He praised the upcoming agreement of the Trans-Pacific Partnership that would encompass 40 percent of the global economy. In many words, he talked of more of the same globalization that impacted US low-skilled workers.

He ended by talking of the universal message of "common interests" and "common humanity", and that there are certain ideas and principles that are universal.

2016

Obama's appearance at the UN General Assembly in September 2016 was less than two months before the elections of 2016. At that time, the Republican candidate Trump was already talking openly against the policies of the Obama administration that had caused unemployment to soar, and suppressed the wages of the low-skilled workers. Obama's speech was actually an election speech addressed to people who were not US voters.

He talked of the "global integration" that exposed "deep fault lines" in the existing international order. Although globalization produced less violence and more prosperity in the world, still societies are "filled with uncertainty, and unease, and strife". He talked of concerns about "immigration and changing demographics" that are present in both Europe and the US.

He mentioned the same junction of making a decision, as he had mentioned in 2014 – either to press forward with "a better model of cooperation and integration", or to go back to a "sharply divided" world, back to "age-old lines of nation and tribe and race and religion".

Not so surprisingly ("external", right?) Obama suggested moving "forward, and not backward". Admitting that globalization is indeed "imperfect", still it remains "the firmest foundation for human progress in this century".

Obama, who describes himself as "fact-based", moved on to cite that billions of men, women and children have a better life, and "extreme poverty" had gone down from 40 percent of humanity to under 10 percent.   True numbers. As the former Canadian prime minister said – globally people gained, in the US people lost.

Again, he repeated his talk against the forces from the far right – which seek to restore what they believe was a better, simpler age free of outside contamination. (It should remind us of the slogan "Make American Great Again".) He admitted that these visions cannot be dismissed and they are powerful. He talked of how he was criticized for his adherence to "international norms and multilateral institutions".   At the same time, these visions fail to recognize "common humanity". He summarized it by saying: "Today, a nation ringed by walls would only imprison itself."

Similar to what he said in his book "The Audacity of Hope", a book he wrote in 2006, Obama acknowledged in 2016, ten years later, that the situation remained the same. Globalization weakened the position of workers and their ability to secure a decent wage. Unions have been undermined, and many manufacturing jobs have disappeared. Moreover, the ones who benefited from globalization used their political power to further undermine the position of workers.

Realizing that globalization was "imperfect", Obama called for "a course correction". That "disruptions" caused by "integration" should be "squarely addressed".

He asked the question: So how do we fix this imbalance?

His answer:

> "We cannot unwind integration any more than we can stuff technology back into a box. Nor can we look to failed models of the past. If we start resorting to trade wars, market distorting subsidies, beggar thy neighbor policies, an over-reliance on natural resources instead of innovation – these approaches will make us poorer, collectively, and they are more like to lead to conflict."

"External", right?

And as he did in 2006 in his book, instead of moving to fix the "system", he suggested fixing the "people".

> "It means investing in our people – their skills, their education, their capacity to take an idea and turn it into a business. It means strengthening the safety net that protects our people from hardship and allows them to take more risks – to look for a new job, or start a new venture."

He acknowledged that these are the policies that he suggested in 2006, and these are the same policies that he "pursued here in the United States, and with clear results. American businesses have created now 15 million new jobs."

[Note: Adding 15 million new jobs sounds like quite an accomplishment. There is only one issue that President Obama forgot to mention. According to Senator John McCain, the US absorbs 2.5 million legal immigrants each year. This means that in the eight years of the Obama administration around 20 million legal immigrants entered the US. Assuming that 50% are children, this means that during the eight years of the Obama administration, 10 million adults entered the US. These numbers do not take into consideration the natural birth rate in the US, which adds millions of young adults into the workforce each year. The bottom line is that adding 15 million new jobs means a practical stagnation in the workforce of the US, and maybe even a reduction of jobs available to the young people entering the workforce. In fact, most surveys in the US showed that young people finishing college today are earning less than their parents a generation ago. No wonder that all surveys showed that around 80% of the population felt that the country is going the wrong way.]

Obama continued to list poverty-going-down as his administration's achievement, hoping that with further investment in infrastructure and early childhood education and basic research, that progress will continue.

And returning again to globalization, he emphasized the importance of more trade agreements, or, in other words, more of the same.

He moved on to discuss his final point: "international cooperation" needs to be rooted in the rights and responsibilities of nations. In many words, countries need to abide by the rules. Remember China?

Actually talking directly to Trump, he ended by saying,

> "And in my own life, in this country, and as President, I have learned that our identities do not have to be defined by putting someone else down, but can be enhanced by lifting somebody else up."

What about lifting ourselves up?

Climate Change

Introduction

One cannot talk about globalization without relating to climate change. After all, climate change is not restricted to one country. It is a global issue.

Background information

Tuvia Tenenbom is a journalist writing for a German newspaper, that contracted him to tour the United States before the elections of 2016, and to interview people at local diners in small towns and villages. His findings are included in a book he published[4]. An interesting observation was that every single person with whom he talked, and who considered climate change to be a major threat, was also in favor of an independent Palestinian state. According to him, there was not even one single exception to this observation. One should note that President Obama, without being interviewed by Tenenbom, fits this observation.

Tenenbom only brings this observation without any attempt to explain it. But the question we can ask is whether to conclude, based upon this observation, that these two different issues are intertwined?

The answer is: definitely not. What we are facing is a "correlation" between these two issues. However, "correlation" does not mean "cause and effect". This means that although A and B are found to occur together, it does not mean that A causes B, or vice versa.

Scientifically, one should check if there is another component, unknown to us right now, component C, that might be behind both A and B, or maybe more than one hidden component.

If we return to climate change, we face two components – A (presence of CO_2 in the atmosphere) and B (climate change). Does it mean that A causes B? Or in other words, are the perceived changes in climate a result of changes in the amount of CO_2 in the atmosphere? Or is there some other issue [C] that causes both?

We can further divide this into more factors, such as: what causes the increase in CO_2 in the atmosphere? Is it the product of more activity by power plants generating electricity through burning of fossil fuels? Or maybe it is due to reduction in forests all over the globe, especially in the Amazon region of South America, and the jungle in southeast Asia, due to increase in habitation and agriculture at the expense of the forests?

---

[4] Tuvia Tenenbom, "The Lies They Tell", Gefen Publishing House, New Jersey, 2017

Another question that we should ask: would climate change take place regardless of increase in CO2?

It is a fact that planet Earth has been going through changes in climate throughout its history. For example, between the years 950 and 1100 there was "the Medieval Warm Period", and in the 17th century there was "the Little Ice Age".

The Earth's climate is strongly influenced by the storms that take place in the sun, in a cycle of 11 years. There are other patterns of rain, wind, and storms that have nothing to do with human influence.

Another important fact is that the pollution today over cities is significantly less than what it was in the past. In the 19th century, the smog over London was so thick that there were times that people couldn't walk outside, as they couldn't see anything in front of them. Although the term "smog" was only invented later, this pollution was picturesquely described as a "pea-soup fog". At that time, people burned wood and coal in every home for heat and cooking, creating large amounts of smoke. Moreover, transportation by horses and horse-drawn carriages created pollution in the streets.

A counter claim supporting the theory of human influence over climate would be that today the world population is double what it was 100 years ago.

There is one point that we should not disregard. When the siren was heard of changes in the global climate, scientists called it "global warming". After it was found that at times several areas were actually colder than in the past, the label was changed from "global warming" to "climate change".

In summary, even if one accepts climate change as a fact, should we at the same time connect climate change solely to human causes, such as an increase in CO2 in the atmosphere?

With these considerations we can now see President Obama's approach to climate change.

Senator Obama on Climate Change

Climate change is not mentioned at all in Obama's first book, "Dreams From My Father".

In his second book, "The Audacity of Hope", climate change is not featured as an independent issue. It is mentioned as one of the issues on which Democrats and Republicans disagree. In two places he equates climate change to the deficit in the budget (BO AOH 16, 126). The only time where he talks about climate change on its own is in one short paragraph:

"And then there are the environmental consequences of our fossil fuel-based economy. Just about every scientist outside the White House believes climate change is real, is serious, and is accelerated by the continued release of carbon dioxide." (BO AOH168)

[Please note that the phrase "just about every scientist" is not the same as "every scientist". It means that there are still some scientists "outside the White House" that do not accept the two assertions mentioned here – climate change (B) connected to release of carbon dioxide (A).]

Even this quote is not in a section relating solely to climate change. It is included in the section dealing with "energy infrastructure". In summary, one can see that as a senator, at least in his writing, Obama did not put a great deal of emphasis on it.

Candidate Obama on Climate Change

After winning the Iowa caucus on January 3, 2008, candidate Obama was interviewed by the editorial board of the San Francisco Chronicle. In this interview, he talked about climate change much more than he had done before, and with more concrete measures to confront its danger.

First, he mentioned that he was proud that he had been the first to introduce the system of "cap-and-trade", according to which every polluter who would emit any unit of carbon or greenhouse gases would incur the financial cost.

He then said that he is not against building new coal-powered plants. However, due to the "cap and trade" charge that would be imposed on this pollution, it is quite likely that it would bankrupt any company that runs a coal-powered plant.

Counting his chickens before they hatch, Obama predicted that the "cap and trade" would produce billions of dollars that could be invested in "alternative energy approaches".

Besides exposing his negativity towards coal-powered plants, in this approach Obama also exposed his disregard for the power of the market place. Any business person knows that imposing higher taxation on businesses does not bring bankruptcy. It only brings higher prices for the consumer, as the business will transfer their cost to the consumer.

Any American who crosses the border into Canada can see right away that everything in Canada is much more expensive, even if you take into consideration the exchange rate of US and Canadian dollars. The reason is due to taxation. Canada provides socialized medicine to all of its citizens, and in order to pay for it, has increased taxation all over the economy. It is clearly evident in the price of gas at the gas station.

Returning to the "cap and trade" proposed by candidate Obama – the not-so-"unexpected consequence" would not be fewer coal-powered plants, but quite likely higher rates for electricity for the average citizen all over the US, a citizen who otherwise enjoys one of the lowest costs of energy compared to any other country.

President Obama on Climate Change

In several speeches that President Obama gave regarding the issue of climate change, he asserted that "the reality of climate change is not in doubt" (Copenhagen 12.18.2009). In 2013 he stated that, "The 12 warmest years in recorded history have all come in the last 15 years. Last year, temperatures in some areas of the ocean reached record highs, and ice in the Arctic shrank to its smallest size on record." (Washington, DC 6.25.2013)

He also stated that 97% of scientists "acknowledged the planet is warming and human activity is contributing to it." (Washington, DC 6.25.2013)

Question: why 97%? Why are 3% still holding tight against this connection? There are other theories in science that were proved, and no scientist would disagree with them (i.e. 100%, not 97%, are in agreement); for example, the "big bang" as the start of the universe, or Einstein's theory of relativity, that has been confirmed in many ways.

At the UN Climate Change Summit in 2014, he described climate change as the single most important threat to humanity (UN 9.23.2014). President Obama even quoted the Pentagon's assertion that climate change poses an increasing set of risks to our national security (Florida, 4.22.2015).

Susan Rice, Obama's National Security Advisor in his second term, said that Obama put climate change "at the very center of our national security agenda". She also said that the Department of Defense calls climate change a "threat multiplier", explaining that even if climate change isn't the spark that directly ignites conflict, it increases the size of "the powder keg". Rice brought Syria as an example. Before the conflict started, Syria had experienced its worst drought on record, causing mass migration from rural areas into the cities, and increasing political unrest (SusanR, Stanford University 10.12.2015).

The main step that President Obama recommended was: "We have to cut carbon pollution in our own countries to prevent the worst effects of climate change." (UN 9.23.2014)

In 2009, President Obama outlined the US commitment to cut emissions by 17% by 2020, and by more than 80% by 2050. In 2013 he stated the goal of reducing emissions to the level of 2005 by 2020. His plan was to reduce carbon dioxide by using less dirty energy and more clean energy, and wasting less energy throughout the US economy (Copenhagen 12.18.2009; Washington, DC 6.25.2013).

In 2013 President Obama quoted a Supreme Court decision from 2007 which stated that greenhouse gases are pollutants covered by the Clean Air Act. The decision instructed the Environmental Protection Agency

(EPA) to determine whether these pollutants are a threat to our health and welfare.

The year 2007 was during the Bush administration, and the bureaucracy took its time to conduct the investigation mandated by the Supreme Court. But in 2009, with the change in the EPA due to the Obama administration, the bureaucracy finally determined that greenhouse gases are indeed a threat to health and welfare, and as such would be subject to "regulation".

In his speech in 2013, President Obama announced that he is directing the EPA to put an end to the "limitless dumping of carbon pollution from our power plants", and to regulate new standards for both old and newly constructed coal-powered plants (Washington, DC 6.25.2013).

There was one point that President Obama mentioned that got lost within his announcement. The greenhouses gases from coal-powered plants in the US are 40% of all the greenhouse gases that the US sends to the atmosphere. What about the other 60%?

A personal note: I am a strong supporter of green energy. I installed solar panels on the top of my mini-motorhome to replace the diesel generator I had before. It is quieter and cleaner. It was a costly move, but I calculated that two years of non-consumption of diesel for the generator would pay for the panels.

When I drive in the US I am in awe, observing the spread of the wind turbines all over the horizon on Highway 40 in Texas. And each time I drive there, I see more and more of them.

Years ago, I read a book by Boone Pickens, the natural gas magnate. He stated that the middle third of the US (the plains) is so windy that it can electrify the entire US just by wind turbines. Anyone who drives through the plains will testify to this fact just by observing the difference on the gas gauge when driving east (a lot less consumption) versus driving west, driving against the wind.

Back to Coal Plants

Guarding health and welfare by limiting greenhouse gases from coal-powered plants sounds very good. There is only one point to consider. The coal mines are a major source of employment for low-skilled employees. And they are concentrated in the states of western Pennsylvania, Ohio, Kentucky and West Virginia, along with several western states that produce coal. In other words, limiting coal-powered plants means closing mines, and they did close, sending large numbers into unemployment.

Note that the above-mentioned states are not in the area conducive to green energy on two accounts. The windy area is in the middle third of the country, and these states are not there. And since the Midwest and mid-Atlantic areas are very cloudy most of the year, they are not suitable for solar energy.

In summary, there was a major impact on the employment of low-skilled employees by this green energy decision.

What about other countries?

Climate change is a global issue. At this point we should check how other countries related to climate change.

In his speech to the United Nations in 2014, Obama said: "Over the past eight years, the United States has reduced our total carbon pollution **by more than any other nation on Earth.**" (UN 9.23.2014)

Obama in 2009 at the Climate Change Conference in Copenhagen said that although global institutions had convened to reach agreements on reducing the carbon dioxide released into the atmosphere, "we have very little to show for it other than an increased acceleration of the climate change phenomenon." He also said that the multinational agreements are not "legally binding"; however, he comforted himself by saying that each country will be able to show the world what they are doing. And even though the Kyoto agreement was "legally binding", still everyone "fell short anyway". He acknowledged that the agreement is only as strong "as the countries' commitments to participate". Since he was not going to be present at the end of the conference, even the US signature was not going to be on the agreement reached in Copenhagen (Copenhagen 12.18.2009).

Obama went on to say that he realizes that the poor countries of the world are not producing that much pollution, but he mentioned three countries which he labeled as "emerging countries" – China, India, and Brazil – that showed "enormous economic growth and industrialization", or, in other words, more coal-powered electricity plants, and a lot of pollution.

Note: just China and India, with over one billion people each, constitute close to one third of the entire global population.

And how do these two countries relate to climate change? President Obama quoted their claims: "per capita our carbon footprint remains very small." Both China and India can easily claim that not all of their people enjoy the amenities of modern life, like running water and electricity, and therefore, they are on their way to rapidly increase the amount of coal-powered plants to bring modernity to all of their citizens.

In Copenhagen President Obama expressed his frustration that the agreement that other countries wanted to sign did not include clauses to require sharing information, and to ensure that the countries would meet their commitments. In other words, he admitted that all these global conventions (Kyoto, Paris) were just "words" with nothing to back them up.

Now we understand why President Obama's message was: It takes time (Copenhagen 12.18.2009, Washington, D.C. 6.25.2013).

Summary

As we saw in regard to "globalization", which is a one-way-street program – raising the standard of living outside the US, while reducing the standard of living inside the US – the same is true of climate change. President Obama embarked on a one-country program of reducing carbon dioxide in the US, impacting the employment of many low-skilled American employees, while the main polluters – India and China – took care of their own people, disregarding the climate change of the globe entirely. China and India gave the US "words", while the US alone moved into "actions".

And President Obama did so, knowing that he presides over a country that took climate change seriously, while the main polluters got a free ticket.

It is another example of moving to solve an issue while disregarding other issues relating to it.

Immigration

Personal background

I was not born in the US. When I requested an immigration visa in 1983, it was based upon the fact that my wife was an American citizen. Before acquiring the permanent visa ("green card") in 1983, my brother-in-law had to sign an affidavit that if by any chance my financial situation would deteriorate, I would not go on welfare. Instead, my brother-in-law would support me financially. Today, the law is different. New immigrants do not need to provide such an affidavit from a relative. Welfare is given to all, citizens and immigrants alike.

Incidentally, today I wouldn't have a need to naturalize. The immigration law was changed, and today grandparents can give US citizenship to their grandchildren. My maternal grandfather was an American citizen. I have a very large family in the US on both sides of my family.

Obama on Immigration

In his book "The Audacity of Hope", it takes many pages (249 out 362) until Obama reaches the issue of immigration. It didn't even deserve an independent chapter. Immigration is included within the section of the book dealing with "Race".

Obama started by distinguishing between two different communities: the African Americans and the Latinos (therein relating to Mexican and Central American people). According to Obama, the focus of the African American community is the inner-city poor, while for the Latinos it is the illegal aliens ("undocumented workers" in Obama's language), and the political debate about immigration (BO AOH 249).

Are these indeed two separate issues?

Obama observed that Latino people dominate the low-wage work that once was dominated by the African Americans. The huge migration of mostly low-skilled workers benefited the economy, Obama says, and keeps the workforce young. At the same time, Obama acknowledged that this migration of low-skilled workers depresses the wages of blue-collar workers in general, who have a large percentage of African Americans (BO AOH 262, 263). In summary, in one sentence, Obama listed the most devastating outcome of low-skilled immigration on US blue-collar employees.

Till this point Obama accurately describes the situation. Indeed, migration of low-skilled workers does not happen in a vacuum. It does have an impact, and later we will see how much.

As he did with globalization, describing the picture accurately, based upon data, and then moving to an evaluation of the future with no foundation backing it up (as to the future of the US), he does the same for immigration.

Obama states that immigration is **not** "loss of jobs" but "loss of sovereignty" (BO AOH 264).

Technically, Obama is right. Immigration does not produce "loss of jobs". It only reduces the "quality of jobs", or in everyday language, it reduces the income from these jobs.

If we really want to see a clear picture of what immigration does to workers in the US, we need to go a little bit outside of the US, to our neighbor on the north – Canada.

Stephen Harper, whose ten-year term as prime minister of Canada overlapped much of the Obama presidency, related in his book extensively to immigration.

Stephen Harper on Immigration

Harper acknowledges that at times a country should consider "humanitarian" issues in deciding who should enter the country. However, for him, immigration policy should be guided by the needs of the country receiving the migration (StephenH 7).

Harper is amazed that both parties in the US, the Democrats and the Republicans, alienated themselves from their own supporters by uniting on two issues that impacted the quality of life of ordinary citizens: trade deals (=shipping jobs out of the country), and unskilled immigration (=reducing income of the jobs that remain in the country). The Democrats did this because of "progressive" social agendas, while the Republicans did so because of corporate interests in having skilled foreign professionals and lower wages for unskilled workers. Each party for its own reasons, but the bottom line was the same – both parties acted against the needs of American low-skilled workers (StephenH 11, 65).

It is no wonder, Harper says, that anger and resentment built up regarding these two issues. Harper quoted polls stating that 80% of Republicans and 50% of Democrats had anger against illegal immigration. Among Trump voters, 80% called illegal immigration a "very big problem", and close to 90% believed it had worsened since 2008 (when Obama was elected President). Harper brought 2015 as an example of a year of the Obama administration. In 2015, one million legal immigrants entered the US, and only 14% of them through a job-based preference. This means that the remainder did not address the needs of the country; or in other words, 85% of all legal immigration into the US disregarded the country's needs. In summary, Harper labeled US immigration policy as a "failure" (StephenH 66, 70).

Harper supported his analysis with numbers. High school dropouts earn about $25,000 annually. According to census data, due to a larger pool of low-skilled workers, the annual earnings of US high school dropouts went down between $800 and $1500. In other words, when a government is guided by "humanitarian" considerations towards people from afar, this same government acts cruelly towards its own citizens (StephenH 71).

Harper summarizes it by saying that if a policy is not working for the benefit of the citizens, a policymaker should not denounce the public, but change the policy (StephenH 74).

Canada, on the other hand, created an immigration policy that was aligned with the needs of the country, and as a result it didn't create any opposition (StephenH 13, 63).

The United States, like Canada, Australia, and Israel, is one of a handful of countries in the world whose history and character has been substantially shaped by immigration. (StephenH 67)

Nikki Haley on Immigration

Haley, a daughter of immigrants from India, was elected as governor of South Carolina, and later served for two years as US ambassador to the UN in the Trump administration.

Haley, like Stephen Harper, advocated vetting people who want to come to the US – both for security reasons, and also to make skills a priority; but not based only on "family connections", which can lead to what is known as "chain immigration" (NikkiH 243).

Haley enlightens her readers by pointing out that poverty in the US is not only "identity politics" (translation: based upon race), as there are white communities in the US that are simply "forgotten". As an example, she mentions Abbeville County in South Carolina, which is mostly white but has a 20% poverty rate. This county has all the issues that plague the poor inner city (the South Side of Chicago comes to mind): "high rates of drug addiction, domestic violence, and under-performing schools". Haley is against making these poor taxpayers pay for illegal immigrants' health care and education, while they are in need of help as well. (NikkiH 245).

Summary

Immigration is not an independent issue. It is an issue that impacts everyone in society at large – a citizen, a legal immigrant, and an illegal immigrant. It is not easy to see the effects right away, or even to connect the dots between one issue and another, especially in the US, which is a very large country, actually a continent. However, when a government implements a policy for one issue, as immigration, other people in society will have to carry the burden of that policy over time. The impacted people might not recognize the connection between the policy and their lives, but their frustration and anger are real, and these build up.

Later we will see other examples of how dealing with one issue while disregarding other issues was evident in several points during the Obama presidency.

Health care

Background information

Both Israel and Canada have socialized medicine – universal health care paid by the taxes of the population, according to income. This means that every citizen has a card that enables him or her to go to a doctor for an appointment, and to receive any necessary treatment, including surgery.

This tax-based universal health care brings a large gap in prices between the US and Canada. Anyone who crosses the border into Canada realizes right away that the prices in Canada for everything are around 30% higher, even if you adjust for the exchange rate of the Canadian dollar.

In Israel, the government has a committee that convenes once a year, and this committee decides which medications would be paid by the universal coverage, and which ones will not. In the US, they call it "rationing", and during the debate about health care, the opponents labeled it as "death committees". In Israel, they call it "the necessity of budget constraints".

There is one activity that both countries – Israel and Canada – share. Many Canadians who need surgery cross the border into the US, pay for the surgery out of their own pocket, and receive the surgery right away. If they would stay in Canada, they will have to enter a "waiting list" for the surgery. Moreover, when the primary care doctor tells the patient that he/she needs to see a specialist, that patient needs to wait for an appointment to see the specialist. This wait can be quite long. Instead of waiting, many Canadians cross the border into the US, pay out of their own pocket, and see the specialist right away.

In Israel, along with the public system, there is a private system. This means that the same doctors working in the public system, also have their own private clinic, and their patients would receive quicker and better care than in the public system. In addition, many Israelis purchase an additional insurance policy to cover surgery in the US, if it ever becomes necessary.

In summary, both countries rely upon the American system as a backup, as plan B. It is not stated formally, but in practice that is what is going on.

My two older children were born in Israel, while the youngest was born in the US. There is no way anyone can even compare the conditions in the hospital between the two countries. Although Israel is a modern western country, the US hospital looked to me as a "space ship" compared to the somewhat old-fashioned and more-crowded hospitals in Israel.

One additional point: in the US hospital, my wife shared a room with a welfare recipient. In Arizona, any citizen on welfare is covered medically by "AHCCCS" at the same level as anyone who has insurance.

This means that the ones who refrain from purchasing health insurance in order to save money are not the really poor people. The really poor people, at least in Arizona, are covered by the state. The ones who "fall between the cracks" are the lower middle class. The ones who are not on welfare, but cannot afford medical insurance.

Question: if the US would adopt universal health care, where would the American taxpayer find his Plan B?

Basic Concept of Insurance

The law mandates having car insurance. Anyone who drives a car without insurance violates the law. Anyone who owns a car knows that the safe drivers pay for insurance all their lives without ever using the policy, and they even hope that they would never have to. But their insurance payments pay for the cost of reckless drivers. It is an axiom in insurance. One might pay for 20 years without the need to use one's car insurance, while another driver might use his car insurance several times.

The same applies to medical insurance. The healthy people who by law must have insurance (Israel and Canada) are paying for the sick people who frequent the medical clinics. In these two countries, there are no "pre-existing conditions". A person starts to pay for medical insurance when he first enters the job market. Your salary slip will include your gross pay and all the deductions, and among them is medical insurance.

Case Study - Massachusetts

Several years before Obamacare, the state of Massachusetts enacted universal health care.   At the time the law was enacted, the estimate of the cost for a small state as Massachusetts was 200 million dollars a year. It didn't take more than a year or two for the cost to rise to 600 million dollars. The reason was that the state did not really legislate a true "universal" health care. Citizens still enjoyed the option not to join. And if one decided not to join, one had to pay $1,000 a year, instead of the $6,000 for an insured person. The young and the healthy, the ones who were supposed to finance the sick, chose not to join, and they only joined if and when they needed medical care.

In other words, one cannot have "universal" health care, if one leaves the decision to the person as to whether or not to join.

Obama on Health Care

Along with the loss of manufacturing jobs, Obama listed "high cost of health care" as one of the major concerns people had. Not only employees struggled with high health care cost, but employers and self-employed people did as well. The US, according to Obama, had a "broken health-care system" (BO AOH 6, 158, 183).

Obama also listed health care as an area where there are disparities between minorities and whites. He mentioned that even when one takes into consideration the income and levels of insurance, there are disparities between minorities and whites in medical care (BO AOH 247).

Therefore, universal health care is not only a medical issue for Obama; it is a social issue as well, as it has the potential to eliminate the gap in health care between whites and minorities, more than any other program designed to address race related issues (BO AOH 247).

Considering health care to be a social issue also mandates that universal health care would include "reproductive health care", a code word which stands for everything except "reproduction". In other words, "reproductive health care" is a euphemism for "prevention of reproduction", whether by contraceptives or elective abortion. (BO AOH 257)

Obama suggested a way to pay for universal health care which included: increasing preventive care, lowering administrative costs, and reducing malpractice lawsuits. These savings would enable the government to subsidize health care for low-income families. Obama estimated that universal health care would provide "decent health care" to the entire population without the two concerns raised by opponents of government-mandated health care: an increase in the government budget, and "rationing" (BO AOH 185, 186).

The Situation before Obama's Presidency

President Obama was not the first president who tried to change the health care as practiced in the US. Seven presidents tried and failed. The one who is most remembered for this is President Bill Clinton, who tried at the beginning of his presidency, along with his wife Hillary, to reform the system, only to be defeated by the strong medical insurance companies (ValJ 206).

When President Obama took office, Axelrod said that 85% of the population was medically insured. However, 15% were not. It was estimated that around 45 million people were not insured, and their numbers were growing (Axe 371).

Valerie Jarrett labeled the system at that time as being "irrational, costly, discriminatory, cruel, and, yes, even deadly" (ValJ 205).

In summary, the new team at the White House felt that this is an urgent issue to deal with, not to mention that for President Obama, it was even personal.

The Plan for Universal Health Care

The main piece of the puzzle, as Jarrett put it, was money. The question was how to pay for the cost of insuring 45 million people. And the natural solution was to have the "mandate", or, in simple terms, to force the insurance on everyone, including the young and the healthy (ValJ 206, 209).

[Note: the assumption held by both President Obama and Valerie Jarrett was that the only reason these 45 million people were uninsured, was because they could not afford to pay for medical insurance. As we go along, we will see if this assumption is "fact based", as President Obama labeled himself.]

According to the health care experts, two issues were on the agenda: The first was the mandate that everyone should buy medical insurance, so that the healthy people would pay for the sick. The second was a tax on high-cost health care plans that some employers give their employees (Axe 371).

[Note: in Israel there is no such tax on additional insurance plans. It means that this was just an excuse to tax "the rich".]

There was a debate in the White House as to whether to go for a universal health care, as the left wing of the Democratic party promoted, which means that everyone would pay into the system – the healthy as well as the sick – or to go with something less. The Vice President agreed with Rahm Emanuel that it would be better to go with less (Axe 371).

Although going with less, to pacify the opposition, was more likely to get the votes in Congress, it would still produce a "reform". The only question was if it would be a positive reform or a negative one.

Obama's Promises

David Axelrod outlined candidate Obama's promises in regard to health care: he promised not to have a health care mandate and not to tax health benefits. Obama also promised that all "heath care stakeholders" would be consulted, and that all negotiations during the legislation process would be broadcasted on C-SPAN, for the public to be updated on the process in real time (Axe 372).

In reality, only the insurance industry and drug companies were consulted, and the negotiations were behind closed doors. The "excuse" given was to enable open and honest discussions. As a result, the interests of these two groups were secured, at the expense of the average health care consumer (Axe 374).

David Litt, President Obama's speechwriter, mentioned a very important promise the president made between 2008 and 2013, and he made this same promise three dozen times: "If you like your plan, you can keep your plan."

David Litt said that any fact-checking person would have flagged this promise as grossly misleading – "Insurance companies might be forced to drop plans that don't meet the law's higher standards." (DavidL 219).

The Legislation Process

Axelrod said that President Obama "desperately" wanted to have a bipartisan legislation to pass the health care "reform". Obama knew that passing this huge change in society on a strictly party line (Democratic) would only widen the gap between the two parties and diminish the public's confidence in the government institutions (Axe 376).

At this point, President Obama had already gotten a backlash from his saying to Republican leaders after his inauguration, "I won" and "I trump you", and it was not easy to get the Republican leadership to join the effort.

Instead of begging for forgiveness for what he had said earlier, which would have enabled him to achieve his objective, President Obama aggravated the Republican leadership even further. He tried to bypass them, fishing for individual senators here and there, so he would be able to say it was "bipartisan".

They started with Senator Chuck Grassley of Iowa, who had supported a health care bill in the past. Grassley was willing to vote for the health care reform if ten other Republican senators would join. The administration realized that it was a nice way to say "No". Then they tried to recruit Senator Olympia Snowe of Maine, only to find out that this moderate senator couldn't go against her own leadership (Axe 376, 382).

And although most of the Democrats supported the bill, Senator Ben Nelson of Nebraska was only willing to go along if he would get a kickback ("Cornhusker Kickback") by the legislation exempting the state of Nebraska from the cost of the reform. When this deal was exposed, the process was "tainted" (Axe 382).

Not only was the process "tainted", but one can imagine how the Republican leadership felt about President Obama trying to "steal" their own people, and even offering a "kickback" (or in criminal language – "a bribe").

Let's see how David Axelrod summed up the impact of the health care legislation on Obama's presidency:

> "Elected as an apostle of change in Washington, he had compromised when he had to, employed the traditional tools of the trade to achieve his goal, and jammed the law through on a straight party-line vote. In doing so, he had ignited a blazing grassroots opposition that would cost him his House majority and bedevil him for the remainder of his presidency." (Axe 389)

The Aftermath

The Supreme Court upheld the "mandate" as legitimate, labeling it a "tax" that Congress can impose on the population.

There was only one main problem with the "mandate". Those who decided not to get medical insurance using Obamacare had to pay a "tax" of $1,000 a year, instead of getting medical insurance that would cost them around $6,000 a year, or even more.

In essence, Obamacare simulated the Massachusetts experience. Due to "Obamacare", 20 million people got medical insurance which they weren't able to get before, under the old system. However, 25 million people preferred to pay the $1,000 a year and not to enter the new system. In other words, the young and the healthy did not consider it necessary to get the insurance, and preferred to cut their losses. The main component of insurance – the healthy paying for the sick – evaporated from the scenery.

As Einstein said once: to repeat something and to expect different results each time is "insanity".

Obamacare's Impact in Arizona

Within two years after Obamacare was passed, the cost of health insurance went up by 100%. The middle class enjoying their medical insurance felt squeezed by Obamacare, without anyone compensating them for their additional expense. Moreover, several insurance companies left the state, as they found out that it is not profitable to operate in this environment.

In other words, Obamacare was not only medical insurance as such. On paper it was, but in reality, Obamacare was the largest "redistribution of wealth", not from the super-rich to the poor, but from the middle class to the lower middle class.

It took time for the middle class to suffer this tight financial squeeze. It might explain why in 2012 President Obama still got elected, while the anger building up only reached its peak before 2016.

Summary

Unlike Canada, or many other countries, the US is a country of individuals. And the way the "founding fathers" framed the constitution was based upon basic mistrust in government. This ethos of "basic mistrust" is still valid today. For an American government to come and tell people what to do is to go against the American ethos.

It is similar to President Obama's suggestion, citing the Chinese example of building high-speed trains all over China, to promote a high-speed train in Florida between Tampa and Orlando, at a cost of four billion dollars.

Only someone who does not understand how American people think and feel, can come up with such an idea. Which American would give up on driving his pickup truck (like the horse of the Wild West) for 90 miles, in order to take a train, and then to find out that he is stranded once he arrives at Orlando and cannot reach Disneyland right away, as he needs a taxi?

Obama's Policies - Summary

After examining these four issues separately (globalization, climate change, immigration, and health care), we can now discuss them together as a "package".

All four of these issues impacted the US economy very seriously. They depleted jobs, sending them away ("globalization"), and they suppressed the wages of the low-skilled workers still residing in the US (immigration).   If globalization was not enough to deplete jobs, the "climate change" agenda came along, and evaporated many jobs by closing mines, due to new regulations that prevented coal-operated power plants from polluting the air. And if this was not enough, "universal health care" came along, and increased the expenses of the middle class for health care. The ones who had medical insurance suddenly saw their bills going up significantly, without any increase in their salaries.

To the "credit" of President Obama, one can say that he was not the only one who acted this way. It started with President Clinton, continued with President Bush, and continued with President Obama. All three presidents acted the same way.

There was one difference between President Obama and the previous two presidents. Obama campaigned on "change", and he raised the expectations of the population to a messianic fever. And as high as the expectations were, so was the disappointment afterwards. And besides the fact that he didn't deliver, he went and continued with the same destructive policies of his predecessors. (See Stephen Harper.)

As an example, we can bring Edward Snowden. Snowden said that when Obama was elected, campaigning on "change", he (Snowden) was optimistic that the system would change. He was very disappointed when he found out that not only didn't President Obama bring the positive change he had promised, but he went even further to erode the civil rights of the population, by invading their privacy more and more. Snowden's disappointment, at least according to what he said, brought him to go to the news media, as he felt that the two parties acted in the same way, and he would not find any change within the government.

There are three characteristics of Jewish culture: family, education, and charity. (See "The Jewish Mind" by Raphael Patai.) Charity is not just "a nice thing to do". Charity is a religious obligation.

[Note: the Bible does not give the poor a right to charity. The Bible only talks of the obligation of those who have, to give to those who don't have. It comes to a point that not only the rich give to the poor, but even the poor give to those who are poorer than they are.]

The Jewish culture emphasizes not only charity, but it emphasizes charity with dignity. This means that the one who gives should do so in a way that will not deprive the receiver of his/her dignity. The stories are numerous, of how people went out of their way to conceal the fact that they are giving charity. Anonymous charity is very important.

For many generations, there were discussions among the rabbis of what does it mean "to give". Maimonides, a very famous rabbi and philosopher of the twelfth century, listed various degrees of charity. The highest degree, which is the noblest way to give charity, is to give someone a job. Not to give money, but to give the person a job. A job maintains the person's dignity.

Sending people into unemployment is a major devastation to their dignity and pride. No unemployment check can restore the blow to the person's self image.

When one reads Barack Obama's books, "Dreams from My Father", and "The Audacity of Hope" one can easily be impressed by his accurate analysis of the situation in the US before the 2008 elections.   The analysis was accurate: jobs had evaporated, wages were suppressed, health care was a problem for many. However, the solutions he offered in his book were "long term" solutions – education, training, etc. – while people still suffered with the impact of losing jobs and suppressed wages.

Moreover, President Obama, due to his personal experience with his mother's struggle with cancer, spent all his political influence to deal with the health care issue, and not with jobs and wages. By doing so, he took one issue, focused on it, emphasized it, and disregarded the real issue that was so important to so many people – jobs and wages. But besides health care not being a "solution", it produced a major blow to the welfare of middle class people.

Four issues with one impact. The bottom line was: no "hope" and no "change".

President Obama – Before and After 2008

Introduction

In this section we will examine the way candidate Obama talked about the issue of unity vs. partisanship in Congress, and compare it to the way President Obama acted and talked after he was elected in November 2008.

Keynote Address at the Democratic National Convention, July 27, 2004

While running for the US Senate from Illinois, Obama was asked by the Kerry campaign to give the keynote address at the Democratic National Convention in Boston, where Kerry would be nominated to run against President Bush.

Obama started his speech by addressing all components of American society: Democrats, Republicans, and independents.

He advocated the idea that each American is his/her "brother's and sister's keeper". He talked about individual dreams, but at the same time as part of one "single American family", quoting the US motto of unity, the Latin expression which is found on every American coin: "*E pluribus unum* – Out of many, one."

He repeated this theme several times in his speech. He negated the idea that there is a liberal or conservative America. There is only one "United States of America."

He talked of the colors representing the Democrats and the Republicans - red states for Republicans, blue States for Democrats. He negated both colors, and gave examples to show that Americans in "blue" (liberal) states and in "red" (conservative) states are "one people", all under the same flag, all defending the same country.

He also asked the question of whether Americans have "a politics of cynicism, or a politics of hope".

"The Audacity of Hope"

Background

Obama published his book "The Audacity of Hope" in November 2006. By then he had already been elected to the US Senate from Illinois. In the book, Obama expanded on the same theme he had talked about in Boston – the theme of unity.

Obama stated his view that politics is the art of convincing each other of common objectives based upon the same reality. It calls for compromise between one's objectives, and what can be achieved. Politics is "the art of the possible". Obama even quoted a friend who stated that he (the friend) avoided entering politics, as it requires compromise, not only on issues, but also on values and ideals. Obama quoted Benjamin Franklin, who wanted to die as "useful" rather than "rich" (BO AOH 219, 360, 361).

Taking into consideration that at the time he wrote his book, Obama was a freshman senator with 99 others senior to him, it is easy to understand why he felt that he couldn't do much in the US Senate. If being in politics is to be "useful", he felt that being a senator with no influence at all, is only "an exercise in vanity, useful to no one." (BO AOH 361)

Obama painted the situation in the political arena as the country being "vehemently" divided. It reached a point that the divide impacted personal relationships between people. The two sides of the divide are extremes, where each side moved into "absolutism". For example, in relation to the environment, the two poles are either "unchecked development" on one side, or "stifling bureaucracy" on the other. Each side of the aisle developed a litmus test to check adherence to "orthodoxy" on every issue. Compromise is rejected as weakness (BO AOH 16, 28, 33, 34).

Obama wrote that when he encountered claims among Democrats that the US is facing "creeping fascism", he had to remind them of the previous administrations of John Adams (the Alien and Sedition Acts) and FDR (internment of Japanese Americans). He said that President G.W. Bush is not a bad man, and that he does what he thinks is best for the country; that Bush is like every other American, who has a "mix of virtues and vices". Obama said that he suggests to these Democrats that they should rethink their claims (BO AOH 21-22, 47,48).

In summary, Obama painted the wide gap between the politics of the present (which is "business") versus politics the way it should be (as a "mission"). Although, as a Democrat, Obama believes that liberals are more based upon "reason and fact", he was aware that both right and left are only mirroring each other. At the time he wrote his book, the Republicans controlled both the White House and the Congress, and therefore didn't feel any need to compromise. Obama criticized them for this, but he also criticized both "radical conservatism" and "perverse liberalism" for not having any feelings of responsibility for the stalemate in politics (BO AOH 22, 23, 24).

The divide between the two sides is illustrated by the different groups that support each side. The Democrats are supported by the unions, the environmental groups, and the pro-choice groups. The Republicans are supported by the religious right, local chambers of commerce, the NRA, and the anti-tax organizations (BO AOH 51, 116).

The politics of the present force the politician to compromise with the truth. Although, according to Obama, the politician would not lie, but he would prefer to avoid the truth (BO AOH 127).

It is time, Obama said, to take a break, maybe even a temporary break, from this division, and bring about a White House based upon "humility and compromise". Such a government should take into consideration the values, the common hopes, and the common dreams, that Americans share (BO AOH 19, 20, 25).

Obama advocated unity among the American people. In his language, Americans should emphasize the understandings that pull them together for the "common good". He also wrote that people "have a stake" in each other. The desired politics should be based upon compromise, common sense, and responsibility (BO AOH 2, 9, 42).

As evidence that this unity is possible, Obama wrote about his experience in the Illinois legislature. As a state senator, he managed to reach understandings with the other party to pass legislation in campaign finance reform, police interrogations, and other categories. His experience told him that person-to-person contact enables bipartisan legislation, even if to the public the two sides will campaign against each other. If it was possible in Illinois, then why is it not possible on a national scale? (BO AOH 17)

Acceptance Speech at the 2008 Democratic National Convention, August 28, 2008

In this speech Obama continued with the unity theme.

Again, he continued with the duality of the hard work of the individual to guarantee success, but at the same time, having the "American family" coming together as one. The American spirit and the American promise are what "binds us together in spite of our differences".

But it is not just the individual's promise that is in play. It is the combination of all dreams that "can be one", quoting Martin Luther King who said, "We cannot walk alone."

Election night victory speech, November 4, 2008

In this speech, Obama again mentioned Democrats and Republicans. However, he went to a wider net: "… young and old, rich and poor, Democrat and Republican, black, white, Hispanic, Asian, Native American, gay, straight, disabled and not disabled".

Again, America is not only "a collection of individuals or a collection of red states and blue states". Americans will always be "the United States of America" – "as one nation, as one people". He added that it was time "…to reclaim the American dream and reaffirm that fundamental truth, that, out of many, we are one…"

Obama also returned to the message of his book – to reject the "partisanship and pettiness and immaturity that has poisoned our politics for so long".

First Inaugural Address, January 20, 2009

Two things changed in this speech.

The first – "On this day, we gather because we have chosen hope over fear, unity of purpose over conflict and discord."

In his book Obama talked about the need for new politics, about the need for compromise. In his speeches before, and on the day of his election, he talked about "out of many we are one". Now he still talked about "conflict and discord", but instead of "out of many we are one", he only talked of "unity of **purpose**". Not unity of people.

The second – "For we know that our patchwork heritage is a strength, not a weakness. We are a nation of Christians and Muslims, Jews and Hindus, and non-believers. We are shaped by every language and culture, drawn from every end of this Earth…"

In his book he talked about the need to reach compromise between Democrats and Republicans, and later on, with a wider net that included not only Democrats and Republicans, but also young and old, etc. Now "Democrats and Republicans" vanished from his "patchwork". He only talked of different religions, invoking for the first time "Christians and Muslims, Jews and Hindus, and non-believers".

What happened between November 4, 2008, the day he was elected, and January 20, 2009, the day he was inaugurated as president, that caused these two changes in the way he talked about the country?

For one – he appointed Rahm Emanuel to be Chief of Staff at the White House.

Chief of Staff Rahm Emanuel

Background information

In the Democratic primaries before the 2008 elections, the two candidates – Barack Obama and Hillary Clinton – campaigned regarding who would be a better candidate to bring about change. While "Hope and Change" were Obama's slogans, Clinton countered that she would be a better choice to bring about change in the Washington establishment, as she had a track record of working together with both sides of the aisle – Democrats and Republicans together. Clinton, as Senator from New York, established very good relationships with many Republicans, to which John McCain, the Republican candidate in 2008, testified in his book as well.

Obama in his book "The Audacity of Hope", published in 2006, talked extensively about the gridlock in Washington, to the point that nothing could be accomplished, as the two sides couldn't get together on anything. Obama also said that as time passed, the animosity between the sides just became worse and worse.

Like Clinton, Obama brought his record of being able to reach bipartisan legislation in the Illinois senate.

And the first step President-elect Obama took, right after the elections of 2008, was to appoint Rahm Emanuel to be Chief of Staff of his upcoming White House. This appointment was so important to the future of the Obama presidency, that we have to look very carefully at this appointment.

Who was Rahm Emanuel?

Rahm Emanuel was not a simple bureaucrat or an administrator. He was a politician of the highest league. He was a congressman from Chicago, and before the 2008 elections he was in charge of electing many Democrats to the House of Representatives, to create a Democratic majority, a project that he managed very well. The Obama victory in 2008 was accompanied by a large Democratic majority in the House of Representatives, a result of Emanuel's work behind the scenes. It came to a point that it was rumored in Washington DC that Emanuel could have become the first Jewish Speaker of the House (BE 39).

Emanuel was also a thinker. He published a book, "The Plan", to outline his ideas about how the Democrats can move the country forward.

And Emanuel didn't want to give up his seat in Congress, and to forgo his chances to become the speaker. But he couldn't refuse the President's calling. He was raised upon responsibility and duty (BE 39).

The Position of Chief of Staff

Leon Panetta, congressman from California, and later CIA Director and Secretary of Defense in the Obama administration, listed in his book two important characteristics a person should have in order to be able to take the position of White House Chief of Staff: the first, it must be a person whom the president trusts completely; and the second, the person should be "candid" with the president. As for duties of the Chief of Staff, Panetta listed the importance of scheduling, access, and **coordination with Congress** (LeonP 192).

Evaluation as Chief of Staff

In talking about Rahm Emanuel, a candidate to be Chief of Staff, David Plouffe said that "In baseball, a five-tool player refers to someone who excels at just about everything." According to Plouffe, Rahm was such a player. (DavPl 372).

Indeed, one White House official was quoted in the *Financial Times* as saying, "If you were to ask me who the real national security advisor is, I would say there were three or four, of whom Rahm is one, and of which General Jones is probably the least important." (RobG 291)

Being Candid

As for being "candid", President Obama did not have to worry about Emanuel.

Rahm's brother Ezekiel described Rahm as "unabashed about saying what he thinks", and said that he spoke bluntly, and frequently raised his voice. Rahm had a reputation of not keeping his opinions to himself, even at the cost of hurting people's feelings (BE 217, 254-255, GQ 12.14.06).

When President Obama convened the White House staff and said that he envisioned the place to be a family-friendly place, Rahm intervened and said that there is only one family in the White House, and that is the First Family. He didn't care that Obama might have been polite to say what he said, to give the attendees a good feeling. Good feeling was not the domain of Rahm Emanuel. He was for the absolute truth, even if it hurts people (DavPl 372).

It reminds me of one of my college professors, Professor Charney, who gave a class on "Conflicts Within the Family". He said that "total honesty is cruelty."

Years later, as mayor of Chicago, Emanuel gave an interview to the Chicago Tribune, in which he told the reporter, "I don't think you have any respect for me so don't worry about it", and "…in all due respect to you, and again since we are lying to each other about respect here…" Nothing is swept under the carpet. Everything, including inner thoughts, are in the open (Chicago Tribune 2.12.12).

This trait of Rahm Emanuel should not be a surprise, knowing that he came from a "temperamentally outspoken" family. Even as a kid, after listening to his friend's father denigrating women, Rahm did not hesitate to say, "F*** you, Uncle Bill", and went on to tell his friend's father that he is actually Archie Bunker himself (BE 84, 171).

The apple doesn't fall far from the tree. Rahm Emanuel's mother was a major influence in setting up his personality.   She herself was bullied by her father, and she used to bully her own children "with her emotional outbursts and extended silences" (BE 269).

Marsha Emanuel, Rahm's mother, was known for her extreme truth, at the expense of being polite. While they were sitting around the table at home, Rahm's mother told Rahm's friend, "We love you, honey, but we don't need you." Rahm's brother Ezekiel, quoting his mother, said that it was a true statement, as the friend was not part of the family, but still the friend felt that she didn't have to say it. We should note that the author, Rahm's brother, didn't see anything wrong with the content of what she said, as he was used to it. The only criticism he produced is what the friend said. Not what she said. As for the mother, and for the oldest son Ezekiel, and for the second son Rahm, truth was a first priority, even when the truth hurts friends (BE 229).

On the back cover of the book published by Rahm's brother Ezekiel, "Brothers Emanuel", there is a quote by their mother Marsha: "It is really hard to believe these boys succeeded. Instead of a doctor we got a bioethicist. Instead of a lawyer we got a politician. Instead of a respectable businessman we got a screaming Hollywood agent. Oy."

In Rahm's interview with the Chicago Tribune, mentioned earlier, Rahm quoted himself telling his mother, "You love Zeke – my older brother – you love Zeke more than you love me…" to which she responded "I hate you all equally."

What mother would say such a thing to her son, even as a joke?

Was she sarcastic? Was she kidding? Or did she actually tell the truth – "the whole truth"?

In the newspaper interview, Rahm said that "It's totally a Jewish mother thing." But the fact is that this is not a "Jewish mother thing". It is a "Rahm's mother thing". And Rahm applied his mother's "total honesty" later on his life.

Rahm Emanuel was not only "candid" verbally. He was also "candid" non-verbally. According to his brother, he showed emotions openly, spoke bluntly, and frequently raised his voice. Rahm showed his feelings to the point that "he could communicate a whole range of emotions – puzzled, content, annoyed, you name it – without saying a word." (BE 254-255, 7)

As the mother was "candid" in outbursts (verbally) and silences (non-verbally) so was Rahm "candid" to the extreme, and always. President Obama confirmed it. In talking at the departure of Rahm Emanuel from his position as Chief of Staff, Obama said, "His advice has always been candid." (President Obama 10.1.2010)

Rahm Emanuel's Past in the Government

Emanuel was no new face to the White House. He had served for years in the Clinton White House. He started as a finance director in Bill Clinton's campaign, moved on to be among the trio who organized the inaugural events of Bill Clinton's presidency, and became director of political affairs (BC ML 376-377, 464, 471).

Bill Clinton gave Emanuel a great evaluation. Emanuel's "great gift" was the ability to move ideas into action. He identified important issues that others missed, and Emanuel possessed a trait of being a detail-oriented person, a trait that was essential to guaranteeing success.

The most important point was that after the Republicans took over Congress in 1994, Emanuel was the one who brought Clinton "back into line with reality". Emanuel was instrumental in reaching a compromise agreement on the budget with the Republican majority, an agreement that allowed President Clinton to avoid being a lame duck president, and to achieve a lot of his political goals (BC ML 821).

Hillary Clinton talked of Rahm as having "sharp political skills". She also listed Rahm among her husband's "most trusted advisers" (HRC LH 103, 467).

Coming to Obamaworld

Unlike others in the Obama White House, Emanuel was not into basketball. However, he was very much into "miles of swimming and biking in his triathlon training schedule" (Fortune 9.25.06).

Joining the first African American president was not a novel thing for Rahm Emanuel. He brought with him to the White House a very rich record of activity in campaigning for civil rights in general, and for racial equality in particular.

At this point, I need to introduce the reader to a concept in Jewish culture, labeled in Hebrew (as well as in Yiddish) as "yichus". It is mostly used in religious circles to refer to the connection between a person and famous ancestry. Usually, one can be proud of being a descendant of a famous rabbi or a leader of a community.

In the US, one can compare it to the organization, Daughters of the American Revolution (DAR). But in Jewish religious culture, it is not a formal "organization" where people meet together, relying on distant ancestry. It is not an abstract concept, as even today, in ultra-religious communities, a person who is a descendant of a famous rabbi would have better chances in matchmaking.

Returning to Rahm Emanuel, his record (or "yichus") in politics was more impressive than that of Obama – the political activity of Rahm's mother, and by extension, also his own, from a very young age.

Rahm's mother marched with Martin Luther King when he came to Chicago (Rahm Emanuel 10.1.2010).   She was also present with 250,000 other Americans to hear MLK's well-known "I Have a Dream" address. Due to her fears of violence (which later turned out to be justified), she didn't join the Chicago movement that went to march with MLK from Selma to Montgomery, Alabama, in 1965, but she contributed money for the cause (BE 108).

The Emanuel family belonged to a congregation led by Rabbi William Frankel, who marched with MLK in Chicago. The Jewish community in Chicago strongly supported MLK's campaign for racial equality, and MLK spoke in three different congregations in the area (BE 161).

Marsha Emanuel was a member of a neighborhood chapter of the Congress of Racial Equality (CORE), and she took her two older sons to join her in her activity, when Rahm was only in a baby carriage. When they were old enough, they joined her walking in the neighborhood, knocking on doors and distributing literature. In short, Rahm started his political life as a baby in a carriage (BE 18, 174).

Dealing with Discrimination

Belonging to a minority (Jewish) in Chicago in the early sixties meant discrimination.
However, the Emanuel family didn't dwell on discrimination. They saw themselves as part and parcel of the US, no different than the descendants of the *Mayflower* families. (BE 68).

Unlike Rahm's older brother, who had fair skin, Rahm and his younger brother had their mother's "skin coloring". By the end of the summer, after spending a lot of time in the sun, the two of them were "almost chestnut brown". Rahm, with curly black hair and a broad, flat nose, looked like an African American (BE 119-120).

He also shared the experience of discrimination that African Americans had. There was a time when boys grabbed his bicycle saying "N*****s cannot ride here." (BE 154)

Foul language

Emanuel was known for his "profanity-laced tirades". David Plouffe gives an example. When Plouffe signed off his conversation with Emanuel, saying "Enjoy your afternoon, Mr Chief of Staff", Emanuel responded with "F*** you." Knowing Emanuel, Plouffe was not offended, and he remarked that for Emanuel to say this was the equivalent of "See ya." Emanuel could tell someone to f*** off, then to hug them.   James Carville said that for Emanuel "Everybody is a f***ing idiot…" He used to leave messages on the phone saying, "Hey, d***head, call me back." The one reporting it said that Emanuel was an "equal opportunity" curser. He talked to everyone like that, including his own mother (Axe 125, DavPl 373, Esquire 2.19.14, GQ 12.14.06, GQ 12.14.06).

Ben Rhodes said that it seemed that the swearing was not meant to put people down. Many times Emanuel swore only "to live up to his caricature, giving in parenthesis what is likely a label that Emanuel gave himself – 'the secretary of f***ing agriculture'". Leon Panetta, relating to Emanuel's colorful language, said that Emanuel had on his desk a brass plate reading – "Undersecretary for Go F*** Yourself" (BenR 56, LeonP 192).

Secretary of Defense Robert Gates said that once he dropped several "f-bombs" of his own, Emanuel seemed to treat him with "new respect" (RobG 294-295).

It was not only swearing. Even his regular language was full of "colorful" metaphors. Michael Oren, Israeli ambassador to the US, born and raised in the US, said that Emanuel described an alleged crisis in the US-Israel relationship as only "a pimple on the ass of the U.S.-Israel friendship" (MicOr 140).

We saw earlier that education and progress in life depends on the parents' message, and we saw the same for political activity, when Emanuel started his political life in his baby carriage. So it was with his "colorful" language – it started at home.

The Emanuel family had an institution – family meetings at the kitchen table, called "powwows" – a time in which everyone was entitled to say whatever was on his/her mind, in whatever language they desired – "Yiddish, formal English, and cursing were all mixed up." Rahm's brother labeled it "family style", and it was not meant to be an "insult" (BE 81,82).

Rahm's brother Ezekiel says that Rahm started cursing around the age of twelve or thirteen. (Note that thirteen is the age when a boy in Jewish culture enters "adulthood".) At times, the father approached his sons with the exclamation – "What are you, a schm***?" And their mother encouraged the sons to say what was on their mind "in whatever language adults might use. If they cussed, we could cuss, too." Many years later, when the three brothers got together, they would tease each other with "F*** yous". Rahm's oldest brother ends his book with a message to his brothers – "I love you, you schm***s" (BE 171, 201, 195, 25, 272).

Rahm Emanuel's Personality

The easiest trait to observe in Emanuel was his hyperactivity. Rahm was not used to sitting in one place for a long time (BE 89). He was on the move constantly. Ben Rhodes described a situation in which Emanuel called him to edit a speech, while Emanuel was swimming (BenR 56).

President Obama described Emanuel as having "an unmatched level of energy and enthusiasm" (President Obama 10.1.2010). His brother said he had "focused intensity" (BE 215). David Axelrod described it as "manic energy" (Axe 178). David Plouffe called it "relentless" (DavPl 372).

David Axelrod described Emanuel as a "super-achiever", for whom "failure of any kind was a terrifying prospect", and "losing… was not an option." (Axe 125) Even if he had a setback or failure, he was known to be very good at coming back (Fortune 9.25.06). His brother described himself as being "incredibly competitive" (BE 249), and said that for Rahm, "Life was about competition." (BE 56)

Rahm Emanuel described himself as having "the rougher edges of my Emanuel personality" (BE 204). Bill Clinton commented that Emanuel's aggressiveness made him, Clinton, seem "laid-back" (BC ML 376-377). When replacing Emanuel, Clinton found someone "who was almost as aggressive as Rahm" (BC ML 821); in essence, Rahm was the ultimate in aggressiveness.

Rahm's brother described his family as having an "aggressive, free-form style of relating" that might look to outsiders as "obnoxious, if not assaultive" (BE 238). Secretary of Defense Robert Gates said that Rahm Emanuel was known to be "terrorizing everyone", and labeled him as "hell-on-wheels" (RobG 294).

Rahm's brother said that their father influenced the three sons in the way they related to women – the father openly dismissed his wife's opinions in front of his sons. (BE 237).

Rahm Emanuel's aggressiveness and attitude towards women brought about an intervention at the West Wing. Valerie Jarrett said he was "intimidating". She gave him credit for being "an equal-opportunity screamer", but women didn't take it easily. It brought Jarrett to convene several women with President Obama to air their complaints, at a meeting that took hours (ValJ 175, 177).

There was more than one side to Rahm Emanuel's personality. His brother said that they could be both "benevolent and belligerent, sometimes in the same moment, as when my brothers say, "I love you, a**hole" (BE 268-269). Michael Oren described Rahm as one who could be "both a misanthrope and a mensch" (MicOr 103-104). Robert Gates said that Rahm made him laugh (RobG 294-295). Rahm could conduct small talk and tell jokes. He could be "funny" (BE 100, 154).

Aggression in Politics

Rahm Emanuel was "a legendarily intense Democratic operative", and "a rough-and-tumble politician" (BE 270). For him, politics is "war without blood". He followed the rule that his father taught him: "Offense is the best defense." (DavPl 372, (Fortune 9.25.06, BE 254-255)

In a well-known incident, he sent a dead fish in a box to another politician (Chicago Tribune 9.4.18).

Rahm's brother reported some of his "outrageous acts", such as naming his opponents and declaring them "dead" while stabbing a table with a steak knife. When CNN projected that the Democrats were going to be the majority in the House, Rahm stood on a desk and told his staff: "The Republicans can go f*** themselves!" (BE 270, GQ 12.14.06).

"But elections ultimately meant something" (BO AOH 83)

Presidential elections determine who will be the president. And the president determines who will be on his team. Some of them need to be confirmed by the Senate, such as cabinet members; and some, serving at the White House, are the president's own decision.

The people whom the president chooses are the ones who will determine US policy domestically and abroad. This is well known, especially in Israel, a small country that is dependent on the support of the US at the UN. For example, the US can use its veto power in the Security Council to reject the constant attacks against Israel in all UN institutions. The Arab block, along with the block of previously-communist countries and "non-aligned" block, can combine together and vote that day is night, or that night is day, or that Zionism is racism.

Michael Oren, former Israeli ambassador to the US, writes in his book "Ally" about Israel's interest in the personalities chosen by the new president for his team.

President Obama appointed former Senate majority leader George Mitchell as his Special Envoy for Middle East Peace. Immediately, the files were opened in Israel to check if this move is "good for Israel", or not.

Mitchell, of Lebanese descent, was involved earlier in the "peace process". He had written a report stating that PLO Chairman Arafat had nothing to do with the violence erupting in Israel in 2000. The report also called for a complete freeze on building in Jewish towns, aka "settlements". This record immediately put Mitchell in the category of "anti-Israel". In Oren's diplomatic language, Israel was "not enthused" by his appointment (MicOr 49)

Another appointment that was important to Israel was the nominee for national security advisor, a position that has a major impact on the US relationship with Israel. President Obama wanted General James (Jim) Jones. Again, the files were opened. Jones had previously filed a very critical report about Israel; again, positioning him as "anti-Israel" (MicOr 49).

Three names that Oren mentioned whose selection "heartened" him were: Rahm Emanuel as White House chief of staff, Hillary Clinton as secretary of state, and Dennis Ross as Clinton's special advisor (MicOr 50).

One should note that the above-mentioned views are from the Israeli perspective, and not from the US domestic perspective.

President-elect Obama was elected on the slogan of "hope and change"; promoting unity between people; saying that there are not Democrats or Republicans, only "Americans"; and bringing his record of being able to achieve bipartisan legislation in the Illinois state senate. Yet he chose the most partisan and belligerent person to run his White House as Chief of Staff, a position that included connections with Congress.

Was it oversight? Negligence? Or, could it have been a cold calculated move?

What Does the Sabbatical Year Have to Do with Mount Sinai?

There is a verse in Leviticus that begins: "And the Lord spoke to Moses on Mount Sinai, saying…" (Leviticus 25:1).

The following section then describes the laws of the seventh year, aka the Sabbatical year, when all agricultural activities in the land of Israel must cease for one year. The well-known Biblical commentator Rabbi Shlomo Yitzhaki (Rashi in acronym) asks: what does the Sabbatical year have to do with Mount Sinai? Why does the text need to tell us that Moses was instructed about these laws when the Israelites were only beginning their long journey through the desert? The commentator's question became an idiom in Hebrew, like asking: what connection is there between apples and oranges?

And in our context, we can ask: what connection is there between foreign policy and domestic policy? If we want to focus even further, we might wonder what connection is there is between President Obama's relationship with Israeli Prime Minister Benjamin Netanyahu, and President Obama's relationship with the Republicans in Congress?

On the surface, it would seem that there is not much of a connection. But if we examine it further, we find that these two relationships have a lot in common, if one knows that Rahm Emanuel was in the picture behind both of them.

Secretary of State Hillary Clinton, in her book "Hard Choices", said that Rahm Emanuel advised President Obama before his meeting with Prime Minister Benjamin Netanyahu "to take a strong position right out of the gate; otherwise he'd walk all over us." Clinton added that President Obama went along with this position, labeling it "both good policy and smart strategy" (HC HC 316).

The First Meeting Between Obama and Netanyahu

When did this meeting start? Did it start when Netanyahu came to the White House in person?

Nor really. The first interview President Obama gave after being elected was to the Arab TV channel in Dubai. In this interview he talked about his Muslim family connections, and his wish for reconciliation with the Muslim world (MicOr 49).

Before his meeting with Netanyahu, Obama was also interviewed by the Arab TV channel "Al Jazeera", located in Qatar.

For anyone who might not know: Al Jazeera is the TV channel that broadcasted Osama Bin Laden's messages to the US. It is a channel that is run by the Qatari ruler, and that criticizes everyone in the Arab world, except, of course, Qatar itself. The Saudis and the Egyptians consider Al Jazeera to be a channel promoting terrorism and unrest all over the Middle East. Both Egypt and Saudi Arabia ban reporters of Al Jazeera from operating in their countries.

In his appearance at Al Jazeera, President Obama talked of his desire for reconciliation with the Muslim world. He said that the Middle East must change – that dictators must disappear and be replaced by new democratic leaders promoting freedom. President Obama labeled the Jewish towns in Judea and Samaria (aka "settlements" in "the West Bank") as an obstacle to peace. He stated that he does not consider them to be "legitimate", and that he intends to talk about it in his upcoming meeting with Prime Minister Netanyahu (Storm 49).

Ilan Kfir, an Israeli journalist, gives us a detailed description of these events in his book "Storm Toward Iran". Quite likely it was reported to him from the Israeli side. He says that this last interview with Al Jazeera brought Netanyahu to understand that he is not going to meet a "friend" at the White House; but that in fact, he is going out to war (Storm 49).

The meeting started in a quite friendly way, with President Obama calling Netanyahu "my friend Bibi", and saying that he is committed to the defense of Israel.

But when the two leaders entered the Oval Office for a private conversation without their teams, President Obama told Netanyahu, "The situation in which you build in the settlements and in East Jerusalem, and create facts on the ground, cannot continue. It has to stop – and immediately. You must decide soon on a total freeze of building in all the settlements in Judea, Samaria, and East Jerusalem, and an encompassing agreement to evacuate them."

[Note: this complete quote was quite likely reported to Ilan Kfir by Netanyahu himself.]

When Netanyahu started to respond to this demand, Obama cut him off in the middle saying, "Enough is enough."

Netanyahu talked with the Israeli reporters, and during the meeting Ambassador Oren got a phone call from one of Obama's advisors, asking that Netanyahu would not tell the reporters about the conflict between the two leaders at the Oval Office. The only thing Oren could say was that the phone call came too late, as Netanyahu had already ended his briefing to the Israeli reporters. (Quite likely Kfir was among them).

From that point on, Kfir reports, everyone in Netanyahu's office in Jerusalem referred to the American president by his middle name – Hussein.

The above description of this meeting is not intended as a discussion of the US-Israel relationship during the Obama administration. That issue will be discussed in a later chapter. The description only comes to show how a "good policy and smart strategy" promoted by an aggressive and belligerent advisor shadowed the eight years of the Obama administration in its relationship to Israel.

Did Rahm Emanuel advise President Obama to deal in the same way with the Republicans in Congress?

Background information – Obama and Congress

Obama served in the US Senate for two years before being elected as president in 2008. In his book "The Audacity of Hope", Obama was very cynical about his experience as a US Senator.

He talked of one senator standing in chamber delivering a statement while everyone else had already left. Then this senator would leave, and another one enters to deliver another statement to an empty chamber. He summarized it by saying: "no one is listening." (BO AOH 14, 15)

His observations of what is going on in Congress: "The longer you are a senator, the narrower the scope of your interactions." In other words, that there is no way a senator can change anything in Washington. However, there is one thing he mentioned as a "good point" for being a senator – the senator flies a lot (BO AOH 115, 137).

When talking to Samantha Power, Obama expressed his frustrations at being in the Senate. He said that as the "ninety-ninth senator" he has no power at all. Once after concluding a speech, he told Axelrod, "Blah, blah, blah. That's all we do around here." In an interview, he summed up his experience at the Senate by saying, "I think it's very possible to have a Senate career here that is not particularly useful." (SamP 147, 148, Axe 168, SamP 152)

Background information - Congress and Obama

If Obama considered his time as a rookie senator to be a waste of time, we can imagine what the other senators felt about him. Here is a rookie senator, who didn't spend much time in the chamber at all, and he already bypassed them, and got elected as president. Moreover, the one who ran against Obama in the elections was a veteran Republican senator, John McCain, who was considered to be a "maverick" and "war hero" – yet an unknown rookie senator defeated him.

It was not easy for them; not only for the Republicans, but also for the Democrats.

With this in mind, President Obama went to meet with the Republican leadership in Congress, the House Republican Caucus. Just before the meeting, the news media reported that the Republicans were already rejecting the recovery plan that had been suggested by the new administration in order to deal with the major financial meltdown that was occurring. Axelrod reported that on his way to the meeting, President Obama said, "This shit's not on the level, is it?" (Axe 353-354).

How would President Obama react to these news reports? Would he try to pacify the Republicans in order to achieve a united front to deal with the crisis, or would he go with the same policy and strategy advocated by Rahm Emanuel on how to treat the visiting Prime Minister of Israel?

President Obama – First Meetings with the Republicans in Congress

Eric Cantor, former Republican congressman, wrote an opinion piece in the NY Times entitled: "What the Obama Presidency Looked Like to the Opposition" (January 14, 2017).

Cantor reports that shortly before his inauguration, Obama met with Republican and Democratic leaders at the Capitol, and asked him and several others to bring suggestions. Cantor and several others tried to find policies that would be agreeable to both sides, and a few weeks later they met with President Obama at the White House. Cantor reports that at first Obama listened attentively to the Republicans' ideas, including a 20% reduction in taxes for small businesses, for which Obama reacted positively. However, when Cantor mentioned that the stimulus package suggested by the Democrats looked like "old Washington," President Obama reacted with: "Elections have consequences, and at the end of the day, I won. So I think on that one I trump you."

The phrase "I won" was also mentioned in the Wall Street Journal (January 23, 2009) and in Politico (January 24, 2009).

Back to our question:

What does President Obama's relationship with Israeli Prime Minister Benjamin Netanyahu have to do with President Obama's relationship with the Republicans in Congress?

To Netanyahu, President Obama said "Enough is enough" and set the tone for the rest of the eight years of his administration. To the Republicans, President Obama said, "Elections have consequences, and at the end of the day, I won. So I think on that one I trump you," and he set the tone for the six years, after the Democrats lost their majority in the House in 2010.

Maybe President Obama should have reminded himself of what he wrote in his book "The Audacity of Hope":

> "…perhaps it was time to put the election behind us, for both parties to store away their animosities and ammunition and, for a year or two at least, get down to governing the country… Maybe peace would have broken out with a different kind of White House, one less committed to waging a perpetual campaign – a White House that would see a 51-48 victory as a call to humility and compromise rather than an irrefutable mandate." (BO AOH 19-20)

Instead, Obama used a different policy and a different strategy – a "good policy and smart strategy" promoted by the most aggressive and partisan politician in Washington DC. One who after the elections of 2008, when the Democrats were projected to have a majority in the House of Representatives, stood on a desk and told his staff : "The Republicans can go f*** themselves!" None other than Rahm Emanuel.

"Elections have consequences" of 2009 is no different from "…elections ultimately meant something" of 2006.

Valerie Jarrett said in her book: "We knew that as much as he campaigned on jobs, health care, and the war in Iraq, the subject of race would always be there, shaping and informing every move we made." (ValJ 133)

Was it really "race" that dominated Washington DC? One can say it was race, only if one is "external". An "internal" would examine himself and his own words and actions, to determine what he/she said and/or did that caused the situation.

Rahm Emanuel Jumping Ship

Question: why would anyone in the center of power in national politics choose to step down, and run for the position of a city mayor, even if it is a large city such as Chicago?

Before becoming White House Chief of Staff, Rahm Emanuel was at the center of power in the House of Representatives, even rumored to eventually become Speaker of the House. He reluctantly agreed to become Chief of Staff, only because the president asked him for his help. And then after less than two years on the job, he decided to give up his position, and move away from Washington DC to the city of Chicago.

And he did this, around one month before the 2010 elections.

David Axelrod, President Obama's strategist, talked of the pressure Rahm Emanuel was under, a few months before the 2010 elections. Although there were major successes in legislation during the first two years, and Emanuel had created a Democratic majority by recruiting the right people to run for Congress in 2008, still he felt that this majority is going to implode. The "political landscape", as Axelrod labeled it, was not conducive for repeating the success of 2008 (Axe 421).

In August 2010, three months before the elections, "potentially explosive issues" came into focus. The first was the wish of a Muslim group to build a mosque near the World Trade Center (Axe 421).

Emanuel felt that this explosive issue would not be received well by swing voters, who would be likely to revolt and vote differently from the way they did in 2008. Emanuel demanded that the scheduled press conference on this issue should be cancelled. However, President Obama intervened, and using the language of a professor of civil rights, went against the wisdom of politics, and championed the principle of religious freedom. He advocated the right of the Muslim group to go ahead and build the mosque at a place considered today in the American psyche as a "sacred" place.

According to Axelrod, Emanuel felt that Obama had sacrificed the chances of the Democrats in the country to repeat their success of 2008. Soon after this incident, Emanuel showed up at Axelrod's office, talking about his wish to run for mayor of Chicago.

It is not said openly in Axelrod's book; he connects it instead to the decision by Richard Daley to not run for re-election as Chicago mayor. But the close proximity of these two descriptions, one talking about the mosque in New York, and the other of Emanuel's wish to run for mayor of Chicago, brings the reader to conclude that Emanuel was certain that President Obama's approach is sabotaging the chances of the Democratic majority he created. Moreover, knowing that traditionally the mid-term elections are usually a vote against the ruling party, and with Emanuel having an "allergy" to failure, he understood that he had better step down, and not take responsibility for that failure. In summary, Emanuel didn't want to have on his record the failure of 2010.

Summary

We can summarize Emanuel's legacy in his less than two years as White House Chief of Staff, as a legacy of aggression and belligerence towards two components: Israel's government, that had been elected with a clear platform viewing the Jewish towns (aka "settlements") of Judea and Samaria as an integral part of Israel; and the Republican minority in Congress during the first two years of Obama's presidency.

On these two fronts, Emanuel moved President Obama into trouble. Is it Emanuel's responsibility?

Only if one thinks that a president is **not** responsible for his own words and deeds (an "external"). If one thinks that the president's advisors are the ones to be blamed, and the president is just exempt from any responsibility, then yes, Emanuel is to be blamed.

Question: Emanuel had a track record from Clinton's administration of being able to negotiate with Congress when it was controlled by the Republicans, an ability that had produced a lot of legislation. This was true even at a time when people considered Bill Clinton to be a "lame duck", when he lost control of Congress. Why couldn't Emanuel do the same during Obama's administration?

Answer: Actually, Emanuel did not produce the compromise between Bill Clinton and the Republicans in Congress. A good employee is only good if he has a good "Number One" above him. When Emanuel had Clinton to guide him, to make decisions, and to accept compromises, Emanuel produced wonders. However, Obama is not Clinton.

Both presidents were Democrats. However, since Clinton is quite likely an "internal", while Obama, is an "external", Obama accepted Emanuel's advice, considering it to be "both good policy and smart strategy". In doing so, he sealed the fate of his presidency for the entire eight years.

David Axelrod's Summary

David Axelrod, Obama's strategist, made a comparison between Netanyahu and the Republicans in Congress. In his words, "Whether it's John Boehner (Republican Speaker of the House) or Bibi Netanyahu, few practiced politicians appreciate being lectured on where their political self-interest lies." (Axe 485)

Axelrod asks whether the Obama team could have done more to gain a bipartisan legislation, with support of the Republicans, and his answer is positive. But he blamed their "haste to pass the plan" as the reason that Rahm and the team worked only with the Democratic majorities in Congress (Axe 354).

Axelrod said that Obama is not "exempt from blame", and he expressed his wish that "If Obama could forge the kind of bipartisan solutions he had promised as a candidate…" – but Obama couldn't. And not only was Obama unable to bridge the divide between the two parties, he went ahead to widen that divide (Axe 485, 483, 487).

The only thing Axelrod didn't do was: he didn't connect the fact that Obama is an "external", and that he had Rahm Emanuel as his Chief of Staff for the first two years.

Jewish Wisdom

Hindsight is perfect vision. When Obama said, "I won" and "I trump you", the Republicans did not have the majority or control of Congress. Instead, Obama should have adhered to a rule stated in Jewish wisdom:

"Do not be scornful of any person and do not be disdainful of anything, for you have no person without his hour, and no thing without its place." (Pirkei Avot, 4:3)

President Obama's speeches – Unity Vs Partisanship

Introduction

At this point, we will examine the way President Obama related to his relationship with the Republicans in Congress, as it is reflected in the State of the Union Addresses he gave during his presidency.

2009

The first speech the President gave was very early, on February 24, a little more than a month after his inauguration, to a joint session of Congress.

He started by expressing his gratitude that Congress had delivered the legislation on the "American Recovery and Reinvestment Act", but the fact was that this legislation was passed by strictly partisan lines. The Democratic majority did not need the support of the Republicans in this project. Moreover, as previously mentioned – during the negotiations between the president and the Republican leadership, the president had been quoted as responding to the Republicans' ideas with: "Elections have consequences, and at the end of the day, I won. So I think on that one I trump you."

President Obama talked of the unity between the Democrats and the Republicans, as both sides of the aisle were upset with the banks.

He did acknowledge that there were some in the audience who were "skeptical" if the recovery plan would work, and that they would not agree in the future on everything, and quite likely they "will part ways".

He talked of the fact that everyone in the audience loves the country, and that this is the "starting point for every debate", and the "foundation… to build common ground".

"To build" – but there was no "common ground".

2010

This State of the Union Address, at the time that the Democrats still controlled both chambers of Congress, was the first in which President Obama talked of the partisanship, and "the shouting and the pettiness".

He talked of the divisions and the "philosophical differences", and "disagreements" between the parties that are "deeply entrenched", but he emphasized the need for both Democrats and Republicans "to work through our differences".

He talked of how "Washington" is a place in which every day is an election day, "a perpetual campaign", and not governing; and that spreading false and malicious information about the other side is "just part of the game". This kind of politics produces more division and distrust in government.

Addressing the Democrats, he reminded them that they still have the largest majority in decades and that the people expect them to solve problems, and "not run for the hills". Addressing the Republicans, he said that insisting on a super-majority of 60 for any legislation is not leadership but "short-term politics".

As in his campaign his slogan was "change", so he committed himself to not giving up on trying to produce a "change".

Returning to same theme of his 2004 speech at the Democratic Convention in Boston, he said, "These aren't Republican values or Democratic values that they're living by, business values or labor values. They're American values."

He also said:

"I campaigned on the promise of change, change we can believe in, the slogan went. And right now, I know there are many Americans who aren't sure if they still believe we can change, or that I can deliver it. But remember this: I never suggested that change would be easy or that I could do it alone. "

In the elections of November 2010 the Democrats lost their majority in Congress.

In summary, even though President Obama faced a Democratic-controlled Congress, it was an election year, and the clouds on the horizon were building up. The president realized that something is not right. Although he initially told the Republican leadership "I won", legislation that is achieved by strictly partisan support does not establish "common ground", as he had hoped for a year earlier. Such a partisan vote is problematic, and therefore his excessive talk of the need for unity and governing.

2011

He talked of the audience facing him as being "part of the American family", but that this in itself "won't usher in a new era of cooperation". He said that sitting together that night is not the issue, but whether they can "work together tomorrow".

Unlike the first two years of his presidency where all the laws were passed only by the support of the Democratic majority, now the country faced a new reality - "a shared responsibility between parties" in which "new laws will only pass with support from Democrats and Republicans".

It is the first time that President Obama talked about a concept he hadn't mentioned in his first two years – "a principled compromise that gets the job done".

2012

This time in his State of the Union Address, President Obama talked about the military, not only to congratulate them for doing a great job, but also to emphasize that they are working to defend the country regardless of the differences between them. "They work together," he said, adding, "Imagine what we could accomplish if we followed their example."

He repeated his theme from his speech at the Democratic National Convention in Boston in 2004 – "What's at stake aren't Democratic values or Republican values, but American values."

As in his inaugural speech, he talked of "common purpose", adding also "common resolve".

However, unlike "I won" and "I trump you" at the beginning of his presidency, now there was a different tone: "As long as I'm President, I will work with anyone in this chamber…" Yet he couldn't refrain from adding a threat as well: "But I intend to fight obstruction with action." He repeated this line again, later on in his speech: "With or without this Congress, I will keep taking actions that help the economy grow."

He acknowledged that regarding the question of climate change, "The differences in this chamber may be too deep right now to pass a comprehensive plan…", but not only for climate change. He said:

> "I bet most Americans are thinking the same thing right about now: Nothing will get done in Washington this year, or next year, or maybe even the year after that, because Washington is broken. Can you blame them for feeling a little cynical?"

He talked of the divide between Washington and the rest of the country, and that it gets worse from one year to another. There is a need, he said, to "lower the temperature in this town", and there is a need "…to end the notion that the two parties must be locked in a perpetual campaign of mutual destruction."

"Washington is broken," he said. "External", right?

2013

We should note that this speech was given after President Obama was reelected to his second term.

Again, he acknowledged that the American people do not expect "…those of us in this chamber to agree on every issue," but they expect "reasonable compromise", adding that "None of us will get 100 percent of what we want."

It is not easy in discussing history to ask the question "What if?" Still, if he would have used the above message in 2009 instead of "I won", and "I trump you", he might have been able to reach bipartisan legislation.

In this speech he exposed for the first time the fact that even though the two parties had the same idea about certain legislation, still they couldn't reach the finish line in voting on the legislation. He urged Congress to vote, even if to vote "no", but to vote. In other words, the party in power, the Republican Party, had frozen the legislation. After the Newtown massacre, President Obama suggested more gun control legislation, and Congress refused to even consider a debate on it.

He said:

> "Hadiya's parents, Nate and Cleo, are in this chamber tonight, along with more than two dozen Americans whose lives have been torn apart by gun violence. They deserve a vote. They deserve a vote. (Applause.) Gabby Giffords deserves a vote. (Applause.) The families of Newtown deserve a vote. (Applause.) The families of Aurora deserve a vote. (Applause.) The families of Oak Creek and Tucson and Blacksburg, and the countless other communities ripped open by gun violence – they deserve a simple vote. (Applause.) They deserve a simple vote."

He was right. All of them deserved a vote. But the one who didn't deserve a vote, at least in the eyes of the Republicans in Congress, and was missing from his speech, was President Obama himself,.

"External", right?

2014

For the first time, Obama was addressing the American people, and not the Congress he was talking to: "Tonight, this chamber speaks with one voice to the people we represent: it is you, our citizens, who make the state of our union strong."

He talked of the "rancorous argument" that had been going on for several years. He said that Americans "are tired of stale political arguments", and that he is "committed to making Washington work better."

Just as he had done a year earlier, he said that his plan is to "take steps without legislation… that's what I'm going to do... I will act on my own…"

He talked of his plan to "issue an Executive Order requiring federal contractors to pay their federally-funded employees a fair wage of at least $10.10 an hour…" But he realized that he needed Congress to legislate the same for all Americans, and he expressed his inability "to convince my Republican friends on the merits of this law."

He realized that he would not have any problem with Congress in regard to reforming the surveillance programs (this was after Edward Snowden surfacing in 2013), but this was national security, and in that area Congress rarely acted in a partisan way.

Later on in his speech, he needed to add the condition, "But if we work together…" something which he was not able to reach at all.

2015

As he had done a year earlier, at one point in his speech, he addressed, "My fellow Americans…"

The rift between Republicans and Democrats was as wide as it had been from the beginning ("I won", "I trump you"), so President Obama needed to say, "Will we allow ourselves to be sorted into factions and turned against one another – or will we recapture the sense of common purpose that has always propelled America forward?"

He also talked of his plan to "crisscross the country" to campaign for his ideas. He couldn't campaign the same way in Congress.

He pointed out that in the past "Democrats and Republicans used to agree…" and he acknowledged that for infrastructure and basic research "there is bipartisan support", but still this "bipartisan support" does not produce any legislation.

As he had done several times before, he mentioned his speech in Boston in 2004 where he had said that "…there wasn't a liberal America, or a conservative America; a black America or a white America – but a United States of America," and "…that we are still more than a collection of red states and blue states; that we are the United States of America."

He mentioned that pundits had concluded that he "hasn't delivered on this vision" and that Washington is entrenched in "partisanship and gridlock", but he felt that "the cynics are wrong."

He moved into flattery – "There are a lot of good people here, on both sides of the aisle."

He referred to the "broad vision" described in the speech and said, "If you disagree with parts of it, I hope you'll at least work with me where you do agree. And I commit to every Republican here tonight that I will not only seek out your ideas, I will seek to work with you to make this country stronger."

He also returned to what he had said in his book "The Audacity of Hope":

> "Imagine if we broke out of these tired old patterns. Imagine if we did something different. Understand, a better politics isn't one where Democrats abandon their agenda or Republicans simply embrace mine. A better politics is one where we appeal to each other's basic decency instead of our basest fears. A better politics is one where we debate without demonizing each other; where we talk issues and values, and principles and facts, rather than

> 'gotcha' moments, or trivial gaffes, or fake controversies that have nothing to do with people's daily lives."

It is a great speech. The only problem is, it was six years too late.

2016

As he had done a year earlier, at one point in his speech, he addressed, "My fellow Americans…"

He realized that with 2016 being an election year, "expectations for what we will achieve this year are low." He acknowledged that "it has been difficult to find agreement over the last seven years," stating that these disagreements had to do with the "role the government should play"; that it was a legitimate disagreement; and that the American people have a choice to make, quite likely referring to the upcoming elections later in the year.

[Note: in this section, only the components that relate to unity vs. partisanship are discussed. This speech included a lot of addressing the issues that were discussed in the campaign. This speech can easily be described as a "campaign speech".]

In spite of all the disagreements, President Obama still hoped for "bipartisan priorities",
adding, "who knows, we might surprise the cynics again."

Again, he repeated the same theme from his 2004 speech in Boston:

> "Voices that help us see ourselves not, first and foremost, as black or white, or Asian or Latino, not as gay or straight, immigrant or native born, not as Democrat or Republican, but as Americans first, bound by a common creed."

Since this was his final address to Congress, he didn't want to talk only about 2016, but he wanted to "focus on the next five years, the next 10 years, and beyond. I want to focus on our future."

Everything will happen ""if we work together", and "if we fix our politics."

The word "compromise" was also mentioned in "Democracy grinds to a halt without a willingness to compromise…"

He said:

> "It's one of the few regrets of my presidency -- that the rancor and suspicion between the parties has gotten worse instead of better. I have no doubt a president with the gifts of Lincoln or Roosevelt might have better bridged the divide, and I guarantee I'll keep trying to be better so long as I hold this office."

Being an "external", he said:

> "But, my fellow Americans, this cannot be my task -- or any President's -- alone. There are a whole lot of folks in this chamber, good people who would like to see more cooperation, would like to see a more elevated debate in Washington, but feel trapped by the imperatives of getting elected, by the noise coming out of your base. I know; you've told me. It's the worst-kept secret in Washington. And a lot of you aren't enjoying being trapped in that kind of rancor. But that means if we want a better politics -- and I'm addressing the American people now -- if we want a better politics, it's not enough just to change a congressman or change a senator or even change a President. We have to change the system to reflect our better selves."

He ended by saying, "I believe in change because I believe in you, the American people."

He believes in the American people. Does he believe in himself?

2017

On January 10, 2017, President Obama gave his "farewell address" in Chicago.

As an "external", he talked of "the rise of naked partisanship" and a "dysfunctional Congress", and that "democracy does not require uniformity. Our founders argued. They quarreled. Eventually they compromised. They expected us to do the same."

As he had done a year earlier, he said, "I'm asking you to believe. Not in my ability to bring about change – but in yours."

He knew he hadn't delivered. It is only the realm of "belief".

The Israel-Arab Conflict

Introduction

This chapter shows the two main reasons that the Israeli-Arab conflict is not dealt with in the right way in the international arena.

The first is that whenever anyone discusses this issue, one only deals with images, and not with the reality on the ground. It is as if reality does not count.

The second reason is that western leaders do not always consider the history of a conflict.

In this chapter we will deal with several seemingly different points.

1. South Sudan and Palestine

2. Geography, Topography, History and Now

3. "A Problem From Hell" by Samantha Power.

The first section compares the recent history of Sudan and "Palestine".

The second section, "Geography, Topography, History and Now", reviews the books "A Durable Peace" by Benjamin Netanyahu, "Breakthrough" by Moshe Dayan, and "Warrior" by Ariel Sharon, who was known as "the father of the settlements". It also includes information from "Prisoners of Geography" by Tim Marshal.

The third section reviews the book "A Problem from Hell" by Samantha Power.

These sections show the difference between people like Netanyahu, Dayan, and Sharon, who live (or for Dayan and Sharon – lived) in the present without forgetting the past, and Samantha Power – a member of the Obama administration – who lives in the present, while disregarding the past.

The tendency of the US and the West is to deal with any conflict as if it is a still picture – the way it is seen at this moment of time – while reality is more like a video. One cannot discuss what is going on right now, without being aware of what happened before. In other words, as any historian would ask: when did the issue really begin?   This is the reason that a review of the book "A Problem from Hell" is included. It shows the tendency in the US media to look upon conflicts as if they are frozen in the present time

Samantha Power was close to President Obama. She worked with him on his book "The Audacity of Hope", helping him to edit the book. She also served as US representative at the UN in the Obama administration second term. Her view of events is important to understand President Obama as well.

South Sudan and Palestine

As we asked the question before, using the Hebrew idiom, What does the Sabbatical Year (Shemita in Hebrew) have to do with Mount Sinai? Or, in our case, what possible connection is there between South Sudan and Palestine?

But the history of South Sudan can be very instructive when we compare it to the solutions recommended for Palestine.

Background Information

Sudan's borders, like those of many other countries in the world, were drawn on the map by the British Empire. On the map it showed up as a huge country south of Egypt. But inward, it was clear that it was not one country. Sudan was divided into two distinct national groups, which differed in many points: social, cultural, and even racial. In the north there was the Arab area, whose inhabitants controlled the country, and in the south were the Africans, who had nothing to do with Arabic or Islam.

The Arabs in the north oppressed the Africans in the south, and it didn't take long for the south to start a rebellion that lasted for many years.

Quite likely the famine and the oppression in Darfur, on the west side of Sudan, brought Sudan to the attention of the world, and also to the attention of President Obama during his presidency.

South Sudan

President Obama pressured the rulers of Sudan to allow a referendum in South Sudan to let the population decide for themselves if they want to be part of Sudan, or, as it was expected, that they would like to branch out on their own, and start a new country.

Susan Rice, the US ambassador to the UN, credited President Obama's intervention of using the carrot (investment and a better relationship with the US) and the stick ("more pressure and deeper isolation") that convinced the Sudanese government to go along with the referendum. As expected, on January 2, 2011, 98.6 percent voted to establish their own new country – South Sudan (SusanR 273, 274).

Rice mentioned that Vitaly Churkin, the Russian ambassador to the UN, told her that in spite of the festivities and the optimism of the population of the new country to be, this country is going to be "stillborn", and that it will be "a mess for many years to come". Of course, Rice objected "strenuously" (SusanR 274).

It didn't take long for the leadership of the new country, and Rice mentioned specifically "Salva Kiir, South Sudan's hard-drinking, do-nothing, demi-dictator president", to transform the new country into a big mess. Moreover, she mentioned that the South Sudan army raped, tortured and killed thousands of citizens.

At this point of time, Rice said, "One of my most bitter regrets is having to admit that Vitaly was right", and she added that in regard to South Sudan one has to be reminded of the saying, "You can't help those who refuse to help themselves." *(SusanR 277)*

But it was not over even then. The conflict in the area of South Sudan continued for years. And Rice said that even at the time of her writing her book (2018), "hundreds of thousands of innocent South Sudanese have been displaced, raped, starved, and killed…"

And as the Russian ambassador told her, "South Sudan remains a stillborn state."

She ended the discussion about South Sudan by saying, "Few things sadden me more, having put my heart and soul into such a worthy cause for so long." (SusanR 397-398)

Establishing an independent state for a group of people can only solve their problem if they have honest leaders.

"Palestine"

Note: in this discussion there will be no reference to the issue of historical arguments of the two sides in the conflict. That is not the focus of this segment. And since I was born and raised in Israel, and one might suspect me of being biased in this issue, I will rely mostly on Palestinian sources, and I will add some clarifying information by Israeli sources (mostly by pro-Arab Israelis), as both of them report the same.

Background information

In 1993, the leftist Labor Government of Israel, headed by Prime Minister Yitzhak Rabin and Foreign Minister Shimon Peres, signed an agreement with Yasser Arafat, Chairman of the Palestinian Liberation Organization (PLO), to establish the "Palestinian Authority" (PA) in the territories that had been occupied (or "liberated" in Israeli rightwing language) since 1967.

Most of the Israeli public opposed the idea of signing an agreement with Arafat, an unrepentant terrorist. However, Rabin and Peres used various political tricks to get the agreement approved by the Knesset.

Note: since the Six-Day War in 1967, when Israel took control of the "territories" (Judea, Samaria, and the Gaza Strip), Israeli politicians and military personnel have had numerous meetings with prominent citizens from inside the territories. However, the agreement that was signed in 1993 was not with people from "inside" the territories, but with people from "outside" the territories. The PLO headquarters was located at the time in Tunis, far away from the territories themselves, after previously being located in Egypt, Jordan, and Lebanon.

In fact, the terms "inside" ("Dachel" in Arabic) and "outside" ("Kharej") are terms used by the Arab population of the territories. The agreement of 1993 allowed Arafat and 10,000 of his armed followers to enter the territories and to establish the "Palestinian Authority".

The idea was that the Arabs would govern themselves, while Israel would maintain control over security on the borders, and in some instances, even inside the territories. The agreement was for a duration of five years, and the intent of the signers to the agreement was that in the meantime the Arabs would establish all the functions of a modern country, ministries that will deal with health, commerce, trade, tourism, etc. After five years, the issues of a "final settlement" would be solved, when the spirit of cooperation between the two sides would help to reach understanding. This was at least the declared intent of the two sides.

Hanan Ashrawi and Sari Nusseibeh

I would like to introduce the reader to these two prominent people from East Jerusalem.

Hanan Ashrawi was the voice of the Palestinian struggle for Palestine. She appeared in numerous TV interviews all over the world, to promote the Palestinian cause. She was an activist for promoting democracy, civil rights, including rights for women (she herself says that women in Palestine do not enjoy equal rights), and other issues that are of interest in any modern and western society.

Sari Nusseibeh is from a very prominent family in East Jerusalem. If one wants to compare the significance of his family, one can easily compare it to the Kennedy family in US life. Mr Nusseibeh is a college professor, and he was instrumental in establishing the Al-Quds University in East Jerusalem.

Both of them published books in English. Hanan Ashrawi wrote "This Side of Peace", and Sari Nusseibeh wrote "Once Upon A Country, A Palestinian Life".

Let's see how each of them relates to the "Palestinian Authority" that Arafat established in the territories.

Ashrawi and several other Arab academics sat down and prepared the outline of "institution building" which is "an essential component of the reconstruction of a nation." (HananA 15) The group discussed for a very long time how to run the future government ministries. They prepared folders on how each ministry in the future Palestine should be created, to the most minute details. In doing so, the best interest of the population was in their mind and heart.

The Reality

Sari Nusseibeh said that once the "Palestinian Authority" was established, the "center of gravity" shifted from the rebellion ("Intifadah") "activists" on the "inside" to the "outsiders" who came from Tunisia. And the "insiders", the ones who had prepared the foundations, were pushed aside, and the functionaries from the "outside" took control (SariN 392).

However, continued Nusseibeh, the "apparatchiks" from the "outside" had no time to study the preparation work that had been done by the "insiders", as they were very "busy" with the "trappings of power". These so-called "ministers" spent their time gathering around Arafat's desk in Gaza, waiting for him to give their instructions, at times even to get his permission just to hire a secretary (SariN 392).

In many words, the "institution building" sought by the "activists" from the "inside", according to Hanan Ashrawi, was relegated to the "circular file". This negligence in building government institutions that would operate according to budget and transparency, created another problem. Funds and assistance by the donor countries slowed down, and private investors did not want to operate in "this unstable environment", dealing with "the leadership's unprofessional economic practices and policies" (HananA 14).

Ashrawi explained why "the Palestinian house was shaky" – instead of "institution building", Arafat gave precedence to security. There was a time in which around 17 different security organizations were operating in this small "Palestinian Authority". Sari Nusseibeh even said that Arafat received American backing to set up one more security force "heavily composed of returning 'outsiders'" (HananA 14, SariN 393).

The legal system was "fragmented". The judiciary was "incomplete". There were no "regulations and work systems". Moreover, "political patronage and inefficiency seemed to prevail", and the people that Arafat chose to head the "ministries" were unacceptable for "political credibility, personal integrity, or professional capability" (HananA 14, 296).

The reader should know that there is a limit to how much both Ashrawi and Nusseibeh could write about the system. After all, many critics of the "Palestinian Authority" were arrested for "defaming" the Authority. Several of them were tortured, and some even found their death in their "interrogations". Both Ashrawi and Nusseibeh mentioned in their books that when they showed some "independence", they got a message that the "chairman" is "not happy", and that they should be careful not to cross the line.

Before we continue, there is one point that everyone agrees on – whether Arabs, Israelis, Americans, or Europeans. Arafat lived a very modest life. Luxury was not his style of living. He lived a very Spartan life, sleeping at headquarters. Food was very minimal. However, he made sure that everyone around him would be corrupt. It was his way to control the rivals around him.

As Nusseibeh described it:

> "The chairman personally came out clean. Arafat lived a monkish existence with few material needs. He never pocketed anything for himself and was personally far less corrupt than most autocrats, or CEOs for that matter." (SariN 404)

The more-free Sari Nusseibeh explains in his book what Ashrawi meant by "political patronage". The PA established a monopoly over "basic commodities such as gasoline". According to Nusseibeh, Israeli tankers protected by PA forces delivered the gas to local stations, and the stations had no choice but to purchase it at "steeply inflated prices" (SariN 405).

Nusseibeh summarized it as follows:

> "Such racketeering forced the man on the street to pay higher prices, and it denied the government legitimate income. Security officials made millions, and their garish villas soon popped up next to squalid refugee camps. Meanwhile, fortunes were flowing into secret Arafat-controlled accounts." (405)

In Israeli sources we get more details.

The monopolies were in areas of petrol (gas), cement, cigarettes, building materials, food for animals, steel, meat, paint, and milk powder. The monopoly bought the merchandise from the importer in Israel, and sold it in the territories at a much higher price. Bergman even gives some of the prices. If before the establishment of the "Palestinian Authority" the food for the animals was 120 Jordanian dinars, once Arafat came to the area with the monopolies, the price went up to 300 dinars. Six kilograms of flour cost 15 dinars before Arafat's time, and went up to 40 dinars after Arafat arrived (Bergman 125, 126).

And the money went to the pockets of the "outsiders". Abu Ala, the one who negotiated with the Israeli side in Oslo, built a house in Jericho for 1.5 million dollars. The son of the "minister" in charge of "Information" received $100,000 to help build his own house. Cash money was flowing to others around Arafat himself (Bergman 156).

Bergman said that the **US State Department** counted 27 monopolies operating in the territories under Arafat's control, and the income from these monopolies was 300 million US dollars a year (Bergman 126).

In other words, the "political patronage" that Ashrawi talks of, meant that instead of "ministries" that were supposed to be created for proper governing, Arafat's "ministries" were the monopolies. And these monopolies raised the prices on the individual by 300%. It is no wonder that Ashrawi said that the standard of living in the Gaza Strip "deteriorated", while her colleague Nusseibeh said that the living standards continued to plummet, and the "the civil service that on paper was supposed to improve the lot of the masses only made things worse." As time went on, despair was building up among the "liberated" population due to "hollow promises of liberation and of a better, more dignified life" (Ashrawi 14, SariN 401, 406).

PA Corruption and Israel

Ronen Bergman in his book "Authority Granted" quoted Hussam Khader, a member of the Palestinian Parliament, who said: "It is actually a Mafia that started in parallel to the negotiations between Israel and the PLO. The same people who talked at Oslo were also the people who started to connect with Israeli companies… These same people would do everything to continue these activities with no supervision or control over it." (Bergman 138)

It is well known that in the financial agreement between Israel and the PLO that was signed in Paris, France, Israel agreed to transfer money directly into Arafat's account in an Israeli bank in Tel Aviv. There was a time that this bank account accumulated over one billion shekels (300 million dollars). This bank account was not under the supervision of the

PA budget or the World Bank. It was money given to Arafat to use at his own discretion.

Bergman in his book talked of other smaller bank accounts that funneled more money, smaller in scope, not in hundreds of millions but in the single digits and double digits of millions.

Personal experience

My colleague and I came to our destination at a city close to Jerusalem. I saw that he left his phone on the console in the car. I told him that he is negligent because if his car will be stolen, he will also lose the phone. He said: that's why I leave the phone in the car. If I return and the car is not there, I can call the thief and offer him money to return the car. The thief will very likely go with it, and the insurance will pay for it. It will be much less for them to pay the thief, than to pay me the full value of the car.

Car Theft

The experience I had only illustrated what happened in Israel after the government signed the agreement with the PLO, to establish the "Palestinian Authority". On paper it sounded nice. In reality, the agreement established "safe havens" for car thieves.

Bergman in his book gives us the statistics of car thefts in Israel. Before the establishment of the "Palestinian Authority" in 1993, around 15,000 cars were stolen each year in Israel. Starting in 1993, the numbers went up significantly. In 1995, close to 34,000 cars were stolen, and in 1996 around 55,000 cars were stolen.

In other words, the "political" agreement between the Israeli government and the PLO had a major impact on crime statistics in Israel.

Bergman in his book gives us additional information in regard to car thefts:

High-ranking officials in the PA were ordering specific cars they liked, and the thieves produced them, and these cars were parked at the various police stations of the PA with new PA Police plates on them. In summary, the higher ranks of the PA Police were car thieves.

In the Gaza Strip, anyone who has in his ownership a stolen car, can go to the local DMV office of the PA, pay 200 shekel per month, get a temporary plate of the PA, and after paying these fees for six months, the car owner can get a permanent plate. In other words, the PA itself was part of the system to launder stolen cars.

The Wall

This "party" came to an end once Arafat decided to start his war against Israel in October 2000. A campaign of suicide bombers flooded the country with buses and restaurants exploding, killing women and children. At first, Israel exercised patience and "restraint", and was passive in dealing with this terror campaign, but when a suicide bomber exploded himself on Passover eve just before the holiday seder (the traditional family meal on Passover) at a hotel in a city north of Tel Aviv, killing dozens and wounding many more, the government unleashed the military to remove the threat from the territories that had been given to the PLO in 1993.

Terror subsided but was not eliminated completely. To guard the country, Israel decided to build a barrier between Judea and Samaria, and pre-1967 Israel. (The barrier is often referred to as a "wall", but in some parts it is really just a fence.) They moved quickly and it didn't take long to construct the barrier.

[Note: the Arabs went to the UN to condemn Israel for building the "wall". They compared the "wall" to their terror campaign.]

It didn't take long, and a very interesting characteristic of this barrier was established. It doesn't just prevent one-way movement. It prevents movements in both directions. People can scale a wall, as long as it is not too high, but they cannot move a car the same way as a person.

This means that once the barrier was built, car thefts in Israel went down significantly, even to the point that it was less than what it had been before 1993.

South Arizona – case study

People think that a wall on the US side on the border between the US and Mexico is only meant to prevent illegal immigration. This impression neglects the characteristic of a two-way barrier. There are places in Phoenix where if one parks a car, it would be in Mexico in four hours. I would imagine that as in the PA, the car thieves would find a way to get Mexican plates for these stolen cars.

When I had a class in El Paso, Texas, the lady at the rental car agency strongly recommended to me to take the full insurance. She said that every day, ten cars of just their agency are stolen, and end up in Mexico.

If a wall would be built on the border, quite likely the cost of car insurance will go down in Arizona. People in Arizona don't realize that the lack of a physical barrier on the border of Mexico has a major impact on their wallet. They don't connect the car insurance fees to the lack of a wall, but if they would study the Israeli experience of building a wall against terror and its impact on car theft, they would get the picture.

Only car thefts?

It is a known point in criminology that one cannot commit one crime and retire. Once a person commits a crime, it is quite likely that the person would go up the "ladder of crime". This means that nobody gets up in the morning and says to himself: today I will kill someone. The natural progression in crime is to commit a small crime, and then a larger one, and an even larger one, and so on. It comes to a point that one can predict where and when a person would end up in crime just by observing the steps of crime.

If we take for example car thefts, it is not going to end with car thefts. Very likely a local organization that deals with car thefts would be upset if another organization would step into their territory. This will now bring about more violent crime between criminals for the control of their territory.

If we go back to the criminal enterprise of the Palestinian Authority, establishing monopolies to extract money from the population by increasing their cost of everything including food, this means that they do not care for their own people.

Arab society is based upon blood relationships – family, extended family, tribe, and so on. In such a situation it is debatable if there would be a perception of "brotherhood" between people of different clans.

In fact, there were reports that elements of the PA Police were terrorizing the population via robbery, and even rape of young women. It came to a point that the Muslim Mufti of East Jerusalem had to issue a religious edict (fatwa) forbidding young newlywed couples from emigrating out of the area. There was a need for such a decree, as every young husband who wanted to guard his wife had to take her out of the area, out of fear that she would be raped.

Summary

Quoting the Palestinian Parliament member Hussam Khader, who called the PA a "Mafia", and reading what two distinguished Palestinians – Hanan Ashrawi and Sari Nusseibeh – wrote in their books (in English), we come to the conclusion that in 1993 the Israeli government signed an agreement with a criminal enterprise to take over certain areas of the country. By doing so, the government endangered the population both security-wise and crime-wise.

This also has a major impact on the so-called "peace process" that has been continued for generations. Is there any possibility that this criminal enterprise would agree to settle anything with Israel?

It reminds me of "The Sopranos", the well-known HBO series. Would the FBI eliminate the problem with the Mafia by giving the Mafia an area that they will control, and would doing so save other areas from crime? Every reasonable person on the street would say that it is not only insanity but it is the epitome of stupidity. Why would a Mafia organization agree to limit their activity to only one area?

It is just like the other HBO series, "The Wire", which is about Baltimore. One of the high-ranking officers in the series decided to move all drug dealings in the city to one area so the other areas would be safe.

It is only a TV show, and it never happened in reality, and it would never happen in the future.

The Israeli government decided that it is a good idea!!!

Personal observation:

When I read the books by Hanan Ashrawi and Sari Nusseibeh, I felt sorry for them. They really wanted to be free and to establish a democratic country alongside Israel. They wanted a country that would have all the legal and social institutions that a modern country has. They wanted a country where each citizen would enjoy the right to live freely, with all the civil rights that any other citizen of a modern country enjoys. That is what they fought for. But they didn't achieve it. It was not "in the cards".

[It should be noted that prior to 1993, for example in the Madrid Conference of 1991, Israel had insisted on negotiating only with local Palestinian representatives and not with the PLO. However, the members of the Palestinian delegation – including Ms Ashrawi – were in constant communication with Arafat during the conference.]

South Sudan and Palestine

We can now return to what Susan Rice said about the new South Sudan military that "raped, tortured and killed thousands of citizens."

Susan Rice said about South Sudan: "hundreds of thousands of innocent South Sudanese have been displaced, raped, starved, and killed..."

The same happened in the territories once they came under Arafat's control. There was a major emigration of anyone who was able to leave, simply to run away. There was a report in the Los Angeles Times that in several Arab cities, classes had to start the school year when they were less than half-full. The middle class, the professionals, doctors, lawyers, accountants, and so on, simply packed up and moved out. Just like Sari Nusseibeh, who decided to move to the US. He knew what was coming.

Susan Rice admitted that the Russian ambassador was right, and that South Sudan became a "failed state".

Question: is there any need to establish another independent country, when we already know that it is a "failed state" to start with?

Did President Obama know all of the above information?

During his presidency, President Obama pressured the rightwing Israeli government (see more later) to compromise and allow the establishment of an independent "Palestinian state". When President Obama pressured Prime Minister Netanyahu to compromise, did he do so with or without the above knowledge about the criminal enterprise of the PA?

He must have known, and for the following reasons:

1. The number of the monopolies in the territories, extorting the population of their meager income by raising the cost of food by 300%, was registered by the State Department.

2. One security organization that was established under Arafat was trained by the US, and quite likely by the CIA.

3. Moreover, the presidents of the US are proud that they are briefed every single morning with top-secret information from all over the globe. These presidential briefings are an institution, employing many people who collect all the information from all over the US intelligence community, to produce a summary for the president of what is going on around the world.

The information that I listed above is not secret. It is from "open sources" (i.e. books), and even by Palestinian dignitaries.

Bottom line: President Obama had to know. And he still pressured Netanyahu to go along with this charade.

To his "credit", we can defend President Obama by saying that he was not the only president who went along with this facade. It started with President Clinton, went on with President Bush, and ended with President Obama.

Why?

Geography, Topography, History and Now

Introduction

In this section we will discuss several books: "Breakthrough: A Personal Account of the Egypt-Israel Peace Negotiations" by Moshe Dayan; "A Durable Peace: Israel and its Place Among the Nations" by Benjamin Netanyahu; and "Warrior" (Autobiography) by Ariel Sharon. Information is also included from "Prisoners of Geography" by Tim Marshal.

Together, these books show us what is behind the Israeli-Arab conflict, which today is often referred to as the Israel-Palestinian conflict.

The Size of Israel

Benjamin Netanyahu wants his readers to know the size of Israel – forty miles wide "(including the West Bank)", and without the "West Bank", it is ten miles wide. In terms of military operations, if Israel would return to the border of pre-1967 War, the borders when the war started, when it was 10 miles wide (at its narrowest point, near Tel Aviv), enemy military could reach the sea in just a few hours (BenN xx, 287).

Netanyahu goes on to describe this distance in terms of walking and running. Netanyahu was a member of the most prestigious commando unit of the Israeli military, with the rank of captain. He describes how it is only a one-day march from the Sea of Galilee (more appropriately described as a "lake" in US terms) to the Mediterranean. From the border of the pre-1967 War (also known as "the Green Line") to the Mediterranean is a run that takes only a little more than one hour. In comparison, Netanyahu brings us the distance between the Warsaw Pact lines and the English Channel – one thousand miles. (BenN 289).

Judea and Samaria, also known as "the West Bank" (i.e. the west bank of the Jordan River; which would be considered a "creek" in US terms), is an area sixty miles long and thirty miles wide. It is located east of the center of pre-1967 Israel (BenN 163).

Judea and Samaria are sparsely populated, about 150 people per square kilometer, compared to 6700 per square km in Tel Aviv. It is equivalent to "rural regions beyond the metropolitan belts" of large cities like New York, London, or Paris (BenN 190).

The above-mentioned numbers, although accurate, do not give the full picture. The book "Prisoners of Geography" gives us the topography of the area:

> "Much of it [the West Bank] compromises a mountain ridge that runs north to south. From a military perspective, this gives an advantage to whoever controls the high ground of the coastal plain on the western side of the ridge [Pre-1967 Israel] and the Jordan Rift Valley to its east." (TimM 155)

Personal experience: I once walked on Jaffa Street, the street that crosses Jerusalem east to west, from Jaffa Gate at the Old City, to the entrance to Jerusalem from the west, at the point that Jaffa Street connects to the highway going downhill towards Tel Aviv. Although it is not a real plateau, i.e. there are times that one has to go uphill or downhill, still it is a walk of only 2 kilometers (1.3 miles) from east to west – this is the width of the mountain ridge, from where one goes down either to the Jordan River on the east, or towards the coastal area on the west.

In essence, nature produced a natural "wall" protecting Israel on its eastern front, the side that faces the narrow "waist" of the country.

Moshe Dayan on Israeli "Settlements" in Judea and Samaria

Introduction

Moshe Dayan was in his earlier years Chief of Staff of the Israeli Defense Forces (IDF). Upon retiring from his military post, Dayan entered politics. Before the Six Day War in 1967, Dayan was appointed as Minister of Defense in the unity government of Prime Minister Levi Eshkol.

Upon the death of Eshkol in 1969, Golda Meir succeeded him, and kept Dayan as Minister of Defense throughout the years. Her government fell several months after the Yom Kippur War of 1973.

Upon victory of the Likud party in the elections of May 1977, Prime Minister elect Menachem Begin offered Dayan, who had been elected to the Knesset (parliament) on the Labor party list, the position of Minister of Foreign Affairs. Dayan accepted the position, and was involved thereafter in the peace negotiations with Egypt, in which the US, presided by President Jimmy Carter, was fully involved.

Upon his election as US President, Jimmy Carter expressed his support for a "Palestinian homeland", and pressured Israel to give up Judea and Samaria to allow "self-determination" to the "Palestinians" in these areas. Prime Minister Begin, who was elected on the platform of keeping hold of these areas, along with Foreign Minister Dayan, who was elected on the Labor Party list, resisted this pressure.

Dayan in his book[5] outlined his view of the Jewish towns, aka "settlements", in Judea and Samaria.

When President Carter pressured Dayan to give up the territories, Dayan replied:

"…there never was and never could be a government in Israel that would fail to establish Israeli settlements in the territories." (Dayan 59)

When American Jewish leaders met Dayan to express to him their hesitation about the new Israeli government moving strongly with "settlements" into the territories, Dayan shared in his book his feelings towards the "settlers":

"I stared straight back at one American questioner who had talked of the 'sabotage' of Zionism by the Gush Imunim settlers, and told him that with all my differences of opinion with Gush Imunim, I saw them as dedicated pioneers, and I preferred them to the 'Zionists' who dwelt comfortably in the United States." (Dayan 118)

Dayan also talked of the importance of Judea and Samaria to Israel:

---

[5] Moshe Dayan, "Breakthrough: A Personal Account of the Egypt-Israel Peace Negotiations", Alfred A. Knopf, New York, 1981

"It was up to us to ensure that neither our armed forces nor our settlements would be removed from the West Bank, and that the territory would not come under foreign rule." (Dayan 129)

It should be noted that unlike Prime Minister Begin, who declared openly that in the future Israel will exercise its right to claim sovereignty over Judea and Samaria, Dayan as a Labor party member was not into "declarations". It didn't matter to him if the area would be annexed to Israel. What mattered to him was that no foreign rule would be established over this area, and that the IDF and the settlers would stay there.

Although being flexible on the issue of sovereignty, Dayan was aware of the historical importance of the area, being the "birthplace of our homeland, in which we could live as of right and not on sufferance." (Dayan 183)

Dayan connected the Israeli settlers to the presence of the IDF in the area. For him, these two were one and the same. In his words:

"I myself viewed an Israeli military presence in the West Bank and Gaza District as inextricably bound up with settlement. I did not believe it politically possible to maintain Israeli troops in these territories unless there is also an Israeli civilian population. I thought that Jewish villages should be established, with army units stationed in or near them. If the population of the territories were exclusively Arab, the role of the Israeli units would appear to be that of an occupation force stationed among a resentful population, and Israel would be under constant pressure to remove it." (Dayan 185)

He also said the area calls for:

"…early-warning system and other military installations, as well as army units, for the sole purpose of protecting the adjacent narrow strip of Israel with its dense population along the Mediterranean" (Dayan 304).

He added that, "We had no wish to deploy our units in the midst of the populated Arab centers of the West Bank. Thus, if we had sizable Jewish settlement blocs, such as the Jordan Valley, the Etzion region south of Jerusalem, and the ridges in Samaria, those would be the places where we could maintain a military presence; and our troops there would not be regarded as foreign conquerors but as a defense element to safeguard Israel." (Dayan 304)

Dayan also had meetings with Arab dignitaries from the area to gauge their attitude toward an agreement with Israel. When he met Anwar al-Hatib, a local Arab dignitary, and they talked of the Israeli "settlements", Dayan told al-Hatib:

"We did not establish settlements at the expense of or in the place of Arab inhabitants, but alongside them. Could he cite a single case of Arabs having to leave their village, or suffer the slightest damage to their source of livelihood, as a result of the rise of a nearby Jewish settlement? On the contrary, our settlement brought with it new sources of employment, development and economic growth." (Dayan 151)

"The Father of the Settlements" Ariel Sharon[6]

Ariel Sharon, a retired high-ranking officer in the Israeli military, was involved in Israeli wars from 1948 till 1973. In the 1973 Yom Kippur War, he was the general who led his troops to cross the Suez Canal and surround the entire Egyptian Third Army. The only thing that saved them was the cease-fire mandated by the UN.

For Ariel Sharon, the "settlements" were a product of geography and terrain. The attack on the coastal area, including Tel Aviv – that was bombed in 1967 – came from Judea and Samaria, the mountain ridge overlooking the coastal area where almost the entire Jewish-Israeli population is concentrated.

The question for Sharon was how to ensure that this high mountain ridge will never again be used to attack Israel, as it was used in 1967. He ruled out stationing military units there, as "military units can be in one place today, while tomorrow they can be moved somewhere else." For him, looking at the history of the Jewish "settlements" since the 1880s, "settlements could secure a claim to land." (403)

---

[6] Ariel Sharon with David Chanoff, "Warrior", Simon & Schuster, New York, 1989-2001

His policy included several considerations: to locate the right strategic places; no expropriation of productive Arab-owned land; to make sure that the land had not been cultivated for many years; and to determine if there was access, or if access was blocked by privately owned land (360, 361).

This was for the central mountain ridge. On the east (the Jordan River), Israel faced the Eastern Front, made of Jordan, Syria, Iraq, and Saudi Arabia. All four of these countries had taken part in the Israeli-Arab wars, in one way or another. Sharon, with his military view of the situation, counted the forces at their disposal: four thousand tanks, a thousand combat aircraft, and twenty-five divisions (357).

The Labor government, from 1967-1977, established Jewish towns, aka "settlements", in the Jordan Valley. By the time the Likud took over in 1977, ten years after the war, there were 25 "settlements" already on the ground along the Jordan River, the line that separated Jordan and Israel, east of Judea and Samaria (358).

For Sharon, this thin line of "settlements" by the actual border was not enough to guarantee strong control. He wanted to broaden the line of "settlements", and to position them on the eastern side of the mountain ridge, from the point where the terrain goes down sharply – descending close to four thousand feet within 10 miles. In addition, he wanted to establish three roads crossing the mountain ridge, from the Israeli coastal area to the Jordan River, to enable quick movement of the military in time of emergency; and to position Jewish "settlements" along these three roads, to guard the roads (358).

For Sharon, in his words, the "settlements" were to "insure that we would keep in our hands the vital strategic terrain and prevent any future possibility that it might fall into someone else's hands." He also said that there were two principles guiding him in setting up the "settlements": "to protect our population centers and to insure the right of Jews to live in historical Israel." (403, 367-368)

In summary, the "settlements" were designed as the Israeli defense plan to prevent a repetition of the 1967 attack from the east – i.e. from Jordan, east of the Jordan River. The plan was designed and carried out by a decorated high-ranking officer of the Israeli military, who used to go around with topographical maps, to show the terrain in three dimensions, and not just two dimensions, that can be quite misleading.

In fact, any traveler in the United States would see upon approaching a town or a city that they all have two common denominators: first, there is a source of water, usually a river (water = life); and second, the city will usually sprawl in a valley, with a mountain ridge to guard it from the wind.

On these two accounts – water and valley – the opposite is true of the Jewish towns, aka "settlements", in Judea and Samaria. Any traveler there would notice that these towns are positioned on the top of the highest mountain, exposed to the harsh environment around. The location of the town was not to guard the inhabitants or residents inside, but to guard the area all around. In Sharon's words – locating the most strategic points in the area. In a way, although the "settlement" is a civilian place, it has a military value, if hostilities would break out.

The second point, very visible to the eye, is that there is no water source close by. Water has to be brought to the top of the mountain. When the "settlements" started, there was no water, no electricity, and no other modern amenities. Water had to be brought by tankers, until pipes and pumps were installed to push the water to the top of the mountain.

The reality on the ground verifies what General Sharon said – the "settlements" were located with defense considerations as primary, and all the rest was relegated to the bottom of the list. In fact, General Sharon said in his book that the main problem they faced was to find people in this modern era who are willing to leave a comfortable life in the city or the suburbs and to move to a barren mountain and live there. Luckily, there was a group of people who could enlist the volunteers to serve as civilian guards in these outposts, turning gradually to villages, and some even into towns and cities.

The relative quiet of the areas of Judea and Samaria, compared to the Gaza Strip, is due to the existence of the "settlements". The "settlements" also served as starting points for military and security operations being executed all over the area, to make sure that there would be no rockets shot at Israel, as there are today from the Gaza Strip.

It is not that the Arab population is more peaceful in Judea and Samaria. The General Security Service puts out periodic reports of how many terrorist plots are prevented in each period of time, and the number is in the hundreds. Still, the area is "quiet".

Question: would the US give up the islands of Hawaii, or even further away – Guam – in exchange for security arrangements, such as 3 aircraft carriers in exchange for Hawaii, and one for Guam? Hawaii is 2000 miles from the California coast, while Judea and Samaria are right on the border of Israel, and adjacent to its major population centers.

The Defense Strategy of Israel

Without entering the issue of history, and rights to the land, one should understand that the "West Bank" is an integral part of the defense strategy of Israel.

Benjamin Netanyahu brings an interesting "round-table discussion" conducted with eight left-leaning former Israeli generals in the newspaper Haaretz in 1988.

[Note: the newspaper Haaretz is read by about 3% of the population in Israel. It is extremely virulently "anti-settlements", advocating strongly for the creation of a "Palestinian state". It is interesting to note that there is German money invested in the newspaper.]

All of these leftist generals were advocating the creation of a "Palestinian state"; however, each one of them also said that due to the terrain, Israel would need to maintain control, so that the military branch that each general came from, would be able to defend the country in case another war would break out. When the generals finished their points, the moderator of the conference summed it up:

> "All of you favor withdrawal, but the conditions are air space, early-warning stations, the right to hot pursuit, the Jordan River Valley, Israeli cantons .... What Arab partner would be willing to enter into negotiations at all with conditions like these??" (BenN 309)

Right after the end of hostilities of the Six-Day War, US Secretary of Defense Robert McNamara asked the Pentagon to produce a map that would outline the minimal territory Israel would need to keep under its control, "without regard to political forces." (BenN 290)

The map, based upon apolitical military planners of the US Department of Defense, includes most of the West Bank and all of the Golan Heights. The only area that the Pentagon thought Israel could afford not to annex was the eastern slope of Samaria, facing the Jordan River.   It should be noted that the eastern slope of the mountain ridge is uninhabitable, and it is not an area that even a 4-wheel drive can pass through. For defense purposes, the top of the mountain, before the slope starts to descend on the east, is the area to be fortified (BenN 290).

In essence, the Pentagon was no different from General Sharon, who based his defense plan upon the terrain, and use of "settlements" to hold the terrain.

Defense of Israel and Peace with the Palestinians

Netanyahu outlines in his book what a future peace agreement between Israel and the Palestinians should be. In essence, Israel cannot afford to compromise with its defense. In other words, Israel cannot give up the natural barrier of the mountain ridge that defends the Israeli population from a future attack coming from the eastern front – Jordan, Syria, Iraq, and even further away, Iran.

Defense consists of three factors: "…its military strength relative to that of the Arabs; the warning time it has to mobilize its forces; and the minimum space that its army requires to deploy in the face of potential threats." (BenN 283).

Since "space buys time", the last two points – warning time and strategic depth – are one and the same. The more distance the attackers must go through, the longer is the time available for the defense to organize (286-287).

The last two points – warning time, and the minimum space mandate that Israel would need in order to maintain "indispensable security zones" – require a buffer of 12 miles west of the Jordan River, an area going from the top of the mountain ridge and descending to the Jordan River. As for the western side of the mountain ridge, the one that overlooks the coastal area, where the overwhelming majority of the Israeli population resides, the buffer zone can be less that 12 miles, but at least several miles. Netanyahu compares these 12 miles of "strategic depth" to the 180 miles that NATO in Europe required to withstand the threat from the east (Russia) (BenN 341-342).

And if anyone suggests to Israel that a future "Palestinian state" would be demilitarized, Netanyahu has one very brief answer for it: "It cannot be sustained." (BenN 305)

Due to the "minuscule" size of Judea and Samaria, where strategic points and the population centers are intertwined, one needs to control the area "both militarily and politically" (BenN 310).

As for international guarantees for a future peace agreement with the "Palestinians", Netanyahu quotes Prime Minister Golda Meir who said, "By the time they come to save Israel, there won't be an Israel." (BenN 337)

Summary

If one takes into consideration the small size of the areas in discussion, and the fact that Israel has already faced in the past an attack from these same areas, and the need to maintain the natural barrier defending Israel, the conclusion is that to reach an agreement with the Arab inhabitants of these same areas – the "Palestinians" – an agreement that would give Israel security is practically impossible.

When Did Everything Start?

As we will see later, the world today concentrates on the Israeli-Palestinian conflict. But this is not how everything started. Netanyahu stresses the fact that if peace is ever to be achieved, it needs to be based upon truth. And Netanyahu in his book moved to set the facts straight (just like President Obama, who described himself as a "fact based person").

Netanyahu started by emphasizing that *"The Arabs do not hate the West because of Israel; they hate Israel because of the West."* (BenN 133) [Italics in the original.]

The Six-Day War in 1967 did not start due to a dispute over territory. At that time Jordan controlled all of Judea and Samaria (aka the "West Bank") and the Old City of Jerusalem; and Egypt controlled the Gaza Strip. The war started for the simple reason that the Arabs were attempting to annihilate and exterminate the State of Israel. Netanyahu quotes several Arab leaders, such as the Egyptian President who said on May 25, 1967, that "the problem before the Arab countries [is] how totally to exterminate the State of Israel for all time." The Iraqi President said on May 31, "Our goal is clear: to wipe Israel off the map." On June 4, a day before the war started, the Algerian President said, "The Arab struggle must lead to the liquidation of Israel", and on the day the war started, on June 5, Radio Damascus exhorted simply: "Throw them into the sea." (BenN 143)

But the conflict didn't start in 1967. Netanyahu quoted the secretary general of the Arab League, Azzam Pasha, who said in 1948, on the day that five Arab countries invaded the newborn country, "This will be a war of extermination and a momentous massacre which will be spoken of like the Mongolian massacres and the Crusades." (BenN 154)

Moreover, Netanyahu also quotes Arab sources telling the truth about the origin of the Palestinian refugees. The Jordanian newspaper Filastin in February 1949 wrote: "The Arab States encouraged the Palestine Arabs to leave their homes temporarily in order to be out of the way of the Arab invasion armies." In 1954 the Jordanian daily Al-Difaa quoted one of the "refugees": "The Arab governments told us: Get out so that we can get in. So we got out, but they did not get in." The Egyptian Akhbar al-Yom wrote in 1963, "May 15th arrived .... [O] n that very day the Mufti of Jerusalem appealed to the Arabs of Palestine to leave the country, because the Arab armies were about to enter and fight in their stead." (BenN 154)

And the conflict didn't even start only in 1948. It started a lot earlier, but I don't want to tire the reader too much. After all, we live in the present, and in the present there is an "Israeli-Palestinian conflict". But the truth is, it is an "Israeli-Arab" conflict.

Netanyahu quoted Yasser Arafat, the head of the PLO, saying, "The question of borders does not interest us. Palestine is only a small drop in the great Arab ocean. Our nation is the great Arab nation extending from the Atlantic to the Red Sea and beyond." Zuhair Mohsin, a member of the PLO executive, said, "There are no differences between Jordanians, Palestinians, Syrians and Lebanese. We are one people." In 1988 The PLO leader Abu Iyad said, "We also insist on confederation with Jordan because we are one and the same people." (BenN 158, 159)

Netanyahu showed that this tune was not only on the PLO side. It came from the Jordanian side as well. Crown Prince Hassan of Jordan said in 1970, "Palestine is Jordan, and Jordan is Palestine. There is one people and one land, with one history and one destiny." Arafat said at the UN in 1974, "Jordan is ours, Palestine is ours, and we shall build our national entity on the whole of this land." King Hussein of Jordan said in 1981, "The truth is that Jordan is Palestine and Palestine is Jordan." And in 1984, he told the Kuwaiti paper Al-Anba that "Jordan is Palestine .... Jordanians and Palestinians must ... realize that their fate is the same," and that "Jordan in itself is Palestine." (BenN 159).

Netanyahu also quoted the Syrian president Hafez Assad, who once told Yasser Arafat:

"You do not represent Palestine as much as we do. Never forget this one point: There is no such thing as a Palestinian people, there is no Palestinian entity, there is only Syria. You are an integral part of the Syrian people, Palestine is an integral part of Syria. Therefore it is we, the Syrian authorities, who are the true representatives of the Palestinian people." (BenN 104)

The bottom line is that if one really wants the truth, then the Arabs of the British mandate of Palestine are not seeking "self-determination", as they already have it in Jordan, as they themselves said. The campaign to get a new country called "Palestine" is only an attempt to force Israel to return to the "green line", the line that separated Israel from the Arab countries at the end of the 1948 War, the same hard-to-defend line that "invited" the Arabs to try again in 1967 (BenN 160-161).

[Note: if one listen to the Arabs very carefully, by the words they actually use, both in English and Arabic, one can realize that "self-determination" and "independence" do not show up in their language. They only want "Palestine". And if one wants to know what "Palestine" means to them, one only needs to go to any Arab school in Judea and Samaria under the "Palestinian Authority" that was established in 1993, and can see on the walls of all classrooms that their "Palestine" includes all of Israel as well.]

Israel is today a powerful country, with a very strong military. So how could a tiny country as "Palestine", living side by side with Israel, be such a mortal danger? Well, if such a country would be established 10 miles from the Tel Aviv seacoast (with the whole Tel Aviv metropolitan area inside those 10 miles), life in Israel would be next to impossible, as it was witnessed by many Israelis when Arafat started his terror war in 2000, killing thousands in Israel by exploding buses, restaurants, and more (BenN 256).

Summary

After being twice defeated, in 1948 and in 1967, the Arabs moved to use a different language. All of the Arab countries fighting one small country, with the objective of annihilating and exterminating it, did not sound very good for PR, at least not in the west. They had to change their tune. And the new tune, the new language, was the language of "self-determination".

Netanyahu summarizes it as follows: "That Palestinian demand for unbridled self-determination is not in itself a demand for greater freedom to insure Palestinian liberties, but a demand for the freedom to extinguish the liberty and life of the Jewish state." The issue, Netanyahu said, is "the persistent Arab refusal to recognize Israel within *any* boundaries." (BenN 162, 163) [Italics in original]

Anyone who reads the speeches that both Rabin and Arafat gave at the ceremony at the White House, when they signed the Oslo agreement, can observe clearly the difference in their approaches. While Rabin talked about the end of bloodshed, Arafat talked of "the peace of the brave".

At other times, Arafat referred to this "peace of the brave" as "the Peace of Saladin".   Netanyahu explains the meaning of it, as history explains it.

Saladin was the Arab military commander who signed a peace treaty with the Crusaders, as a tactical ruse to allow his people a break in the war, only to continue the war at a later time, when they got stronger, to be able to drive the Christians out of the Holy Land (BenN 133, 331).

In a speech Arafat gave at a mosque in Johannesburg, South Africa, on May 10, 1994, not long after the signing of the Oslo agreement, Arafat said:

"This agreement, I am not considering it more than the agreement which had been signed between our prophet Mohammed and Koraish, and you remember the Caliph Omar had refused this agreement and considered it a despicable truce."

The agreement that Arafat referred to was an agreement that Mohammed had signed with the Koraish tribe. He kept the agreement for two years, until he became strong enough to attack the Koraish and take over Mecca. In essence, what Arafat said was: I was weak and I had no choice but to go along with this "despicable" agreement. But all of you should know that when I will get stronger this agreement is meaningless.

Learning from history? – Hitler and Czechoslovakia

Netanyahu in his book makes a clear analogy between Judea and Samaria, and the Sudetenland of Czechoslovakia. Hitler coveted the Sudetenland of Czechoslovakia, and the Arabs covet Judea and Samaria.

Before the Second World War started, Hitler wanted to take over Czechoslovakia. There were two obstacles in Hitler's way: first, Czechoslovakia had a very strong military; and second, western Czechoslovakia, the Sudetenland area, was a very mountainous area – high mountains that the German military high command figured they would not be able to attack.

[Note: the Sudetenland area should remind the reader of the natural barrier that Israel has on the east – the mountain ridge of Judea and Samaria.]

Hitler figured that he needs a political solution, if the military one does not exist. He decided to take advantage of the fact that in the Sudetenland area there was a large German minority; and therefore, instead of attacking Czechoslovakia, he would promote "self-determination" for the Germans who live under Czechoslovakian "occupation".

Hitler and his propaganda machine started to drum out the card of "self-determination". It didn't take long, and the European countries agreed with Hitler, and pressured Czechoslovakia to give up the natural barrier between them and Germany.

After a long-term pressure, Czechoslovakia relented and gave up the Sudetenland area. And the rest is history.

Netanyahu labels "self-determination" as "the Achilles heel of the West". People in the US and other western countries easily identify with inalienable rights and national freedom, and therefore identify with the "Palestinians" of today. Just like the Europeans who identified with the Germans in Czechoslovakia (BenN 170-174).

The "Palestinian Principle"

Observation: Catalonia, a region in Spain, has its own culture and its own language. The majority of people in Catalonia voted for separation from Spain, and establishing their own independent country. Spain, a country that strongly supports the right of the "Palestinians" for "self-determination", moved quickly to violently crush the Catalonian movement, declaring it "illegal", and putting the leaders of this independence movement into prison. The top leader ran away, and is in exile in Belgium. Spain issued a "European Arrest Warrant" against him, but later dropped it, leaving only a national arrest warrant that prevents him from returning to Spain.

This is what Benjamin Netanyahu calls "The Palestinian Principle", which stands for the idea that any minority that does not want to be a minority does not have to be one. (BenN 163).

Personal experience: I had a class in Phoenix, where one of the students was a Hispanic American police chief. During one of the breaks, I told him that it is quite likely that once the Hispanics in the southwestern United States would reach a majority in any one state, they might demand to secede from the US. The police chief responded, "I am a third-generation American, and I am a very proud American, and I don't want to be anything else but American." I replied, "This is you, but the younger generations of Hispanics are militant, and pride is more important to them than convenience in life." The police chief was quiet for a little bit, absorbing what I said, and then he said, "You are right. The younger generation is more militant. They might call for it."

Netanyahu talks of this danger in his book (BenN 164).

The Civil War started when the southern states decided by popular vote among them to secede from the US and to create their own confederacy. The Union moved to crush them in a bloody war, that consumed more than all other casualties in all the other wars combined, including the First and Second World Wars. The fact is that the South wanted to use "The Palestinian Principle".

Netanyahu talks of the danger of "the Palestinian principle" not only as a danger to Israel, but a danger in general for many other countries that have minorities, and Netanyahu gives a long list of these countries and minorities. (BenN 166, 167)

The most visible minority in the Middle East is the Kurds, who are Muslims but not Arabs. They have their own culture and their own language. If the Kurds would be an independent country, they would constitute the largest country in the region – made of eastern Turkey, northern Syria, northwestern Iran, and northern Iraq.

Why not to advocate "self-determination" for the Kurds? Is it because it would upset Turkey, a member of NATO?

Two Types of Peace

According to Netanyahu, there are two kinds of peace. The first is between countries that have open borders, commerce, tourism, and more. Such a peace is between the US and Canada, for example. It is a peace between democratic countries. Although the west wants such a peace everywhere, Netanyahu comments that such a peace is nowhere to be seen anywhere else (BenN 259-260, 261, 262).

The reason is that such a peace can be achieved only between two democratic countries. When a country has an "internally enforced" peace, that same country would seek an external peace as well. Netanyahu gives the Falkland Islands as an example. The war started when Argentina was ruled by a military dictatorship. When Argentina returned to be democratic, it moved to negotiate with Britain to resolve the dispute. In summary, "democracies tend toward peace, while despotisms tend toward war." (BenN 262, 264)

Moving to discuss the Middle East, Netanyahu points out that no Arab country has democracy. No free elections, free press, civil rights, or the rule of law (BenN 269).

Instead of pressuring the Arab countries to democratize, the west does the opposite – focusing on Israel to criticize it for the way it deals with the violence on the streets in Arab neighborhoods, while Israel is "a democracy at war" (BenN 271).

Netanyahu gives the numbers of victims of violence in the Middle East. While the victims of the violence in the Israeli-Arab conflict were 70,000 over fifty years, the victims of violence in internal Arab wars were: the Egyptian invasion of Yemen – 250,000 dead; the Algerian civil war – one million dead; the Lebanese civil war – 150,000 dead; the Libyan incursion into Chad – 100,000 dead; the Sudanese civil war – at least half a million dead; and the Iran-Iraq War – one million dead.

The Arabs promote the idea that if the Israeli-Arab conflict would be solved, peace and tranquility will reign over the Middle East (BenN 115).

The bottom line, according to Netanyahu, is that one can achieve peace between Israel and the "Palestinians" only with "peace through strength" (BenN 272).

Dealing with US Pressure

At the time Benjamin Netanyahu wrote his book (1993), he was not in government. He updated his book in 2000, and by then he had already served as prime minister for three years, after winning the elections in mid-1996. So, at the time he wrote the book, the issue of US pressure on the Israeli government was not new to him. He faced it during the Bill Clinton administration.

He quoted Israelis who doubt if Israel can withstand US pressure. But the fact is, he stated, that it is "the basic purpose of foreign policy for any country – to pursue one's own interests, not those of others." (BenN 388)

Even if there is US governmental pressure, all is not lost. Netanyahu analyzes the centers of power in the US, of which there are three: the administration, the Congress, and especially popular opinion. Netanyahu said that the US attitude towards Israel is a "synthesis" of these three centers of power (BenN 388).

This should remind us of what UK Prime Minister David Cameron said in his book, that although President Obama wanted to pressure Israel, it "was rejected by Congress" (DavCam 534).

Netanyahu is aware that there are people who are against "activist opposition to the policies dangerous to Israel that may come out of Washington", but Israel should not sacrifice its own interests just to be nice (BenN 388).

Netanyahu on Himself

Netanyahu in his book labels himself as having an "unabashed and passionate partisanship in seeking to assure the Jewish future." (BenN xi) He realized that he became the "new villain" when it comes to the Middle East – that all evil that comes out of the Middle East, including radicalism and fundamentalism, is attributed to one person: himself. He knows that his critics say that if he were less "obstructionist" then the Middle East would reach a state of nirvana (BenN 322).

To counter this claim, Netanyahu says that it is possible to reach peace, but this is not the issue. The question is: can one reach a "durable peace" (the title of his book)? For such a peace, one needs to base everything upon security and justice, and most importantly, upon truth. Throughout the book, Netanyahu shows that truth is absent from all the claims against Israel (BenN 321-322).

US Administration People on Benjamin Netanyahu

Introduction

Benjamin Netanyahu won the elections of 1996, after the Labor party preceding him signed the Oslo agreement that brought Arafat from Tunisia into the center of the country. Netanyahu was strongly against the Oslo agreement. At the same time, he promised before the elections, that he would not negate previous commitments made by previous governments. Therefore, throughout his three years as prime minister, he went along with the so-called "peace process" that produced a lot of terrorism in the country, even though he objected to it. His solution was to keep the accords to the letter, and require the "Palestinian Authority" to fulfill their obligations.

Two of the people from the US administration who dealt with Netanyahu during his leadership were Dennis Ross, the US envoy to the Israeli-Palestinian "peace process", and Secretary of State Madeline Albright.

Madeline Albright on Netanyahu

Since Netanyahu had previously spent years in the United States (he graduated from MIT in economics), he spoke "idiomatic English with no noticeable accent", to the point that she had to remind herself that she is not talking with an American. She saw Netanyahu as "pugnacious, partisan, and very smooth", reminding her of the Republican Speaker of the House Newt Gingrich. (She was not the only one to make this connection.) Netanyahu, according to her, could be "both disarming and somewhat disingenuous". At times, she believed that she had reached an agreement with him, only to find out that it was not his intention to reach any agreement. (After all, he was against the entire process to start with.) (Albright 375)

Correctly, she said that when Netanyahu felt "trapped", he called for new elections in 1999, in which he was defeated (Albright 602).

Dennis Ross on Netanyahu

Ross admits that the US received the news of Netanyahu's election with "collective dread" (Ross 258). After all, it was no secret that he was against the process.

And sure enough, "Netanyahu was not willing to concede anything." The funny point is that Ross accused Netanyahu, a prime minister elected in free, democratic elections, of going according to his political base instead of the "needs of the process" (Ross 267, 324, 331, 367, 492).

Henry Kissinger said once that Israel does not have a foreign policy. Israel has only domestic policy, and everything else is secondary. This is true, but at the same time it is true of the US as well, and of any other free, democratic country.

As for Netanyahu's personality, Ross labeled him as very intelligent, and that Netanyahu saw himself in "historic, grandiose terms". When he was "agitated", he spoke "a mile a minute" (Ross 337, 339, 347).

Ross summarized the three years of Netanyahu's term as prime minister, that for Netanyahu "the deal really was land for security, not land for peace" – just as he had written in his book. Ross also correctly described Netanyahu as "a leader who had two legs walking in different directions" (Ross 399, 493).

The problem the Americans were facing with Netanyahu was that he didn't have a "design" for the process. I wonder if it is criticism at all, taking into consideration that Netanyahu didn't want the process to start with, and he only went along due to politics (Ross 339).

Book Review – "A Problem from Hell: America and the Age of Genocide" by Samantha Power[7]

Introduction

In November 2004, Samantha Power sent Senator Obama an inscribed copy of her book, "A Problem from Hell". This brought Senator Obama to call her and to set a meeting with her, resulting later in her working for him. She also helped him to edit his book, "The Audacity of Hope".

Samantha Power served throughout the eight years of the Obama administration – in the NSA during Obama's first term, and as US ambassador to the UN in his second term.

I didn't plan to read Power's book "A Problem from Hell". I had embarked on a search of books written by people who worked closely with President Obama, with the goal of finding out how he was perceived by the people who were close to him. In reading Samantha Power's autobiography, "The Education of an Idealist", I was struck by one huge omission in her book.

Power mentioned Israel very sporadically in her account of the four years when she was US ambassador to the UN. One should note that 50% of the decisions of any UN organization are devoted to condemning Israel in one way or another. To mention Israel only as a side remark would be to dismiss 50% of UN activity.

One only needs to compare Power's book to the one written by Susan Rice, who preceded Power as US ambassador to the UN for four years, and the book by Nikki Haley, who was US ambassador to the UN for two years under the Trump administration. Both Rice and Haley wrote extensively on the UN preoccupation with Israel.

This brought me to read and study Power's book, "A Problem from Hell".

---

[7] Basic Books, 2002, 2003, 2007, 2013

Background information

It is not simple for any historian to write history. At which point would the historian start his/her account of what happened? For example, in relating to the short Israeli history, what was the time that the Six Day War started? Was it on June 5, 1967, when Israel started its preemptive military campaign? Was it in April of that year, when there was an air battle over northern Israel, in which the Israeli air force shot down several Syrian fighter planes? Or, was it the Arab campaign that tried to prevent Israel from using the water of the Sea of Galilee? This campaign went on for quite a while, and caused several battles on that front. Or, was it in 1949, at the end of Israel's War of Independence, when ceasefire agreements were signed by Israel and several Arab countries (Iraq didn't sign), and left Israel with indefensible borders? An American journalist who covered the war in 1948, predicted in his book that it is only a matter of time until Israel will "complete" the unfinished war and reach the Jordan River.

The Armenian Genocide and the Holocaust

Power starts her book with a very long chapter dealing with the Turkish campaign against the Armenians during the First World War. An estimated one and a half million Armenians were killed. There is plenty of evidence that the Turks' intent was to annihilate the Armenians. Some of the Turks even boasted about it in the open.

Power writes in her book that Hitler commented on the world's silence about what happened to the Armenians, as a claim that he can do the same to the Jews during the Second World War, and still the world would be silent. It is sad to note that on this account Hitler was right. The world was silent during the Holocaust, in which 6 million Jews were killed.

The Holocaust

After describing in very minute details what the Turks did to the Armenians, Power moved on to describe the Holocaust. But something is missing from her book.

In her list of contents, the first chapter is "Race Murder" (relating to the Turkish-Armenian tragedy), moving on to "A Crime without a Name", and on to "A Crime with a Name", and to "Lemkin's Law". (Lemkin was a Jewish attorney who coined the word "genocide".) These three chapters related to the Holocaust committed by Nazi Germany against European Jewry. She didn't label the first chapter "Turkey" or "The Ottoman Empire" for the Armenian tragedy, and she didn't label the three chapters dealing with the Holocaust by the country name: "Germany" or "Nazi Germany".

She started naming countries in chapter 6, with Cambodia. And then on to Iraq, Bosnia, Rwanda, Srebrenica, Kosovo, and ending with the last chapter "Lemkin's Courtroom Legacy".

Why the lack of consistency in labeling the chapters? Why there are no chapters that are labeled "Turkey" or "Nazi Germany"? Are we facing here negligence, or are we are facing a bias of the author?

Cambodia

Two million people were killed in Cambodia after the extremist Khmer Rouge (KR) took over. The KR embarked on a campaign of social surgery and rehabilitation. They moved to abolish the middle class, and bring collectivization into the country. In their campaign, they emptied the big city of Phnom Penh of its population, and moved the people into the country, where they established concentration camps to put the people in. Due to the collectivization process, food was scarce, and starvation ruled. In this cruel process two million died.

We should ask what Power did not mention. If she called the KR brutal rule over Cambodia "genocide", why didn't she mention the collectivization process in the Soviet Union during Stalin's rule, in which an estimated 40 million people died of starvation? Why to mention the concentration camps in Cambodia, and to dismiss the entire Gulag in Siberia, in which concentration camps were all over the map? Moreover, there were reports that prisoners in the Gulag were forced to work in uranium mines with their bare hands, guaranteeing a slow death to all of them. Actually, Stalin killed more of his own people than Hitler killed during the entire Second World War. And Stalin is hardly mentioned in Power's book.

Not only Stalin is missing. What about the process in Zimbabwe in which the whites were driven out, and the food basket of the southern part of the African continent became desolate? Starvation was rampant; many people died, and many fled out of the country, mostly to South Africa.

What about the collectivization that went on in Venezuela, that brought starvation into the country to a point that people are dying due to lack of food and medicine?

Why to single out one country, Cambodia, and at the same time to ignore other countries in which the same brutal process was enacted, and dismiss these countries altogether?

"A problem from Hell"? Yes!!! But Power singles out Cambodia, and dismisses the 20 times more powerful and vicious attack of Stalin against his own people. Two million in Cambodia vs. 40 million in the Soviet Union.

Iraq, Rwanda, and the Balkans

After Cambodia, Power goes on to describe massacres in Iraq, Bosnia, Rwanda, Srebrenica, and Kosovo. But while she describes the massacres in detail, she does not give any background information to give the reader a more complete picture.

The fact is that the examples of Iraq, Bosnia and Rwanda are examples of two parties to an armed conflict, and the bloodshed reported in Power's book is just the most recent part of this conflict. In each case, the war between the two groups goes back for decades and even generations, with mutual bloodshed on both sides. Focusing on the most recent massacre, while ignoring all those that preceded it, omits an important part of the history of the conflict.

The Nazi extermination of the Jews was different from the other massacres described in Power's book. The Jews were loyal citizens in Germany and other countries. The Nazis used the pretext of the war to kill a group of bystanders, people who were not even a party to the conflict. This distinction is missing from Power's book.

Epilogue

Samantha Power in her book "A Problem from Hell" compared the Holocaust to other massacres committed in other parts of the globe. But her book merges oranges with apples. Her book does not stand the scrutiny of any objective reader.

In President Obama's address in Cairo to the Muslim world, he said:

> Around the world, the Jewish people were persecuted for centuries, and anti-Semitism in Europe culminated in an unprecedented Holocaust. Tomorrow, I will visit Buchenwald, which was part of a network of camps where Jews were enslaved, tortured, shot and gassed to death by the Third Reich. Six million Jews were killed – more than the entire Jewish population of Israel today. Denying that fact is baseless, ignorant, and hateful. Threatening Israel with destruction – or repeating vile stereotypes about Jews – is deeply wrong, and only serves to evoke in the minds of Israelis this most painful of memories while preventing the peace that the people of this region deserve.

The Israeli ambassador to the US during the Obama administration, Michael Oren, was upset that President Obama linked the Holocaust to Israeli legitimacy (MicOr 65-66). In fact, President Obama did so. But Oren has no reason to complain. Any dignitary who visits Israel is expected to visit the Holocaust memorial, as if this were the reason for Israel's existence. Instead of requiring a visiting dignitary to visit the cradle of Jewish culture, the Cave of the Patriarchs in Hebron (located south of Jerusalem in Judea, aka "the West Bank"), or the Shrine of the Book at the Israel Museum, which houses two-thousand-year-old Hebrew manuscripts from the Dead Sea Scrolls, the secular Israeli government prefers to put the Holocaust memorial on the list of locations to visit.

Israel was not established because of the Holocaust. After the First World War, the League of Nations gave the British government a mandate, or assignment, to rule over the Land of Israel, aka "Palestine", with the objective of re-establishing a homeland for the Jewish people. This was years before the Holocaust, and even at that time there were a significant number of Jews and Jewish towns in Israel. Jerusalem had a Jewish majority already in the mid-19th century.

Part of the instructions of the League of Nations were that the British should encourage settlement by Jews in Palestine. But instead, starting in 1939, the British prevented Jews from entering, thus making it impossible for them to flee the Holocaust. The Holocaust is not the reason for Israel's establishment, but lack of an independent Israel is one of the main reasons that the Holocaust occurred.

Personally, I don't feel that Jews should visit Auschwitz or any other concentration camps. Jews do not need to be reminded of their tragedies. They are aware of them. The ones who need to be reminded are the nations who killed the Jews during history, and first among them is Germany.

When in the 1980s I taught my class to the American military in Germany, my hosts insisted that I should visit the concentration camp in Dachau, close to the location of the class in Munich. I didn't want to go, but they insisted, so I went. The only thing that went through my mind during the visit was that I am lucky to have been born after Israeli independence, at a time that Israel is in charge of its own security. Lucky me!

Summary

Samantha Power's view of events freezes the video of an event to a still picture. It is a journalistic approach to world events: describing what is going on right now, without taking into consideration that maybe some previous events might have caused the events in the present.

Generally speaking, it is recommendable for people to live in the present. But nobody said that living in the present means to forget the past. For Samantha Power, the past does not exist.

Since she worked closely with Senator and later President Obama, it is a point to realize what happens when two leaders meet to discuss an issue – one who is restricting himself to the present, and the other lives in the present, but does not forget the past. This clash of views will produce fireworks.

President Obama and Israel

1. Do American diplomats really know Israel?

2. Israel – US Defense Relationship

3. Candidate Obama and Israel

4. President Obama and Israel

5. President Obama – Israel's Friend

6. The Iran Deal

Do American Diplomats Really Know Israel?

Introduction

President Jimmy Carter, in his book "The Blood of Abraham"[8], described a meeting he and his wife had with Prime Minister Golda Meir when they visited Israel. The meeting was on Friday, and they were having "an extended talk". Meir noticed that Carter was bothered by something, and she asked him what was on his mind. He responded that it was something of a "religious nature". She encouraged him to go on, and he told her that during Sabbath services at the kibbutz Ayelet Hashahar, there was no interest among the members in religious services. He added that during Biblical times, the Israelites triumphed "when they were close to God and were defeated when unfaithful."

Meir laughed and she agreed with him, but she told him that he should not be concerned because there are enough religious people ("Orthodox") in Israel. Carter wrote that they were "a real thorn in her side" (Carter 27-28).

Is this the reason that Carter wrote afterwards in his book that "Israel cannot reconstruct the Kingdom of David"? (Carter 191)

In 2006, President Jimmy Carter published another book, titled "Palestine: Peace Not Apartheid"[9]. Once the book was out for sale, Jewish groups in the US openly accused Carter of being anti-Semitic. Carter was genuinely surprised. How can it be? The most he did in his book was to quote what the Israeli pro-Arab left was saying, not just in content, but also in language.

Anyone who reads the daily newspaper "Haaretz" ("The Land" in Hebrew) would see the same content and language all over its editorial and news items. There are people on the rightwing side of the political divide who refer to "Haaretz" as "Al-Bilad" ("The Land" in Arabic).

Moreover, the idea that Israel is establishing "apartheid" in Judea and Samaria is an invention of Israeli academics. There are even professors

---

[8] Jimmy Carter, "The Blood of Abraham: Insights into the Middle East", The University of Arkansas Press, 1993
[9] Simon and Schuster, New York.

in universities in Israel who are openly calling on foreign universities to boycott their own universities. They even support the "BDS" (boycott, divestment, and sanctions) movement that operates against Israel in many countries.

If so, why would Carter be labeled as anti-Semitic, if he only quoted Israeli Jews who say the same?

The problem is that President Carter met a very distinct component of the Israeli community, and according to statistics, it is not very representative of the Israeli Jewish population.

Israeli Population – Statistics

If a poll would be conducted in Israel asking people if they are religious or not, only around 30% would describe themselves as "religious". However, if one looks at the two most distinct Jewish observance – observance of the Sabbath, and eating kosher food – around 60% of the Jewish population would answer in the affirmative. For them, keeping the Sabbath and eating kosher food is not "religion". It is "family".

There are other statistics. Among Israeli Jews, 99% circumcise their baby boys on the eighth day after birth, as Jewish law requires. And 93% have a family "seder" (the festive meal on Passover eve, including a ceremonial reading of the story of the exodus from Egypt). They don't consider it "religion". It is a "family holiday".

Many years ago, the Saudi king was quoted in the news media saying that time is against the Arabs. The reason, he said, was the fact that Israel is moving more and more into religion, and therefore the population is more attached to the "territories" (Judea and Samaria) to the point that it would prevent any "peace" agreement in the future, at least not an agreement based upon the "two state solution".

It takes a Saudi king to read Israel correctly.

Jewish Self-hatred – Case Study

In his book "The Audacity of Hope", Senator Obama described his first visit to Israel. He said that he took a helicopter flight over Judea and

Samaria, and he could not distinguish Jewish towns from Arab towns. All of them looked to him "like fragile outposts against the green and stony hills" (BO AOH 322).

On the other hand, Ben Rhodes, who accompanied President Obama for eight years, and joined him on his presidential trip to Israel, gave a very different description of the area:

"I looked out at rolling hills and could see where Israeli settlements were splitting the West Bank in two. We were in the air for less than ten minutes, but the contrast could not have been starker: Israel from the air resembles southern Europe; the settlements looked like subdivisions in the Nevada desert; the Palestinian towns looked shabby and choked off." (BenR 201)

Which description is accurate? The description of Senator Obama, who couldn't distinguish between the two? Or, maybe the one seeing such a striking difference between Jewish and Arab towns, a description that Ben Rhodes gave?

We need to know who is Ben Rhodes to understand the difference in description.

Rhodes said that when Rahm Emanuel got tired of Rhodes's arguing that President Obama should show more sympathy to the Palestinians, Emanuel gave him a nickname – "Hamas". One should know that "Hamas" is the Muslim "violent extremist" (in Obama's language; or "terrorist" in Israel's language) organization that rules the Gaza Strip and launches rockets attacks against the Israeli civilian communities surrounding the Gaza Strip. To call someone "Hamas" is to label someone as the worst enemy of Israel (BenR 57).

Rhodes quotes a conversation with President Obama in which Rhodes labeled himself, saying, "I know, I'm the self-hating Jew. Or half self-hating."

Why only "half self-hating"? He explains it in another place in his book. His mother's family consisted of secular Jews living in New York. His father was not Jewish. That's why he said that when he worked on President Obama's speech to be given in Israel, he felt "a bit like a bystander, aware of my own half heritage, neither full Jew nor non-Jew." (BenR 146, 201)

How can it be that a Jewish person would be anti-Semitic, or in other words, having self-hatred? The anthropologist Raphael Patai in his book "The Jewish Mind" [recommended reading] related to this phenomenon. It is present in every minority group that lives with a large majority surrounding it.

The fact is that in early times, Senator Obama's description of the Jewish towns in Judea and Samaria was very unemotional and detached. It was not so later on, during his presidency. Something happened in between these two points. What happened?

Israel – US Defense Relationship

Personal Experience: I had a class in Qatar, a small Arab country on the Persian/Arab Gulf. The class was given at a branch of a Canadian university that was contracted to bring its expertise so young Arabs from Qatar would have access to a high-quality higher education.

Upon arrival I was assigned an entire house for my accommodation, for the duration of the days I was scheduled to be there. I was amazed at the vast empty spaces inside the house.

There was one "tiny" problem. The faucet in the bathtub and the shower was not working. I reported it the next morning to the secretary of the section where the class was held, a Canadian lady, who wrote down the problem, and promised me that it will be taken care of right away. But on the evening of that day, the problem persisted. When the secretary asked me the next morning if everything is now to my satisfaction, I had to disappoint her and say that the problem is still there. And so it was every single day.

This experience opened my eyes to the problem of maintenance in the Arab world. True, it is only anecdotal evidence, just one example. But I told myself, if such a small problem of plumbing cannot be fixed within a day, it has to be meaningful.

"Armies of Sand"

It appeared to be anecdotal evidence in my mind until I read the book "Armies of Sand"[10] by Kenneth M. Pollack, which was recommended to me by someone in Israel who is involved in security issues. Not only did I read the book, but I actually "studied" it. It is a "must-read book" for anyone in Israel or in the US dealing with the strategic defense alliance between the two countries.

Pollack, in his words, was in his earlier years a "young military analyst at CIA". He stated that the book was screened both by the CIA and the DIA prior to publication, and it got approval that it does not contain any classified material. These two agencies did not even ask to take anything

---

[10] Oxford University Press, 2019

out, or to edit anything. They found the material in the book to be "open" (xiii).

"An early manuscript version of this work was reviewed by both the Central Intelligence Agency and the Defense Intelligence Agency prior to publication to ensure that it contained no classified material. Neither agency altered the text in any way." (xvi)

There are many issues discussed in the book, including cultural, psychological, and military aspects. In this discussion I would like to relate to only two points – maintenance and performance.

Maintenance

In all Arab air forces there are "low sortie rates". This means that each fighter plane can only fly one sortie a day, due to poor performance of ground crews. This is not just a historical problem, as the Saudi Air Force faced this problem when they started their war in Yemen in 2015 (Pollack 35).

Most of the Arab armed forces had a poor track record of keeping their weapons, vehicles, and other equipment up and running. (Pollack 35)

Pollack said that the Egyptian Air Force cancelled the US maintenance of their US-built fighter planes, and as a result, it didn't take long for the aircraft to become "non-operational". The reason was that there is no emphasis on "preventive maintenance", and due to "poor repair capabilities" (Pollack 70, 244).

This problem is not restricted only to Egypt, or only to planes. The same applies to any weapon system, such as tanks, and by any other Arab country, such as Syria. Pollack said that during a battle, if a tank would malfunction, they need to pull it out from the battlefield to move it back to a "small number of central depots around Damascus" manned by Cuban mechanics (Pollack 271).

[Note: Here comes a not-very-well-known fact into the open. Cuba had an active part in the war against Israel.]

This does not mean that the Cubans were exceptional mechanics. Pollack said that they were "not outstanding", but they performed better than their Arab counterparts (Pollack 334).

Pollack summarized this problem by saying that this poor maintenance had a major impact on the Arab militaries' "operational readiness", and that's why they showed poor performance (Pollack 401).

Poor Performance

Maintenance was not the only problem. The other problem in combination with "poor maintenance" was also "poor performance".

Pollack gives the numbers to show that the Arab air forces could not maintain a ratio of one pilot per one aircraft. This means that in Egypt in 1956, they had 30 pilots for 120 MIGs, a ratio of 1:4. In 1973, Libya had 25 pilots for 110 Mirages, and in 1978 they had 150 pilots for 550 aircraft.

Pollack shows that the same poor ratio was not restricted only to aircraft but also to tanks and armored vehicles (Pollack 29).

In 1973, the Israeli air force faced the problem of the massive anti-aircraft missiles that the Egyptians deployed on the banks of the Suez Canal. However, Pollack gives the ratio of missiles deployed vs. aircraft downed – an average of 40 SAM and 150 SA-7 missiles were used per aircraft downed (when the Russians estimated it would take only 5-10); and an average of 0.006-0.0075 aircraft downed per sortie. Pollack even exposed that the Egyptians shot down between 45 and 60 of their own aircraft (Pollack 140).

During the 1973 Yom Kippur war there 52 major dogfights between the Israeli and the Egyptian aircraft, in which the Egyptians shot down 5-8 Israeli aircraft, while Israel shot down 172 Egyptian aircraft (Pollack 141).

People in Israel thought that the Egyptian military would be better in 1973 than in 1967, but Pollack said that the kill ratio in 1967 was 1:7 in favor of Israel while in 1973 it went down to 1:25 (Pollack 141).

In the Lebanon war in 1982, the kill ratio was labeled by Pollack as "a slaughter". Israel shot down 82 Syrian aircraft without losing even one (Pollack 263).

Former Secretary of Defense Robert Gates describes in his book a conversation he had with Israeli Prime Minister Netanyahu, who came to discuss the upcoming sale of sophisticated aircraft to Saudi Arabia. Among other questions that Gates asked Netanyahu was: "How long would those planes continue to work without U.S. support?" (RobG 397).

Gates was aware that selling the aircraft to Saudi Arabia is meaningless if the Saudis would be the ones to maintain the planes.

Nobody asked the question, but I will present it here: over the years, Saudi Arabia purchased hundreds of billions of dollars' worth of sophisticated weaponry, including aircraft as well. In the early eighties, when President Reagan approved the sale of four AWACS surveillance planes to Saudi Arabia, there was a major fight in Congress to block the sale. The fight was defeated and the sale was approved.

If so, when Saddam Hussein invaded Kuwait in 1991, and the Saudis were afraid that Saddam is on his way to invade Saudi Arabia as well, why did they need the US to do the job, while all the sophisticated weaponry was idle on the ground? The same question can be asked of the Saudi campaign in Yemen that started in 2015, with no results to show for it.

"Qualitative Military Edge" (QME)

When US Defense Secretary Robert Gates describes in his book the objection of Israeli government officials regarding the sale of sophisticated aircraft to the Saudis, Gates brings up the concept of "Qualitative Military Edge" (QME) (RobG 396).

Since the United States is selling weaponry to both Israel and its adversaries in the Arab world, there is an understanding between Israel and the US that the US will maintain Israel's QME – i.e., that Israel will always maintain an advantage of sophistication in terms of weaponry.

[Note: in his counter claim, Gates says, "I also pointed out that not once in all of Israel's wars had Saudi Arabia fired a shot." Although technically it is a true statement, it is very misleading. It is a fact that Saudi Arabia sent two battalions to Syria to take part in the 1973 war. They might not have fired any shots, but just their presence was enough to raise the morale of the Syrians, and in this way to assist them in their war against Israel. Moreover, Prince Bandar, who was the Saudi ambassador to the US from 1983 to 2005, wrote in his book that during the 1973 war he was a pilot in the Saudi air force, and they were already on the planes ready to go out to attack Eilat on the southern point of Israel, only to find that their mission was cancelled at the last minute. Bandar was so relieved, since he realized that to attack Israel was a one-way mission, and in his words, a suicide mission.]

Israel-Arab Ratio of Weaponry

Knowing the above, should Israel relate to the accumulation of sophisticated weaponry in Arab militaries as a threat to its defense?

The US sold to both Israel and Egypt around 600 F-15 and F-16 fighter planes. Does it mean that Israel has parity in fighter planes with Egypt? If maintenance is an issue, the most the Egyptian Air Force has is 150 planes in reality, if even that number. And if a fighter plane can do only one sortie a day, while the same aircraft in Israel can do many sorties a day, then what would be real ratio between the two air forces?

The Sale of F-35s to Israel – Case Study

When the US defense industry completed the development of the new aircraft, Israel got an "invitation" to order this aircraft for its arsenal.

The newspapers in Israel reported that the Foreign Affairs and Defense Committee of the Knesset (Parliament) established a special sub-committee to look into the idea of whether Israel even needs such a sophisticated plane. The sub-committee concluded that there is no real need for this new aircraft, as Israel on its own is refurbishing the "old" F-15 and F-16 planes to lengthen their actual life by many more years. However, how can one refuse such an "invitation", especially when it is understood that the plane would be purchased by the annual defense aid that the US gives Israel each year. Therefore, the sub-committee concluded that Israel should "order" 12 of these new aircraft.

The Americans were upset with this decision. According to them, 12 will not be a meaningful number to actually operate the plane. They suggested that Israel would "order" 30 of this new aircraft. Eventually, the number went up to 50.

In fact, the newspapers in Israel are reporting that fighter pilots have the highest accolades for this new aircraft that takes their operations to such a higher level, that they could not believe it that it was even possible.

But the fact is: it is a simple "overkill". It is totally unnecessary in the existing environment, and this is not my conclusion, but the conclusion of the experts of that sub-committee.

The Annual US Defense Aid to Israel

In 2016, President Obama signed a memorandum allocating a budget of 3.8 billion US dollars per year for the next ten years, for Israel to purchase weapons, mainly fighter planes.

Due to the development of the "Iron Dome" system that can shoot down rockets shot at Israel, some of the money is given to Israel in cash to pay for these systems.

[Note: when Israel came up with the idea of developing such a system, the US Defense Department sent a delegation of experts to Israel to check the feasibility of developing it. The conclusion of the US experts was that it would take Israel 15 years to develop such a system. Instead, they suggested that Israel should purchase an existing US system. Israel declined and it took 3 (three) years to have the system operational.]

In essence, the US annual defense aid to Israel is actually a subsidy that the US federal government gives the US defense industry.

In effect, it corrupts the decision-making process of the Israeli military High Command. If you get something for free, why use brains? If the US offers sophisticated planes, why refuse them, even if you don't really need them?

Moreover, there was a time when Israel was working on development of its own fighter plane. The research and development had already been done, and the project had almost reached the manufacturing stage. But there was a lot of pressure from Israeli and US lobbyists to cancel the project. Why to develop such a plane, if it can be "purchased" for free from the US? Eventually Prime Minister Rabin decided to cancel the project.

It was a major blow to the Israeli defense industry, and to all the engineers who had been employed by the project. Many of them left the country to work for foreigners. Not to mention that the development of a fighter plane in a small and threatened country like Israel also has political implications. Once you establish dependency on a foreign country, your own decision-making is limited.

In recent years, natural gas deposits were found in the Mediterranean Sea close to Israel. Israel became a net exporter of energy to Egypt and Jordan, and there are now discussions of setting up a pipeline to move the natural gas to Europe.

This means that if several years ago the annual US defense aid was less than 2 percent of the Israeli government annual budget, it is even much less today. The bottom line is: Israel can easily pay for what Israel finds to be necessary, and not to be asked to "purchase" what it doesn't need.

There are many people in Israel, and I am among them, who call to approach the US and to give up this annual aid. There was a time in which Prime Minister Netanyahu talked of this idea openly. It didn't take long, and he "forgot" this idea altogether.

As the saying goes: "The cow wants to suckle more than calf wants to drink."

Candidate Obama and Israel

Introduction

We can divide the way Barack Obama related to Israel into two periods of time: the era before he became president, and during the eights years of his presidency.

Senator Obama

Before he announced his decision to run for president, Senator Obama combined a tour in Baghdad with a tour in Israel. He related to this tour in his book "The Audacity of Hope".

He talked with people from both sides of the conflict, and he mapped in his mind the place that has so much "strife". He concluded by saying that he "…pondered the possible futility of believing that this conflict might somehow end in our time, or that America, for all its power, might have any lasting say over the course of the world." (BO AOH 322)

Two points should be noted in his description: one is language and the other is content.

Language

Obama said:

"I talked to Jews who'd lost parents in the Holocaust and brothers in suicide bombings; I heard Palestinians talk of the indignities of checkpoints and reminisce about the land they had lost." (BO AOH 322)

Please note the following:

1. With the Jews he **talked**, while he **heard** the Palestinians talking.

   As we already learned of Obama, the characteristic of "listening" is very important to him. He did listen to the Palestinians (he "heard" them) while he didn't listen to the Jews.

2. He did not use the same equivalent language for the two sides. Either one says "Israelis" and "Palestinians", or "Jews" and "Arabs". But he related to the Israelis via the religion, while he related to the Arabs via their newly claimed nationality – "Palestinians".

He also said:

"I flew by helicopter across the line separating the two peoples and found myself unable to distinguish Jewish towns from Arab towns..." (BO AOH 322).

Note that, again, he talked of "Jewish" and not "Israeli", while now he used "Arabs" and not "Palestinians".

In summary, Senator Obama in both quotes avoided using the word "Israelis".

Content

"I talked to Jews who'd lost parents in the Holocaust and brothers in suicide bombings; I heard Palestinians talk of the indignities of checkpoints and reminisce about the land they had lost."

Please note the following:

1. Senator Obama equated the suicide bombings, and the Israeli response to the suicide bombings – "indignities of checkpoints". It is actually the view of the Arab side of the political divide.

   Checkpoints started only after buses and coffee shops and restaurants started going up in the air. There were no "checkpoints" before the mass murder started in the area.

   And how is it possible to equate "the indignities of checkpoints" to actual deaths? (Note, by the way, that not only Arabs need to go through checkpoints. Everyone, Jewish and Arab, must go through a checkpoint and have their bags examined at the entrance to every supermarket and mall.)

2. People didn't lose only "brothers" in suicide bombings. Suicide bombings killed old people, women, and babies. No one was spared.

   The description Senator Obama gave, in a way, diminished the gruesome pictures of what happened on the streets.

Summary

On two accounts, both language and content, Senator Obama showed a slight leaning to the Palestinian side.

Second Visit to Israel

In July 2008, now-candidate Obama visited Israel. It was during a multi-country trip that Obama made during the campaign, with the objective of raising his status in foreign affairs. The campaign team suggested visiting Iraq, Israel, Germany, and Britain. Obama insisted on adding France as well (DavPl 271, 272).

Eventually, the highlight of the trip was the speech that candidate Obama gave in Berlin, Germany, a speech that invoked memories of the speech President Kennedy had given there in 1963. That speech raised the candidate Obama to the status of celebrity.

The stop in Israel, according to Plouffe, was meant to show Obama's commitment to Israel, and to emphasize his intent to seek peace between Israel and the Palestinians (DavPl 272).

During the short visit, Obama met Prime Minister Benjamin Netanyahu, and President Shimon Peres.

[Note: the position of "president" in Israel is not equivalent to the US president. The Israeli president is a figurehead, equivalent to the Queen of England. The center of political power is in the prime minister.]

This was not the first time Obama met Netanyahu.

In March 2007, Benjamin Netanyahu, a former Prime Minister and at the time a Knesset member from the opposition, gave a speech in

Washington DC, to the annual convention of the Israeli lobby in Congress – AIPAC. Obama requested to meet Netanyahu, and they met before Netanyahu departed Washington DC.

Obama told Netanyahu that it was important for him to meet the well-known Israeli politician, and Obama asked for a picture of them together, a picture that he used later on during the primaries, to help Obama defeat Clinton. Netanyahu shared with Obama the security issues that Israel faces. Netanyahu was impressed by the knowledge Obama exhibited. To his assistants, Netanyahu commented after the meeting "He has got it." (Storm 45).

Obama of July 2008 was a very different person. He was more secure and confident in himself, and after Netanyahu shared his views of the situation, unlike a year earlier, this time Obama presented to Netanyahu his view that a general and encompassing peace in the Middle East could be achieved only after settling the Israeli-Palestinian conflict, a line advocated by the Arab side.

Netanyahu didn't share this Arab view of the situation, putting the Israeli-Palestinian conflict at the center of all problems in the Middle East. It goes along with the Arab characteristic of looking for the cause of their problems on the outside instead of the inside.

Former Israeli Defense Minister Moshe Yaalon said in his book that it is amazing to find that there is a total agreement between the Israelis and the Arabs. The Arabs blame Israel for everything that goes wrong in their countries, and the Israelis blame themselves for everything that goes wrong in Arab countries.

In fact, there are so many problems in the Middle East that it makes the Israeli-Palestinian conflict miniscule in caparison. It took several additional years for the "evidence" to show up in the form of the "Arab Spring" (called in Israel "The Arab Winter").

The conversation between Obama and Netanyahu and their teams turned into a "discussion", with the two sides expressing their views. Still, according to the report, it was "in good spirit", except for the national security advisor on Obama's team, Susan Rice, who remained "frozen, cold, with a constant cold stare at Netanyahu and his assistants." (Storm 46)

After the meeting, Netanyahu's assistant gave an interview to Newsweek magazine, in which he talked of the positive impression Senator Obama had on Netanyahu and his team. Two days later the magazine came out with the headline: "Tensions in Obama-Netanyahu Meeting". Such a headline could have only come from Obama's team (Storm 46).

David Axelrod, candidate Obama's strategist during the campaign, gave another piece of information about Obama's visit in Israel – Israel's "venerable" president Shimon Peres welcomed Obama very warmly, and according to Axelrod, "almost endorsed" him as his favorite for the elections (Axe 291).

At this point, Axelrod said that the visit would help candidate Obama with Jewish voters. In spite of the fact that he talked the right way, many Jewish voters wanted to know more than what he said. They wanted his "kishkes" (Axelrod's language; "guts" in Yiddish), meaning, they really wanted to know if the way he talked is just campaign talk, or would he act as president the same way he talked during the campaign. According to Axelrod, Peres's "almost endorsement" solved this issue.

[Note: when Prime Minister Netanyahu hosted candidate Romney for a festive dinner just before the 2012 elections, President Obama's team accused Netanyahu of "interference" in the US elections. No such complaint came from them in 2008.]

Back to Candidate Obama

Orly Azoulay, an Israeli journalist, followed candidate Obama during his campaign for presidency. The book that she published covered the time till the elections of 2008.

While on the campaign trail, having several Jews serving on his campaign, Obama talked very warmly about his ties with the Jewish people.

To the well-known Jewish journalist Jeffrey Goldberg, Obama said that the Jewish authors Philip Roth and Leon Uris had both impacted his emotional world. Azoulay quoted Obama from this interview:

> "So when I became more politically conscious, my starting point when I think about the Middle East is this enormous emotional attachment and sympathy for Israel, mindful of its history, mindful of the hardship and pain and suffering that the Jewish people have undergone, but also mindful of the incredible opportunity that is presented when people finally return to a land and are able to try to excavate their best traditions and their best selves." (Azoulay 218; Jeffrey Goldberg, "The Atlantic", May 12, 2008)

Orly Azoulay also describes a campaign speech that candidate Obama gave at a synagogue in Boca Raton, Florida. She quotes him as saying, "There is no deeper friendship than the one between Israel and the United States. I will keep this friendship and strengthen it. There is also an unshakeable commitment of the American people to the Jewish and the Israeli people." (Azoulay 226) All in all, a great presentation of the US-Israel relationship, and according to this, candidate Obama committed himself to continue with this heritage.

But is that what he actually said?

From a transcript of the speech, given at the B'nai Torah Congregation on May 23, 2008[11], we can summarize the attitude of candidate Obama towards Israel with three components: the US-Israel bond, the "Palestinians", and Iran.

US-Israel bond

In the speech, candidate Obama expressed his "…deep affinity with the ideal of social justice that was embodied in the Jewish faith."

---

[11] https://www.jta.org/2008/05/23/culture/obama-goes-to-shul-in-florida; https://www.youtube.com/watch?v=BLZF2mQvhuw

He went on to express the sense of community "embodied in the kibbutz – that we all have a responsibility to each other, that we're all in this together…"

One should note that candidate Obama chose an example, the kibbutz, which is from the far left of the political and social life in Israel. It might be interesting for former candidate Obama of the time to know that the kibbutz movement had already cancelled the idea of "everyone according to his needs", as they found that such a mantra tends to corrupt people.

Candidate Obama went on to talk of the bond between the US and Israel as "…none is deeper…"

Although many people consider the bond between the two countries to be rooted in shared Judeo-Christian values, it is interesting to note that Obama sees this bond as "…rooted in the millions of Jewish immigrants who sought opportunity on America's shores; in the liberation of those awful Nazi death camps in World War II; and in the courageous stance of President Harry Truman, who bucked the counsel of his own advisors in recognizing the Jewish state."

[Note: there is a striking mistake in his talk. The United States did not let any Jewish people enter the US when they were fleeing Nazi Germany. Not during the Holocaust. Moreover, a ship that came to the US shore with hundreds of Jewish refugees was turned around and was forced to return to Germany, where all the refugees were sent to perish in Auschwitz. Obama himself said that he read many books about the Holocaust, and quite likely he knew that what he said was untrue.]

Obama went on to talk of "a values bond and an ideals bond, and an intellectual bond", and "this special relationship". He does mention that it is "a relationship that's rooted in shared interests and shared values", but he then defines those values as, "democracy and opportunity, and tolerance and community" – i.e. liberal humanism rather than Judeo-Christian values. He concluded this part of his speech by saying, "…when I am in the White House, I will bring with me an unshakable commitment to maintaining that bond between the United States of America and an unshakable commitment to Israel's security."

One should wonder why candidate Obama did not say, "…when I am in the White House, I will bring with me an unshakable commitment to maintaining that bond between the United States of America **and Israel**…"

Was it an oversight? A mistake in writing? A mistake in editing? All reports from the campaign said that candidate Obama wrote his important speeches himself, in his own handwriting.

Note also the distinction between two different issues that candidate Obama said in this last section: "…unshakable commitment to maintaining that bond…" and "…unshakable commitment to Israel's security."

In fact, during his presidency, President Obama sharply distinguished between support for Israel, and support for Israel's security.

One point to note is that due to historical reasons, the entire cadre of high ranking officers and officials of the Israeli military and security establishment is overwhelmingly represented by the far left of the political map.

Candidate Obama and "Palestinians"

In his speech, candidate Obama said, "I intend to strengthen **Palestinian partners** who support that vision and renounce terrorism and recognize Israel's right to exist."

A point to observe is that this was the only time during his speech that candidate Obama used the word "Palestinian". Later on, he preferred other labels.

Moreover, one can ask a simple question: are there such "Palestinian partners"?

Candidate Obama contrasted the purported "Palestinian partners" with Hizbollah (Lebanon) and Hamas (Gaza Strip) – but isn't he aware that even the non-Hamas "Palestinian partners" (i.e. the PLO, who were brought into the country in the 1993 Oslo Accords) do not accept Israel's right to exist? This can be seen in all the textbooks that have been used, from 1993 to this day, in the schools of the "Palestinian partners".

Since this speech was given in 2008, we should remember that Arafat "renounced terrorism" in 1993, only to start a very cruel terrorist war against Israel seven years later.

Iran

Candidate Obama acknowledged that "the gravest threat to Israel today obviously comes from Iran."

However, when he came to talk of Iran's animosity to Israel, he preferred to label them as "disturbing **denunciations** of Israel".

Were they only "denunciations", or were they open and blatant threats to annihilate Israel from the map?

Summary

As usual, it is not what a person says that counts, but what they don't say. And as candidate Obama did his best to avoid using the word "Palestinian" (substituting instead the word Hamas), and by minimizing the Iranian threat to Israel, candidate Obama set the stage for his strong support of the Palestinians during his presidency, and for his "signature achievement" of reaching the Iran deal in the second term of his presidency.

Although candidate Obama proclaimed "an unshakeable commitment to Israel's security", UK Prime Minister David Cameron wrote in his book:

> "Obama was, I believed, the most pro-Arab, pro-Palestinian president in history. But, as ever, his careful analysis – 'They both need to want peace more than we do,' as he put it to me – meant a reluctance to take risks in order to achieve progress. Plus, he was understandably distracted by the Arab Spring, and anything he *did* propose to put pressure on Israel was rejected by Congress." (DavCam 534)

How can one have "an unshakeable commitment to Israel's security" and still be "the most pro-Arab, pro-Palestinian president in history", when the Arabs at large, and the Palestinians in particular, at least in public, call for the elimination of Israel?

As we go along, we will see how President Obama could hold the stick from both ends.

President Obama and Israel

President Obama took office in the midst of a major financial crisis, with the potential of being as severe as the Great Depression. Still, in his first address to the Joint Session of Congress, a month after he took office (February 24th, 2009), he related briefly to Israel by saying, "To seek progress toward a secure and lasting peace between Israel and her neighbors, we have appointed an envoy to sustain our effort."

On April 1, 2009, the White House put out a summary of a phone call between President Obama and Prime Minister Netanyahu.

There are two points to note in this report.

The first, the text says: "The President <u>spoke with</u> Israeli Prime Minister Benyamin Netanyahu today."

There are three ways to report a conversation, language-wise:

"President Obama called Prime Minister Netanyahu and they spoke…"
"President Obama and Prime Minister Netanyahu spoke…"
"President Obama spoke with Prime Minister Netanyahu…"

These three ways report the same event, but each one relates to a different description of the relationship between the two people. In the first two, the relationship is okay; but in the third one, use of the word "with" indicates some distance between the two.

The text continues, "…and <u>reaffirmed</u> the United States' steadfast commitment to Israel and its security."

Why there was any need for this "reaffirmation"? Is it because of President Obama's interview to the Dubai TV station Al Arabiya on January 27, 2009?

In the interview, the new President repeated the US support for Israel and its security, but he also added that he wants to begin by listening and talking to all parties involved in the conflict without prejudging their concerns. He also praised the Saudi peace plan, a plan that called for Israel's withdrawal from all the territories taken in 1967, to include East

Jerusalem, Judea, Samaria, the Gaza Strip, and the Golan Heights. (Al Arabiya website
https://www.alarabiya.net/articles/2009/01/27/65096.html).

Note that Israel rejected the Saudi plan upon its deliverance, stating that Israel is not going to return to what former Foreign Minister Abba Eban had called "Auschwitz borders". Therefore, to praise the Saudi "peace" plan, and to listen to the parties "without prejudging their concerns", quite likely raised the alarm in Israel.

The report on the content of the phone call ended with: "The President said he looked forward to working closely with Prime Minister Netanyahu and his government to address issues of mutual concern, including Iran and Arab-Israeli peace."

This is the first time that the two issues were packaged as one. Later on, President Obama would elaborate on this linkage quite a bit.

The first meeting – May 18, 2009

Earlier, we already saw that in this meeting, President Obama – on the advice of his aggressive and belligerent Chief of Staff Rahm Emanuel – decided on a frontal attack against the Israeli towns (aka "settlements") in Judea and Samaria, along with the Jerusalem area, annexed after 1967.

Let's see how President Obama talked to the press after the meeting (as reported on Obamawhitehouse.gov).

He started by talking of the "extraordinary relationship" and "special relationship" between the US and Israel. He labeled Israel as "a stalwart ally" of the US. He talked of the historical and emotional ties, and praised Israel as "the only true democracy of the Middle East" and "a source of admiration and inspiration for the American people."

After the general flattery, he continued with "**my** policies" – that "Israel's security is paramount", and it is "in U.S. national security interests" to maintain "an independent Jewish state".

Note: it sounds as if President Obama is strongly on the side of Israel. However, by advocating the maintaining of a "Jewish state", President

Obama is adopting here the claim of the pro-Arab Israeli left, with its prominent figure of Shimon Peres, the architect of the Oslo agreement with Arafat. This claim alleges that for Israel to remain a "Jewish state", Israel must refrain from annexing Judea and Samaria, since doing so would require it to give full citizenship to "millions" of Arabs, and would transform Israel into a bi-national state. In other words, the Israeli left's main claim is that to maintain Israel as a Jewish state, Israel must give up Judea and Samaria – the historic heartland of the land of Israel.

In essence, in this last quote President Obama set the stage for what would come later. One might wonder if by using the phrase "my policies", President Obama comes to say publicly, what he told Prime Minister Netanyahu in private: "Enough is enough." "My policies" comes to signify the personal attachment President Obama had to the Palestinian cause.

Obama continued with, again, the agenda of the pro-Arab Israeli left: "…it is I believe in the interest not only of the Palestinians, but also the Israelis and the United States and the international community to achieve a two-state solution in which Israelis and Palestinians are living side by side in peace and security."

[Note the grouping: he did not say "in the interest of both Palestinians and Israelis", but "in the interest not only of the Palestinians, **but also** the Israelis and the United States and the international community." The benefit of the Palestinians is first, and the benefit of Israel is relegated to a secondary status along with all the rest of the world.]

President Obama continued:

"…and to move forward in a way that assures Israel's security, that stops the terrorist attacks that have been such a source of pain and hardship, that we can stop rocket attacks on Israel…"

Background information

Historically, no conflict between countries has ever been resolved by "talks" between the two sides to the conflict. It is a sad observation to realize that historically, bloodshed has been the only way to resolve conflicts.

For example, the American colonies did not get independence just by negotiations with the British monarch. Although there were prior attempts at negotiation, these were rejected, and the matter was resolved only by declaring independence and going to war. The leaders of the American revolution realized, as Benjamin Franklin said, "We must, indeed, all hang together or, most assuredly, we shall all hang separately."

The same applied to the Second World War. Chamberlain tried to sign an agreement with Hitler to bring "peace for our time", but this did not prevent Hitler from trying to overrun all of Europe. When the war was in progress, the leaders of the Allies convened together, and decided that they would not let Germany surrender, although there were approaches by Germans to secure a respectable end to the war. The Allies knew that if they wanted that war to be the end of bloodshed, they needed to physically behead the Nazi regime.

Moreover, towards the end of the war, the Allies moved to destroy the German cities, in retaliation for Germany's bombing of London at the beginning of the war. Actually, more Germans were killed in these bombings than the number of Japanese who were killed by the two atomic bombs. And when the Russians conquered Berlin, they did it in a very savage way. They killed practically everything that moved, and raped thousands of women.

But both Germany and Japan – which were responsible not only for the Second World War, but also for several prior wars – were transformed from countries of cruel warriors to peace-loving countries thereafter. The defeated Germans and Japanese had a new lesson to transmit to their children and grandchildren.

I admired President Truman, who asked his generals how many soldiers would have to be killed for the US to conquer Japan by conventional means. When they told him that the estimate was around one million American soldiers, he responded with: drop the bomb. [About 250,000 Japanese died as a result of the bombs on Hiroshima and Nagasaki; but the estimate of how many Japanese would have died trying to defend their islands from invasion, based on the number who died defending isolated Pacific islands, ranges from 5 to 10 million.]

I visited the Truman Presidential Library in Independence, Missouri, and I recommend to everyone, if they are passing there on Interstate 70, to make a stop there. At the end of the tour there is a place for visitors to write what they think about President Truman's decision to drop the bomb on Japan. I wrote down that by doing so, he brought peace to the region.

There is a saying in the Israeli left that "you only make peace with enemies." This is true on only one condition, and history proves it. One can make peace with enemies only after the enemy has been so thoroughly defeated that the enemy is transformed into a peace-loving friend.

The Arabs lost in 1948. The Arabs lost in 1967. For all practical purposes, the Arabs lost in 1973. And Yasser Arafat lost the war that he started in 2000.

But even though the Arabs lost every war they fought against Israel, the international community – and particularly the US – continued as if their defeat on the battlefield was not a political defeat. In essence, Israel won tactically but not strategically. And as a result, the Arabs never lost their hope to destroy Israel in the "next round".

Yet US Presidents, from Truman to President Obama, wanted to continue negotiations to establish two peace-loving states living side by side. It is a historical joke!

Back to President Obama

It was not in his initial speech on May 18, 2009, but he left it for the Q & A segment. There President Obama elaborated on what was said earlier in the summary of the April phone call: "…to address issues of mutual concern, including Iran and Arab-Israeli peace."

In answer to a question by a journalist about the "peace process", Obama said, "In order for us to potentially realign interests in the region in a constructive way, bolstering, to use the Prime Minister's word, the Palestinian-Israeli peace track is critical."

In other words, "interests in the region" (Iran?) mean that "the Palestinian-Israeli peace track is critical."

President Obama then talked about the "Palestinian Authority" that had been established in 1993, and now in 2009 they still needed "…to gain additional legitimacy and credibility with their own people, and delivering services."

In other words, 16 (sixteen) years after the "monopolies" were established, raising the expenses of the population by 300%, President Obama still hoped that the Palestinian Authority would transform itself to be like the US government, with transparency of budgets and expenses.

President Obama also brought up an issue that hadn't been mentioned, and to bring it into the open – the "settlements".

"Now, Israel is going to have to take some difficult steps as well, and I shared with the Prime Minister the fact that under the roadmap and under Annapolis that there's a clear understanding that we have to make progress on settlements. **Settlements have to be stopped in order for us to move forward**. That's a difficult issue. I recognize that, but it's an important one and it has to be addressed."

Background information – "settlements"

The "Palestinian Liberation Organization" (PLO) was established in 1964, when Jordan ruled Judea and Samaria, and Egypt ruled the Gaza Strip.

In the Six-Day War in 1967, Israel requested from King Hussein of Jordan to not attack Israel, as Israel didn't want to face three fronts simultaneously. Two was more than enough. But King Hussein went ahead and attacked Jerusalem, and Israel was forced to defend itself, and in the process it took over Judea and Samaria.

Right after the war, Israel declared that the territories were like a deposit to return to the Arabs when peace will be achieved. The Arabs refused.

Please note one important point: the Biblical Israel was not on the coast, as modern Israel is. The Biblical Israel was on the mountain ridge going through the country. The area of Judea and Samaria is in fact Biblical Israel. Even the "Arabic" names of the various places are an Arabization of the original Hebrew names of the places mentioned in the Bible.

There is an area in Judea just south of Jerusalem, where several Jewish towns had been built before 1948. This group of towns, called the Etzion Block, was conquered by the Arabs in 1948; many of the residents were killed, and the survivors were "ethnically cleansed" by Jordan.

Right after the Six Day War in 1967, the survivors of the Etzion Block – including many who had been orphaned and exiled as children – asked the government to allow them to return to their homes, and permission was granted.

Except for these few towns, the rest of the area was empty. But in 1968, a group of people rented a hotel for the Passover holiday, in Hebron, the city where the burial cave of the Jewish Patriarchs is located. The Israeli military wanted to evacuate them, as they were at the center of a large Arab city, but there were ministers in the government, including Prime Minister Golda Meir, who said that there is no Jewish government that can prevent Jewish people from residing close to their ancestors' cemetery.

[Notes:

1. Until 1929, there was a peaceful Jewish community in Hebron, consisting mostly of rabbis and their students. In August 1929, the Arabs rioted and murdered many of the Jews, and the British, who controlled Israel at the time, forced the Jewish survivors to leave. Since then, Hebron has been an "Arab city".
2. Arafat once said that Hebron is apparently more important to the Israelis than the Temple Mount. He brought as evidence that Israel insisted on the right of Jews to pray at the Cave of the Patriarchs, but Israel did not insist on the same right at the Temple Mount. In that sense, Arafat was right. For Israelis, Hebron is "family", while the Temple Mount is "religion".]

Except for these two spots, the area of Judea and Samaria remained untouched by Jewish "settlements". After the Yom Kippur War of 1973, when Secretary of State Henry Kissinger shuttled around trying to reach cease-fire agreements between Israel and Egypt and Syria, a group of people got organized with the idea that it is time to settle the land. They tried to settle a place in Samaria that had historic Jewish roots, and they were evacuated by the Israeli government seven times, until the government relented in their eighth attempt.

In essence, the "settlement" movement did not start as a government project. It started as a grass-roots movement, from the people. There were many people from all over the country who came to help this group, including people from both the right and left sides of the political map.

Only after 1977, when the government changed from the Labor party to the Likud, Prime Minister Menachem Begin appointed Ariel Sharon to be in charge of settling the land.

Back to President Obama

President Obama, in his remarks, included the following:

"But the one thing that I've committed to the Prime Minister is we are going to be engaged, the United States is going to roll up our sleeves. We want to be a strong partner in this process."

In essence, President Obama told the world that Israel will not be negotiating with the Palestinians; Israel would negotiate with the US.

Not knowing the Arab culture, President Obama absolved the Palestinians from talking with the Israelis. In doing so, President Obama killed the peace process that he so desired. In fact, during the Obama presidency, the Palestinians did not want to enter any negotiation over the territories. Does this remind anyone of the Republicans in Congress?

This is not just my own conclusion. Abu Mazen, the leader who replaced Yasser Arafat after the latter's death, said it himself: the US gave me a tall ladder to climb on, and I climbed; they stepped down, and took the ladder, and left me hanging at the top of the tree.

The "unexpected" expected consequences!

Returning to the linkage between Iran and the Israel-Arab Conflict

As in the statement about the phone call earlier, linking the Iran nuclear effort to the Israeli-Arab conflict, President Obama said:

> "To the extent that we can make peace with the Palestinians – between the Palestinians and the Israelis, then I actually think it strengthens our hand in the international community in dealing with a potential Iranian threat."

In other words, he told Netanyahu openly: if you want us to deal with Iran, you need to compromise on the Palestinian front. Choose between an existential threat of an Iranian bomb, and an existential threat of losing the natural mountain range guarding Israel on the east.

President Obama's Cairo Speech

On June 4, 2009, a little over two weeks after the first meeting between President Obama and Prime Minister Netanyahu, President Obama went to Cairo to give his famous speech approaching the Arab world.

President Obama started his speech by talking of the existing tension between the US and Muslims. The tension is "rooted in historical forces", "fed by colonialism", by the "Cold War", and by "modernity and globalization".

President Obama is a person who believes in telling the whole truth, complete honesty. Since he came to Cairo to "seek a new beginning", he felt that it is time for the US and the Muslim World to not "ignore sources of tension", and it is time for him to "speak as clearly and plainly as I can" about "specific issues" that must be "confronted".

The "first issue" was "violent extremism in all of its forms". Although the US is not and would not be at war with Islam, still the US will "relentlessly confront violent extremists who pose a grave threat to our security." He gave examples to indicate that this refers to Afghanistan, Iraq, and elsewhere.

Note: "violent extremism" and "violent extremists", but not "terrorism" or "terrorists".

Statistics

From the beginning of his speech till this point, President Obama used 2,417 words out of 5,802 of the entire speech = 41%. At this point of time, he moved to talk about Israel and the Palestinians – 1,020 words, or 17.5% of the entire speech.

In essence, all the history of tension between the Muslim world and the west, to include the last two wars in Afghanistan and Iraq on the one hand, and the Israeli-Palestinian conflict on the other, received 3,437 words. This means a ratio of 2 to 1. At least, Israel got only 30% of the text till now, compared to 50% of all the UN discussions and decisions. Compared to the UN, quantity-wise, President Obama was not as bad.

The Israeli-Palestinian Issue in the Speech

Due to the importance of this text to our discussion, I include the text as an appendix to this chapter.

President Obama started by saying,

> "The second major source of tension that we need to discuss is the situation between Israelis, Palestinians and the Arab world."

The first paragraph is an "introduction" to the issue.

Please note two points:

The first, President Obama related to the first two as peoples – Israelis and Palestinians. If he were to be consistent, he should have related to the rest of the Arabs as "the Arabs", i.e. "to discuss the situation between the Israelis, the Palestinians, and the other Arabs." But he didn't. The first two are "peoples", while the rest is an abstract entity – "the Arab world". The fact is that in all the wars that Israel had to deal with, Israel needed to defend itself, but not from an abstract entity – the Arabs were a side to the conflict.

The way President Obama phrased it, it sounds as if the Israeli-Palestinian conflict is more personal to him, while the rest of the Arab world remains in the abstract.

The second point is the way President Obama introduced the sides to the conflict. One would have expected that he would refer to "the situation between the Israelis and the Palestinians and the Arab world."

Instead, he piled together the Israelis and the Palestinians in one group, and the Arab world in another group. As if the Palestinians and the Arab world are two distinct entities, unrelated to each other. It is true that the Israelis and the Palestinians are in dispute over the same territory, however, nobody can claim that the Arab world is an outside observer to the conflict.

It is another point to indicate his closeness to the issue.

President Obama continued with three paragraphs talking about Israel, before moving on to talk of the Palestinian issue. The first paragraph of the three started by expressing the "strong" and "unbreakable" bond between Israel and the US.

It is interesting the way President Obama chose to approach the Muslim world with a message of peace, and talking about the need of the Palestinians to have their own homeland.

The analogy that comes to mind is a man who wants to convince a woman to go on a date, telling her: "I would like to be honest with you. I am deeply in love with another woman. At the same time, I would like you to go out with me."

Would anyone like to imagine what the woman would reply?

In other words, President Obama said, "I am your enemy's best friend, but I want to be your friend as well." This approach will not work, not only in the Middle East, but anywhere on the globe. Only a person who believes that all humans are brothers, that all humans are one group, an ideal utopia that doesn't exist, can come with such naivety.

Alyssa Mastromonaco, who worked with the Obama campaign before 2008, and then worked at the White House for several years, wrote a book titled: "Who Thought This Was a Good Idea?" It is not openly said in the book that this was a question that President Obama used to ask, but the picture that accompanied the title, showed her sitting on a seat on the plane, with President Obama sitting on the arm-rest. Both of them are serious, not smiling, not looking at each other, and President Obama is folding his hands on his chest. The body language shows it is not a good moment between the two.

Reading the text of President Obama's speech in Cairo, one can easily ask: "Who Thought This was a Good Idea?"

As we saw earlier in the book, President Obama is a person who believes in telling the truth, and the whole truth, even if it hurts the listener. But designing such a prominent speech, and bringing the listeners to shut down to him, closing their ears to the rest of his message, was definitely the wrong approach.

President Obama had a large team preparing his speeches. For this particular speech, he had an Egyptian-American working at the State Department, Gamal Hilal, who helped to put the right touches on the speech. In fact, when I read the text of the speech for the first time, without knowing of the Egyptian-American's input, it was clear to me that this is not American language. There are several points in the text that were quite likely phrased by an Arab. And this is the product?

If President Obama really wanted to reach his audience's hearts, he should have started with the Palestinian issue, omitting altogether the talk about Israel, and if he would have talked about Israel at all, he should have done so only after he had completed the discussion of the Palestinian issue.

Question: is it possible that he wasn't really talking to the audience in front of him?

The second paragraph of the three about Israel discussed the Holocaust:

> "Around the world, the Jewish people were persecuted for centuries, and anti-Semitism in Europe culminated in an

unprecedented Holocaust. Tomorrow, I will visit Buchenwald, which was part of a network of camps where Jews were enslaved, tortured, shot and gassed to death by the Third Reich. Six million Jews were killed – more than the entire Jewish population of Israel today. Denying that fact is baseless, ignorant, and hateful. Threatening Israel with destruction – or repeating vile stereotypes about Jews – is deeply wrong, and only serves to evoke in the minds of Israelis this most painful of memories while preventing the peace that the people of this region deserve."

Israeli ambassador to the US Michael Oren had the most difficulty with this description – the linkage between Israel's legitimacy and the Holocaust. For Oren, it was "the most damaging part of his speech". It is the Arabs' complaint throughout the years of the conflict – that the Arabs were displaced from their homeland just to make room for the Jews who were displaced from their countries in Europe. Oren asks the question: "Why should the Arabs make peace with a country that even its ally, the United States, seemed to label alien?" (MicOr 65, 66).

In fact, the establishment of the homeland for the Jewish people was recognized by the League of Nations (preceding the United Nations) in 1922, a long time before the Holocaust, and the Jews had begun to develop and rehabilitate the empty parts of the land already in the 19th century. The permission that the League of Nations gave Great Britain to establish its mandate over the area called "Palestine" was with the specific goal of "the establishment in Palestine of a national home for the Jewish people" due to "the historical connection of the Jewish people with Palestine and to the grounds for reconstituting their national home in that country." (League of Nations Mandate for Palestine, July 24, 1922)

President Obama on the Palestinians

He started with,

> "On the other hand, it is also undeniable that the Palestinian people – Muslims and Christians – have suffered in pursuit of a homeland. For more than sixty years they have endured the pain of dislocation. Many wait in refugee camps in the West Bank, Gaza, and neighboring lands for a life of peace and security that they have never been able to lead. They endure the daily humiliations – large and small – that come with occupation. So let

there be no doubt: the situation for the Palestinian people is intolerable. America will not turn our backs on the legitimate Palestinian aspiration for dignity, opportunity, and a state of their own."

"Undeniable"

For the Holocaust, President Obama said, "Denying that fact is baseless, ignorant, and hateful". For the Palestinian "suffering" it is "undeniable".

Did the "Palestinians" suffer due to "pursuit of a homeland"? Or, maybe they suffered due to their negation of the "pursuit of a homeland" for others? After all, they were offered a homeland in the UN partition plan of November 1947, which would have given them more than half of the land – a plan that they rejected, while the Jews accepted it.

The "undeniable" that President Obama talks of is not based upon historical truth. Not at all. Saying that it is "undeniable" does not mean that it is "undeniable".

And President Obama continued:

"For more than sixty years they have endured the pain of dislocation."

Again, the fact is that around 700,000 Arabs decided to leave the country. Most of them due to encouragement by the Arab leaders; some, because they did not want to be in a place where a war was being fought; and some, which is "undeniable", were forced to leave, but mainly in places where they were attacking their Jewish neighbors.

At the same time, around one million Jews were dislocated from Arab countries, and since most of them were middle class, and they were forced to leave (or fled from massacres), they had to leave behind them a large amount of property. They came to Israel with practically nothing. In effect, in 1948-1951 there was an exchange of population between the new country of Israel and the entire "Arab world".

There was one difference between these two groups. While Israel absorbed and resettled the Jewish refugees, the Arab countries refused to settle the Arab refugees. Moreover, there are numerous UN decisions that forbade Israel from settling the so-called "refugees" in permanent homes once Israel took control of Judea, Samaria, and the Gaza Strip.

To say that the "Palestinians" endured "dislocation" for sixty years is a travesty of the truth.

And Obama continued:

"They endure the daily humiliations – large and small – that come with occupation."

The fact is that the "daily humiliations" President Obama talked about are only due to the terror campaign that they lodged against Israel after 1993. After suicide bombers started to come into Israeli cities to blow up buses and restaurants, Israel had to put up checkpoints at the entrance to its cities. At first, emergency vehicles like ambulances could pass the checkpoints without inspection, but after Arabs started to use ambulances to transfer terrorists and weapons on their way to commit suicide bombings, Israel had to stop and inspect Arab ambulances as well.

"Occupation"? As Benjamin Netanyahu said in his book, "A Durable Peace" – since when was the Jews' right to the land negated by the League of Nations, or by the UN that had accepted all previous decisions of the League of Nations as binding?

"Occupation" is a term used by the Israeli pro-Arab left, and by the Arabs themselves. It is a term that is not used by many legal scholars, including Americans, who are familiar with the subject. At most, one can call the area "disputed".

President Obama continued:

"…the only resolution is for the aspirations of both sides to be met through two states, where Israelis and Palestinians each live in peace and security."

The Arabs' Traditional "No"

The Arabs rejected the so-called "Two State Solution" in 1937 with the British Peel Commission. The Arabs rejected the UN decision of 1947 to partition the land between Arabs and Jews. The Arabs rejected the Israeli call in 1967 to return the territories in exchange for peace. The Arabs rejected Mr Begin's Autonomy Plan in 1977. At Camp David in 2000, Arafat rejected the offer of the entire area of Judea, Samaria, and the Gaza Strip, with minimal border changes, and started his terror campaign. Abu Mazen, his successor, rejected Prime Minister Ehud Olmert's plan offering him everything in 2008.

After rejecting this plan repeatedly, why would the Arabs accept it only because an American president repeats what others have already said a long time before him? Moreover, why would Israel accept such a plan, knowing that the only reason the "Palestinians" exist as a "separate nation", distinct from all other Arabs, is to eliminate Israel?

And Obama continued:

> "Palestinians must abandon violence. Resistance through violence and killing is wrong and does not succeed. For centuries, black people in America suffered the lash of the whip as slaves and the humiliation of segregation. But it was not violence that won full and equal rights. It was a peaceful and determined insistence upon the ideals at the center of America's founding. This same story can be told by people from South Africa to South Asia; from Eastern Europe to Indonesia. It's a story with a simple truth: that violence is a dead end. It is a sign of neither courage nor power to shoot rockets at sleeping children, or to blow up old women on a bus. That is not how moral authority is claimed; that is how it is surrendered."

President Obama compared the fate of the slaves in America, to the fate of the Palestinians. The Arabs in the "disputed" territories were never slaves. By doing so, he exposed his own bias in this historical conflict.

The Arabs' standard of living went up dramatically after Israel took control over the areas. Their life expectancy went up significantly, not only in comparison to Arabs in Arab countries, but even in comparison to Arabs in European countries, like France. Their education became better to the point that the Palestinians are now the most educated among all the Arab world.

People aren't aware, or don't want to accept, that for the Arabs this is a zero-sum game. The Arabs' ideology can be described as "I am OK only if you are not OK."

In essence, western academia posits that poverty breeds violence, and they do not want to accept this is not so. Highly educated Arabs, with college degrees, coming from very wealthy families, committed 9/11.

Personal experience: Many years ago, I had a conversation with an FBI agent. He asked me: "What are you doing to the Palestinians?" I responded with: "What we are doing to the Palestinians is nothing compared to what you did to the Indians. Most of them you killed, and the ones you didn't kill, you sent to reservations in the middle of nowhere." He said: "But it was a long time ago." And I told him, "Let's stop the conversation, and continue it 50 years from now, and I will tell you that "it was a long time ago."

President Obama continued:

> "Now is the time for Palestinians to focus on what they can build.
> The Palestinian Authority must develop its capacity to govern,
> with institutions that serve the needs of its people."

The Palestinian Authority was established in 1993. President Obama was speaking in Cairo in 2009. This is 16 years after the Palestinian Authority was established, with generous funds pouring into them from all over the world, including the US. And "now is the time for Palestinians to focus on what they can build"? Hello? Were the Palestinians in hibernation? Or, maybe they were busy abusing their own population, taking all funds in the billions and living a life of luxury at the expense of their population.

And the fact is that President Obama knows all of this. What does he expect? That now they will change because he asked them so nicely to change?

President Obama continued:

> "At the same time, Israelis must acknowledge that just as Israel's
> right to exist cannot be denied, neither can Palestine's. The United

States does not accept the legitimacy of continued Israeli settlements. This construction violates previous agreements and undermines efforts to achieve peace. It is time for these settlements to stop."

Actually, the construction of Jewish towns, aka "settlements", does not, and did not, violate any previous agreement. The Oslo agreement was signed, only after Arafat agreed that the "settlements" are a "final agreement issue". It was set aside so they could reach an agreement.

To say that the "settlements" violate any agreement is simply untrue – a simple lie, not even used by the Palestinians. They reject the "settlements", but they do not say that the "settlements" violate the Oslo agreement. They know it is no violation.

In summary, President Obama set up a new reality that did not exist till his speech.

Summary

In the first meeting President Obama had with Prime Minister Benjamin Netanyahu, President Obama exposed his bias in favor of the Palestinians. He did so again, even much more so, in Cairo, by being the main advocate for the Palestinians' distortions and lies that have gone on for so many years.

But if this was not enough, President Obama went even further to show his bias in deeds, not only in words.

There was no balance in President Obama's itinerary in his trip. He visited Cairo, Egypt. Then he went to Saudi Arabia and Turkey. Dan Shapiro, one of the people on Obama's team, was quoted in a book saying, "The President was aware of the criticism that he bypassed Israel on his way to Cairo." (Storm 53).

The journalist Marvin Kalb, who joined Air Force One, found it difficult to understand why Saudi Arabia and Turkey were included in the itinerary, yet there was no time for a 45-minute flight to Ben-Gurion Airport. In a TV message from Cairo, Kalb said, "The President will lose

Netanyahu." Even the leftist Israeli journalist Nahum Barnea said that Obama is losing Netanyahu (Storm 54).

Was President Obama "going to" lose Netanyahu (future tense)? Was he "losing" Netanyahu (present tense)? It seemed that he had already lost him (past tense). Netanyahu was quoted as saying (apparently in a private conversation, after the above-mentioned treatment from Obama), "We are at war, and the way to win is to move it to the enemy's territory… This president is an existential threat to Israel. Barack Hussein Obama is the first Muslim president in the White House. There is a need to fight him with all means possible." (Storm 56)

For Netanyahu, Obama had become "the enemy", and "an existential threat to Israel". Worse than that nobody can get. The rightwing news media in Israel portrayed Obama with an Arabic kaffiyah on his head, and emphasizing his middle name Hussein (Storm 61).

Netanyahu's Response to the Cairo Speech

If indeed President Obama was "an existential threat to Israel" and even an "enemy", and if President Obama is going to serve eight years, what would Prime Minister Netanyahu do to confront this threat?

Political Power

In his book "A Durable Peace", Netanyahu attributes importance to "political power", unlike "military power".

Netanyahu brings two events in history as examples. The first is the fact that the Czechs allowed Hitler to push them into a political corner, forcing them to surrender their country's defenses without firing a shot. The second example is no less than Saddam Hussein of Iraq. He invaded Kuwait, and after taking over Kuwait in several hours using military power, he neglected to wage the war in the political arena, to address public opinion and convince the public that his cause to take over Kuwait is just (BenN 373).

Netanyahu summarizes it as follows: to win one must win not only on the battlefield. One needs to win over the public opinion (BenN 374).

Netanyahu even cynically said that it doesn't matter if your cause is "just or unjust, moral or immoral". What matters is whether you win over the public opinion. It is no wonder that Netanyahu had Churchill's picture in his office, as he admired Churchill's speeches that mobilized the western world to his cause (BenN 374).

Netanyahu said: "…a powerful message powerfully delivered and powerfully broadcast to public opinion has become an indispensable element in the waging of political and military struggles." (BenN 375) If President Obama could do it in Cairo, why couldn't Netanyahu do it in Ramat Gan, Israel, at Bar-Ilan University?

Netanyahu quoted Israel's first Prime Minister, David Ben-Gurion, who said, "What matters is not what the goyim (Gentiles) say, but what the Jews do." Netanyahu said that Ben-Gurion was wrong by dismissing what the Gentiles say. As an example, after the 1956 campaign when Israel took over the Sinai desert, Ben-Gurion declared that Israel will not evacuate it for a thousand years, only to find that he had to evacuate it within several months due to American and Soviet pressure (BenN 377).

Netanyahu also brings as a mistake Israel's lack of public relations efforts after the Israeli bombing of the Iraqi nuclear reactor in 1981. Israel neglected to establish in the public opinion why the bombing was necessary, and as a result Israel was condemned by everyone, including the US, only to get thanks from the US ten years later – before, during and after Operation Desert Storm (BenN 380).

Netanyahu addresses language as well: "I have found over the years, again contrary to the popular wisdom, that occasionally one word can be worth a thousand pictures, rather than vice versa. For example, the word occupation. Or the expression homeless people. Or Arab land. Or land for peace." (BenN 383)

Four days after his speech in Cairo, on June 8, 2009, President Obama had a phone call with Netanyahu.

In the White House briefing it was said:

The President and Prime Minister had a constructive, 20-minute conversation. The President reiterated the principal elements of his Cairo speech, including his commitment to Israel's security. He indicated that he looked forward to hearing the Prime Minister's upcoming speech outlining his views on peace and security…"

Four days after Obama's Cairo speech, Netanyahu had already prepared his own response speech. And as President Obama decided to give his speech at a religious academic institute in Cairo, Prime Minister Netanyahu decided to give his response speech at a religious university in Israel – Bar Ilan, a stronghold of the National Religious movement, from which the majority of the earlier settlers in Judea and Samaria came.

Netanyahu's Bar-Ilan Speech

Netanyahu started by saying that peace is the Jewish people's "most ardent desire", and he listed the three "immense challenges" of the unity government that he had established about two months before: the Iranian threat, the economic crisis, and the advancement of peace.

He talked of the Iranian threat that is "the greatest danger confronting Israel", talked briefly of the global economic crisis, and went on to discuss regional peace in the Middle East.

He addressed the Arab leaders, saying that he is willing to meet them in any Arab capital city to establish "economic peace" that would lead to "political peace". He commended the Gulf states on their economic success, and suggested the development of industrial areas that would generate thousands of jobs and more.

Then he said: "I turn to you, our Palestinian neighbors, led by the Palestinian Authority, and I say: Let's begin negotiations immediately without preconditions."

He talked of peace in which Israelis and Palestinians would live in peace, "as good neighbors", not knowing anymore the agony of losing loved ones. He personally knew "the face of war"; he doesn't want war, and "no one in Israel wants war."

He summed up the "root of the conflict" that had prevented peace for over sixty years: "the refusal to recognize the right of the Jewish people to a state of their own, in their historic homeland."

He moved to give a short history of the Arab hostility towards Israel, starting from 1920 to show that the Jewish presence in Judea and Samaria is not the reason for the conflict.   That for close to 50 years (1920 to 1967) there were many attacks against Israel "before a single Israeli soldier ever set foot in Judea and Samaria".

And when others pressure Israel to withdraw, Israel only gets "massive waves of terror, by suicide bombers and thousands of missiles". When Israel twice suggested full withdrawal in return for "end of the conflict", the Palestinians rejected it. The bottom line, he said, is that the claim that territorial withdrawals will bring peace, or advance peace, did not stand "the test of reality."

Before peace can be achieved, the Palestinian leadership needs to declare openly: "Enough of this conflict. We recognize the right of the Jewish people to a state of their own in this land, and we are prepared to live beside you in true peace."

He emphasized it again by asking for "a public, binding and unequivocal Palestinian recognition of Israel as the nation state of the Jewish people."

Before moving to talk of the rights of the Palestinians, he devoted time to talk of the right of the Jews to their historical homeland: "This is the land of our forefathers," he said.

He disputed what President Obama had said in his Cairo speech (actually an Arab claim), pointing out that the right of Jews to the land does not come from "the catastrophes that have plagued our people."

He recognized that there are who say (President Obama?) that if the Holocaust had not occurred, Israel would never have been established. He said that the opposite is true: if the state of Israel would have been established earlier, the Holocaust would not have occurred.

He quoted from the Israeli declaration of independence, delivered by Israel's first Prime Minister, David Ben-Gurion:

> "The Jewish people arose in the land of Israel and it was here that its spiritual, religious and political character was shaped. Here

they attained their sovereignty, and here they bequeathed to the world their national and cultural treasures, and the most eternal of books."

And he moved on with the "bombshell":

"But we must also tell the truth in its entirety: within this homeland lives a large Palestinian community. We do not want to rule over them, we do not want to govern their lives, we do not want to impose either our flag or our culture on them."

His "vision of peace" is "two peoples live freely, side-by-side, in amity and mutual respect."

But peace has to be "peace with security." Therefore, he continued with the points that would give Israel security:

1. Recognition – Palestinians must clearly and unambiguously recognize Israel as the state of the Jewish people.
2. Demilitarization – without an army, without control of its airspace, with effective security measures to prevent weapons smuggling into the territory, and no military pacts.
3. Defensible borders
4. Jerusalem must remain the united capital of Israel with continued religious freedom for all faiths.

He ended by saying, "With God's help, we will know no more war. We will know peace."

Aftermath

The speech was received with total rejection by the Israeli right, and with doubt by the Israeli left. The right accused Netanyahu of betrayal of the Biblical prophecies that promised the return of the Jewish exiles to their historical homeland. The left simply said that they believe that Netanyahu was lying, and that he didn't mean even one word that he said.

In fact, years later, President Obama said that Netanyahu was indeed lying to him about his wish for peace.

It is ironic that Obama made this accusation after he had told Netanyahu in their first meeting regarding the "settlements" that "enough is enough", and then came the Cairo speech in which President Obama repeated many distortions and lies that the Arabs have been saying throughout the conflict.

Actually, Netanyahu's speech is a replica of his book "A Durable Peace", plus one more point: his requirement that the Palestinian side would openly declare that they recognize the right of the Jews to their historical homeland in Israel of pre-1967.

But the question of whether Netanyahu was "truthful" or not, actually misses the point. In his book "A Durable Peace", he devoted a chapter to discuss "political power". As previously described, there he said that it doesn't matter if your cause is just or unjust, moral or immoral. The only question is how you are perceived in the arena of public opinion. And the struggle is not about reality, but about how reality is being perceived.

It is quite likely that Netanyahu saw the danger that President Obama is trying to corner him into being the one who resists "peace". Netanyahu blamed the Czechs and Saddam Hussein for neglecting the public opinion, and true to the message he gave in his book, he was not going to leave the focus of the news media on President Obama and his attempt to deprive Israel of its most important defensive barrier – Judea and Samaria.

Therefore he talked the language of "peace", with added conditions. After the speech, he didn't need to convince the world that he is 100% sincere. That was not his objective. His objective was to create at least a 1% possibility that he might be sincere. And he accomplished his goal.

We know for a fact that in Israeli terms, the speech remained a speech. Netanyahu did not bring the agenda of the speech to the government for a vote, or even to the Knesset (parliament) for a vote.

Moreover, when the right attacked him, very fiercely, he remained silent. He didn't respond. He didn't have to. The attacks of the right only served his cause. The right labeled Netanyahu a "traitor", and by doing so, they gave him a "certificate" of sincerity, at least in the eyes of the west.

We should remember what Dennis Ross accurately said about Netanyahu, that he might come up with an idea only to let himself out of a trap, and he did come out of the trap that President Obama had set for him.

It is no wonder that out of all the world leaders, the one that irritated President Obama the most was Benjamin Netanyahu. President Obama wanted to manipulate him, but Netanyahu manipulated him in return.

When the American ambassador to Israel David Friedman was asked in an interview what would happen if the Palestinians would accept President Trump's plan, the ambassador responded: Then they will not be Palestinians. They would be Canadians. He used the term "Canadians" as he is from the US. In Israel the saying goes that if the Palestinians would accept Netanyahu's plan they will be "Scandinavians". With them, there would be no problem to compromise and make peace.

Personal experience: In 1981 I had a class in the Washington DC area. This was at the time that the Israeli lobby in DC fought against the sale of four AWACS planes to Saudi Arabia. Eventually, the Senate approved the sale. During one of the breaks, a student asked me for my comment on the struggle in Congress, and the outcome. I told him that a nation that is 4,000 years old, does not measure itself by a US president who is in power for eight years.

In retrospect, this was the struggle between President Obama and Prime Minister Benjamin Netanyahu.

President Obama – Israel's Friend

People consider President Truman to have been a friendly president to Israel. After all, he recognized the new country only 11 minutes after its declaration of independence. But there are two points that people don't know about President Truman.

The first is that when Israel's 1948 war of independence ended, Israel had new borders, further than what the UN partition plan had designated for the Jewish state. Joseph McDonald, the first US ambassador to Israel, appointed personally by President Truman, reported a very heavy pressure on Israel in the early fifties to withdraw to the partition plan borders. Israel withstood that pressure.

The second point is that just as President Truman appointed a personal ambassador to Israel, he also appointed a special US ambassador to the Palestinian "refugees", to take care of them. Unknown to many, most of the budget of UNRWA, the UN agency supporting the Arab refugees, is solely an American budget.

In a way, President Truman eternalized the Arab refugee problem, to the extent that it couldn't be resolved by settling them in the countries they had fled to. By Truman's supporting the refugees with a special envoy and a special UNRWA budget, he prevented the refugees from the necessity to adjust.

President Truman said in his memoirs that he was not pro-Jews or pro-Arabs. He was pro-fairness. And if the British had promised the Jews a homeland in what was then called "Palestine" (Balfour declaration) then they should have delivered on their promise.

When President Eisenhower wanted to pressure Israel to withdraw from the Sinai after the 1956 war, he threatened Israel with cutting off the tax-free Jewish donations to Israel, and to legislate a ban on any money moving between the US and Israel. At the time, being only 8 years old, with the need to absorb a destitute immigrant population, Israel could not withstand that pressure, and withdrew from the Sinai.

President Kennedy pressured Israel to stop its effort to develop nuclear capability. The book "The Bomb" by Avner Cohen reported this pressure. One should note that President Kennedy only authorized selling defensive weapons to Israel, such as the Hawk anti-air missiles.

Rabin said in his memoirs that after the Six Day War, the US retaliated against Israel and froze all discussions on future defense contracts. Moreover, the US also cancelled contracts that had already been signed, and were already in the process of being carried out.

After the 1973 Yom Kippur war, Israel and Egypt negotiated regarding a partial retreat of Israel from the Sinai. When Israel didn't agree to the terms, Secretary of State Henry Kissinger suggested that President Ford would announce the "reassessment" of the relationship between the US and Israel, and practically froze all defense contacts and contracts between the two countries.

When Israel bombed the Iraqi nuclear reactor in 1981, President Reagan – who was otherwise very friendly to Israel – still froze for a while the defense relationship between the two countries.

When the influx of Jewish immigrants from the Soviet Union flooded Israel in the early nineties, Israel asked the US to provide guarantees for loans that Israel would take from banks to provide housing for all these new immigrants. President George H. Bush and his Secretary of State James Baker conditioned the guarantees on Israel stopping the building of Jewish towns, aka "settlements", in Judea and Samaria. Prime Minister Shamir didn't want to commit to such a move, and preferred to give up on the loan guarantees. The open conflict with the US is considered today as one of the reasons Prime Minister Shamir lost the elections in 1992, that brought Prime Minister Rabin and his Foreign Minister Shimon Peres to power, and soon thereafter they produced the agreement between the Israeli government and the PLO.

In essence, throughout the years, there was US pressure on Israel, tying the defense relationship to other issues that the US wanted Israel to comply with.

President Obama

President Obama **did not** act that way. Throughout his presidency, in spite of the disagreements about the "settlements" in Judea and Samaria,

President Obama not only kept the defense relationship between the two countries intact, but he strengthened it to a point unparalleled in the past.

In an appearance of President Obama's National Security Advisor Susan Rice before the American Jewish Committee Global Forum on June 06, 2016, Rice said that President Obama is "fiercely devoted to Israel and to the well-being of the Jewish people"; and that when President Obama labeled US commitment to Israel's security "unshakeable," that it was not just talk.   She listed the help that President Obama gave to Israel:

Close to $24 billion in defense aid. Close to one billion dollars to develop and produce the Iron Dome anti-rocket system, and this one billion dollars was given in cash to the Israeli defense industry. Support to develop other anti-missiles system. Defense industries in both countries develop the "Underground Iron Dome" – anti-tunneling technology.

Special Forces of both countries train together. Air forces and navies of both countries drill together. American National Guard troops will be going to Israel for a joint disaster response exercise.

Michael Oren, Israeli ambassador to the US, said that when Israel faced a major forest fire consuming life and property, Israel asked President Obama for emergency aid, lending Israel planes to fight the fires, and President Obama gave the emergency aid right away.

When President Obama visited Israel in March 2013, he gave a speech in Jerusalem to university students. In his speech, President Obama talked of Israel in superlatives that only a real admirer would use.

> "I have borne witness to the ancient history of the Jewish people at the Shrine of the Book, and I have seen Israel's shining future in your scientists and entrepreneurs. This is a nation of museums and patents, timeless holy sites and ground-breaking innovation. Only in Israel could you see the Dead Sea Scrolls and the place where the technology on board the Mars Rover originated."

His visit was close to the Passover holiday, and he talked of how the story of the Exodus was so meaningful, especially to the African-American community – the history of people "emerging from the grip of bondage";

and how meaningful this story was for him personally, a person "growing up in far-flung parts of the world and without firm roots", yearning for a "home".

> "Israel has built a prosperous nation – through kibbutzeem that made the desert bloom, business that broadened the middle class, and innovators who reached new frontiers – from the smallest microchip to the orbits of space."

> "Israel has established a thriving democracy – with a spirited civil society, proud political parties, a tireless free press, and a lively public debate – lively may even be an understatement."

With all the accolades, he still had to comment on his problematic relationship with Netanyahu saying:

> "But just so you know, any drama between me and my friend Bibi over the years was just a plot to create material for Eretz Nehederet."

[Note: "Eretz Nehederet" ("Great Country" in Hebrew) is a satirical TV show in Israel.]

President Obama's critics in Israel commented on two negative points: the first, he didn't address the Knesset (parliament) as dignitaries in the past did, like President Sadat of Egypt, and others. Instead, he preferred to talk to university students, and not just to anyone. According to reports, the US embassy required each student who wanted to attend to write an essay about politics of the day. They wanted to make sure that only one side of the aisle would be there, so President Obama will not face disturbances from his critics during the speech.

But the fact is that he did talk very nicely, and he did act upon his commitment to the security of Israel, above and beyond any previous president.

Susan Rice and Israel

Introduction

Besides repeating his declaration of "unshakeable" commitment to the security of Israel, and at the same time expressing strong opposition to the "settlements" in Judea and Samaria, we don't know much about how President Obama actually feels about Israel – what Axelrod labeled in his book "the kishkes" (the inside "guts").

We do have a window to these inside feelings, by looking into what his National Security Advisor (NSA) in his second term, Susan Rice, said about Israel. During President Obama's second term, Susan Rice gave dozens of speeches in four years, standing in for President Obama. In comparison, her predecessor gave one speech in two years. In every speech one can read several times that she quoted President Obama: "As President Obama said…"

In essence, Susan Rice was more than just NSA. She was President Obama's extension to the outside world, talking even on issues that were not directly connected to national security.

Susan Rice said in her book that she had an amazing trait of knowing exactly what President Obama was thinking. She could even finish his sentences verbatim, as if she were him. This clearly indicates closeness, and quite likely the way she feels about Israel might be either identical, or similar, to the way President Obama feels.

Susan Rice

When Susan Rice was 14, her father took her and her brother on a visit to Israel. She loved Israel "with its energy, bustle, and idealism". It was a place she labeled as "one of the most hopeful places on earth". Her memories from this visit "are etched in my soul". She even learned the "Sh'ma"[12] by heart. (SusanR 89, Speech 6-6-2016)

Rice on the US-Israel Relationship

In a speech Rice gave at an Israeli Air Force base she said:

---

[12] "Hear O Israel, the Lord is our God, the Lord is one."

> "The American people care deeply about the people of Israel. We admire your commitment to advancing the values of a free and open society, while facing the uncertainties of living in a very challenging neighborhood." (5-9-2014)

In a speech she gave to the AIPAC Annual Meeting on March 2, 2015, she attributed the US-Israel alliance to sharing the values of "freedom and democracy". It is not a relationship between states and leaders. "It is between two peoples and the millions of intimate, personal connections that bind us." This alliance is "rooted in the unbreakable friendship between our two peoples."

The US-Israel Relationship in the Eyes of Israelis

Many times during the years, people in my classes asked me how Israelis see the United States. There is a "Truman Village" in Israel commemorating the US recognition of Israeli independence. There is a Kennedy Forest close to Jerusalem. Martin Luther King Day in January is a day when many schools in Israel assemble the students to discuss civil rights.

When Kennedy was assassinated, there was a shock all over Israel. 9/11 was not only an attack on the US. The impact was felt all over Israel. One could go and hear people talking about only one point: "The Twins" – the twin towers, that's how they call them in Israel.

One has to go for a walk on Israeli streets to see the impact of the US, not only in branches of American companies, but also many stores that name themselves in English, written in Hebrew letters.

When I was in the police polygraph, I had subjects who told me that they wanted their lawyer to be present in the room. I asked them: from where did you get the idea that you have such a right? And they answered: I saw it on TV. I needed to tell them that the TV shows are American, but they live in Israel, where there is no such right.

[Note: they can go out and consult their lawyers, but the lawyer cannot be in the interview room with them.]

In essence, Israelis look up to the US as a role model.

Rice at the UN

When she was the US ambassador to the UN in the first four years of the Obama administration, Susan Rice was a very strong defender of Israel, a role she embraced "with passion". She had no problem to attribute the UN hostility to Israel as "crass prejudice", and stating that anti-Semitism and racism for her is personal, and she loathed it.

She talked of the Israeli ambassador to the UN Gabriela Shalev, a professor of law and a jurist. She also found it important to note that Shalev was an appointee of Israel Foreign Minister Tzipi Livni, with whom she had previous acquaintance. [Interestingly, Tzipi Livni was a Knesset member who started her political life in the Likud, only to move to the extreme "left", becoming an advocate of an independent Palestinian state.]

Rice talked of Shalev, who was old enough to be her mother, who became her "sister" even at the time of writing her book.

Rice listed all her activities at the UN to defend Israel, and to prevent resolutions condemning Israel for its defensive activities against Hamas rockets attacking Israeli communities (SusanR 252, 253).

In the speeches she gave as National Security Advisor, she gave a lot more details on US defense of Israel at the UN.   The UN has "spurious resolutions and initiatives designed to isolate Israel" that the US struggles against. She had to defend Israel "from a drumbeat of hostility".

"Israel is not alone," she declared when talking of Israel being "singled out time and again on the floor of the United Nations", or when "angry voices attack Israel's right to exist." Not only it is wrong, she said, but "it's ugly." (ADL 6-17-2015, AJC 6-6-2016)

Rice and Netanyahu

With all her defense of Israel at the UN, Rice singled out Netanyahu to be negative towards him. She mentioned that Netanyahu's policies gave "daily fodder to Israel's critics". When talking about foreign leaders visiting the White House, she singled out some as an exception: the Chinese with "paranoia over protests", "the entitled Saudis, provocative Israeli prime minister Netanyahu, and the prickly Pakistanis" (SusanR 252, 381).

Note the way she singled out Netanyahu in this list of exceptions. All the rest are mentioned by their nationality – Chinese, Saudis, Pakistanis. Only Netanyahu is mentioned as an individual. It goes along with her supporting Israel, but being against Netanyahu personally. (Does this remind you of President Obama?)

Her criticism against Netanyahu is long. When she talked about her arranging the increase of defense aid to Israel, making it 3.8 billion instead of the previous 3 billion a year, she again mentioned Netanyahu who "wanted more and strongly resisted changes to the traditional terms of the grant." She criticized him for it, as the money could go for other US domestic needs. Although she said that the two parties to the Israeli-Palestinian conflict were not interested in peace, still she criticized Netanyahu's "settlements" policy as making it impossible to reach peace with the "two-state solution" (SusanR 430).

She said that because of the Iran negotiations and deal, the relationship between President Obama and Prime Minister Netanyahu "deteriorated", and Netanyahu's supporters "leveled dishonest ad hominem attacks against the president and his closest advisors, including me." These attacks frustrated her, and she saw them as "unfair", especially after she had worked so hard at the UN to defend Israel (SusanR 431).

Note to the Reader

At this point of time there is a need to take a detour and to be introduced to a very important figure who played a part during the Obama-Netanyahu "drama" (President Obama's language).

President of Israel Shimon Peres

Introduction

Shimon Peres served as President of Israel (2007 till 2014) during six years of President Obama's presidency. It should be noted that Israel is a parliamentary democracy, and the power rests with the Prime Minister, who gains a majority in the Knesset (Israeli parliament). The President is not elected by popular vote, but by members of parliament. The office of president in Israel is equivalent to the Queen of England, a figurehead who unites the people above politics.

Prior to becoming president, Peres was in politics for most of his life, as a parliament member from the Labor Party. He started his political journey at a very young age, as Director General of the Defense Ministry, when Israel's first Prime Minister, David Ben-Gurion, was in office. Peres was charged by Ben-Gurion to be the one to connect with the French, who supplied Israel with the know-how in Israel's campaign to achieve nuclear capability.

In later years, Peres was the one who designed and was in charge of the negotiations with the PLO at Oslo, that brought about the agreement, later signed at the White House, between the Israeli Prime Minister Yitzhak Rabin and PLO Chief Yasser Arafat. Both Rabin and Peres, along with Arafat, received the Nobel Peace Price for the Oslo Accords.

The Oslo Accords were very controversial in Israel. It brought Arafat from Tunisia into the country. It didn't take long and terrorism was raining bombs and suicide bombers all over the country.

The Oslo Accords also produced the first political assassination of a prime minister in Israel. In November 1994, Prime Minister Yitzhak Rabin was killed at a public square in the center of Tel-Aviv. The confessed killer was sentenced to life in prison.

President Obama on Peres

On June 13, 2012, President Obama awarded President Peres of Israel the Medal of Freedom at the White House.

President Obama started his remarks by saying that "…no individual has done so much over so many years to build our alliance and to bring our two nations closer…", calling him "our friend".

President Obama commended Peres for looking for security for Israel, quoting the first Prime Minister of Israel, David Ben-Gurion, who said,

"An Israel capable of defending herself, which cannot be destroyed, can bring peace nearer." President Obama said that Peres knows that security is not only dependent on strength but also "upon the righteousness of its deeds – its moral compass." And Peres's energy is to achieve "peace, security and dignity, for Israelis and Palestinians and all Israel's Arab neighbors."

President Obama commended Peres for always looking to achieve the world – as it should be, and not to accept it as it is. He quoted Peres as saying, "A good Jew can never be satisfied."

Rahm Emanuel comes to mind when he commented on his own mother saying to her sons, "I hate all of you equally," as a saying attributed to all Jewish mothers. Here, Peres's saying only exposes his own view from his own life, projecting it on all other Jewish people.

[Note: In Pirkei Avot ("Ethics of the Fathers" – a section of the Talmud that is a collection of proverbs from various Talmudic rabbis) it is said, "Who is rich? The one who is **satisfied** with what he has."]

Summary

One can understand the need for pleasantries at such an occasion, but to say of Peres that "…no individual has done so much over so many years to build our alliance and to bring our two nations closer…"?

There had to be something that Peres had to do to bring such accolades from President Obama. What was it? In order to find what it was, we need to go back to Peres's history, the way he was seen by both Americans and Israelis.

Back to the Late Eighties

When George Shultz served as Secretary of State in President Reagan's administration, Shimon Peres served as Israel's Foreign Minister in the unity government established between the Likud Party (the party that Prime Minister Benjamin Netanyahu now heads) and the Labor party. Since the elections produced a stalemate between the two, they decided to split the government between them. The first two years, Peres (Labor) would be prime minister and Yitzhak Shamir (Likud) would be foreign minister, and they would reverse roles in the other two years.

Secretary of State George Shultz on Shimon Peres

Shultz reported in his book[13] that Peres organized a meeting with King Hussein of Jordan in London on the weekend of April 10, 1987. The meeting was with the knowledge of the US State Department, and Shultz designated an ambassador to be present at the meeting (Shultz 937).

Shultz reported that an emissary from Peres, Yossi Beilin, came to inform him of the meeting and the agreement that the two sides reached. The emissary portrayed the agreement as a "breakthrough", and Peres felt, as Beilin described it, that it was "the most historically significant step for Israel" since even before Israeli independence.

Although Peres and King Hussein didn't sign any paper, still they shook hands, and as Beilin labeled it, "This handshake had the feeling of an historic event." (Shultz 938)

At this point, came Peres's request. The initiative should not be presented as either an Israeli or Jordanian initiative, but as a US initiative. Peres requested that Shultz should visit the area, and present this agreement to the Israeli government and the Israeli public as his idea (Shultz 938).

At this point, Shultz said in his book:

> "Yet this urgent request was extraordinary: the foreign minister of Israel's government of national unity was asking me to sell to Israel's prime minister, the head of a rival party, the substance of an agreement made with a foreign head of state – an agreement revealed to me before it had been revealed to the Israeli government itself! Peres was informing me, and wanting me to collaborate with him, before going to his prime minister. The situation was explosive, especially because Shamir and his Likud party were vociferously denouncing the idea of an international conference of any kind." (Shultz 939).

---

[13] George P. Shultz, "Turmoil and Triumph: My Years As Secretary of State", Scribners, 1993

Shultz didn't want to be "deceiving", a behavior he labeled as "a deadly practice in diplomacy and one that would inevitably be discovered." Shultz wanted to capitalize on this development, but he did not want to deceive Shamir, as Peres had requested him to do. Shultz insisted that Peres should be the one to present it to Prime Minister Shamir (Shultz 939).

Shultz called Prime Minister Shamir and informed him that Peres had approached him, and that he wanted to come to the area to discuss the new agreement. Shamir asked Shultz for time to think about it, and then sent his emissary to give his negative answer to Shultz (Shultz 940).

Shultz ended his description by saying, "By early May, Jordan had disclaimed the London agreement, leaving Peres out on a limb, testy, and tending to blame me." (Shultz 941)

Yitzhak Rabin on Shimon Peres

Rabin served as prime minister for 3 years (1974-1977) after the Golda Meir government collapsed after the 1973 Yom Kippur war. Rabin did not want to, but he had to appoint Shimon Peres as defense minister, due to the power structure within the Labor Party. However, for this decision he said, "It was an error I would regret and whose price I would pay in full." (Rabin 241)[14]

Rabin talked extensively about Peres. When the two of them were competing for the post of head of the party, later to become prime minister, Peres offered him a gentlemanly agreement: "Let's conclude a gentleman's agreement to hold a fair contest. Whoever loses will accept the decision in good spirit and be loyal to the winner."

Rabin's response was: "…my inclination was not to believe a word he said." (Rabin 239)

Rabin said that what bothered him the most was not his disagreements with Peres, as it is natural for members of the same government to disagree. What bothered him was that once a debate in the government is done, and a vote is taken, all members of said government should support

---

[14] Yitzhak Rabin, "The Rabin Memoirs", University of California Press, Berkeley, 1979

the decision. But this was not Peres's behavior. His tendency was to go to the news media and talk against the decision of the government of which he himself was a member. Rabin listed two major examples. (Rabin 307).

When there was a leak of a very sensitive diplomatic development, polygraph was used to find who had leaked the information. When nobody was found as the culprit among the bureaucrats, Rabin, Peres, and Foreign Minister Yigal Allon met to discuss the matter. When Allon suggested that all three of them should take the polygraph, Peres threatened to resign (Rabin 308).

Although it is not in the English version of his memoirs, but only in the Hebrew edition, Rabin gave Peres the label of "indefatigable schemer", a label that stuck with him during his years in politics. Once he became president, allegedly leaving politics behind him, the label faded into the past, and he was very likeable, and even loved by the public.

Yitzhak Shamir on Shimon Peres

Yitzhak Shamir in his book[15] gave the same description as Secretary of State George Shultz had given of the so-called London agreement between King Hussein and Peres.

Peres came to Shamir's office, read him aloud the document of the agreement (remember? it was not signed), and refused to give Shamir a copy to study it. Shamir received a copy from the US ambassador in Israel (Shamir 208).

Shamir also echoes the same complaints that Yitzhak Rabin had of Shimon Peres.

Shamir said that Peres had good connections in the news media, and also with intellectuals in western Europe. Peres knew how to talk with people, and to convince them of his ideas, but Shamir labeled him as "a man one cannot work with, and he is completely unreliable" (Shamir 200).

---

[15] Yitzhak Shamir, "Summing Up", Yedioth Ahronoth, Tel-Aviv, 2015

Like Rabin, Shamir also complained about Peres who, despite being a minister in the unity government, still fought the government "with any means and to scheme against, if it serves his political needs." (Shamir 201)

Shamir also gave details of Peres's behavior. Peres talked with "foreign elements" without the knowledge of the members of the government of which he himself was a member.

When Secretary of State James Baker demanded that Israel would agree to let the Arabs of east Jerusalem, and expelled Arabs from the territories, take part in the future planned negotiations, Peres demanded that the government would accept this demand right away. Shamir couldn't understand why the Israeli government had "to act with a stopwatch and to be so excited by the wishes of an American Secretary of State…" This crisis brought the unity government to dissolve (Shamir 259).

Shamir also gave Peres's attitude towards the Jewish towns (aka "settlements") in Judea and Samaria:

> "…he was extreme in his opposition – that reached the level of hatred – to the towns that were established beyond the green line. For reasons I could never understand, they simply angered him, literally." (Shamir 202)

Back to the question:

What did Peres do that brought such accolades from President Obama?

Peres had the reputation in previous US administrations, and also among his Israeli counterparts, of being "a loose cannon". He conducted his own foreign policy, regardless of who was in the government in Israel, and regardless of whether he had signed any agreement for a coalition government. And even after moving to the symbolic position of being a figurehead (President), he still continued with such behavior.

And knowing now his attitude towards the "settlements" in Judea and Samaria, an issue that brought him to hatred and even anger ("literally" according to PM Shamir), it is quite likely that Peres indeed was considered by President Obama as the one who did the most to strengthen the alliance "between the two countries", by opposing the "settlements" as Obama wanted.

While President Obama was in office, he encountered two types of Israel. One was represented by Prime Minister Netanyahu, heading the elected government of Israel, and the other was represented by President Peres, running his own foreign policy that suited President Obama. It was no surprise that by President Obama's standards Peres deserved the Medal of Freedom. He was "free" of all constraints of standards and of the accepted behaviors that are called for by politicians in office.

In fact, President Obama's approach to the "settlements", stating that they are eroding the Jewish character of the country by preventing the creation of "two states for two peoples", is an Israeli leftist mantra advocated by Peres.

Back to Susan Rice

Rice and Peres

NSA Rice labeled Israeli President Shimon Peres as "my cherished friend" and "hero",
"one of Israel's greatest sons and a walking global treasure" (SusanR 254, 431, Speech 6-25-2014).

The two met in 2009 at a luncheon in his honor hosted by a Jewish organization. Both of them spoke at the occasion, and at the end, "he held me by my shoulders, looked deeply into my eyes with his piercing blues, and thanked me for my words and my service." (SusanR 254, 431)

Of her relationship with Peres she said:

"Peres was warm, energetic, charming, funny, and, all told, the sexiest senior citizen I have ever known. I loved Shimon Peres like a father figure but can only imagine what a devil he might have been in his prime." (SusanR 255)

Rice said that Peres "…loved President Obama like a son, and saw in him so many qualities of greatness, as he often told me. He worried about

Obama's security and political fortunes and cared deeply for those of us close to him." (SusanR 255)

There are two things that she said in her book that indicate a constant connection throughout the years. The first was: "I could always rely on one phenomenal Israeli man to be in my corner" – indicating that he supported her against criticism, quite likely from Netanyahu and his supporters. She referred to this criticism elsewhere, and it aggravated her a lot, especially since she had defended Israel so strongly at the UN (SusanR 254).

The second was: "He would write or call when he sensed from afar that I might need moral support" – again, "moral support" when such was needed (SusanR 255).

In a speech she gave on June 25, 2014, she said:

"On more than one occasion, when from very far away, he sensed that perhaps I was having a bit of a rough patch, he would call or write or find some other special way of letting me know that he was there, and that I was in his thoughts…"

In that same speech, she gave two quotes that she labeled as a "Peres-ism". The first was: "Polls are like perfume – nice to smell, dangerous to swallow." This might relate to the fact that he always got high percentages in the TV exit polls on election day, only to lose when the real results came in. The second saying, which she also quoted in another speech addressed to non-Jewish people was: "There are no hopeless situations, only hopeless people."

Obama's Duality on Israel

As we saw earlier in the book, in almost every characteristic and trait Obama shows duality. And the same applies to Israel. On the one hand, he is a strong supporter of Israel's security, unparalleled by any previous president; and on the other hand, harsh and public criticism against Israeli "settlements" in Judea and Samaria.

President Obama was not new in this criticism of the "settlements". All previous administrations were against the Jewish towns, aka "settlements", and very strongly.   One only needs to remember President Bush 41, who froze all loan guarantees to Israeli absorption of Russian immigrants as a means of pressure on Israel to stop the building of Jewish towns in Judea and Samaria.

It is the concept that Israeli ambassador to the US Michael Oren labeled as "daylight". This means that "daylight" refers to taking the argument openly into the public, and "darkness" means to keep the argument behind closed doors, without the public having any hint of such an argument.

From the beginning, President Obama, with his extreme "honesty", advocated taking the argument over the "settlements" into the open – "daylight". Oren quoted Obama saying, "When there is no daylight, Israel just sits on the sidelines and that erodes our credibility with the Arabs." (MicOr 87).

The problem with this approach, Oren said, that it simply doesn't work.

In the Middle East, security is "largely a product of impressions". The bottom line is that "a friend who stands by his friends on some issues but not on others is, in Middle Eastern eyes, not really a friend." (MicO88)

The only thing I wonder about what Oren said, is whether this saying is only true of the Middle East. It might be true all over the globe, and it might be true for any relationship, whether between countries, or even between people.

As a result, Oren said, "In the Middle East, when the White House pressured Israel on peace, the enemies of peace could conclude that America might not stand beside Israel in war." (MicOr 89)

According to news media reports in Israel, there was pressure from the White House on Netanyahu to stop the publication of Oren's book. Netanyahu refused, saying that Israel is a democratic country, and there is no way to censor people.

Now we can understand why, after Obama's speech in Cairo in 2009, addressing the Muslim world, his approval rating in Israel was only 4%. Note that in sociology research, a result of 4% is equivalent to zero, because in the social sciences one never gets results of 0% or 100%. A result of 4% is negligible, and thus equivalent to zero. Many people in Israel were certain that he is a Muslim (and Obama himself described himself as "Christian and skeptic"). Moreover, his insistence that Israel should freeze the "settlements" painted him as being negative to Israel, at least in the eyes of Netanyahu and his supporters, and perhaps even by people more towards the center of the map.

Even his friendly speech while visiting Israel ("you are not alone") didn't change the perception at all. As Oren said, supporting a friend in one issue, and going against the same friend in another issue, is not really a "friend".

In essence, President Obama sent the Arab world a message of betrayal of Israel. If this was not enough, when the "Arab Spring" started, and he demanded the immediate resignation of President Mubarak of Egypt, he sent another message of betrayal – in this case, betrayal of his Arab friend.

Amos Gilead, a former high-ranking officer in the Israeli intelligence commented[16] on the fact that there were only three countries that the Arab Spring didn't "touch": Saudi Arabia, Jordan, and Morocco. These three countries are monarchies, and each king considers himself to be a descendant of the prophet Muhammad. This is the reason that the population didn't rebel against these three kings. After all, blood relationship to the prophet Muhammad is more important than the American-advocated democracy.

President Obama's speech in Cairo did not accomplish its objectives. The Arabs at large still detest the west, and see the west as trying to impose a foreign culture on them.

But President Obama did accomplish something. I am almost certain he didn't have it in mind, but it is a so-called "unexpected consequence". He managed to bring the Sunni Arab countries closer to Israel, to the point that there are many reports of high-ranking Saudis visiting Israel to meet their Israeli counterparts.

---

[16] Shimon Shiffer, "The Warning: Conversations with General (Ret.) Amos Gilead", Yedioth Ahronoth, Rishon Letzion, 2019

By signing the JCPOA agreement with Iran in 2015, he sent the Sunni Arab countries a message that "the enemy of my enemy is my friend" – i.e. that Israel must be their friend because, like the Sunni Arab countries, Israel is the enemy of Iran. It is like the story of the Gentile prophet Balaam, mentioned in the book of Numbers, who was contracted to curse the Israelites, but the poetry he produced about the Israelites is wonderful. There is an expression in Hebrew referring to this: "He wanted to curse, and he came out blessing."

Again, only about the "settlements".

UN Security Council Resolution 2334

Nikki Haley served as US Ambassador to the UN during the first two years of the Trump administration. In her book[17] she gives the long history of the UN anti-Israel agenda, to include even the resolution in 1975 declaring Zionism to be "racism" (NikkiH 80).

[Note: the resolution was reversed a few years later.]

Haley explains that there is a difference between the Security Council, where the US and the other four powers – Russia, China, Great Britain, and France – enjoy veto power, and the General Assembly, where they do not have this power, and all countries are equal. Therefore, the decisions condemning Israel, which consume around 50% of all UN decisions, are voted in the General Assembly and other UN agencies, such as UNESCO. "Zionism as Racism" was voted in the General Assembly, while in the Security Council the US voted many times against resolutions condemning Israel (NikkiH 80-81).

On December 23, 2016, during the transition time between the elections of November 2016 and the end of the Obama presidency, the Security Council approved Resolution 2334 condemning Israeli "settlements" in the West Bank (NikkiH 81).

Haley added information that the news media didn't report. First, the resolution not only condemned the existence of the "settlements" in Judea and Samaria. It actually "declared illegal all Israeli activity in all

---

[17] Nikki R. Haley, "With All Due Respect: Defending America with Grit and Grace", St. Martin Press, New York, 2019

the territories that are disputed by the Palestinians" ["all" in italics in the original], to include the Western Wall at the site of the Temple Mount.

Haley said that not only did the US mission not veto the decision. The US mission privately told the other members of the council that they will not veto, and by doing so, the US "affirmatively participated" in the resolution (NikkiH 82).

Haley summed up the Obama administration's policy towards the Israeli-Palestinian conflict as "almost exclusively in terms of Israeli settlements in the West Bank".

She added that when she came to the offices of the US State Department in Washington DC, the walls were covered with maps of Israeli "settlements" (NikkiH 138).

Haley added one more point that the Obama administration did at the UN. Not only did it abstain in the UN in the anti-"settlements" resolution, but the US also abstained when a resolution was accepted blaming the United States for the poverty and oppression in Cuba (NikkiH 94-95).

If one can abstain on a resolution against Israel, why not to abstain on a resolution against the US? After all, there is an "unshakeable" bond between the two countries.

There is one point that Haley neglects to mention. There have been numerous UN Security Council resolutions against Israel that deal with Jerusalem and the "settlements". They are meaningless. Dead letters. The only UN Security Council resolutions that are meaningful are Resolutions 242 and 338, both voted after the two wars – 242 after the Six-Day War, and 338 after the Yom Kippur War. Both decisions are meaningful for one reason: Israel accepted them as binding. The rest are forgotten and nobody even mentions them. It is likely to be the same fate for 2334.

President Obama naively thought that he would leave a "legacy" that would haunt Israel in the future for its "settlements" in Judea and Samaria. The only thing that he managed to accomplish with this decision is to paint himself as anti-"settlements" person.

The "Settlements" in Jewish History

When a trickle of secular Jews started to arrive in Ottoman Palestine in the early 1880s, the Jewish population was small, estimated to be around sixty thousand among a quarter of a million Arabs. As time passed, more and more Jews came in. They purchased land that the Arab landowners considered worthless (because the landowners would not sell any other type of land to Jews). The Jews rehabilitated and cultivated the land, and built infrastructure, and provided more and more jobs. Therefore, not only Jews immigrated into Israel, but also Arabs immigrated in from all neighboring countries, looking for work in Jewish farms and factories. At the time of Israeli independence, there were six hundred thousand Jews in Israel. Today (2020) there are over seven million Jews in the country.

The return of the Jews to their historical homeland is a historical process. The only reason that people do not see it as such, not even Israelis, is that unlike Moses, who took the Israelites out of Egypt – one leader taking all the people behind him – in modern times there was no individual leader. Every Jew who came to Palestine/Israel did so for his own reasons. It was not community-organized, but an individualistic venture. Still, it is the returning of the exiles to their homeland.

From the time the Israelites entered the land, crossing the Jordan River with Joshua, till the kingdom of David, 480 years passed. From the trickle of Jews who entered the land in the 1880s till today (2020) 140 years passed.

One only needs patience.

The Iran Deal

Wendy Sherman and the Iran Deal

Wendy Sherman was the lead negotiator for the United States on the 2015 Iran nuclear deal, and has held other government positions over the years. She wrote a book about her experiences, titled "Not for the Faint of Heart".[18]

The Iran Deal

In 2015, the five permanent members of the UN Security Council (the US, UK, France, Russia, and China – also known as "the P5"), along with Germany (therefore P5+1) reached an agreement with Iran, by which Iran would suspend its efforts to build an atomic weapon for a duration of ten years, in exchange for the P5+1 canceling all sanctions that had been imposed on Iran, and the unfreezing of all Iranian assets in US banks.

Although several countries were involved in the negotiations, the main country facing the Iranian negotiators was the US. In fact, the "Iran deal" was considered as the "signature achievement" of President Obama during his eight years of presidency, maybe even rivaling "Obamacare".

Wendy Sherman was the US State Department official who represented the US among the P5+1. In her words, she had "the burden of representing the sheer might of the United States." (WendyS 63)

Brief History

In 1979 the western US-leaning regime of the Shah of Iran was deposed in a very violent revolution, that brought into power the Shiite religious establishment of Iran, headed at the time by the Ayatollah Khomeini. Since then Iran has been virulently anti-US (which it calls "the Big Satan") and anti-Israel (which it calls "the Little Satan").

---

[18]Wendy R. Sherman, "Not For the Faint of Heart: Lessons in Courage, Power, and Persistence", Hachette Books, New York, 2018

Iranian leaders held annual demonstrations against the US, with hundred of thousands of people marching and holding banners that said "Death to America".

At this point, it is interesting to note how Ms Sherman related in her book to this Iranian hostility towards the US:

> "It was 'Death to America' that was chanted at Friday prayers in Tehran, not 'Death to the United Nations' or any other country." (WendyS 62) [Emphasis added]

What Ms Sherman does not want the reader to know

Hello? Did her hands shake when she wrote this blatant lie? She cannot be ignorant to the Iranian hostility towards Israel. Being at the State Department, she must be more knowledgeable than a person on the street.

To set the record straight, let me share with you the information that Ms Sherman did not share with her readers:

Once Khomeini took power in Iran, the Israeli embassy building was transferred to the PLO, and the PLO flag was raised on the building. This act was symbolic, as the Khomeini regime supported the PLO's objective to replace the State of Israel.

Iran holds an annual "Jerusalem Day" in which marches are held calling for the annihilation of Israel from the face of the globe. Moreover, throughout the years, Iranian political leaders and military commanders said that their aim is to eradicate what they called "the Zionist entity" which is a "cancer" in the Middle East. Iran has also held international conferences advocating Holocaust denial.

An Iranian general was quoted once as saying that Israel is a "one bomb country" (referring to the size of the country) in which one atomic bomb is enough to finish off the whole country, while Iran, much bigger in size, can absorb an atomic bomb without it being annihilated.

This Iranian general was not wrong. In terms of an atomic attack against Israel, Israel indeed is "a one bomb country". Moreover, most of the population of Israel is not even spread over the entire length of the country. Although the country is 500 km (350 miles) long from north to south, most of the population is located in the center of the country, on a strip of 120 miles (close to 200 km) long, and at the most 40 miles (60 km) wide, although in many places it is a lot less.

When Hitler talked against the Jews, people said it was rhetoric. Well, it turned out not to be just "rhetoric". He did exactly what he said he would do.   Should Israel assume that the Iranians' talk is only "rhetoric"? Or, should Israel take what they say very seriously?

It is no wonder that the Israeli leadership, along with the entire population, live in constant fear. There is no margin for error. Israel is not a country that can take risks. One serious mistake, and the country is lost.

Back to Iran

This Iranian virulent "rhetoric" was accompanied by Iran enriching uranium, while at the same time developing their missiles, with the help of North Korean knowledge.

Iranian hostility towards Israel is not only "rhetoric". Iran finances Hizbollah in Lebanon, a terrorist organization that has attacked Israel numerous times. Iran is also financing Hamas (a Sunni terrorist organization in Gaza) and encourages it to attack Israel from the south, paying Hamas for its "service" to Iran in attacking Israel. In essence, Iran is conducting an ongoing war by proxy with Israel on two fronts, Hizbollah in the north, and Hamas in the south.

The above-mentioned information is well known all over the western media, and in diplomatic circles all over the globe. Ms Sherman decided to gloss over all this information.

We should not be surprised. Experience shows that most people do not lie by commission, but by omission. This is the reason for the most fundamental rule of SCAN – "Total Belief in the Subject".

"Total Belief in the Subject" does not mean that the person is innocent. Most deceptive people mislead us by omission. Therefore, the listener/reader should ask: "Is it possible that the statement in front of me is true, and with this true statement, the person is misleading me, and what the person does not say might turn the statement upside down by 180 degrees?"

Is this the only information that Ms Sherman decided to withhold from her readers? No!
Once she is on a campaign to mislead the reader by omission, there is no way to stop this trend.

Let's go to another issue in which Ms Sherman is doing exactly the same.

The Oslo Accord

Introduction

In 1993 the Israeli government, headed by the leftist side of the political map in Israel, signed an agreement with the PLO, headed by Yasser Arafat, to agree to mutual recognition of the two parties, and for the PLO to renounce terrorism in all its forms. In return, Israel allowed the PLO to establish the "Palestinian Authority" in the Gaza Strip, and later on in six more Arab cities in Judea and Samaria (also known as "the West Bank" of the Jordan River).

It didn't take long and major terrorist attacks started against the civilian population of Israel, in which suicide murderers blew themselves up in crowded buses, restaurants, and public places.

Israeli Prime Minister Yitzhak Rabin announced that he will pursue peace as if there is no terrorism, and he will fight terrorism as if there is no peace process. Rabin was just paraphrasing a well-known quote of David Ben-Gurion from before Israel's independence. But history moves on, and not every situation is the same.

This mantra by Rabin brought major depression over the country, to the point that Rabin was physically attacked whenever he showed up in public. The public was enraged that he, for all purposes, had deserted them. His approval ratings went to close to zero. There was no doubt that if he were to reach the elections, he would have lost them in a major defeat unheard of in the history of the state.

But Rabin was "rescued" from such defeat, as he was assassinated by an extreme rightwing young man. This assassination brought into power Shimon Peres, the one who had initiated the Oslo Accords, and was regarded as the advocate of "a new Middle East".

At the time Peres became Prime Minister, his approval ratings were very high, mainly due to the public opposing the violence that had brought about the assassination. Peres decided to bring the elections forward, before their due date, in hopes that he would get the mandate to rule on his own merit. But soon after he announced the elections, a major suicide bombing campaign started all over the country, a campaign that demolished Peres's standing with the public. He lost the elections to Benjamin Netanyahu at a very razor-thin margin.

Ms Sherman on the Events

Let's see how Sherman described the Oslo Accords:

"But what was signed that day on the South Lawn was only a framework for peace. It detailed a series of show-me steps intended to build confidence on both sides. It laid out a schedule of Israeli troop withdrawals from Palestinian-claimed territory (minus, crucially, Jerusalem and the existing Israeli settlements)." (WendyS 96)

Anyone who has read the speeches given by both Rabin from the Israeli side, and Arafat from the Arab side, could have gotten the picture quite clearly. While Rabin talked about having "enough" of bloodshed, and time to make peace, Arafat had a different tune. He talked about "peace of the brave", and not even once in his speech did he talk of "enough" to bloodshed.

In essence, it was not "a framework for peace". It was an agreement to allow Arafat to take control of the territories, and to postpone the negotiations on the "final status" of the territories for later. In essence, it was an agreement not to agree, and leave the dispute for later.

Sherman continued:

"The confidence-building steps themselves depended on a minimum level of trust before either side was willing to take them." (WendyS 97)

The "confidence-building steps" that Sherman is talking about were an idea of Peres, the one who dreamt of a "new Middle East". But in a "neighborhood" where the weak is annihilated, and the strong prospers, one does not take "confidence-building steps" with an unrepentant terrorist.

An American reader who reads this paragraph written by Sherman, should ask if the US would have reached an agreement with Al-Qaeda to "reform" the organization after 9/11.

Sherman continued:

"But progress on the Oslo Accords was excruciatingly slow. Both Arafat and Rabin faced increasing dissent about taking the interim steps that Oslo mandated. Protests turned into street violence, and not only the nagging disruptions from the Palestinian side that Oslo was designed to end." (WendyS 97)

Hello? I had to slow down my reading to make sure that I am not making a mistake in seeing how she labeled the cruel terrorist campaign that killed women, children, babies, and old people, who just were taking a bus in the city or eating pizza at a restaurant. That's how one refers to terrorism? "**Nagging disruptions** from the Palestinian side…"

And to equate the anger of the victims' families about the carnage going on in buses, restaurants, and other public places, to the "nagging disruptions" from the Palestinian side? This is the ultimate in hypocrisy.

Sherman was "right". There was violence on the Israeli side. One young man took the law into his own hands, and decided on his own to commit murder, and to assassinate the prime minister. Both the right and left vilified this one man. It was a different picture on the other side, the Arab side. According to polls conducted by the Palestinian entity, 70% of Arabs supported suicide bombings. And whenever a bus with all its innocent passengers was blown up, cheers of happiness were heard on Arab streets, and sweets were distributed to celebrate. No different from what happened in "Palestinian" cities after the attack in the US on 9/11. In essence, the Arab side was on a campaign of genocide.

Ms Sherman found one man on the Jewish side who took the law into his own hands. And this one man was equivalent for her to all the murderers on the Arab side.

She continued by saying that the assassin was "opposed to peace with the Palestinians in general and withdrawal from the West Bank in particular." (WendyS 97)

Really? I don't think that anyone in Israel is or was opposed to peace. Not the left and not the right. Not even the extreme right. Not even the one who was convicted for the assassination of Rabin. People only opposed the bloodshed that went on in the public arena, and what infuriated them the most, was that the left found a label for these victims – "the victims of peace".

I would like to share with the readers that one year before the assassination I told my brother-in-law that Rabin is going to be assassinated. Not Peres who initiated the Oslo Accords, but Rabin. My brother-in-law was in shock. How can I say something like that?

I explained to him that Peres was a gentleman. He treated people with respect. Peres treated the settlers who opposed the Oslo Accords with respect. Rabin, who was known to use excessive alcohol, and who was a constant smoker, was very demeaning to people. He used vulgar language against the people who protested the carnage on the street. Many protestors were immigrants from the US, and Rabin said that they should return to the US. (On previous occasions, Rabin had similarly insulting comments for other groups as well. He was an "equal-opportunity insulter".) As if protesting wrong government policy that produced murders in the public arena is wrong.

Since I assessed that Rabin would be assassinated, I talked with my children and warned them very seriously not to be involved in any illegal activity. To protest peacefully – yes. But not to do anything that would call for an arrest, for example, blocking streets. Nothing!!!

Back to Sherman

Does her attitude tell us that she can understand Arab violence, but she cannot understand Jewish violence? It seems that what she said is based upon this assumption, that leads her to equate these two situations.

Let's go to Sherman's other "mistakes".

She described Rabin as one who was "…pushing his own people toward the settlement imagined in the Oslo deal…", and she added that Rabin "…was a chief pillar of support for Arafat too." (WendyS 98)

Actually, from the start Rabin criticized the Oslo Accords. He was the one who labeled it as "Swiss cheese", as a metaphor for the holes that the accords left without moving to resolve them. To come and label Rabin as the "chief pillar of support for Arafat" is doing a major injustice to the memory of Rabin. This was not how Rabin perceived Arafat. Rabin himself was quoted by his aides as one who was on the verge of canceling the Oslo Accords.

If this is not enough, let's see how she perceived Arafat's position. She said, "It soon became clear that, without Rabin, Arafat would not be able to stand his ground against the hard-liners in the PLO." (WendyS 98)

Arafat, the architect of terrorism, had a track record of almost destroying the country of Jordan, until he was ejected in a bloody fight in September 1970. He then moved to Lebanon, and did the same there. He took the quietest Arab country, with a beautiful capital of Beirut that had been labeled all over the Middle East as the "Paris of the Orient", with a banking industry that served all the rich Arabs from the Gulf, and destroyed it totally. During the 1970s Arafat turned Lebanon into a base for terror attacks against Israeli citizens, and as a result Israel invaded Lebanon in 1982 and ejected Arafat. He moved to Tunisia, but he was under constant surveillance by the local authorities as they didn't want him to import his terrorism into their own country.

This same Arafat, the chief terrorist of the Middle East, who was loathed by all the Arab leaders of the Middle East, due to his blackmailing them, this same Arafat had a problem, according to the "knowledgeable"

Sherman, to deal with "hard-liners in the PLO". If this is not a joke, one might wonder what it is.

If her knowledge of the Arab side is so minimal, one might wonder what is her knowledge of the Israeli side.

She labeled Benjamin Netanyahu as "Rabin's successor as prime minister..." (WendyS 101).

But the fact is that Netanyahu was Peres's successor, and not Rabin's. It is true that Peres was only an interim prime minister, but he could have been prime minister for several more years. His position as prime minister was cut short only because of his haste to try to establish his own mandate, and he brought the elections earlier.

Before we leave the Middle East, let's see how Ms Sherman related in her book to the conflict in Syria.

Syria

Introduction

Syria is not actually a "country" in the western meaning of a "country". Before the beginning of the so-called "Arab Spring" (which in Israel was labeled as the "Arab Winter"), Syria was a country of 90% Sunni people and a 10% minority of Alawites, who were concentrated in the northwest part of the country, on the Mediterranean Sea. These 10% took over the power of the country, ruling it with an iron fist. When many years ago, the Sunnis in the city of Hama rebelled, the government forces leveled the city, killing an estimated 20,000 people.

When the "Arab Spring" started igniting the conflict in Syria, it became very clear from the beginning that the world was not facing a "civil war" in the traditional sense of the word, but a war between two different populations that had no connection between them. Moreover, it was not a war between good people fighting bad people, but a war between bad people fighting worse people.

President Obama

After reading Samantha Power's book "A Problem from Hell" [See review of that book earlier in this book], and working together with her on his own book, President Obama should have known to keep quiet about Syria, and not say anything. But he chose to say something, something that he shouldn't have said, according to Susan Rice, his own National Security Advisor.

President Obama declared a "red line" in regard to the bloodshed that went on in Syria. He said that if this "red line" would be crossed, it would be a "game changer" for him. The "red line" was the use of chemical weapons in the conflict by the Syrian government against the opposition.

[Note: One might wonder what is the scale of morality for President Obama? According to him, the massacre that went on in Rwanda was not a "game changer" as people there were killed by knives and machetes. So if killing takes place, even on a large scale, without using chemical weapons, it is ok for the morals of President Obama. But chemical weapons were not.]

Actually, by President Obama declaring this "red line" he "invited" the brutal Syrian regime to cross the line. The Syrian regime could have killed the opposition by many other means available to them. After all, they used the air force to bomb residential areas. But quite likely they used the same "game changer" weapon to notify the Arab world that they can defy the American president with impunity. And in fact, they were right, as President Obama showed it, by his making this "red line" a very changing and dimming light from one day to the next, until there was no color at all, and eventually no light.

Ms Sherman on Syria

Let's see how Ms Sherman related to this debacle of President Obama.

First she said that "Many of us… were devastated that he chose not to follow up on his red line…" (WendyS 162). This in itself tells the reader that the "many of us" knew that it was a major debacle.

Still, at the same time, she concluded that for President Obama – who had vowed not to enter "stupid wars", for whom "success was not having another major new military commitment on his watch" – that "in that sense, perhaps, Obama had won Syria already – by keeping us, by and large, out of it." (WendyS 210)

Ms Sherman, the "great diplomat", can describe a debacle as "success". As if President Obama had only one option of entering a full war to defend the helpless civilian population of Syria. According to her, and that's what she implies, the Commander in Chief of the US did not have any other forceful means, besides a full war, to deter the brutal Syrian regime.

Ms Sherman and North Korea

After seeing her track record of total ignorance about what is going on in the Middle East, let's go farther to see Ms Sherman's track record in telling us about another US foreign policy issue – North Korea.

She says that she "had been negotiating with the North Koreans since 1997…" (WendyS 103).

And if the reader would like to know why with all the negotiations going on since 1997 there was no agreement, Ms Sherman enlightens the reader by saying, "**I believe** that Kim Jong-Il was ready in 2000 to complete a deal over his missile program." (WendyS 105) [emphasis added].

She believes? Based upon what? Did she have any evidence to support such a "belief"? It is known in intelligence that one can estimate **capabilities** but not **intentions**. This truth is even more evident in a dictatorial regime than in a democracy. How can Ms Sherman know what went on in the North Korean dictator's mind? Is she a mind reader? No professional intelligence analyst would say something like – "I believe".

And she continued: "Unfortunately, my country was not ready." (WendyS 105) So, she blamed her own country for not reaching an agreement. Interesting. The innocent and naïve North Korean who so much wanted peace with the US was victimized by Ms Sherman's country! Again, if this is not a joke, what is it?

Who is Wendy Sherman?

Introduction

The Jewish affiliated community in the US is divided into three main branches: the Orthodox, Conservative, and Reform. One should note that there are many Jews in the US who are not affiliated with any of these three organized groups.

The Orthodox are the ones who adhere to all the rules and regulations mandated by the Torah to act in a certain way (called "Halakha" – the way to walk). This includes Shabbat (Sabbath observance), kosher food, and other laws. Adaptations to modern times are made according to precedents and Halakha.

The Conservative movement, although accepting the religious mandates, are more liberal in what they consider to be "adjusting" these mandates to modern times. The Reform movement is the most liberal one, and in fact this is the largest branch among the three.

Sherman labeled herself as a "Reform Jew" (WendyS 200). Let's see what it means for her to be a "Reform Jew".

The main feature of the Reform movement shows up in her book: "I still carry my parents' faith that the world can change for the better if you have the courage to keep trying…" (WendyS 216). It is known in the Reform movement as "Tikkun Olam" – "repairing the world". (i.e., after discarding many of the Torah's laws and principles, the Reform movement replaced them with a form of liberal humanism that they call "Tikkun Olam.") We will see later how she perceived the Iran deal within her "Tikkun Olam".

The division between the three main branches in American Judaism comes across with Sherman saying that her being a "Reform Jew" meant that she "carried less weight than two devout Orthodox Jews…" (referring to two specific individuals in the Obama administration) in trying to convince Jewish groups to accept the administration's Iran policy (WendyS 200).

What about her knowledge of Jewish heritage?

She talked about the Passover holiday as being one that "…challenges Jews of every generation 'to regard himself as though he, in his own person, had been a slave unto Pharaoh.'" (WendyS 2)

She is wrong. She should take a Haggadah (the book read during the Passover seder ceremony), even a Reform one, and open it, to find out that the Passover holiday is not about slavery in Egypt. The Passover Holiday is about the Exodus – **coming out of Egypt**. That every Jew in all generations should perceive himself as the one who **came out of Egypt**. It might be that she was influenced by President Obama, who used this same line, celebrating Passover as the holiday of slavery, while it is not.

Does her lack of knowledge end here?

Let's see how she related to the Holocaust. She said, "World War II didn't end conflict in the world – or even, painfully, fascism or **anti-Semitism.**" (WendyS 167)

I am not sure she actually meant what she said. But SCAN does not deal with what people mean. SCAN only deals with what people say. Her saying actually implies that the Holocaust was in the sphere of anti-Semitism.

Can anyone equate the average anti-Semitism to what the Nazis did in the Holocaust? Was the Holocaust **only** anti-Semitism? The Holocaust was something above and beyond Sherman's "anti-Semitism".

As for the Iran deal – one might wonder why she found it "particularly painful, personally" that there was "mistrust from some members of the Jewish community, at home and abroad, who sat on the far opposite side and could not see the necessity for the deal that I saw." (WendyS 170) [emphasis added]

She, the **individual**, could not understand why the **many** "who sat on the far opposite side" could not see what she saw. Maybe it would be more accurate to say that she couldn't see what they saw.

She continued by saying that "The best we could do was explain why the agreement with Iran was the best, safest option for Israel." (WendyS 200)

If the Israeli leadership found the deal very dangerous to Israel, how can Ms Sherman decide that the deal is "the best, safest option for Israel"? Does she know something that Israelis, who will later need to suffer the consequences of such a deal, do not know?

An administration that is in power **for eight years** is moving to approach a deal to prevent the most existential enemy of Israel, the one who advocates the annihilation of Israel, no different from Hitler and the Nazis, this **eight-year** long administration is signing an agreement to prevent Iran from developing a nuclear bomb **for ten years**. And what would happen after these ten years? Once Iran will develop the bomb after these ten years, should the Israeli population come to Ms Sherman to complain?

To show that there is support for the deal, even in Israel, Ms Sherman brought two Israeli "sources". The first was Meir Dagan, then chief of the Mossad, who was quoted in *The New Yorker* as if attacking Iran would give the Iranians more reason to develop the bomb (WendyS 25).

Dagan was known in Israel to be "anti-Netanyahu". Whatever Netanyahu said, Dagan would say the opposite; yet he is a reliable "source" for her. In fact, Israel had already bombed two Arab nuclear reactors, one in Iraq, and one in Syria, and amazingly enough, demolishing their reactors didn't bring these two countries to continue their efforts to achieve the bomb.

Ms Sherman brought another source to support her "help" to Israel. She attended a conference at "The Institute for National Security Studies" (INSS) in Tel Aviv in January 2016.

She mentioned the head of this institute, retired general Amos Yadlin, as being "among the most helpful Israelis as we negotiated the Iran deal." (WendyS 210-211)

She also mentioned that after her speech, "several attendees told me that they had never understood what we had done and thanked me for our

work. I couldn't have felt better or more successful than I did just then."
(WendyS 211).

She omitted a simple fact. Due to various historical reasons, the
high-ranking officials in the intelligence and the security organizations in
Israel are extreme leftists, to include both General Amos Yadlin and all
the attendees in that conference.   It is no wonder that they supported the
leftist US President. And in fact, as it is shown in this book, President
Obama supported the security (leftwing) of Israel while he was against
the elected government (rightwing) of Israel.

Iran Deal – Tikkun Olam

In essence, Ms Sherman told the reader that her "Tikkun Olam"
(repairing the world), via the Iran deal, came with a warranty of only ten
years.

Let's see how Ms Sherman herself relates to the weakness of the Iran
deal.

Diplomacy

The Iran deal was reached via diplomacy. Ms Sherman says that
"Diplomacy is not for the faint of heart." (WendyS 156)

She goes on to explain why. First, diplomacy "rarely achieves its
objectives in a linear fashion." Moreover, once an agreement is reached,
"words you agree to will be interpreted and reargued by both sides as
they carry out the terms amid the jostle of events." (WendyS 156)

She explains to the reader how failure should not be attributed to the
diplomats – "Failure in diplomacy can sometimes be attributed to a lack
of what I call 'ripeness.'"
She then explains what "ripeness" means – "The term has been adopted
by the legal world to mean a situation that can't be resolved." (WendyS
102)

One might wonder, if a "situation" "cannot be resolved", then why would
diplomats even try to resolve it? Ms Sherman has an answer.

"We diplomats live in denial… We are eternal optimists, continuing to bring groups together or shuttling from one to the other, even as those looking on can see that nothing is going to change." (WendyS 102).

Reading the above, brings one to wonder whether Ms Sherman is talking against the Iran deal.

And when agreement is reached – "…an agreement that fixes one problem should not be sacrificed even though other problems remain or arise."

In this sentence, Ms Sherman explains why the Iran deal dealt only with Iran's developing of the bomb, and not dealing with Iran developing the means to deliver the bomb, i.e. developing ballistic missiles, even for a range that can reach Europe, not to mention Israel, and they are on the way to develop missiles that can reach the US. No different from North Korea.

And if one thinks that this was an oversight, Ms Sherman explains to the reader that this was intentional, directed by President Obama.

"The Iran deal, for instance, was designed to keep Iran from ever getting a bomb. This definition, set by President Obama, was met, and we resisted attempts to extend the deal's purview to stopping Iran's activities in Syria or Yemen…" (WendyS 194-195).

One should note that she mentioned Iran's spreading terrorism all over the Middle East, but neglected to mention Iran's development of ballistic missiles.

But even when one has "success" in diplomacy, Ms Sherman says that "…success in diplomacy is so vulnerable to changing circumstances", and she adds that agreements can be "…overrun by events, undermined or declared invalid by succeeding leaders, or simply disregarded." (WendyS 194)

She mentions three options for "changing circumstances":

1. Overrun by events
2. Undermined or declared invalid by succeeding leaders

3. Simply disregarded

While the second option relates to President Trump canceling the US participation in the agreement, Ms Sherman lists two more options that make agreements invalid, and these two are not related to President Trump.

In other words, Ms Sherman is telling the reader that "success" in diplomacy is temporary, and over the long run is actually meaningless.

The bottom line is that she really convinced me that any limits placed on Iran in the Iran deal were meaningless.

The Iran Deal – Opposing View

Introduction

H.R. McMaster, who was National Security Advisor to President Trump at the beginning of the Trump administration, published his book[19], giving us insight into the Iran deal "achieved" by President Obama.

The advantage of McMaster's book is the fact that unlike Wendy Sherman, McMaster is also a historian, and therefore he does not tend to look at events as if they happen in a vacuum. He consistently takes into consideration the historical background of events and people, as well as of countries.

Two concepts are featured in his book: "Strategic Empathy" and "Strategic Narcissism". McMaster quoted the historian Zachary Shore to define "Strategic Empathy": "the skill of understanding what drives and constrains one's adversary". "Strategic Narcissism" is the exact opposite. Quoting the definition set by Hans Morgenthau and Ethel Person in their essay "The Roots of Narcissism", it is "the tendency to view the world only in relation to the United States and to assume that the future course of events depends primarily on U.S. decisions or plans." (McM 16, 15)

---

[19] H.R. McMaster, "Battlegrounds: The Fight to Defend the Free World", HarperCollins, 2020

According to McMaster, "…Strategic Narcissism leads to policies and strategies based on what **the purveyor prefers**, rather than on what **the situation demands.**" (McM16) [emphasis added]

McMaster also described past US policies as being "…over-optimistic, they also led to complacency and hubris," and defines the word "hubris" as "extreme pride leading to overconfidence, often results in misfortune." (McM 11)

The word "hubris" appears very early in McMaster's book, and I feel obligated to remind the reader that this word also appeared in Michelle Obama's book to describe Barack's behavior in being late to meet her in their initial encounter.

However, McMaster does not discriminate between Democrats and Republicans. In his view, all past US administrations suffered from this malady, starting with President Clinton, on to President G.W. Bush, and on to President Obama.

Knowing McMaster's approach to world events, we can move now to examine how McMaster views the Iranians.

Iran – background

Unlike Wendy Sherman, McMaster goes back in history and gives the reader information about the Iranians, starting from the 1930s. At that time, the ruler of Iran, Reza Shah, maintained connections with Germany, Italy and Turkey, or in other words, with the Axis who later fought the Allies in the Second World War. Many years later, in November 2017, the Saudi prince Mohammad bin Salman labeled the Iranian leader Khamenei "the new Hitler of the Middle East" (McM 320, 325).

It is a point to note that like the Saudi prince, the Israeli Prime Minister Benjamin Netanyahu saw the Iranian President Ahmadinejad, who advocated the annihilation of Israel, as a "twin of Hitler" (Storm 66).

McMaster concludes by saying that the Iranian regime's hostility to the US, Israel, Arab countries, and the west is "permanent", and the slogans "Great Satan," "Death to Israel," and "Death to America", are "not mere bluster" (McM 296, 320).

McMaster also brings the reader information which is missing from Sherman's book, that when the Ayatollah Khomeini returned to Iran in 1979, "the crowds that greeted him chanted anti-Western and anti-Israel slogans." McMaster added, "resentment toward American and Britain… remains a principal emotional determinant of Iranian foreign and military policy…" (McM 321).

McMaster summarized the situation in Iran by saying that the "so-called moderates in Iran were moderate mainly in American and Western imaginations, but rarely at home." (McM 306)

Moreover, McMaster says that during the Bush administration, Iranian agents in Iraq killed 600 American soldiers, "over 17 percent of all U.S. deaths in Iraq from 2003 to 2011", and McMaster concluded that "it was implausible that Iranian leaders were not responsible" for these American deaths (McM 308).

But Iranian aggression towards the US was not only restricted to Iraq. McMaster brings the information that the Iranians plotted the assassination of the Saudi ambassador to the US at a restaurant in Washington DC. This was supposed to take place in November 2011, three years into the Obama administration, a plot that was foiled before it took place (McM 309).

McMaster said that from 2008, the year that President Obama was elected, till 2018, two years into the Trump administration, "Iran spent nearly $140 billion on its military and combat operations abroad." (McM 325)

This was the Iran that President Obama decided to engage in giving them "permission" to delay **by only ten years** their effort to produce a nuclear bomb.

Iran – corruption

Although the Iranian regime is run by Ayatollahs, who are allegedly pious clergy, these Ayatollahs only prove the axiom that power corrupts, and absolute power corrupts absolutely.

McMaster brings the reader the information that the "pious clergy" established "bonyads" – "religious foundations" that "control businesses, receive government contracts, launder money, operate without any external audits, and pay no taxes." Many of the children of Ayatollahs are running these "religious foundations". The largest bonyad controls more than 100 businesses in all areas of the economy (McM 313).

McMaster said that journalists found out how the bonyads squandered the wealth of the country, in spite of the "educated population, geostrategic location, and natural resources". Right after the Iran Deal was reached, and the US gave the Iranians $1.7 billion dollars in cash, "at least 90 of the 110 commercial agreements and approximately $80 billion in outside investment went to state-controlled companies." (McM 323, 315)

McMaster added that during the presidency of the ultra-conservative Ahmadinejad, "the **kleptocratic regime** wasted an estimated $800 billion in oil wealth." [emphasis added] This endemic corruption in Iran produces a major "brain drain" on the country. "Approximately 150,000 educated Iranians emigrate every year, costing the country up to $150 billion annually." (McM 337) Interestingly, many years ago, the Los Angeles Times reported the same phenomenon in the "Palestinian territories" once Arafat established his regime there.

McMaster draws parallels to "the tyrannical Communist totalitarian regimes of the Cold War era" (McM 323). But why to go so "far" in time, 30 years? One only needs to read the book published by Senator McCain[20] who labeled the Russian president Vladimir Putin as a "corrupt strongman" who established "endemic corruption" in Russia, the "crooked ex-KGB colonel…", for whom "crime has most certainly paid…" (McCain 241, 252, 310, 236).

Reading about the corruption in Iran, reminds me of the "monopolies" established by the corrupt Arafat regime in the "Palestinian Authority", discussed earlier in this book, a regime that extorted the population of their meager income, and raised the prices of food by 300%. This was the regime that President Obama urged Israel to make peace with. It is no wonder that the Iranians and the "Palestinians" were in bed together. Yet both of these regimes were favorites of President Obama to talk with.

---

[20] John McCain, "The Restless Wave: Good Times, Just Causes, Great Fights, and other Appreciations", Simon & Schuster, 2018.

The Iran Deal according to McMaster

McMaster starts his analysis of the Iran deal by mentioning his two main concepts – "strategic empathy" and "strategic narcissism". He said that the Iran deal was "…an extreme case of strategic narcissism… that U.S. actions were the principal source of Iranian attitudes and behaviors." He went on to quote Wendy Sherman, who said in her book, "…we need to see our adversaries not as eternal enemies or as dispensable ones, but as virtual partners." (McM 294, 315)

This "strategic narcissism" "…was based on wishful thinking – wishful thinking that led to self-delusion and, ultimately, the deception of the American people." (McM 294)

McMaster wrote that it would be "an a-historical fantasy" to assume that bringing the Iranian Islamic Republic into the world of nations would be "a force for stability in the Middle East" (McM 317).

His indictment of the deal goes even further: "A superficial understanding of history is often more misleading than complete ignorance." He explains it by saying that the Obama administration was "sympathetic to the New Left's interpretation of history, in which the modern ills of the world are attributed mainly to capitalist imperialism and an overly powerful United States." (McM 315, 316)

True to his profession as a historian, McMaster's indictment is not addressed only to the Obama administration. According to McMaster: "Across six administrations, goodwill never begot goodwill with Iran. Conciliation has never brought moderation or a shift in the regime's permanent hostility to the United States, Israel, Europe, and the Arab monarchies." And the main problem with the Iran deal reached by the Obama administration was that it did not take into consideration "…the underlying problem: the Iranian regime's hostility…" In essence, according to McMaster, by signing the Iran deal, the Obama administration sided "…with a repressive regime against its own people and the peoples of the region." (McM 318, 332, 318)

McMaster indicts also the way the Obama administration "marketed" the deal to the American people. One can summarize his approach by saying that the Obama administration lied to the American people.

Instead of carefully examining the deal with all its defects, the Obama administration focused on "selling" it. McMaster specifically disagrees with President Obama's deputy national security advisor, Ben Rhodes, who equated those who opposed the deal to those who were in favor of the Iraq war. Moreover, Rhodes presented the situation as if the choice was either the deal or war, a presentation that McMaster labeled as "false" (McM 317).

Rhodes was also the chief architect who designed the campaign to "market" the deal by emphasizing that the deal was intended to address only the nuclear issue, and not other issues. McMaster defines what were these "other issues": "…the regime's tyrannical repression of its own population, its support for terrorists, and the perpetuation of violence in the Middle East." In short, all the holes that the deal left unaddressed. (McM 318)

The Iran Deal – Problems

McMaster listed all the issues that the deal did not address, but were essential in order to curtail Iran's aggression.

But the first problem is that the deal did not even cover all the nuclear issues. It only dealt with stopping the development of the actual nuclear bomb (for only ten years), but at the same time, the Iranians were free to develop all the means to ship this future bomb to its destination – developing the ballistic missiles that would carry the nuclear warhead. In fact, once the deal was reached, Iran concentrated all its efforts in this "department" while adhering to the deal's constraints on developing the bomb.

Moreover, the deal did not concern itself with "the very nature of an Iranian regime that was fundamentally untrustworthy…" Even Wendy Sherman in her testimony before Congress said, "deception is in their DNA." And since "enforcement mechanisms were far from foolproof", the deal was a major concern to the people who were familiar with "the regime's long record of hostility and duplicity" (McM 293, 294).

In fact, in the words of US Central Command commander Gen. Joseph Votel, after the deal was reached, Iran grew "more aggressive in the days [after] the agreement." And the 1.7 billion dollars in cash that was shipped on planes to Iran only intensified the Iranian "proxy wars in the region" (McM 295, 314).

If these were the only problems with the deal, one could counter them by saying that hindsight is always perfect. But the Obama administration did something more sinister. When the rebellion started in Syria against the tyrannical regime, and ISIS established itself in both Syria and Iraq, the Obama administration started a "train-and-equip" program to help opposition groups to fight ISIS.

However, the Obama administration imposed on the fighters who received the training and the equipment to sign a contract that they will not use their training or their equipment to fight either Syrian or Iranian forces, and to only attack ISIS (McM 274).

I was shocked to read this information. I could understand why the Obama administration wanted the opposition groups to concentrate on fighting ISIS. But to prevent these opposition groups from attacking the Iranian forces in Syria? The existential threat to Israel is the Iranian regime. And the Iranians were moving their forces from being far away from the border of Israel, to bring them close to the Israeli border.

In fact, just a few months after the deal was reached, Iran shipped hundreds of soldiers to Syria to help the regime fight the opposition (McM 312).

And President Obama, who professed so strongly his commitment to the security of the state of Israel, is helping the Iranians to bring their forces closer to Israel? If this is not "duplicity" (Iranian's trait), what is it?

But this is not all that the Obama administration did. According to McMaster, in order to reach the deal with Iran, the Obama administration curtailed "Project Cassandra", that was designed to prevent "Iran's ability to fund its proxies abroad, including Lebanese Hezbollah" – Israel's enemy on the north, that instigated a major war in 2006. McMaster quoted Treasury official Katherine Bauer as saying that "the investigations were tamped down for fear of rocking the boat with Iran and jeopardizing the nuclear deal." (McM 311)

In summary, in several ways President Obama, while declaring his strong support for Israel, actually helped Iran, and its offshoot Hizbollah in Lebanon, to fight Israel.

Did he do it intentionally? Did he do it out of ignorance? As any military intelligence knows – intentions do not count. Only behavior and capabilities count.

The Elections of 2016

Introduction

Susan Rice started the chapter in her book labeled "The Fourth Quarter" by quoting President Obama, who said: "We are entering the fourth quarter and really important things happen in the fourth quarter." (SusanR 426)

In this section we will discuss several issues that led to the end of the "fourth quarter".

1. Secretary of State Hillary Clinton
2. The Decision to Run in 2016
3. President Obama the Politician
4. President Obama against Donald Trump
5. President Obama against Candidate Donald Trump
6. The End of President Obama's Presidency

Secretary of State Hillary Clinton

Hillary Clinton served for four years as Secretary of State during the first term of the Obama administration. At the end of the four years, President Obama approached her and asked her to continue serving as Secretary of State during his second term.

The response she gave him was, "I'm sorry, Mr President, but I can't."

It should be noted that she didn't say that she doesn't want to. She said that she couldn't.

It is interesting to compare how she responded four years earlier, when President-elect Obama offered her the position of Secretary of State. At that time she talked of "the call to service" that helped her decide to join his team (HRC 18).

There are several clues as to the reason for the change.

The first clue is her explanation in her book: "But diplomacy is a relay race, and I was nearing the end of my leg." (HRC 593)

Is it a figure of speech – "I was nearing the end of my leg"? Or should the listener take it literally to mean that she had some problem with her leg?

It should be noted that during her campaign in 2016 there was a time when she "collapsed" upon entering the car. Was it "collapsing", or is it that her leg couldn't hold her?

There are other clues to support some "suspicion" that there might have been some medical issue that brought her to quit as Secretary of State.

SCAN Information - The Verb "Left"

Introduction

The verb "left" is associated in society (in all languages on the globe) with a 70% chance of some time pressure playing in the background. The other 30% is associated with some sensitivity.

Generally speaking, it is average to see the verb "left" up to three times in an "open statement". Once the number goes up beyond the average three, the frequency of the verb "left" would indicate extreme sensitivity.

The following are the sentences in which Hillary Clinton used the verb "left" in relating to the end of her tenure:

1. "When I began this book, shortly after **leaving** the State Department…" (HRC xii)
2. "…initiatives begun during my years at the State Department have borne fruit since my **departure**…" (HRC 21)
3. "Near the **end of my tenure as Secretary**…" (HRC 28)
4. "In January 2013, as I prepared to **leave** the State Department…" (HRC 243)
5. "In January 2013, as I prepared to **leave** the State Department…" (HRC 297)
6. "By the time I **departed** the State Department in early 2013…" (HRC 464)
7. "In March 2013, little more than a month after I **left** office…" (HRC 465)

8. "When I **left** government…" (HRC 467)
9. "As much as I loved being Secretary of State, I was looking forward to **leaving** public life…" (HRC 593)

Discussion

There are 9 times in which Hillary Clinton referred to the end of her tenure as Secretary of State using the verb "left", or an equivalent. We should note that in the last quote, she even said that she loved serving as Secretary of State, but still she was looking forward to "leaving" public life.

Moreover, for this book, focusing on President Obama, many books were covered, and all of the people involved had to leave the government upon the end of the Obama presidency. But none of them had such excessive use of the verb "left", except for one person – Alyssa Mastromonaco, who was on candidate Obama's campaign team, and later on moved to the White House in charge of scheduling and trips.

Alyssa Mastromonaco broke the linguistic record of the verb "left" with 27 times in which she referred to "leaving" the White House. If this would have been the only signal, it would not be enough. In using the SCAN technique, one should not go by one signal only. A definite conclusion should always be based upon more than one signal, and the more signals we have, the more confident we should be that the conclusion is the right one.

There are two more signals to indicate that Alyssa Mastromonaco was strongly emotionally attached to President Obama, and quite likely vice versa.

The first signal was when she looked for a job after her time at the White House. She met the mayor of NYC, who offered her a position at the city. She told him that she had promised the president that she would give him enough time to find a replacement for her. She was in shock when the mayor told her that she didn't need to keep the promise. How could he even suggest that she should do something like that to "*my* POTUS" (the italics in the original).

When there was a trip to England to meet the queen, there was no place on Air Force One for her, but POTUS kicked somebody out of the group that was going, to give her the opportunity to meet the queen, although her presence was not necessary.

When she was already out of the White House, her cat died, and she mourned for her beloved cat. Suddenly she got a call from Air Force One, and President Obama comforted her for the loss of her cat.

Towards the end of her book, Alyssa Mastromonaco said, "If you would like to know my personal favorite part of the book, it's when Obama walks in on Alyssa doing sit-ups in her office during a Senate Voterama and goes, 'Good for you.'" (AlyM 217)

Back to Hillary Clinton

Alyssa Mastromonaco was first place on the "left" scale with 27 times, while Hillary Clinton had "only" nine times. Nobody else got even close.

Hillary Clinton related to her excessive travel right at the beginning of her book – "visiting 112 countries and traveling nearly one million miles" (xi).

Other people on the Obama team related also to the excessive travel. For example, President Obama's bodyman Reginald Love (Reggie) related to his excessive travel with President Obama by noting that he visited 65 countries and traveled 1.8 million miles (Reggie 201).

In contrast to Reggie, Clinton complained about her travel:

"But none of those experiences could prepare me for what it would be like to spend more than two thousand hours in the air over four years, traveling nearly a million miles. That's eighty-seven full days of recycled air and the steady vibration of twin turbofan engines propelling us forward at more than 500 miles per hour." (HRC 39)

She mentioned two points that aggravated her: "recycled air" and "steady vibration". Is it possible that "steady vibration" caused problems for her with balance and equilibrium? Perhaps this is an issue that brought her to be "...nearing the end of my leg"?

Summary

Quite likely Hillary Clinton "left" the government, not because she wanted to. She loved her work as Secretary of State. "Leaving" her position was very sensitive for her, as she had to leave. She needed rest from the "recycled air" and "steady vibration".

The Decision to Run in 2016

In her book "What Happened"[21], Clinton said that one month after she "left" her position as Secretary of State, the Obamas invited both of the Clintons for a private dinner at the White House (HC WH 52).

At the dinner, President Obama told her that he believed that she was the Democrats' best chance to continue holding the White House in the next presidential elections of 2016, and that he wanted her to prepare to run (HC WH 53).

President Obama's Third Term

The idea that Clinton's run in 2016 is an extension of President Obama's presidency was expressed openly at a "show" written by President Obama's speechwriters, and presented to the news media on April 25, 2015 at the White House Correspondents' Association Dinner.

This gathering is for the president and the news media to get together, and it is an opportunity for the president to give funny remarks, and at times even poking fun at himself. David Litt, President Obama's speechwriter, labeled this event as "a bilateral summit between Hollywood and Washington, D.C.", and it is "a comedy monologue" given by the president (DavidL 60, 61).

During the show at the "comedy monologue", there is a conversation between President Obama and the actor "Luther".

The exchange:

---

[21] Hillary Rodham Clinton, "What Happened", Simon & Schuster, New York, 2017

The President: The nonstop focus on billionaire donors creates real problems for our democracy.
LUTHER: And that's why **we're running for a third term!**

After talking about money playing in politics, President Obama mentioned the Republican Senator Cruz from Texas, and also balancing it with talking of the need of Clinton to collect money, the actor is saying "**we're** running for a third term!"

Note: this is not the actor talking. President Obama's speechwriters wrote it. David Litt said in his book that there were times that President Obama took suggested jokes out of the script. This is to say that the president approved every single word showing up at this "comedy monologue". As the saying goes, a lot of true information is given within a jest.

During his farewell speech in Chicago on January 10, 2017, the following exchange took place between the public and the outgoing president:

Audience: Four more years! Four more years! Four more years!
The President: I can't do that.
Audience: Four more years! Four more years! Four more years!

"I can't do that", but not "I don't want to."

Back to Clinton

Although she shared with the president the "same values and policy goals", and the urgency that there is a lot at stake in 2016, still her inner thought was not definite that "running was the right decision for me" (HC WH 53).

Clinton's View of the Situation

She talked of the "challenges facing Democrats" that President Obama was aware of, and that the "the obstacles were daunting" (HC WH 8, 48).

She listed these "challenges" and "obstacles". Although there were 75 months of job growth, the fact was that the bottom 80 percent were only "starting to go up". In other words, there had been a "job growth" but with suppressed wages (HC WH 8).

She said that the economic recovery was "…still anemic, with wages and real incomes stagnating for most Americans." She talked of Americans being "alienated", to include both white voters and "black men and women". In essence, she said that everyone was "alienated", and she included also the "Dreamers" and "patriotic Muslim citizens" who "…were made to feel like intruders in their own land." (HC WH 8, 48)

[One should note that the "Dreamers" are non-citizens who were brought illegally into the country as children, and to call it "their own land" is an interesting use of the English language.]

She talked of the Affordable Care Act (Obamacare), labeling it "the greatest legislative achievement of the outgoing administration", that gave medical insurance to 20 million Americans who didn't have it before. She didn't forget to mention that the administration "botched" the Obamacare website, but she did leave out the fact that 25 million other Americans were still left with no medical insurance (HC WH 8).

She and her husband were campaigning for "endangered Democratic incumbents" in the 2014 midterms elections. They encountered "anger, resentment, and cynicism" among the voters, and blamed the Republicans for "fueling it" – but it was there already (HC WH 49).

As we saw earlier, in the chapter "President Obama's Policies", the situation she talked of was quite likely due to the policies of the president relating to globalization (trade treaties), climate change (eliminating jobs in the energy sector), and immigration (bringing in low-skilled immigrants).

She mentioned that President Obama knew that his "legacy" was dependent on the Democrats keeping the White House in 2016 (HC WH 53).

The reason for it was that except for the first two years of his presidency, when the Democrats ruled Congress, the other six years the Republicans took over, and they refused to cooperate with President Obama on any legislation. (Remember Rahm Emanuel with his aggressive and belligerent attitude?) President Obama had to govern with "executive orders", signed by the president alone, as the path of legislation was blocked to him. This way of government was only good for the short term, as any incoming president could reverse these "executive orders" with just a simple pen, if he would wish to do so.

[Note: candidate Trump promised that during the first hour of his potential presidency, he would be busy reversing all of President Obama's executive orders.]

She left the State Department with very high approval ratings (69% in early 2013), attributing it to her ability to work in a bipartisan way, working with Republicans in Congress.   Although she didn't say it, she compared her high approval ratings to those of President Obama that were "stuck in the low 40s" (HC WH 48).

Summary

Clinton's description of the situation is actually an indictment of President Obama's presidency, and her description did not promise any good results for any Democrat, whoever it would be, running in 2016.

Clinton's Strategy in Running for President

After such a description of the situation, and a major indictment of President Obama's years, one would have expected that Clinton would run opposing President Obama's policies. She didn't. She did the exact opposite.

As President Obama had done in appointing her as Secretary of State, so President Obama played a "decisive role" in her decision to run for president. In late 2013, she was contacted by David Plouffe, who had been candidate Obama's campaign manager in 2008, and who offered her his "help and advice" (HC WH 52, 53).

She hired help, and except for one, all the people she mentioned were working for either President Obama, or his wife Michelle, at the White House (HC WH 69).

From the beginning, she designed her future campaign with President Obama's values and policies, and with people who were working for him. At least, in terms of organization, and the general message, it was a continuation of President Obama's presidency – his unconstitutional "third term". Clinton was going to be his surrogate.

Historically, it is known in the US that it is very rare for people to win the presidency if they were associated with the outgoing president. (In recent years, Bush 41 was an exception; but he did disassociate himself from President Reagan.) In most cases, a candidate who was part of the previous administration must disassociate himself from the president, to establish his own independence, and to act differently. Candidate Hillary Clinton acted against all historical data. In a way, she ran for president openly as a surrogate for President Obama.

President Obama the Politician

Introduction

In the UK or any other democratic country in the west, there is a prime minister elected by the majority (even if it is 51% vs. 49%), and there is also a unifying figurehead – either a king/queen, or president.

The US does not have such a unifying figurehead. The president is the head of the country, and being elected by the majority of the voters (and usually less than 50% of the voters vote in presidential elections), the minority is left to lament for four or even eight years.

One can see that the president, while in office, would be involved in the political process going on in the Senate and the House of Representatives. This activity would take place outside the White House, and it is quite accepted behavior for Air Force One to take the president to rallies going on in different parts of the country. But it is not common to see this activity from the pulpit of the White House.

President Obama did use his position as president to talk against running Republicans while he was in Washington DC, and he did so at annual dinners he had with the news media people.

Following the targets he chose to make fun of, one can get the history of who was the one that presented the most threat to the president.

Obama and the White House Correspondents' Association Dinner

This gathering is for the president and the news media to get together, and it is an opportunity for the president to give funny remarks, and at times even poking fun at himself. David Litt, President Obama's speechwriter, labeled this event as "a bilateral summit between Hollywood and Washington, D.C.", and it is "a comedy monologue" given by the president (DavidL 60, 61). President Obama labeled the event in 2011 as "the prom of Washington D.C."

Obama Making Fun of Himself

David Litt, President Obama's speechwriter, who was also involved in preparing several funny lines for the White House Correspondents' Dinner, said in his book that President Obama had a reason to make fun of himself – "…it earned him the right to mock people who genuinely pissed him off." (DavidL 236)

Let's examine the way President Obama made fun of himself. There are a few themes that were included:

Birth Certificate – Facing the rumors that he was not born in the US, and therefore not eligible to become president, President Obama had to show the public his birth certificate. He related to it in 2011, and returned to it twice more – in 2013, and 2104.

His personality – In 2011 he quoted people who said that he is "too professorial" and "arrogant", for which he responded with his poll numbers. He returned to this issue again in 2015 when he quoted people who said he was "arrogant and aloof, condescending". For this he said, "Some people are so dumb. No wonder I don't meet with them."

His age – He related to it in 2012, and twice in 2016 – his last year in office.

Discussion

In his first term, President Obama "made fun of himself" relating to three issues – his birth certificate, his age, and his personality.

It should be noted that showing his birth certificate was not President Obama's initiative, or even the speechwriters' initiative. It was forced upon them by the conspiracy theories, promoted by well-known people, like Donald Trump, and even other conservatives in the far right media.

As for his personality – he only quoted others talking of him, and even went aggressively to show that he disrespects them. As for his age – it is a natural process, and there is not any fun talking about it.

In summary, in his first term, President Obama's "jokes" served his political purpose talking to a very friendly audience.

Second Term

There are funny lines that didn't show up during his first term, and only showed up after he was reelected in 2012.

On making fun of himself – In 2013 he said that he had already exhausted all the jokes about himself so "not much was left". In 2014 he said that he usually starts his monologue with "a few self-deprecating jokes". However, after his "stellar" previous year, "what could I possibly talk about?"

His appearance – In 2013 – using it to blame the sequester – the forced cuts in the budget.

Temporary job – Starting in 2014 he talked about the time remaining for him in office and what he would do once he is done. He did the same in 2015, only to use the opportunity to say that he will govern by executive orders. In 2016 he talked of possible work at a financial institution once he is out of office.

Being Muslim – He started to joke about it in 2013, talking about himself as not being "the strapping young Muslim socialist that I used to be." In 2014 he talked of the need "to pray five times a day" (mandated by Islam), saying "Which is strenuous." In 2015 he talked about his middle name, "Hussein."

Being black – This issue entered the monologue only during his last year in office. In 2016, he talked about "jokes that white people should not make." He also talked about his trip to meet the queen of England and the UK Prime Minister, saying "just in case anybody is still debating whether I'm black enough."

Discussion

It should be noted that two very sensitive issues dealing with race and religion surfaced only during his second term. Once President Obama secured his second term in November 2012 there was no danger that raising these two sensitive issues would be used against him in the upcoming elections.

This might indicate the political awareness behind the "jokes". Quite likely they were not simple "jokes". They were written with the awareness of the political environment surrounding President Obama.

As David Litt said, making fun of himself gave the President the permission to go against his opponents. But there was a limit to it.

Summary

The White House Correspondents' Association Dinner was a very carefully crafted political show meant to send messages to the audience of people who are influencing others via their writings (newspapers, magazines) or talking (talk shows).

Obama Talking Against Others

May 1, 2011

He started his "comedy monologue" by talking about the controversy of his place of birth. [See more about it in the section dealing with "Obama and Trump".]

He talked against the GOP trying to stop funding to public radio. Then he moved to make fun of Paul Ryan, Michele Bachmann, Tim Pawlenty, and Mitt Romney.

April 29, 2012

The presidential elections would take place in November of that year. President Obama said, "I'm not going to attack any of the Republican candidates," and then moved to do exactly that.

He talked against Sarah Palin, joking about the difference between a hockey mom and a pit bull, talking about his "likely opponent" Newt Gingrich, and targeting excessively (three times) Mitt Romney, who was quite likely the presumptive Republican candidate.

March 9, 2013 - the Gridiron Dinner

This time it was after he was reelected to his second term, and based upon his performance from previous years, it is was expected that there would be no Republican targets.

He mentioned both Republican senators John McCain and Chuck Hagel, although not in a negative way, but still it aroused laughter from the crowd.

He made fun of his new Secretary of State John Kerry (his clothing), and his Vice President Joe Biden (his age).

The only Republican who got a negative remark was Senator Ted Cruz from Texas. This rare mentioning should bring us to wonder if at that time the Obama team perceived Senator Ted Cruz as a possible candidate in the future 2016 elections. In fact, he did run in the Republican primary before the 2016 elections.

April 27, 2013 – White House Correspondents' Association Dinner

He talked against the Republicans in Congress, mentioning by name Senator Mitch McConnell, the leader of the Republicans in the Senate. He also mentioned briefly Senators Ted Cruz (twice) and Rand Paul, and Congresswoman Michele Bachmann. A new name came into his list –

Senator Marco Rubio from Florida, comparing him to himself, a first time senator who wants to run for president.

It seems as if the Obama team was canvassing potential candidates to run in the future 2016 elections. In mid April 2013, Senator Rubio deserved attention. In fact, he did run in the Republican primary before the 2016 elections.

May 3, 2014

The Republicans that he mentioned were Rand Paul, the Koch brothers, Republicans in general (several times), Eric Cantor, John Boehner (Republican Speaker of the House), and Chris Christie (former governor of New Jersey).

2014 is the first time that President Obama associated Putin of Russia with the conservative side of the aisle. The importance of it calls for a full quote:

> "You would think they'd appreciate a more assertive approach, considering that the new conservative darling is none other than Vladimir Putin. (Laughter.) Last year, Pat Buchanan said Putin is "headed straight for the Nobel Peace Prize." He said this. Now I know it sounds crazy but to be fair, they give those to just about anybody these days. (Laughter.) So it could happen.
>
> But it's not just Pat – Rudy Giuliani said Putin is "what you call a leader." Mike Huckabee and Sean Hannity keep talking about his bare chest, which is kind of weird. (Laughter.) Look it up – they talk about it a lot. (Laughter.)"

Question: is it a coincidence that the association of Putin with the far right of the political map came in the speech (supposed to be funny) in conjunction to reaching the end of his term?

The importance of this theme is that it showed up very early in mid 2014, a long time before any Russian attempt to smear the name of Hillary Clinton before the elections of 2016.

Stay tuned, as this theme is going to return again later on.

April 25, 2015

This year he talked, again, against John Boehner, saying that he "has already invited Netanyahu to speak at my funeral."

He talked against Dick Cheney, Mike Huckabee, and Michele Bachmann.

He produced a list of the contenders fighting for the Republican nomination – Jeb Bush, Ted Cruz, Rick Santorum, and Donald Trump.

Note: the listing of Donald Trump at the bottom of the list reflected his low priority at the time among the Obama team. At that time, he still didn't deserve that much attention.

He continued by piling up the potential pick of the Koch brothers – Marco Rubio, Rand Paul, Ted Cruz, Jeb Bush, and Scott Walker, asking "Who will finally get that red rose?"

To balance the picture, he mentioned Hillary, whose "private emails got her in trouble," and Bernie Sanders, that if he would win – "We could get **a third Obama term** after all."

Note: this is the third time we find the phrase "third Obama term" in his language.

April 30, 2016

This annual dinner was around six months before the November 2016 elections. At that time, the Republican contest was more or less decided, as many of the Republicans who had started the race had dropped out. Very few still stayed in, and among them was Donald Trump. On the Democratic side, the contest was still going on very strongly between Hillary Clinton and Bernie Sanders.

President Obama started his "comedy monologue" by saying, "It is an honor to be here at my last – and perhaps the last – White House Correspondents' Dinner."

President Obama was reaching the end of his second term, and it was clear that this annual dinner was going to be his last one. But he added one more point – that this might be the last annual dinner in any event.

How could he say this? Did he know something that the audience didn't know?

If we think of it, on the Democratic side there were two contenders, both of whom were not against the news media, while it was clear that on the Republican side, the one who constantly and belligerently fought the news media, accusing them of being "fake news" and more, was Donald Trump.

If a Democrat would win the elections, either Clinton or Sanders, there was no question that the tradition of this annual dinner would continue. However, if Donald Trump would win, it was clear that he wouldn't set foot at this event, to be with his "sworn enemies". In fact, once he won the elections, President Trump cancelled his participation in this event.

Did President Obama already have a poll in April 2016, indicating to him that there is a good chance that candidate Trump might win the elections? From this "slip of the tongue" it seems that he had such information.

Later on, in his monologue, President Obama said, "Next year at this time, someone else will be standing here in this very spot, and it's anyone's guess who **she** will be," winning laughter and applause.

President Obama is telling the crowd, his crowd, that there is no doubt in his mind that Clinton is going to take the elections, a saying to which the crowd responded as faithful Democrats.

As he did in previous years, he talked against the Republicans who restrict his freedom of decision.

He added that it was not only the Republicans that were eager to see him gone – "Even some foreign leaders, they've been looking ahead, anticipating my departure."

There were several foreign leaders, especially in the Middle East, who felt that President Obama had betrayed them with his agreement with

Iran. Foremost among them were the Saudis. But even the Egyptian President A-Sisi quite likely felt betrayed by President Obama. President Obama had favored the deposed president from the extremist Muslim Brotherhood, who was elected in free elections, only to be deposed by the military headed by General A-Sisi. However, the Saudis and the Egyptians were not the only ones "waiting in line". Since President Obama had already in the previous year talked against John Boehner who "has already invited Netanyahu to speak at my funeral," it is quite likely that by "foreign leaders", President Obama included Netanyahu as well.

This sentence – "Even some foreign leaders, they've been looking ahead, anticipating my departure" started a relatively short section in his monologue in which the verb "left" is supreme.

1. "Even some foreign leaders, they've been looking ahead, anticipating my **departure**."
2. "Key staff are now starting to **leave** the White House."
3. "Even reporters have **left** me."
4. "Savannah Guthrie, she's **left** the White House Press Corps…"
5. "Norah O'Donnell **left** the briefing room…"
6. "Jake Tapper **left** journalism to join CNN."
7. "But the prospect of **leaving** the White House is a mixed bag."

Within a section containing 160 words, President Obama used the verb "left" seven times. The point of people leaving him towards the end of his presidency was a very sensitive issue for him – he might have felt that he was being abandoned by them.

He moved on to talk against the Republicans, addressing GOP Chairman Reince Priebus, who was present in the audience. He congratulated Priebus on the success of the Republican Party nomination process, telling him "…it's all going great. Keep it up." This earned him laughter and applause, confirming that he was talking sarcastically.

He addressed Mike Bloomberg, who was sitting at the same table as GOP Chairman Reince Priebus, comparing Bloomberg to "a combative, controversial New York billionaire" who leads the GOP primary. It took him a long time to be able to actually mention the name of this billionaire, and he uttered the name only at the end of the paragraph, by saying, "Although it's not an entirely fair comparison between you and the Donald."

He added:

> "After all, Mike was a big-city mayor. He knows policy in depth. And he's actually worth the amount of money that he says he is" – implying clearly that "the Donald" was not. This one also earned him laughter and applause.

He rested with "the Donald", and let the audience rest from "the Donald", and continued by talking of both Bernie Sanders (making fun of his fundraising campaign) and Hillary Clinton (making fun of her age).

He continued by turning back to the Republican side, criticizing the nomination process as being "more loose", mentioned Paul Ryan again, and mentioned that "some candidates aren't polling high enough to qualify for their own joke tonight."

He made fun of Senator Ted Cruz, who was not familiar with basketball language (a major sin in Obamaworld), and then returned to talk against Donald Trump. [See more about it in the next section.]

He ended his monologue by saying, "And with that, I just have two more words to say – Obama out," while dropping the microphone.

President Obama against Donald Trump

Donald Trump was among those who promoted the conspiracy theory that President Obama was not born in Hawaii, and therefore was not eligible to serve as president.

In the White House Correspondents' Association Dinner on May 1, 2011, President Obama responded to it by opening his monologue with, "As some of you heard, the state of Hawaii released my official long-form birth certificate. Hopefully this puts all doubts to rest."

He moved on to present his "official birth video", showing a "Secret Birth Video" which was actually a clip from the Disney children's cartoon, "The Lion King". It should be noted that he felt the need to tell the audience that it is not his real birth video, but a cartoon, and added, "Call Disney if you don't believe me."

If this was not enough, later on he talked directly to Donald Trump, who was in the audience. He said that now that the birth issue had been put to rest, "the Donald" would be able focus "on the issues that matter – like, did we fake the moon landing? What really happened in Roswell? And where are Biggie and Tupac?"

Till this point he had been referring to conspiracy theories, among which was his place of birth. But he went further against "The Donald": "we all know about your credentials and breadth of experience", mentioning an episode of "Celebrity Apprentice". He then spoke directly to Trump:

> "But you, Mr. Trump, recognized that the real problem was a lack of leadership. And so ultimately, you didn't blame Lil' Jon or Meatloaf. (Laughter.) You fired Gary Busey. (Laughter.) And these are the kind of decisions that would keep me up at night. (Laughter and applause.) Well handled, sir. (Laughter.) Well handled."

And he ended this section of his monologue with, "Say what you will about Mr. Trump, he certainly would bring some change to the White House. Let's see what we've got up there," and on the screen there was a slide showing "Trump White House Resort and Casino."

It should be noted that he didn't talk directly to anybody in the audience in the entire series of monologues from 2011 to 2016, unless it dealt directly with "the Donald".

When he said "…he certainly would bring some change to the White House," one should wonder if President Obama might have been the one who planted the seed for "the Donald" to run for the real White House.

President Obama didn't let go with his anger towards Trump. The next year, he started his monologue at the White House Correspondents' Association Dinner (April 29, 2012) with:

> "My fellow Americans, we gather during a historic anniversary. Last year at this time – in fact, on this very weekend – we finally

delivered justice to one of the world's most notorious individuals."

Reading the transcript found on President Obama's website would give the reader the impression that the president was talking about the successful mission to capture and kill Osama Bin Laden, who had died exactly one year before, on May 2, 2011.

But the book written by David Litt, President Obama's speechwriter, gives the full story:

"Last year at this time – in fact, on this very weekend – we finally delivered justice to one of the world's most notorious individuals." **The giant screens on either side of the podium displayed a picture of a sneering Donald Trump**" (DavidL 123-124).

President Obama equated Donald Trump to Osama Bin Laden!

I wonder if any American citizen, regardless who that person might be, should be compared to a mass murderer who attacked the US and killed three thousand people and wounded many others. Even an ordinary criminal or murderer would not be compared to Osama bin Laden – and Trump was neither a criminal nor a murderer.

It only comes to reflect President Obama's anger towards "the Donald", anger that did not decrease during the years. Actually, his anger was only increasing as time went on – even after he had made fun of "the Donald" a year earlier, talking in the third person, and even talking to him directly in the second person.

President Obama against Candidate Donald Trump

By early 2016, it was beginning to be clear to the President and his speechwriters that the candidacy of Donald Trump is an issue to reckon with.

Starting on January 13, 2016, President Obama had already related in his State of the Union Address to the issues raised by candidate Trump.

The President said:

"Will we respond to the changes of our time with fear, turning inward as a nation, turning against each other as a people? Or will we face the future with confidence in who we are, in what we stand for, in the incredible things that we can do together?"

Later on, he said, "Anyone claiming that America's economy is in decline is peddling fiction." And he went on to acknowledge that "a lot of Americans feel anxious" due to the fact that "the economy has been changing in profound ways, changes that started long before the Great Recession hit; changes that have not let up."

An "outer score-card" person is telling the country that the fact that they are "anxious" has nothing to do with him serving already for seven years as president. It is the "economy", as if the "economy" is an independent entity, not connected at all to his policies as president.

He related to the fact that the workers are "squeezed" and that they have "less leverage for a raise", or, in other words, suppressed wages. He cited, again, that it was due to outside influences, e.g., "Companies have less loyalty to their communities. And more and more wealth and income is concentrated at the very top." ("external", remember?)

He disputed the argument that immigration suppressed wages: "Immigrants aren't the principal reason wages haven't gone up; those decisions are made in the boardrooms that all too often put quarterly earnings over long-term returns."

According to former Canadian Prime Minister Stephen Harper, the decision to allow low-skilled immigrants to flood the country and to suppress wages of low-skilled workers is not a decision made in the boardroom. It is an administrative government decision.

He talked against those who "dispute the science around climate change" (Donald Trump?), and talked about "all the rhetoric you hear about our enemies getting stronger and America getting weaker (Donald Trump?). He talked against "ignoring the rest of the world" ("Make American Great Again"?).

Responding to Trump's Message

If the above-mentioned was not sufficiently clear, he went further to say:

"And that's why we need to reject any politics – any politics – that targets people because of race or religion. (Applause.) Let me just say this. This is not a matter of political correctness. This is a matter of understanding just what it is that makes us strong."

He also said, "When politicians insult Muslims, whether abroad or our fellow citizens… that doesn't make us safer."

"And then, as frustration grows, there will be voices urging us to fall back into our respective tribes, to scapegoat fellow citizens who don't look like us, or pray like us, or vote like we do, or share the same background."

Discussion

Although not mentioning Trump by name, President Obama used the pulpit of Congress, and the fact that his State of the Union Address is broadcasted all over the country, to dispute and contradict messages that candidate Trump had been using since summer of 2015 in his campaign to earn the nomination of the Republican party.

The White House Correspondents' Dinner

By April 30, 2016, it was already apparent that candidate Trump is someone to take seriously in the Republican contest for the nomination. And therefore he was also to be taken seriously again at the White House Correspondents' Dinner, after a break in which for four years (since 2012) the President didn't find the time or energy to focus on Trump. However, in late April 2016, the time was "right".

He started by acknowledging the presence of Mike Bloomberg in the audience. He then mentioned that "a combative, controversial New York billionaire is leading the GOP primary" and that one "is not you" (Bloomberg).   He went on to say:

"Although it's not an entirely fair comparison between you and the Donald. After all, Mike was a big-city mayor. He knows policy in depth. And he's actually worth the amount of money that he says he is."

By comparing them, he implied that while Bloomberg was "worth the amount of money that he says he is", the "combative, controversial New York billionaire" is not.

After moving to other topics, he came back by saying, "You know I'm going to talk about Trump!" And telling the audience, "We weren't just going to stop there," referring to his earlier comparison between Bloomberg and Trump.

He started by saying, "Although I am a little hurt that he's not here tonight. We had so much fun the last time." He wanted to be trashtalking him to his face, but since he was absent, it wouldn't be as "much fun".

Trump's absence bothered him, as he found the need to talk about it extensively:

> "You've got a room full of reporters, celebrities, cameras, and he says no? (Laughter.) Is this dinner too tacky for The Donald? (Laughter.) What could he possibly be doing instead? Is he at home, eating a Trump Steak – (laughter) – tweeting out insults to Angela Merkel? (Laughter.) What's he doing?"

He went on to make fun of him:

> "The Republican establishment is incredulous that he is their most likely nominee – incredulous, shocking. They say Donald lacks the foreign policy experience to be President."

Discussion

This a theme that President Obama would be extensively repeating during 2016, up to the elections on November 8. It is true that the Republican establishment was very strongly against candidate Trump, whom they accused of hijacking the party. But for a Democratic president to come with this theme is to shoot himself in the foot. If indeed the Republicans are against Trump, Democratic voters would find the justification to vote for him. In fact, many Democratic voters did vote for Trump.

In summary, to use this theme was a huge mistake on the part of President Obama.

And President Obama continued:

> "But, in fairness, he has spent years meeting with leaders from around the world: Miss Sweden, Miss Argentina, Miss Azerbaijan."

He talked of Trump's business enterprises:

> "And there's one area where Donald's experience could be invaluable – and that's closing Guantanamo. Because Trump knows a thing or two about running waterfront properties into the ground."

After he devoted so much time to talking against Trump, he said, "All right, that's probably enough. I mean, I've got more material – (applause) – no, no, I don't want to spend too much time on The Donald."

After he devoted extensive time to denigrate "the Donald", he came to summarize it by saying that he doesn't want to do it.

Since his audience was mostly news media people, he addressed them by saying:

> "Following your lead, I want to show some restraint. (Laughter.) Because I think we can all agree that from the start, he's gotten the appropriate amount of coverage, befitting the seriousness of his candidacy."

Discussion

President Obama addressed an interesting point: the excessive coverage the mainstream media gave candidate Trump, which was estimated by the Trump campaign at a value of 2 billion dollars of free exposure.

President Obama ended by saying:

> "I hope you all are proud of yourselves. (Laughter.) The guy wanted to give his hotel business a boost, and now we're praying that Cleveland makes it through July."

It was supposed to be a "comedy monologue", and in fact the message was written in funny lines, bringing laughter and applause from the audience. But it reflected two major points:

The first, President Obama was preaching to the choir. They were on his side, and they were very busy attacking Donald Trump on all fronts.

The second, the amount he devoted to Donald Trump only reflected the seriousness of the Trump candidacy in President Obama's eyes. Donald Trump was a threat to him.

The United Nations General Assembly

On September 20, 2016, a month and a half before the elections, President Obama gave his address to the UN.

He produced an accurate description of the effect of globalization to "expose deep fault lines in the existing international order" and that "financial disruptions continue to weigh upon our workers and entire communities", bringing about the situation that "our societies are filled with uncertainty, and unease, and strife."

He talked of the choice the world faced. Either "to press forward with a better model of cooperation and integration. Or we can retreat into a world sharply divided, and ultimately in conflict, along age-old lines of nation and tribe and race and religion."

His choice would be to "go forward, and not backward," although he admitted that "the existing path to global integration requires a course correction."

Till this point, he talked in general terms, but he couldn't avoid addressing the issues raised by the Trump campaign – even though he was talking in the global arena, where his audience didn't have the power to vote.

> "…the politics of ethnicity, or tribe, or sect; aggressive nationalism; a crude populism – sometimes from the far left, but more often from the far right – which seeks to restore what they believe was a better, simpler age free of outside contamination."

Talking a month and a half before the elections, he said:

"We cannot dismiss these visions. They are powerful. They reflect dissatisfaction among too many of our citizens. I do not believe those visions can deliver security or prosperity over the long term, but I do believe that these visions fail to recognize, at a very basic level, our common humanity."

If it was not clear to the audience that he was talking against Trump, he added, "Today, a nation ringed by walls would only imprison itself."

He mentioned the fact that "Sometimes I'm criticized in my own country for professing a belief in international norms and multilateral institutions." And that he recognized that "history tells a different story than the one that I've talked about here today."

Discussion

The speech President Obama gave at the UN was not a speech addressed to American voters. It was a speech for listeners all over the globe. But it seems that for President Obama, the UN was his "home base". There he felt at home. It is no wonder that he said that he was criticized for being in favor of "international norms and multilateral institutions."

Personal observation: in the months before the elections of 2016, I gave several classes overseas, and it was interesting to realize how citizens from far away countries, like Australia or Singapore, felt that the elections in the US were "their" elections. These people's emotions were no different from the ones expressed by US voters.

President Obama's speech was meant for these global people looking up to the US.

Summary

His address at the UN was not that much different from the State of the Union Address he gave in January. Both of them were the same in content. There is only one difference between these two addresses (State of the Union, and addressing the UN) and his "comedy monologue" of that year. While the two addresses did not mention candidate Trump by name, in the "comedy monologue" he went full steam ahead to talk against candidate Trump, very seriously, although with funny lines.

Hillary Rallies

Five days before the elections of November 2016, President Obama started a round of rallies in which he campaigned for Hillary Clinton.

The first one was in Jacksonville, Florida, on November 3, 2016.

He started by outlining his accomplishments during his presidency. He moved on to say that there is "only one candidate in this race who has devoted her entire life to that better America, and that is the next President of the United States, Hillary Clinton."

If there was any doubt as to why he campaigned for Clinton, he clarified by saying, "Because all the progress we've made these last eight years goes out the window if we don't win this election."

He twice repeated this message: "So I have confidence that Hillary will continue the progress we've made," and "I'm not on the ballot. I'm not on this ballot. But everything we've done these last eight years is on the ballot."

In many words he showed that he was campaigning for a third term.

He talked against Donald Trump who "is uniquely unqualified to be President. Donald Trump is temperamentally unfit to be commander-in-chief."

He talked against Trump's business record, citing "Trump Towers in Toronto in Canada going bust."   The only candidate "in decades who's refused to show his tax returns." He quoted "a Republican senator", according to whom "we can't afford to give the nuclear codes to somebody that erratic."

The only time that he showed a sign of emotion was when he said:

> "But you know, the thing that really gets me is this notion that he's going to be a voice for working people. Now, what's – and look, let's face it, I mean, he's got some support right here in Florida. He's got support around the country – in some cases from working folks."

He compared his run in 2008 (against McCain) and in 2012 (against Romney) saying that he was not as concerned those two times as he was concerned in 2016, since he felt Trump "would do damage to our democracy" and that these coming elections are unique since they are about "the character of this nation."

He invoked the name of Russian Putin in his address – "I just want some consistency. If you say that we should be tougher on the Russians, then how do you nominate a guy who admires Putin?"

On November 5, 2016 at Charlotte, North Carolina, he repeated the same message. Again, he said that "…I want everybody to understand, all the progress we've made, everything we've fought for, everything we aspire to – all of that goes out the window if we don't win this election."

Again, twice he repeated this message: "So if you want Hillary Clinton to continue the progress we've made…" and "My name won't be on the ballot this time. But everything we've worked for is on the ballot."

As he did in Florida, twice he mentioned the fact that "Republicans and conservatives, who aren't running for office so they feel it's safe to do so, to denounce Donald Trump." He also said, "I have Republican friends who don't think or act the way Donald Trump does, and they don't intend to vote for him because they understand this is somebody different who is uniquely unqualified to hold this job."

As he did at the White House Correspondents' Dinner, he went full steam against Trump's business record:

> "The idea that this guy claims to be the voice for working people;
> someone who exploits working people, who probably doesn't
> know any working people – except the guy who's cleaning up in
> his hotel and the guy who's mowing the lawn in his fairway.
> Come on. I know a lot of successful businesspeople. They don't
> go around cheating people to be successful."

He talked of how he is frustrated to "see the degree to which Hillary's reality diverges from what you see in the media and on the news and on the blogs and all that…"

He ended by saying, "Tell them, don't succumb to fear. Tell them to lift up hope. Tell them to choose hope. Choose hope. Carolina, choose hope. Carolina, choose what's best in us. Choose hope. Get out there and vote."

Back in Florida, this time in Orlando, on November 6, 2016, he repeated the same messages.

As he did before, campaigning for an "Obama Third Term", he said four times: "I need your help to help finish what we started eight years ago," "…all the progress we've made goes out the window if we don't win this election," "Let's continue this amazing journey that we started…", and "Let's finish the job!"

He talked against Trump's use of Twitter, and he again connected Trump to Putin by saying, "Maybe he admires Vladimir Putin and some other folks who think that's okay, but this is the United States of America. We can't have that."

As he had done before, he said that the upcoming elections were about "our values" and "It's about the character of this country."

He ended by repeating his battle cry: "Choose hope! Choose hope! Choose hope! Choose hope! Choose hope!"

One day before the elections, on November 7, 2016, President Obama appeared in Durham, New Hampshire.

He repeated his message of running for an "Obama Third Term": "Tomorrow you can choose whether we continue the journey of progress or whether it all goes out the window," and "But make no mistake – all that progress goes down the drain if we don't win tomorrow," and "You know, I've got to say, since my name is not on the ballot…"

He repeated his point that Donald Trump is temperamentally unfit to be Commander-in-Chief, an opinion supported by some Republicans as well.

He repeated the point of Trump and Putin: " You know, his buddy, Putin, may think that's okay," and he also added that "…there are times where I've been just kind of trying to bite my tongue. But there is a lot about this election that has not been on the level. But I'm going to level with you right now."

The same day, November 7, 2016, President Obama also appeared in Ann Arbor, Michigan.

He repeated his message, running for an "Obama Third Term": "But tomorrow, tomorrow, you will choose whether we continue this journey of progress, or whether it all goes out the window," and "But, Michigan, all that progress goes down the drain if we don't win tomorrow."

If this was not clear enough, he went on to say:

> "So, Michigan, I ask you to do for Hillary what you did for me. I ask you to carry her the same way you carried me. I ask you to make her better the same way you made me better.
>
> And tomorrow, if you're willing to stand with me again, if you're willing to get your friends and neighbors and coworkers to the polls again, if you're willing to reject fear again, if you're willing to embrace hope again – then we will finish what we started. We will elect Hillary as President."

He repeated that "Donald Trump is temperamentally unfit to be Commander-in-Chief," and "He's unqualified to be America's chief executive," and "So Donald Trump is uniquely unqualified to hold this job."

He continued with the message that something is not right: "There's a bunch of it that has not been on the level," and he moved to expand on this point:

> "But I want to tell you something right now. The way campaigns have unfolded, we just start accepting crazy stuff as normal. And people, if they just repeat attacks enough and outright lies over and over again, as long as it's on Facebook and people can see it, as long as it's on social media, people start believing it. And it creates this dust cloud of nonsense."

Michelle Obama

On October 20, 2016, Michelle Obama addressed a Clinton Rally in Phoenix, Arizona.

As her husband campaigned for his "third term", so did she.

"Well, Barack and I – and our friend, Hillary – (applause) – we have a very different perspective on this country…", and "That's what Barack and I believe. That's what Hillary believes too."

She talked extensively against Donald Trump, but one major point was missing from her speech: she didn't say, as her husband had repeatedly said, that Trump is "unqualified" to be president.

Summary

The main themes of President Obama's speeches were that the elections are unique, as they are crossroads of voting on the "values" and "character" of the country. That the elections are either to continue with the policies and vision for the country that he, President Obama, had begun, and that Hillary Clinton would continue with the same course, or to reverse course altogether, and choose one who is "uniquely unqualified", in his words, to be president. In short, although he was not on the ballot, President Obama expressed openly that he was.

The End of President Obama's Presidency

Valerie Jarrett, the Obamas' close friend from their time together in Chicago, who had been with President Obama at the White House during the eight years of his presidency, described in her book a meeting she had one evening with President Obama several months before the election.

She said that she wanted him to indulge in her fantasy of having a third term: "I am so going to miss this place. Don't you wish we could just stay for four more years? Just imagine how much more we could get done."

President Obama responded by listing his accomplishments during the eight years, and he ended by saying, "I'm alive. My family is alive. You're alive… We did our best." Then she said that he paused, lowered his voice, and said, "It's time for us to go." (ValJ 291-292)

Before the Elections

Generally speaking, there was an expectation among the people around President Obama that Hillary Clinton would win the elections. Samantha Power, who was US ambassador to the UN, even arranged a party for the election night at the ambassador's residence, and invited all female UN ambassadors. As the night progressed, "evidence mounted that Trump was on the verge of a shocking upset." (SamP 532, 533)

Trump's Victory

Samantha Power brought numbers to express Trump's victory. About 63 million people voted for him. There were 9 percent who voted for President Obama in 2012, and voted for Donald Trump in 2016. Another 7 percent stayed at home and didn't vote, and 3 percent voted for a third-party candidate. In total, 13 million people – close to 20% of those who voted for President Obama in 2012 – did not vote for Hillary Clinton in 2016.

In essence, 13 million voted against a "third term" for President Obama.

To diminish the importance of the numbers, Power said that fewer than 80,000 votes in "three critical swing states of Michigan, Pennsylvania and Wisconsin" determined the outcome. (SamP 534, 535)

Valerie Jarrett said, "nearly 43 percent of eligible voters did not vote." She shouldn't have been surprised, as historically these are the average numbers in all presidential elections in the US. When it comes to local elections, the numbers are even much lower.

It puzzled her how so many people had decided not to vote, and stay at home. It seems that she believed that those who stayed at home would have voted for Hillary Clinton, an assumption that has no basis. Since the Republican establishment was very strongly against candidate Trump, quite likely many Republicans avoided voting, just as many voters who had supported Bernie Sanders decided not to vote for Hillary Clinton (ValJ 300).

Why?

Power attributed Trump's win to the fact that he had "successfully spoken to deeply-felt and entirely legitimate grievances" relating to globalization (SamP 535). She ended her book by saying that "dignity is an underestimated force in politics and geopolitics." As "dignity" played a role in the outbreak of the Arab Spring, and in Russians supporting Putin, so did millions who supported Donald Trump because "many said that they felt ignored, as though their country was moving on without them." (SamP 535, 551)

Susan Rice, National Security Advisor during President Obama's second term, said that she saw the outcome "coming". She even expressed it during the Republican primary contest when President Obama's team ridiculed the idea that Trump might win the nomination. Rice, on the other hand, said: "There is a lot of hate out there. You know some people just can't get over where we are now." (SusanR 453)

Rice said that before the elections she expressed her assessment to foreign dignitaries – to the French representatives, and to the Emirati Crown Prince Mohammed bin Zayed – and she told them that she believed that "Trump had a decent chance." (SusanR 454)

Ben Rhodes, President Obama's advisor and speechwriter, said that candidate Trump replicated the message that candidate Obama himself had used during the Democratic primary contest in 2008: that Hillary Clinton is "part of a corrupt establishment that can't be trusted to bring change." He also said, "Trump was a product of the same forces I'd seen aligning against us for ten years" (BenR 403).

The Morning After

Valerie Jarrett said that the election results were "soul crushing". She had to go through "the five stages of grief". Her team in the White House office had a "distraught look of shock and pain, and yes, tears." (ValJ 288, 300)

Susan Rice talked of "the enormity of this loss and its inestimable consequences." "Trump's election felt like a stinging rebuke of all we believed in."

Rice said that the day after the elections, President Obama "played consoler-in-chief, bucking up the White House team as best he could with the same stiff upper lip." (SusanR 456)

Ben Rhodes said that President Obama was smiling. "The sun is shining," he joked. He quoted Ben Rhodes, who had sent him an email the night before saying, "history doesn't move in a straight line, it zigs and zags." (BenR 403-404)

Obama on the elections

In the early morning of the day after the elections, President Obama told Ben Rhodes, "There are more stars in the sky than grains of sand on the earth." (BenR xiii)

But President Obama was not that philosophical about the results. Ben Rhodes reported that as time passed, the impact of the results came across to him.

While on a trip to Lima, Peru, President Obama asked Ben Rhodes, "What if we were wrong?" When Rhodes asked him, "Wrong about what?" President Obama quoted an article he had read in The New York Times stating that "liberals had forgotten how important identity is to people", and President Obama said, "Maybe we pushed too far. Maybe people just want to fall back into their tribe." (BenR xvi)

The president who advocated global brotherhood, for whom the UN was his "home base", found that Americans really care first of all about what is going on in their own country. Not they disregard the rest of the world, but when they come to vote, they look around, and examine their own life.

Former Secretary of State Henry Kissinger said that Israel doesn't have a foreign policy. For Israel, he said, everything is domestic policy. He was right, but only partially. His observation is true not only for Israel, but for any democratic country, whether it is Israel, or in Europe, or the US. The voters vote for what is important for them. To label it as "falling back into their tribe" is to have a major misunderstanding about what democracy is. Former Canadian Prime Minister Stephen Harper illustrated it very nicely in his book. For Harper, "nationalism" is not a bad word.

Note: It is said in Jewish Law that when giving charity, the poor of your own city take preference over the poor of other cities. When President Bush announced that the US would give five billion dollars to fight AIDS in Africa, I couldn't understand why he wasn't spending this money to fight AIDS in the US – especially since he was spending money he didn't really have. He was working with a deficit budget, printing money to finance the government.

When Ben Rhodes said, "But you would have won if you could have run," President Obama responded, "I don't know. Sometimes I wonder whether I was ten or twenty years too early." (BenR xvii)

Note: Ben Rhodes showed a total misunderstanding of what had happened. President Obama **did** run. He had campaigned and run for his "third term" using a surrogate, Hillary Clinton, and he lost. President Obama was right in grieving for his loss. To comfort him by saying that the loss was not his, was not a comfort at all.

Rhodes also quoted President Obama, who told him, "I feel like Michael Corleone. I almost got out." (BenR xix)

Rhodes said that between meetings in the days after the elections, President Obama "expressed disbelief that the election had been lost." It was one of the "stages of grief" that Valerie Jarrett had talked about: the "denial" stage.

Listing President Obama's accomplishments – unemployment at 5 percent, economy humming, Affordable Care Act working, graduation rates up, most of our troops back home – Ben Rhodes concluded: "…maybe that's why Trump could win. People would never have voted for him in a crisis." (BenR 405)

Note: it is interesting to note that while both Susan Rice and Samantha Power identified the "crisis" (the anger in the population) that the country had to face, Ben Rhodes was oblivious to it.

Rhodes also talked about President Obama's "flashes of anger". When Rhodes told President Obama during a trip to Germany, after the election, that it is quite likely "the last time a U.S. president would defend the liberal international order for a while," President Obama responded, "I don't know. Maybe this is what people want. I've got the economy set up well for him. No facts. No consequences. They can just have a cartoon." (BenR 405)

"They"? Not "we"?

Summary

For President Obama, the elections were not between Hillary Clinton and Donald Trump. The elections were between President Obama running for his surrogate third term, and candidate Trump, who talked against the system that had reigned supreme during the previous three presidencies, a point that former Canadian Prime Minister Stephen Harper had talked about. Candidate Trump did not run only against President Obama. He ran against President Clinton and President Bush as well. He ran against all three of them. He ran against the system at large.

President Obama's Farewell Address

On January 10, 2017, President Obama gave his "Farewell Address" in Chicago.

He talked about change, saying that change "only happens when ordinary people get involved and they get engaged, and they come together to demand it." He went on to say that "after eight years as your President, I still believe that. And it's not just my belief."

Whether "belief" or "knowledge", it seems as if he is saying that he didn't deliver on "change".

He listed the accomplishments of his eight years in office: "reverse a great recession, reboot our auto industry, and unleash the longest stretch of job creation in our history", opening up "a new chapter with the Cuban people, shut down Iran's nuclear weapons program without firing a shot, take out the mastermind of 9/11…", winning "marriage equality", securing "health insurance for another 20 million of our fellow citizens." He ended the list by saying, "But that's what we did. That's what you did. You were the change."

He elaborated on this idea of "change".   The fact that "America is exceptional" is due to the fact that it showed "the capacity to change".

With all the accomplishments achieved, he still realized that "it's not enough."   Here, he moved to describe the problems that are still present: "the laid-off factory worker", and "our trade should be fair and not just free." Then he went on to blame "the next wave of economic dislocations" due to the "relentless pace of automation that makes a lot of good, middle-class jobs obsolete." And the list continued: race "remains a potent and often divisive force in our society", and "the rise of naked partisanship."

Reading his list, one has a feeling that we are reading his book "The Audacity of Hope" all over again. It is an identical description of the situation. There is only one striking gap between the book and the description in his farewell address: his eight years of presidency.

He then returned to the idea of "change": "But laws alone won't be enough. Hearts must change. It won't change overnight."

He ended the speech by saying, "I'm asking you to believe. Not in my ability to bring about change – but in yours."

In many words, he admitted his inability to bring "change".

David Litt, President Obama's speechwriter, summarized it very accurately: "Barack Obama's election was a triumph of hope. But his presidency was a triumph of persistence" (DavidL 303).

Michelle Obama dedicated her book to several people, starting with her parents, and ending with, "…and finally, Barack, who always promised me an interesting journey."

He promised. Did he deliver?

Epilogue

In the summer of 2008, I read the two books published by President Obama before he was elected, and I read them again (2020) for the purpose of this book. I found that, amazingly, both President Obama and President Trump talked in the same way about the problems of the US economy. It is almost as if President Trump read President Obama's books. Identical.

The diagnosis was the same, but the way to deal with the situation was very different. President Obama talked of hope and change, and he raised the expectations of the population to a religious fervor. These high expectations led to a great disappointment.

This is exactly what Edward Snowden said that brought him to go to the news media. He expected President Obama to change (remember "change"?) only to find out that not only did President Obama do the same as had been done in the past, but he went even further to increase the use of technology surveillance. By doing so, he eroded even more the civil rights of the population.

One might suspect that Edward Snowden is just saying this to justify his actions; but he talked in the same way as David Litt, President Obama's speechwriter, who said that President Obama's election was a "triumph of hope", while his presidency was a "triumph of persistence". He knows. He was on the inside.

It was not only President Obama. President Obama was no different than President Clinton and President Bush. All three came from the political side of the map, people who are used to writing policies. But writing policies is a venture for the long term, and it can take a whole generation to find out whether the policy was correct. And even if the policy is not productive, it has the tendency to stay put, and never to change.

This is the reason that all three of the previous presidents perceived "globalization" as engraved in stone, something that cannot be changed. Senator McCain wrote in his book that "globalization" is not a "policy". It is here to stay. Former Canadian Prime Minister Harper said in his book that if a policy is no good, you don't change the people, you change the policy.

And for any policy, it takes time for its failure to register among the voters. There was an economic boom at the time of the Bill Clinton administration, so NAFTA was not an issue. It took another eight years of President Bush, and he moved with CAFTA – Central America trade agreement, an agreement that Senator Obama supported in his book, in spite of the fact that the unions tried to recruit his opposition to it. Democratic Senator Obama, who labeled himself as "a proud Democrat", a politician for whom the unions were a strong component of his political base, voted against their interest.

President Trump came from the business environment, where success and failure are measured very quickly by the bottom line of profit and loss. President Obama talked against Candidate Trump by citing several of his projects that had failed. He simply didn't realize that in the business environment, closing a failed project is not considered "failure". To just keep going with a failed project, and absorbing the losses, is not an option in business – only in a government project.

President Obama is a very likeable man. People love him. He is charming. He knows how to smile. He knows how to talk and captivate his audience. But what he didn't have was – he didn't have the right policies.

President Obama spent most of his political capital on health insurance, while many in the population suffered for lack of jobs; and if they did have a job, their suppressed wages didn't compete with the rise in the cost of food.

One of my neighbors in Phoenix, a retiree, told me that each time he goes to the supermarket, he needs to pay more and more for the same food he usually buys. But his income, quite likely social security, is fixed, and not changing much. So he was squeezed – slowly, gradually, but surely. He was not the only one in the US who faced this same situation.

After diagnosing the US economy correctly, President Obama should have invested his time and energy to bringing jobs to the country. Not health care but jobs. Healthcare does not give people dignity. Jobs do.

One can understand why President Obama went for healthcare. He wrote in his book that his mother, struggling with cancer, had to fight insurance companies. So, his personal experience clouded his judgment.

If people ask me: what was President Obama's legacy? My answer is: Trump.

Without President Obama (and Clinton and Bush), Trump would not have been elected president.

It is important to realize that even though the United States is over 200 years old, historically it is still a very young country. The reason is that once in around fifty years, a President comes into office and changes the rules of the game. It is true for Lincoln with the Civil War. It is true for President Theodore Roosevelt in the early 20th century, who was labeled "the great reformer". It is true for President Franklin Roosevelt after the Great Depression, who brought social security and medicare. It might be true also for President Trump.

People remember presidents who influenced their life. When you go to Mount Rushmore, you will see four Presidents that most Americans recognize and remember. But they don't remember others, as they were presidents who moved by inertia, or, as David Litt called it, by "persistence".

President Obama ran for his surrogate "third term" and he lost. It was time for "change", as he had promised eight years earlier.

Scientific Content Analysis (SCAN)

The SCAN technique is the result of many years of research into verbal communication, and the linguistic behavior used by people when talking or writing. SCAN analyzes a text or statement strictly according to the words used. SCAN has a long track record of successful results in law enforcement investigations, and is currently being used in many police departments and other government agencies in many countries.

The basic concept of the SCAN technique is that no human being can say everything that is in his/her mind. Before a person can write or talk, the person needs to decide if the information (or opinion) present in mind at that specific moment is important enough to transmit to the listener or reader. Or maybe it is not important enough, and therefore the person will not transmit it. This is "the editing process" which is the engine behind every statement. As the speaker or writer goes through this process, so the listener or reader can step into the person's shoes, and reach conclusions about what was present in the person's mind at the time that the text was delivered.

The editing process does not end in choosing which information is important enough to enter the statement. After this stage the person needs to move into another phase, still before delivery, and this is phrasing the information. Here the person needs to decide how to lay out the story, how to build the sentence (syntax), in what order to write the sentence, and which words to use to describe the event or the information.

All these points are taking place in the person's mind at a very fast speed, a speed that is measured in milliseconds. This fast speed might even prevent the person later on from knowing why he/she chose this particular way to describe the event. There are times in which the **statement** itself gives the answer while the **person** cannot do so.

If one were to ask the person, "why did you choose this way to write the sentence?" or, "why did you choose this word and not another word?" in most cases the person would say, "Just because," or, "I don't know." However, when the analyst brings the person the reason for the language in the story, the person is able to confirm if the explanation is the right one. The reason behind the choice of information, and its wording and phrasing, are present in the person's mind; however, this information is "background information" or "passive information." It is not present in the front of memory, or in other words, "active information."

This above-mentioned description of what is going on in the person's mind brings us to an important and basic rule in SCAN: "The Subject is Dead. The Statement is Alive."

People who are not familiar with the SCAN technique ask me, "Don't you need to know who is the person giving the information – their personality, behavior, and/or facial expressions during the delivery of the text?" The answer is no. The analysis does not deal with **people** but with **the statement**.

Here we can move to another basic concept, and this is the "copyright" the person has on the text. This means that the analyst cannot add to or subtract from anything in the text, either from outside sources, or even from logic. In front of the analyst there should be only the text. In a way, the text of every statement is "sacred." The analyst cannot change it, nor can the person who delivered the text. The words have a life of their own. "The Subject is Dead. The Statement is Alive."

In order to be analyzed with SCAN, a statement must be an "open statement". This refers to information that a person gives, without being guided by any questions of the listener to lead the story in a certain direction. The only question the listener is allowed to ask is, "What happened?"

The memoirs analyzed in this book fit the requirement of being an "open statement", as the listener or reader did not lead the statement at the time of delivery.

The language used in an open statement is a "linguistic mirror" of reality. In other words, if we compare the language to the lens of a camera that takes a picture of reality, then the language of the text is the linguistic lens: how the person giving the statement perceives reality.

Another major concept of SCAN is the "unity" of the text, and the "unity" of the analysis. By this I mean that the analyst must maintain **consistency**. The analyst cannot explain one word in a certain way in one place, and give a different explanation of that same word in another place in the text. As the text is "sacred," so should be the analysis: unity for the text, and unity for the analysis.

This means that if one place in the statement contradicts the analyst's explanation, the explanation is wrong, and there is a need to either search for another explanation, or to fine-tune the original one. It is like a crossword or a sudoku puzzle. As the numbers in the sudoku puzzle need to fit up and down, left to right, and within the section, so it is with the analysis of the text. If a person finds a contradiction in their solution of a sudoku puzzle, the person needs to know that the solution is mistaken. The same applies in the analysis of a text. Although it involves words and not numbers, sentences and not squares, the concept is the same.

Change of Language

The Human Brain

It is very easy to underestimate the power of the human brain. It was once mentioned in the newspaper that scientists took several supercomputers and put them together, and they succeeded in simulating the brain of a cat. To emphasize it – the brain of one cat equals the power of several supercomputers combined together.

In the same piece of news it was stated that scientists do not see any time in the future to be able to simulate the power of a human brain. The reason is that there are not enough supercomputers on this globe, to put all of them together to be able to simulate the power of one human brain.

Fifty percent of the human brain is devoted to accommodating the ability to communicate. A well-known linguist in the US, Steven Pinker, says in his book "The Language Instinct" that there is enough evidence to conclude that grammar is found on the DNA. There is a gene that controls grammar. And if this gene is faulty, that person would never be able to communicate properly. The book gives the example of three generations of one family in the UK who couldn't talk English properly due to the fact that they inherited a faulty gene.

The human baby does not need to study grammar. The only thing the baby needs to learn is the sounds of the language. (For example, English has 26 letters but 40 distinct sounds.) During the second year, the baby puts the sounds together into words. By age 3 the baby talks in grammatically correct sentences, without anyone teaching the baby proper grammar.

The Brain and the "Open Statement"

Realizing the speed at which the brain is functioning to accommodate communication, we can now come to see the connection between the physiology of the brain and the delivery of information in an "open statement" (i.e. a statement given in reply to an open question such as "what happened?" with no other input by the interviewer).

When a person begins to give an "open statement", the person needs to go through two stages. In the first stage, the person needs to decide what is important, and what is not. Once the person decides that the information is important enough to enter the statement, the person would deliver that information, either by writing or by speaking.

This is the "editing process", which is an innocent process. Everyone does it upon giving an "open statement" (=free flow). This is a very quick process – so much so, that at the end of delivering the statement, the person will not be able to trace his/her own steps as to why they wrote something.

Upon deciding that something is important enough to enter the statement, the person needs to go through another stage before the information reaches the paper and/or the mouth. The person needs to phrase the information – to take something from memory and to transfer it into words. This is also a very quick process, and in this case as well, the person would not be able to explain, even to himself/herself, why they chose a certain way to phrase a sentence, and why they chose a certain word to describe something. In most cases, if the person would be asked after delivering the statement, why did you change your language (i.e. using two different words to refer to the same person or object) from point A in the statement, to point B, in almost all cases the person would say either "I don't know", or "I was told in school not be redundant." However, if the SCAN analyst would suggest to the person a reason for the change of language, based upon the content of the text, and mainly the location where the change of language took place, the person would be able to relate to what the SCAN analyst was saying and confirm the conclusion. (I do this all the time with the statements of students in my classes, and the students think I am a mind-reader.)

The Human Brain and Emotions

Again, going back to the human brain, it is important to know that the location where a person stores memory for long term is the center of emotions in the brain. This is the reason that people say that if a person wants to remember something for a long time, that person should attach an emotion to the information, and that would guarantee that the person would remember it forever.

Take for example the day of 9/11. No matter where the person was, even not in the US, it is quite likely that the person would be able to tell us what happened in his day from the time he got up till the time he went to sleep.   Very accurately, and to the tiniest details.

In fact, we find out that most changes in language are due to emotions. People trasmit emotions by changing their language. For example, "I **started** the laundry," and later on, "I **began** watching TV." The emotions are different during these two events.

Changes of language and detecting deception

In view of the high speed at which the brain functions, and knowing that most changes in language are due to emotions, we can now see how changes of language are the most accurate way to determine truth and/or deception.

The idea is that we expect a person to maintain consistency in his/her language.   This means that people do not change language for no reason. In other words, we rule out the option of synonyms. If a person changes language, something in the past must have been different, before the language would change in the present. And as discussed, most changes of language are due to emotions.

For example, I had a student who changed his language while writing a statement about the Saturday before he came to the class. In the statement he said that he was going out on his motorbike to enjoy his time on the snow. However, throughout the statement he changed his language in the following way – three times he referred to the "motorbike", twice he called it "sled", once more he called it "motorbike", and then back to "sled".

I asked him my routine two questions: Did you know at the time of the writing that you changed your language? He answered in the negative. My second question was: do you know now (the time of discussion) why you changed your language? Again he answered in the negative.

I told him: I will tell you why you changed your language. While you were out on your "motorbike", the engine failed (so it turned into a sled = no engine), and you tried to fix it, and you believed that you fixed it

(=back to "motorbike"). You went back on the "motorbike", only to find out that you still hadn't fixed it (=back to "sled").

He asked me, how did you know all of that? And I said, "I must have been there."

The main point is that at the time of writing the statement, the information was in his mind. However, later on, when we talked about his statement, the event was not there anymore, and he couldn't relate to it.

Please note that the problem with the engine was not mentioned anywhere in the **content** of the statement. It only entered the **language** of the statement.

In summary

There are two channels of communication.   The first channel is the content – the sequence of events. The second channel is the language being used to describe the sequence of events.

We expect **consistency** between the language and the content. When a change of language is justified by the sequence of events, as it is described in the statement, then the conclusion is that the person is likely to be truthful. However, if we encounter **inconsistency** – a change of language that is not justified by the sequence of events – the conclusion is that the person is likely to be deceptive.

Change of language is the strongest signal by language to determine if a person is truthful or not. It has been found to be a reliable indicator by many investigators in many police and security organizations.

"I don't know / I don't remember" – Background Information

When we come to analyze a statement, whether of a witness or a suspect, we need to know whether the answer was given to a specific question, or if it is an answer to an "open question," making the answer an "open statement." For example, if we ask a person, "Do you know if such-and-such took place?" and the person answers, "I don't know," this might be a legitimate answer. When we direct the person's attention to a particular point and the person says, "I don't know" (or "I don't remember") such an answer cannot bring us to conclude anything.

However, when we deal with an "open statement," for example, when we ask a person to tell us "what happened [on a particular day]," then in the person's mind "the editing process" starts to determine what should be included in the "open statement" and what should not be included. The person needs to bring the event to the front of his mind and to ask one question all the time: "Is it important enough for me to include in my answer?" If the person answers in the affirmative, the person includes it in the open statement. However, if the person answers in the negative, the person does not include it in the open statement.

We should note two major points in regard to this "editing process." One, it is a very innocent process. The truthful person does it as well. Two, it is **a very quick** process in the person's mind, to the point that after giving the statement, if the person is asked about a certain point in the text, the person is not able to reconstruct the thoughts that were present in his/her mind at the time of delivering the statement. This quick pace of the mind brings the feeling that the process is subconscious, but actually it is not subconscious. If the SCAN analyst would bring the information derived from the text to the knowledge of the person, the person would confirm it.

The "editing process" means that any information a person includes in an "open statement" is labeled "important enough to enter the statement." This also means that the sentence "I don't know" or "I don't remember" is **illegitimate** when it is found in an "open statement." If a person does not know something, the person does not include it in an "open statement." However, if a person knows that he/she doesn't know, it should be considered a signal of concealing information.

"Concealing information" is not the same as deception. Both a truthful and deceptive person will conceal information. The information is simply something that the person didn't want us to know.

List of Sources

The Obamas

BO DFMF - Barack Obama, "Dreams from My Father", Three Rivers Press, New York, 2004

BO AOH - Barack Obama, "The Audacity of Hope: Thoughts on Reclaiming the American Dream", Three Rivers Press, New York, 2006

MichO – Michelle Obama, "Becoming", Crown, New York, 2018

Michelle Obama's thesis in college - https://www.politico.com/story/2008/02/michelle-obama-thesis-was-on-racial-divide-008642

Cabinet Members

HRC HC - Hillary Rodham Clinton, "Hard Choices", Simon & Schuster, New York, 2014

HRC WH - Hillary Rodham Clinton, "What Happened", Simon & Schuster, New York, 2017

JohnK - John Kerry, "Every Day is Extra", Simon & Schuster, New York, 2018

LeonP - Leon Panetta, "Worthy Fights", Penguin Books, New York, 2014

RobG - Robert M. Gates, "Duty: Memoirs of a Secretary at War", Alfred A. Knopf, New York, 2014

Candidate Obama's campaign

Axe - David Axelrod, "Believer: My Forty Years in Politics", Penguin Press, New York, 2015 (also served at the White House)

DavPl - David Plouffe, "The Audacity to Win: The Inside Story and Lessons of Barack Obama's Historic Victory", Viking, 2009

White House Personnel

ValJ - Valerie Jarrett, "Finding My Voice: My Journey to the West Wing and the Path Forward", Viking, 2019

SusanR - Susan Rice, "Tough Love: My Story of the Things Worth Fighting For", Simon & Schuster, New York, 2019

BenR - Ben Rhodes, "The World As It Is: A Memoir of the Obama White House", Random House, New York, 2018

Reggie - Reggie Love, "Power Forward: My Presidential Education", Simon & Schuster, New York, 2015

SamP - Samantha Power, "The Education of an Idealist: A Memoir", Dey St., 2019

Samantha Power, "A Problem from Hell: America and the Age of Genocide", Basic Books, 2002, 2003, 2007, 2013

BE - Ezekiel J. Emanuel, "Brothers Emanuel: A Memoir of an American Family", Random House, New York, 2013 (This book relates to Rahm Emanuel, Obama's first White House Chief of Staff)

DavidL - David Litt, "Thanks, Obama: My Hopey, Changey White House Years", Harper Collins, 2017

Pat Cunnane, "West Winging It: An Un-presidential Memoir", Gallery Books, New York, 2018

Alyssa Mastromonaco, "Who Thought This Was a Good Idea? And Other Questions You Should Have Answers to When You Work in the White House", Twelve, New York, 2017

FCO – Beck Dorey-Stein, "From the Corner of the Oval: A Memoir", Spiegel & Grau, New York, 2018

The Clinton Administration

BC ML - Bill Clinton, "My Life", Alfred A. Knopf, New York, 2004

Albright - Madeleine Albright, "Madam Secretary: A Memoir", Miramax Books, New York, 2003

Ross - Dennis Ross, "The Missing Peace: The Inside Story of the Fight for Middle East Peace", Farrar, Straus and Giroux, New York, 2004

Previous Administrations

Jimmy Carter, "The Blood of Abraham: Insights into the Middle East", The University of Arkansas Press, 1993

Jimmy Carter, "Palestine: Peace Not Apartheid", Simon and Schuster, New York, 2006

George P. Shultz, "Turmoil and Triumph: My Years As Secretary of State", Scribners, 1993

US dignitaries

BenC - Ben Carson, "Gifted Hands: The Ben Carson Story", Zondervan, 1990

DPatrick - Deval Patrick, "A Reason to Believe, Lessons from an Improbable Life", Broadway Books, New York, 2011

US Intelligence Personnel

JC   James R. Clapper with Trey Brown, "Facts and Fears: Hard Truths from Life in Intelligence", Viking, New York, 2018

MH1   Michael V. Hayden, "Playing to the Edge: American Intelligence in the Age of Terror", Penguin Press, New York, 2016

MH2   Michael V. Hayden, "The Assault on Intelligence: American National Security in an Age of Lies", Penguin Press, New York, 2018

Foreign Leaders

DavCam - David Cameron, "For The Record", William Collins, GB, 2019

StephenH - Stephen J. Harper, "Right Here Right Now: Politics and Leadership in the Age of Disruption", Penguin Random House, Canada, 2018

François Hollande, "Les leçons du pouvoir", Le livre de poche, Librairie Générale Française, Editions Stocks, 2018- 2019

BenN - Benjamin Netanyahu, "A Durable Peace: Israel and its Place Among the Nations", Warner Books, 1993, 2000

Ariel Sharon with David Chanoff, "Warrior", Simon & Schuster, New York, 1989-2001

Yitzhak Rabin, "The Rabin Memoirs", University of California Press, Berkeley, 1979

Yitzhak Shamir, "Summing Up", Yedioth Ahronoth, Tel-Aviv, 2015

Others

WillB - William J. Burns, "The Back Channel: A Memoir of American Diplomacy and the Case For Its Renewal", Random House, New York, 2019

MicOr - Michael Oren, "Ally: My Journey Across the American-Israeli Divide", Random House, New York, 2015

Michael B. Oren, "Power, Faith, and Fantasy: America in the Middle East 1976 to the Present", W. W. Norton & Company, New York, 2007

NikkiH - Nikki R. Haley, "With All Due Respect: Defending America with Grit and Grace", St. Martin Press, New York, 2019

Tuvia Tenenbom, "The Lies They Tell", Gefen Publishing House, New Jersey, 2017

Kenneth M. Pollack, "Armies of Sand", Oxford University Press, 2019

Ashrawi - Hanan Ashrawi, "This Side of Peace", A Touchstone Book, New York, 1995

SariN - Sari Nusseibeh , "Once Upon a Country: A Palestinian Life", Farrar, Straus and Giroux, New York, 2007

Raphael Patai, "The Jewish Mind", Hatherleigh Press, New York, 1977, 2007

Daniel J. Levitin, "Successful Aging: A Neuroscientist Explores the Power and Potential of Our Lives", Dutton, 2020

DanielL - Daniel J. Levitin, "The Organized Mind: Thinking Straight in the Age of Information Overload", Dutton, 2014

David G. Dalin and John F. Rothmann, "Icon of Evil: Hitler's Mufti and the Rise of Radical Islam", Random House, New York, 2008

Wendy R. Sherman, "Not For the Faint of Heart: Lessons in Courage, Power, and Persistence", Hachette Books, New York, 2018

McM - H.R. McMaster, "Battlegrounds: The Fight to Defend the Free World", HarperCollins, 2020

Uzrad Lew, "Inside Arafat's Pocket", Kinneret, Zmora-Bitan, 2005 (in Hebrew)

OA – Orly Azoulay, "Obama: He Has a Dream", Yedioth Ahronoth, Tel-Aviv, 2009 (in Hebrew)

Storm – Ilan Kfir, "Storm: On the Way to Iran", Yedioth Ahronoth, Rishon Letzion, 2019 (in Hebrew)

Bergman - Ronen Bergman, "Authority Granted" Yedioth Ahronoth, Tel Aviv, 2002 (in Hebrew)

Shimon Shiffer, "Warning Lights: Conversations with General (Reserve) Amos Gilead", Yedioth Ahronoth, Rishon Letzion, 2109 (in Hebrew)

Moshe Yaalon, "A Long Short Journey", Yedioth Ahronoth, 2008 (in Hebrew)

APPENDIX 1 – Michelle and "country" and "nation"

"Forever more, in the halls of one of **our country's** greatest monuments of liberty and equality…"
[Remarks by the First Lady at the Sojourner Truth Bust Unveiling, April 28, 2009]

"That's why I'm here, because we want to continue this conversation that I've been having around **the country**…"
"…we know that here in Mississippi, kids struggle with these issues sometimes even more than in other parts of **the country**."
[Remarks by the First Lady at Brinkley Middle School, Jackson, MS, March 03, 2010]

"And we're already spending billions of dollars in **this country** a year to treat these conditions…"
"It's one that is affecting every community across **this country**."
[Remarks by the First Lady to the NAACP National Convention in Kansas City, Missouri, July 12, 2010]

"… and that is the epidemic of childhood obesity that affects every community in **this country**…"
"And these grants, made possible through the health care reform law, will go to 11 communities and states across **the country**."
[Remarks by the First Lady at the Congressional Black Caucus Foundation Legislative Conference, September 15, 2010]

"Over the past few years as First Lady, I have had the extraordinary privilege of traveling all across **this country**."
"While I believed deeply in my husband's vision for **this country**…"
"And as I got to know Barack, I realized that even though he had grown up all the way across **the country**…"
"Barack knows the American Dream because he's lived it. (Applause.) And he wants everyone in **this country** -- everyone -- to have that same opportunity"

"I love that for Barack, there is no such thing as "us" and "them" -- he doesn't care whether you're a Democrat, a Republican, or none of the above; he knows that we all love **our country**."
"It is who we are as Americans. It is how **this country** was built."
"**...** surely we can give everyone in **this country** a fair chance at that great American Dream."
"Because in the end, more than anything else, that is the story of **this country**..."
"And we must once again come together and stand together for the man we can trust to keep moving **this great country** forward..."
[Remarks by the First Lady at the Democratic National Convention, Time Warner Cable Arena, Charlotte, North Carolina, September 4, 2012]

"They came because they believe that there is no higher calling than serving **our country**, no more noble a cause than that of our fellow citizens."
"Whether our sons and daughters who wear **our country**'s uniform..."
"It's about who we are as Americans."
"It's about doing everything we can to carry on the legacy that is our inheritance not just as African Americans, but as Americans -- as citizens of the greatest country on Earth."
[Remarks by the First Lady at the Congressional Black Caucus Gala, Washington Convention Center, Washington, D.C, September 23, 2012]

"And that story -- the story of Hadiya's life and death -- we read that story day after day, month after month, year after year in this city and around **this country**."
[Remarks by the First Lady at the Joint Luncheon Meeting: Working Together to Address Youth Violence in Chicago, Hilton Chicago, Chicago, Illinois, April 10, 2013]

APPENDIX 2 – President Obama's Cairo Speech, Section Dealing with the Israeli-Arab Conflict

The second major source of tension that we need to discuss is the situation between Israelis, Palestinians and the Arab world.

America's strong bonds with Israel are well known. This bond is unbreakable. It is based upon cultural and historical ties, and the recognition that the aspiration for a Jewish homeland is rooted in a tragic history that cannot be denied.

Around the world, the Jewish people were persecuted for centuries, and anti-Semitism in Europe culminated in an unprecedented Holocaust. Tomorrow, I will visit Buchenwald, which was part of a network of camps where Jews were enslaved, tortured, shot and gassed to death by the Third Reich. Six million Jews were killed – more than the entire Jewish population of Israel today. Denying that fact is baseless, ignorant, and hateful. Threatening Israel with destruction – or repeating vile stereotypes about Jews – is deeply wrong, and only serves to evoke in the minds of Israelis this most painful of memories while preventing the peace that the people of this region deserve.

On the other hand, it is also undeniable that the Palestinian people – Muslims and Christians – have suffered in pursuit of a homeland. For more than sixty years they have endured the pain of dislocation. Many wait in refugee camps in the West Bank, Gaza, and neighboring lands for a life of peace and security that they have never been able to lead. They endure the daily humiliations – large and small – that come with occupation. So let there be no doubt: the situation for the Palestinian people is intolerable. America will not turn our backs on the legitimate Palestinian aspiration for dignity, opportunity, and a state of their own.

For decades, there has been a stalemate: two peoples with legitimate aspirations, each with a painful history that makes compromise elusive. It is easy to point fingers – for Palestinians to point to the displacement brought by Israel's founding, and for Israelis to point to the constant hostility and attacks throughout its history from within its borders as well as beyond. But if we see this conflict only from one side or the other, then we will be blind to the truth: the only resolution is for the aspirations of both sides to be met through two states, where Israelis and Palestinians each live in peace and security.

That is in Israel's interest, Palestine's interest, America's interest, and the world's interest. That is why I intend to personally pursue this outcome with all the patience that the task requires. The obligations that the parties have agreed to under the Road Map are clear. For peace to come, it is time for them – and all of us – to live up to our responsibilities.

Palestinians must abandon violence. Resistance through violence and killing is wrong and does not succeed. For centuries, black people in America suffered the lash of the whip as slaves and the humiliation of segregation. But it was not violence that won full and equal rights. It was a peaceful and determined insistence upon the ideals at the center of America's founding. This same story can be told by people from South Africa to South Asia; from Eastern Europe to Indonesia. It's a story with a simple truth: that violence is a dead end. It is a sign of neither courage nor power to shoot rockets at sleeping children, or to blow up old women on a bus. That is not how moral authority is claimed; that is how it is surrendered.

Now is the time for Palestinians to focus on what they can build. The Palestinian Authority must develop its capacity to govern, with institutions that serve the needs of its people. Hamas does have support among some Palestinians, but they also have responsibilities. To play a role in fulfilling Palestinian aspirations, and to unify the Palestinian people, Hamas must put an end to violence, recognize past agreements, and recognize Israel's right to exist.

At the same time, Israelis must acknowledge that just as Israel's right to exist cannot be denied, neither can Palestine's. The United States does not accept the legitimacy of continued Israeli settlements. This construction violates previous agreements and undermines efforts to achieve peace. It is time for these settlements to stop.

Israel must also live up to its obligations to ensure that Palestinians can live, and work, and develop their society. And just as it devastates Palestinian families, the continuing humanitarian crisis in Gaza does not serve Israel's security; neither does the continuing lack of opportunity in the West Bank. Progress in the daily lives of the Palestinian people must be part of a road to peace, and Israel must take concrete steps to enable such progress.

Finally, the Arab States must recognize that the Arab Peace Initiative was an important beginning, but not the end of their responsibilities. The Arab-Israeli conflict should no longer be used to distract the people of Arab nations from other problems. Instead, it must be a cause for action to help the Palestinian people develop the institutions that will sustain their state; to recognize Israel's legitimacy; and to choose progress over a self-defeating focus on the past.

America will align our policies with those who pursue peace, and say in public what we say in private to Israelis and Palestinians and Arabs. We cannot impose peace. But privately, many Muslims recognize that Israel will not go away. Likewise, many Israelis recognize the need for a Palestinian state. It is time for us to act on what everyone knows to be true.

Too many tears have flowed. Too much blood has been shed. All of us have a responsibility to work for the day when the mothers of Israelis and Palestinians can see their children grow up without fear; when the Holy Land of three great faiths is the place of peace that God intended it to be; when Jerusalem is a secure and lasting home for Jews and Christians and Muslims, and a place for all of the children of Abraham to mingle peacefully together as in the story of Isra, when Moses, Jesus, and Mohammed (peace be upon them) joined in prayer.